Flying the Line
Volume II:

The Line Pilot in Crisis:
ALPA Battles Airline Deregulation
And Other Forces

Flying the Line
Volume II:

The Line Pilot in Crisis:
ALPA Battles Airline Deregulation
And Other Forces

By George E. Hopkins

Air Line Pilots Association, International
Washington, D.C.

International Standard Book Number: 0-9609708-3-5
Library of Congress Catalog Card Number: 82-73051

Copyright © 2000 by the Air Line Pilots Association, International,
Washington, D.C. 20036

First Printing May 2000

CONTENTS

FOREWORD

The famous James H. "Jimmy" Doolittle, first to fly an aircraft entirely on instruments, racing trophy winner, World War II hero, and an honorary member of the Air Line Pilots Association, was an extraordinary figure in the history of aviation. In the sunset of his life, while I was working with him on his autobiography (*I Could Never Be So Lucky Again*), I asked him why he waited until he reached his mid-90s to tell his life story. He replied, "There is an optimum time to write history. That is after the emotions have cooled down and before memory has started to fade. Very frequently when an individual writes history immediately after the event, he is still knowingly or unknowingly emotionally involved. I think only after those emotions have cooled down can you have a real rationalization. Rational thinking and emotions don't go together."

Past, present, and future members of ALPA will find that this second book on the history of their union follows this premise. The emotions of the past have cooled somewhat, and it represents the "rational thinking" of many leading participants as stated by a professional historian, George E. Hopkins, Ph.D., who, in 1982, wrote *Flying the Line: The First Half Century of the Air Line Pilots Association*. That book covered the air mail pilots' strike of 1919, the Association's subsequent founding in 1931, and the incumbency of the first three presidents to the midpoint of Capt. J.J. O'Donnell's 12-year term.

This volume explores in great depth the Association's history from that time through the incumbency of Capt. Henry A. Duffy and the assumption of the ALPA presidency by Capt. Randolph Babbitt. It takes the reader behind the scenes of the political battles that were fought internally and presents a rare, uninhibited evaluation of the motives, emotions, and personalities involved in the traumatic issues that threatened to destroy the organization.

As Hopkins explains in his preface, he is a Navy-trained pilot who nearly became an airline pilot but elected to pursue a career as a historian. He examines the internal political workings and hidden mechanisms of ALPA from an informed, omniscient viewpoint that is rarely found in a history of any organization, much less that of a labor union. After interviews with, and having the consent of, ALPA's past leaders, he reveals and comments freely on their quarrels with pilot groups before and after the passage of the Airline Deregulation Act of 1978. Here will be found frank revelations of the power of the "elephant" pilot groups and the influence that "ants" have had on the union's recent history. And the reader will see the disruptions that occur and the bitterness between pilot groups about seniority that has proven inevitable when airlines merge.

Those who have read *Flying the Line, Vol. I,* will recall the villainy of E.L. Cord in his dealings with pilots in the 1930s. They will see that there was a modern-day equivalent in the person of Francisco Lorenzo, who willfully and ruthlessly broke the laws of labor/management relations and was determined to destroy ALPA as a viable union. ALPA spent $200 million to fight the war against this tyrant and finally witness his downfall. The book contains a straightforward examination of the motivations of some of the airline pilot group leaders during this dismal period and their influence on the transition of leadership from O'Donnell to Duffy as well as the behind-the-scenes political machinations that led to Duffy's victory by a mere 129 votes. The rise and influence of Randolph Babbitt in ALPA's internal affairs and his controversial election to the presidency are discussed with equal candor.

Pilots who have joined ALPA in recent years will learn the origin and meaning of such terms as suspension of service, labor protective provisions, blue skies contract, Mutual Aid Pact, Project Acceleration, B-scale wages, withdrawal of enthusiasm, stovepipe standalone seniority lists, Major Contingency Fund, family awareness programs, and ALPA's fragmentation policy. And readers will grasp what Capt. Frank Mayne, former ALPA executive vice-president, meant when he said, "Whatever goes wrong, ALPA will get the blame. Whatever goes right, the company will get the credit."

Members will gain an assessment of the role of the Reagan and Bush Administrations and the judiciary in labor negotiations and in the disastrous effects of deregulation on the pilot profession. There are interesting "names" encountered here, including such unlikely personalities as Donald Trump and Michael Milken, Lorenzo's junk bond friend who was convicted of securities fraud and sentenced to 10 years in prison.

Nowhere else will readers get such a valuable, unvarnished, inside view of the downfall of Braniff and Eastern, two of the nation's proud airlines, and the sad effects that mergers caused for airline employees. Hopkins traces the troubles and the drastic changes in the industry to a new breed of corporate wheeler-dealers who had no airline experience and minimal qualifications for leadership and who gleefully tried to break the unions. Men like Lorenzo typified everything that is wrong about airline deregulation and caused Sen. Ted Kennedy, a one-time proponent, to admit that deregulation has been a failure.

As a staff member and editor of *Air Line Pilot,* I was privileged to witness, but not to participate in, many of the political events discussed so vividly in the following chapters. My first experience with ALPA might be said to have been when I met my flying instructor at Army Air Corps primary flight school in 1941. He was Verne Treat, known as "Mr. U" on that list of ALPA's founding members who had to keep their identities secret and are listed on that impressive brass plaque in the lobby of ALPA's Herndon, Va., office. He would not discuss those early days with cadets, but he taught me the basics of piloting, and I owe a successful, accident-free flying career to his instructional skills. When I joined the ALPA staff 36 years later, I learned why his name is so permanently memorialized. That is revealed in Hopkins's *The Airline Pilots: A Study in Elite Unionization* and reinforced in *Flying the Line*. I had joined an organization with a proud heritage formed by men of great courage and vision.

This current work of Hopkins should be required reading for all present and future ALPA members. It is a study of crisis and effect and contains priceless lessons that can be learned from past mistakes and successes. The book illustrates the lasting truth of the author's statement that "no victory ever stays won" and should be an incentive for members to get involved in the internal affairs of their union and use the experience of the past as preparation for the future.

C.V. Glines
Former Editor
Air Line Pilot

PREFACE

W hy another book on the history of ALPA and pilot unionization? Weren't my two previous books enough? What has happened since 1970?

The short answer is "history." Over the last three decades, change in the airline industry has been remorseless and revolutionary. Ask any former Braniff, Eastern, or Pan American pilot about that "change."

When Hank Duffy approached me about writing a sequel to *Flying the Line*, I was skeptical. I wasn't sure ALPA (or airline flying as a "profession," for that matter) would survive long enough for anybody to care! That's how bad things were in the 1980s, a decade dominated by Frank Lorenzo and the decertification of ALPA after a lost strike at Continental Airlines. Pilots flying the line today, most of whom began their careers after the trauma described in this book occurred, need to know their history, or they run the risk of repeating it.

But why should I write it? How did the study of airline pilot unionization become my life's work? Thereby hangs a tale.

In 1964, after five years as a naval aviator, I opted for an academic career. It was a tough choice, for I became a Navy pilot because I saw it as the best way to become an airline pilot. I even requested multiengine training because I had heard that airlines preferred pilots with that background.

In 1966, after two years of graduate studies in history at the University of Texas at Austin, I faced the Ph.D. "comprehensive" exams. If I passed, I would go on to write a dissertation, receive my doctorate, and then become a college professor. If I flunked, I would have to find a new career (while presumably taking up history as a hobby!) I had a wife and child, I was nearly 30 years old, and I was feeling uneasy about the future.

At just this time, Dick Russell, an old Navy friend then flying for Braniff, phoned. "If you ever want to fly again, now's the time," Dick said. Braniff needed pilots— I needed career insurance. So I interviewed with Braniff, got hired, and was assigned a class date.

Career insurance safely in hand, I passed the comprehensive doctoral exams and reluctantly wrote to Braniff declining employment. But to this day, I keep that framed Braniff job offer on my office wall, a constant reminder that I could have chosen another career.

I then had to write a "dissertation." A dissertation is supposed to be a "significant contribution" to the field of history. Selecting a dissertation topic takes months—researching and writing one often takes years. An old joke holds that there are two kinds of dissertations: good ones—and those that get finished!

My dissertation adviser, Robert A. Divine, suggested that because I had a background in aviation, and because as a graduate student I had already published an article on American bombing policy in World War II, I ought to continue in this vein. My Navy experience, combined with an aviation specialty, would make me an unusual academician, Divine believed.

My first thought was to write the history of an airline. With the help of Professor Joe B. Frantz, a business historian who knew the president of Braniff, Harding L. Lawrence, I got an interview with Lawrence in his opulent office atop "One Braniff Place" in Dallas. I needed access to Braniff's records. Lawrence was cordial, but he insisted that Braniff would have to retain control over my work. That was quite impossible for a dissertation.

After several more blind alleys that lasted into 1967, I remembered Dick Russell saying: "You won't believe this, Hopkins, but I'm now a card-carrying union member." Dick, a Naval Academy graduate and staunch Republican, gave me an idea.

I discovered that no history of ALPA was listed in any bibliography. So I wrote to ALPA, still located in Chicago, asking permission to use any records the union might have. Almost immediately I received a phone call from W. W. ("Wally") Anderson, ALPA's executive administrator under Charley Ruby. Wally's first comment was: "We've been wanting somebody to write our history for a long time. How much would you charge?"

I explained that my services would be free, but that I needed unrestricted access to ALPA's records. So I came to Chicago in the summer of 1967, and after a brief interview with Charley Ruby, I got his approval—no strings attached. "He seems all right to me" was all Ruby said to Wally Anderson after the interview.

In 1971, Harvard University Press published *The Airline Pilots: A Study in Elite Unionization*, the book that resulted from my dissertation. It took four years to write and covered only the first seven years of ALPA's history, from its formation in 1931 to passage of the Civil Aeronautics Act of 1938. I guess ALPA liked what I wrote, for in 1978, J.J. O'Donnell asked me to write another history commemorating the union's 50th anniversary. With the understanding that I would give ALPA its history "warts and all," I agreed.

The result was *Flying the Line: the First Half-Century of the Air Line Pilots Association*, published in 1982. My interpretation of ALPA's history was not censored. I work for Western Illinois University specifically and for an abstraction called "history" generally. Although frankly nervous about the book, O'Donnell understood that prettified "court history" praising the King (so to speak) would be worthless. If pilots were to derive insight from my book, it had to be free to go wherever truth took it.

Insiders understood that Hank Duffy's interest in a sequel to *Flying the Line* signaled his decision not to seek reelection as ALPA's president in 1990. Duffy never quibbled about my independence.

And so I plunged anew into the thicket of the profession's history, and into its crucible—ALPA. This book offers my best judgment of events spanning two decades, from 1970 to 1990. It is written primarily for contemporary airline pilots, but I believe anybody interested in the history of the airline industry can benefit from it.

My interpretation of significant events that have made the profession what it is today is leavened by my experience as an academic observer since the 1960s— a time when many of the Old Guys, ALPA's founders, were still alive. In some cases, I got to them with my tape recorder near the ends of their lives. I was fortunate to know them, and I am still honored that the Old Guys, men like Homer Cole and John Huber (who served alongside Dave Behncke as ALPA's first national officers), found me a worthy vehicle to pass on to posterity their stories. Had they not trusted me, I doubt that contemporary pilots, many of whom appear as principal figures in this book, would have been as candid with me.

This book is dedicated not only to the Old Guys who built ALPA, and in the process transformed a mere "job" into a "profession," but also to their successors who have kept ALPA alive through some difficult years. Without their help, this book could not have been written. Without their perseverance, ALPA would not exist.

My special thanks goes to the *Air Line Pilot* magazine staff who have worked to prepare this manuscript for publication. When I began this project, Esperison Martinez, Jr., was the magazine's Editor-in-Chief, and he served as book editor for Volume II. Gary DiNunno, the current magazine editor, served as publisher, editor, and production manager. William A. Ford created the page and cover design and photo layouts. Jody McPherson and Susan Fager provided their editing and proofreading expertise. In addition, Cathy Sobel indexed the final manuscript. Chris Sorenson photographed the cover image.

George E. Hopkins
Western Illinois University
March 2000

Flying the Line Volume II:

The Line Pilot in Crisis:
ALPA Battles Airline Deregulation
And Other Forces

CHAPTER I

THE WORLD OF THE AIRLINE PILOT
A Profession at Century's End

The day begins at "Oh dark-thirty." The sun rides high over the Atlantic Ocean. The North American continent still slumbers.

Thousands of professional airline pilots are awakening in the predawn darkness, fumbling toward full alertness. Soon they will sit in the noses of winged metal tubes, marvels of late 20th century technology, which will hurtle through the air at speeds that were inconceivable just a generation ago. Behind these professional airline pilots, completely oblivious to their technical skills and the rigors of the occupational world they inhabit, will sit *hundreds of thousands* of passengers, strapped to their seats, trapped and trusting.

In the span of one lifetime, commercial aviation has made progress that would shame the wildest flights of science fiction fancy. What might a pioneer aviator of the 1920s have thought of a prediction that before the century ended, the few hardy fools who entrusted themselves to the cramped passenger compartment of a Boeing 40B mailplane, would become today's *millions* of routine travelers? And what would that pioneer aviator have thought of his profession, transmuted through the decades to century's end?

The world of modern airline pilots, like the world of the first airline pilots, who turned a mere job into a profession, still begins with the ritual of flight preparation. For every flight, whether predawn or at midnight, professional airline pilots draw on a legacy passed down through the decades. The preflight ritual, almost religious in its intensity, is full of obeisances to costly lessons learned in other eras by other pilots, who flew vastly different aircraft, primitive by today's standards. Modern preflight preparation is more than a routine—it is a rite as old as the professional aviator's calling; and like nothing else in the workday, it links modern airline pilots to their forebears who flew the ungainly aircraft of yesteryear. Just as in 1927, airline pilots at century's end carefully apply the skills of their craft, checking a thousand details, each with the potential of life and death, as they set about making the nation's air transportation system actually work.

Pilots who flew airliners in the era of wooden wings would recognize instantly the physical stresses modern airline pilots face. If a grizzled old captain of a Ford Trimotor lumbering along between Omaha and Chicago should suddenly, by some sci-fi time-warp, find himself at the controls of the latest generation glass cockpit, fly-by-wire marvel, he would be utterly lost, in a technical

1

sense. So much has *changed*—equipment, procedures, the very language of flight.

But the basic *process* of flight, of readying both pilot and airplane, would be eerily familiar. The "Old Guy" would understand. The wrenching impact of interrupted sleep, the physical and psychological tricks by which airline pilots have always deceived their bodies into functioning in mid-day form, these would be the same. Men like Dave Behncke and Rube Wagner, "Doc" Ator and Walter Bullock, Homer Cole and John Huber, Byron Warner and John Pricer—legendary pilots from the dim days of the industry's infancy—these men would understand cold dawns and protesting bodies. They would understand the physical toll an airline pilot's calling exacts, for they lived lives of too many mornings begun too early, and too many days extended too long. They knew their profession robbed the footstep of its spring, prematurely creased the face, and accelerated the complaints of age. It still does—all the technological progress in aviation at century's end hasn't changed that.

But what one of these ancestral pilots would have thought of the flying environment, we can only imagine. What would A. M. "Breezy" Wynne, the American Airlines pilot who fought so hard to stave off the defection of his airline from ALPA in 1963, have thought of the ground control chatter at Chicago's O'Hare? A somewhat younger contemporary of ALPA's founders, Wynne would likely have found the machinegun delivery of O'Hare ground controllers too exasperating to tolerate. Airline pilots of the 1990s are so inured to the self-consciously rapid hyperventilations of today's tower-to-cockpit communications that they routinely tolerate such tart admonitions as: "951, DON'T YOU *DARE* TURN LEFT BEFORE THE STUB!"

Old Breezy Wynne, a man of commanding presence, might well have turned on the tower's verbal scattergunners with withering effect: "Sonny, what the hell is a *STUB*?"

But modern pilots, taxiing in a queue of perhaps a dozen aircraft for takeoff, are almost obligated to respond with a "Roger" to even the most confusing, nonstandard instructions. If they can't figure out for themselves what "the stub" is, they'll take further measures to ensure the safety of their flight—certainly they won't trust the verbal show-offs running ground control for that! But they won't halt the frenetic pace of operations to correct a single ambiguity that is strictly local in its application. The *system* has to flow, and without the daily adjustments applied to this imperfect *system* in the cockpit, it just won't work. The "Old Guy" would remember that, all too well.

But the pace of operations before takeoff is only a prelude to the rapid-fire world aloft. From the moment a modern pilot enters the company operations area, the task at hand is subject to a peculiar interface where aviator meets computer, meets machine, meets programmed response. At bottom, modern airline pilots must still do what the pilot of a Ford Trimotor did in 1929—meet the professional responsibility of getting the airplane aloft and the passengers to their destination, *safely*. The biggest change is that airline pilots of yesteryear suffered from an information *deficit*—modern airline pilots are besieged by an informational *overload*.

Danger has many faces, and the most insidious is the one that presents multiple threats, subtly masked. Modern airline pilots get *so much* information that they have the constant problem of separating what's nice to know from what's absolutely necessary to know. In a world aloft, where computers control everything from preflight plans to enroute sequencing, modern pilots are enmeshed in a system of *dependency*. Pilots depend on controllers, flight dispatchers, weather forecasters, and an almost unlimited array of auxiliary players. Yet just like pilots of 1930, modern pilots are ultimately responsible for the safe and effective functioning of the crucial apex of the air transportation system—the single point at which the vast array of supporting staff concentrate their efforts—the cockpit. All the gewgaws of computerized modernity haven't changed that—or lessened the essential danger each pilot faces in making this crucial apex work.

Danger, of course, is inherent in the professional airline pilots' calling and is not the real issue. Every pilot understands danger, instinctively, as have pilots in all eras, old as well as new. Even among their mutely trusting passengers, few perceive flying today as *really* dangerous. Scratch the surface of "Joe Public's" perceptions, and a fanciful airline pilots' world emerges, where fabulously rich aviators take lengthy vacations and only occasionally "work" while flying to glamorous places—not dangerous in the least! Perhaps flying was dangerous once, but not now, not *today!* Such is the "conventional wisdom."

If a popular news magazine were to feature the question, "Is Your job Killing You?" which era would it represent, 1930 or 1990? If the news magazine, in its lists of the most dangerous occupations, cited "timber cutters/loggers," with 129 deaths per 100,000 people employed, as the most dangerous of all jobs, nobody would be surprised—in 1930 or 1990. If the next most dangerous job classification was "airplane pilots," with 97 deaths per 100,000, then surely the magazine must be of 1930 vintage, or thereabouts. How could it be otherwise, when the third most dangerous job is "asbestos worker," with 79 deaths per 100,000? Being a pilot is more dangerous than working with asbestos? Surely the news magazine must date from some bygone era, one in which pilots regularly engaged in wing-walking and rum-running—a 1920s period piece of Jazz Age journalism.

The news magazine is *Parade,* the popular supplement to Sunday newspapers. The date is Jan. 8, 1989!

Of course, not all the pilots in this survey of dangerous jobs were *airline* pilots. Many were crop dusters, charter pilots, flight instructors, helicopter emergency medical pilots, military jet jockeys. But few pilots arrive in the cockpit of an airliner without serving a long apprenticeship in this extended aviation system. Before pilots can become airline pilots, they must pass through the dangerous years of initiation, while they build the necessary pilot time and qualifications.

But danger is not the point. Pilots, for reasons psychological and practical, have always made light of flying's dangers. For professional airline pilots today, unlike the "Old Guys," danger lies not in the routine hazards, or even the *hazards of routine.* The most consistent danger confronting pilots today, *as pilots,* is something that outsiders are only vaguely aware of—the *hazard of change*—rapid, remorseless, unremitting change. This change assaults pilots in the way they live, the equipment they fly, the conditions of their employment, and the structure of their corporate world, once so immutably secure, now so fragile and shifting. For airline pilots at century's end, change is a condition of daily life; and while an old pilots' adage holds that no two flights are ever quite the same, the *variety of original experiences* that each pilot endures on an almost daily basis is unlike anything any previous generation of pilots has known.

Despite all the changes that have occurred in what is now nearly a century of commercial aviation history, one unvarying constant links modern professional airline pilots to their professional forebears. That constant is the undeniable fact that airline flying is a physically demanding profession that inevitably takes its toll—whether in 1930 or at the century's end.

"If this job is so easy," a familiar lament of contemporary airline pilots goes, "then why am I always falling asleep at the dinner table after a three-day trip?"

Critics who charge that airline pilots are "overpaid and underworked" should follow a typical airline crew through a routine workday.

First, consider the question of *pace*. In some ways, modern airline pilots confront physical challenges that the men who flew in open cockpits never knew. Rising at 03:30 for a dawn takeoff from Chicago to Cincinnati would be just as tough on the pilot of Boeing "Monomail" in 1930 as on a Boeing 757 pilot today. But the "Old Guy" who flew a Monomail would be home after one roundtrip. The hours would be long. He might have to battle the terrible mix of low-altitude weather a modern jet captain can generally avoid (except during the critical terminal phases of flight); but once finished, the "Old Guy" could take what was left of the day off. He wouldn't suffer from multiple crossings of time zones, or exposure to high-altitude radiation, or the possibility of errant electronic impulses from his cathode-ray–laden cockpit.

"Acute circadian rhythm disfunction" (a physiological complaint modern flight surgeons see all too often) wouldn't trouble the airline pilot of 1930 after a long hard flight in a Monomail. The modern flight deck crew, however, will find their work day extending far beyond the limited time zones that encompass a Chicago–Cincinnati trip. Unlike the "Old Guy" in his Monomail, their day will not end with a return to Chicago. Their trip will continue, perhaps to another intermediate stop (say Minneapolis, with a four-hour ground wait interspersed—perhaps planned, perhaps caused by a faulty food service cart that can't be secured in its bay and might come hurtling out to cripple a cabin attendant during takeoff). Next, they fly across the continent in either direction, perhaps easterly one day, westward the next. Time zones blur during a three-day trip, the diurnal rotation of the earth advances or retards a pilot's physiological mainspring, and eventually the circadian rhythm will take its revenge on human biology, ravaging the most basic functions of the human organism, sleep efficiency first, other more sinister effects later.

By the time our modern B-757 crew has checked into a hotel, three time zones and 12 to 14 hours after waking up, only a sadist would say that they have been "underworked." And the day is but a prelude to tomorrow, when they will have to do it all again. The tempo is wearing, and the physical response to the time compression that is so much a part of modern airline piloting rivals anything pioneer pilots endured.

James H. "Jimmy" Roe, ALPA stalwart and friend of Dave Behncke, was a man whose career on TWA spanned the spectrum of aviation from props to jets. When Roe retired in 1961, he admitted that the new era of jet aviation was too much for him. Roe was no shrinking violet, and he was in good shape for his age, despite a lifetime of personal high flying to complement his reputation as a bachelor *bon vivant*. Near the end of his life, Roe declared that the *pace* of jet aviation had made him accept retirement with equanimity.

"There was a graciousness to the old days," Roe said in the late 1970s from his Arizona retirement home. "Flying was an adventure for the passengers, high style, like an ocean voyage, and the captain was like an ocean liner captain. We had *time* to actually get to know our passengers, to mingle. All that ended with the jets."

A hint of disgust crossed old Jimmy Roe's face. Perhaps these were just the ravings of a septuagenarian, doting on a dimly remembered past that never was. Perhaps not.

Roe, like many of the first generation of professional pilots who survived into the dawn of the jet age, knew that the *pace* of modern aviation was taking a toll on pilots that was mysterious and unsettling. These transitioning pilots instinctively knew that the *pace* of modern jet operations was taking something out of them that the great piston queens of the 1950s, the DC-7s, and Superconnies hadn't. Their speculations were haphazard and intuitive, based more on their own anecdotal evidence than on science. But the Old Guys knew that despite the physical dangers of flying a Monomail in 1930 over rough terrain at low altitude, something far more sinister and insidious was lurking over the horizon for airline pilots. These airmen had never heard the phrase "jet lag" before they began flying the new jets. But they discovered what jet lag was soon enough.

Modern pilots are only now beginning to come to terms with the physiological stresses of a workplace the Old Guys barely glimpsed. Most pilots believe that the lives they live, in the cockpit *and* in the stressful environment of airline deregulation and corporate thimble-rigging that has trailed in its wake, are being shortened by hazards that ordinary people only dimly perceive. It is an article of faith among pilots, particularly those who fly international routes, that long hours of exposure to high-altitude natural radiation, combined with the new cockpit environment that emits substantial amounts of radiation on its own, has combined to put them at serious risk. Pilots believe that the medical establishment simply lacks the scientific tools to define the hazards they face, and they point out convincingly that it took years for the doctors to "prove" that smoking was a health hazard. Pilots flying the line today, almost without exception, believe that they face health risks that medical experts either misunderstand or ignore.

As for the *psychological* hazards of working in an industry that moves at the whim of capital-investment decisions, that shows scant regard for the personal and professional effects these decisions have on pilots whose cockpits are at the critical apex of modern air transportation—perhaps that is the greatest change of all.

The Old Guy flying the Boeing Monomail in 1930 would understand—he lived in the same kind of world—and he hated it! He hated it so much that he decided, collectively, with all the other Old Guys who flew similar planes under similar circumstances, to do something about it. They formed a union called the Air Line Pilots "Association" (being somewhat uneasy, owing to the conservative habits of most pilots, about using the "U" word in their title). They formed ALPA because they _had_ to. They used it to protect themselves against exploitation by their employers—as a kind of insurance policy for their budding profession. Many of the Old Guys (whose names are mostly unknown to modern airline pilots) didn't like the idea of forming a union. They _hoped_ that their employers would recognize their contributions and reward them accordingly. They wanted _desperately_ to make their companies succeed, and they hoped against hope that the sacrifices they made to this end (and they weren't just _financial_ sacrifices either) would win for them the kind of fair play that pilots traditionally expect of each other. But when that fervent hope failed, the Old Guys closed ranks, and they marched—not always in a straight line—toward a future for themselves that would be secure and that they believed airline pilots of the future would inherit.

If the future didn't turn out exactly the way the Old Guys hoped, it wasn't because they didn't know about financial sharks who swim in troubled economic waters. Commercial aviation during the 1920s and early 1930s, when the Old Guys were establishing the traditions that modern airline pilots still honor (often without knowing it) and creating the profession of airline piloting out of thin air and dreams, had more than its share of shifty operators who appreciated only the "bottom line." The Old Guys fought them, insisting constantly that aviation was qualitatively _different_ from other kinds of business— that the bottom line wasn't all there was to it—that some things couldn't be quantified neatly on a balance sheet. The Old Guys knew all about economic chaos—deregulation, if you will. They had grown up in a deregulated world, as barnstormers, jackleg charter operators, fly-by-night mail contractors. If a job existed, and it had anything to do with flying an airplane, the Old Guys had done it. They knew about being exploited—about working long hours under dangerous conditions for low pay. They knew Frank Lorenzo's predecessor— his name was E. L. Cord.

When the new airlines began forming during the late 1920s and early 1930s, the first generation of airline pilots seized the opportunity to build a "profession" for themselves. The Old Guys, through ALPA in all its multitude of activities—lobbying, politicking, and cultivating a favorable public "image" of themselves—had almost single-handedly created the regulated system of air transportation that made the American industry the standard by which all other commercial airline systems of the world were measured.

Modern airline pilots confront a world as difficult and dangerous as anything the Old Guys faced at the dawn of commercial aviation. The threat comes as much from erosion of the profession's status as from the normal hazards of aviation. People who opt for a career in an airliner's cockpit do so because they are pilots—men and women who know how to fly an airplane. But to make a "profession" out of the mere job of flying that airplane, these same men and women are learning that, in aviation's brave new world, mere technical excellence is not enough. They must, willy-nilly, become experts in corporate restructuring, financial analysis, mergers, acquisitions, and leveraged buyouts.

"I haven't flown an airliner in a year," said TWA First Officer Larry Garrett in the late 1980s. Assigned then by the TWA Master Executive Council to track the maneuvers of Carl Icahn, Garrett described himself as a "Committee Puke" who would much rather have been flying. "I didn't sign up for flight training to be a financial analyst. If I'd wanted to do that, I would have done it. I didn't, but here I am. The only way I can keep my job as a pilot is to become a financial analyst."

The world of the modern airline pilot is in some ways a more intractable one than the Old Guys faced, because the *political* climate is so much more unfavorable than the one they faced. Luck had a lot to do with it. The Old Guys were fortunate that, just as they began to build ALPA, American public opinion began to change, evolving into one friendly to organized labor. It was a time when a popular bias against big business ran strong. The Great Depression of 1929 left most Americans firmly convinced that corporate power was dangerous when too concentrated and that the leavening hand of government regulation was necessary to control it.

Modern airline pilots have inherited a world the Old Guys would hardly recognize. Instead of a pro-labor bias, the popular climate is decidedly hostile to organized labor; instead of a bias against big business, the public seems to lavish affection on mere wealth, no matter how sleazily acquired. Flashy real estate moguls, Wall Street sharpies, and illegitimate manipulators of paper empires caught the public's fancy during the era of deregulation—not the builders of *real* wealth. The country, instead of distrusting corporate power, seemed (if the results of national elections since 1980 are an accurate guide) to worship it.

The airline pilots of the 1930s in many respects had it easier than modern airline pilots. C. R. Smith and Eddie Rickenbacker were no less predatory than Frank Lorenzo and Carl Icahn, but social and political circumstances restrained their instinct for the jugular. Nothing illustrates this better than the comments of Representative John Martin, a Colorado politician who, following passage of the Civil Aeronautics Act of 1938, weighed in with his view of government's role in protecting airline pilots from the vagaries of free market capitalism.

"In my opinion," Martin said, "the piloting of these great airplanes, which hurtle through the air at 200 miles per hour, loaded with human lives, is the most responsible, the most skillful, and the most dangerous occupation that mankind ever engaged in.

"Nothing in the past history of the world," he said, "nor anything today is equivalent to the position of a pilot at the controls of one of these gigantic airplanes. They are the picked men of the country. It is a profession in which many are called but few are chosen. *These men ought to be as free from worry or concern about their economic condition or future as it is humanly or legislatively possible to accomplish. If there is anything we can put in the* _legislation that will keep worry from the air pilots, it ought to be done"_ [emphasis added].

Could any _serious_ politician at century's end make this kind of statement? Things have changed, and these changes extend far beyond the overheated political rhetoric from the half-remembered days of 1938. Modern airline pilots live in a different, far more dangerous world—professionally.

But perhaps there is a bright side. Billy Joel, that eminent philosopher of rock music, has a lyric every contemporary airline pilot ought to keep securely tucked away for reference in these tough times: "The good old days weren't all that good, and tomorrow's not as bad as it seems."

Pilots are _still_ pilots, ALPA is _still_ here, and _most_ pilots _still_ see ALPA as the bedrock upon which their profession rests today—just as they did in 1931, the year of ALPA's birth. Critics scoff at the notion of unity among pilots, calling ancient notions of a "brotherhood" of the air outdated and naive. They point to the internal stresses that nearly fractured the profession in the 1980s as sure harbingers of ALPA's demise. Perhaps they should remember Mark Twain's letter of correction to a newspaper that had printed his obituary prematurely: "Reports of my death are much exaggerated!"

Despite everything, pilots still are part of a tangible community, just as they were in 1927, with a community mentality born of shared experiences and a perception that the things they have in common outweigh the things that divide them.

Certainly, anybody who knows the history of ALPA understands that the union was built on broken bones. A lot of forgotten aviators paid the price required to build the wages, working conditions, and traditions of modern airline pilots. History is not pretty, and it is not an uninterrupted success story. ALPA's history is full of martyrs and lost causes. But ALPA has survived.

The Old Guys who built ALPA dealt with managers who were no more inclined to give anything away than are today's. A single-minded pursuit of the concept of unity across company lines was almost obsessive among the Old Guys. It came naturally to them, for they shared a set of common experiences. The Old Guys had flown the mail together, barnstormed together, gone through flight training at Randolph or Pensacola together, or they all knew somebody who had, and thus psychologically felt as if they had shared these rites of passage. These shared sets of common experiences gave the Old Guys a "brother pilot" mentality that might sound corny today, but was much more than a mere abstraction to them. The sense of kinship was tangible, meaningful, and it linked them to each other like no other experience save war. Indeed, the shared experiences of the Old Guys often _did_ include war. More than any other factor, this shared experience is what allowed the Old Guys to put aside their parochial interests and act collectively. They thought of themselves as a "band of brothers." Brother pilots. With unity across company lines, they conquered.

Ancient history? Enter any room where airline pilots gather to work or talk today. Attend an Executive Board meeting of the many MEC chairmen of ALPA. Then participate in an MEC meeting. Listen to the conversation, the concerns, the jokes. Whether it's Delta, TWA, United, US Airways, or code-sharing airlines like American Eagle, *they're the same*! Despite all the changes wracking the profession since the Old Guys first began imagining ALPA during conspiratorial meetings at the Troy Lane Hotel in Chicago in 1931, this one indisputable fact remains—pilots are *still* pilots! Something links them together, and airline pilots of today are *still* part of this ancient league, no matter which uniform cap hangs in the cockpit. They are *pilots* who happen to work for different airlines.

After Continental? After the demise of Braniff, Eastern, and Pan Am? Aren't these old notions now outdated, an abstraction, irrelevant in the era of deregulation, Frank Lorenzo, and alter-ego airlines?

Hardly! How else can the cohesion that has linked the *overwhelming* majority of professional airline pilots be explained? In the 1980s, through two terrible ordeals—on Continental and Eastern—an astounding percentage of ALPA members *voluntarily* paid crushing assessments to sustain... *the brotherhood*. The fact that *most* ALPA pilots continued to pay their assessments to the bitter end, and that non-ALPA groups, like the Southwest Airlines pilots' company union, which contributed $50,000, and the American Allied Pilots Association, which contributed $90,000, to help support the Eastern strike of 1989, proves that the ancient idea of a kinship of the air *still* exists.

ALPA remains the living embodiment of that sense of kinship. Despite all the changes afflicting the world of modern airline pilots, despite B-scales, and the multiple tribulations of deregulation, internal disaffection, and external enemies, most pilots *still* recognize ALPA for what it is—the last redoubt of the most formidable weapon remaining to them, the capability to act together *across company lines* to protect their profession in times of crisis. That weapon springs from a fundamental sense of shared interests—"brotherhood," if you will. The vehicle that transports that weapon to war is ALPA.

So long as most airline pilots are willing to pay the price, ALPA will remain viable. So long as airline pilots realize that unity across company lines is a formidable weapon, and that ALPA is the *only* keeper of that faith, that ALPA is "us," not "them," then ALPA will survive. So long as *most* professional airline pilots continue to defiantly wear their ALPA tie tacks and lapel pins in public, ALPA will live.   ✈

CHAPTER 2

THE LEGACY OF FOUR GOLDEN DECADES, 1938–1978
Flying the Line under Regulation

In 1990, as the last decade of commercial aviation's first century began, three professional airline pilots took stock of their careers. Each man was in his early 50s. Their lives dramatize much of what had happened in the 1980s, the tumultuous decade of "deregulation."

Richard D. "Dick" Russell of Miami, Fla., who once criss-crossed Latin America as a DC-8 captain for Braniff International, knew he would never fly the line again. In his own mind and in his inner conception of *who* he was, Dick Russell would always *think* of himself as an airline pilot, even though he was running a maritime machine shop instead of commanding a flight deck. A compact man with a muscular build and startling blue eyes, this Naval Academy graduate still wore his Navy wings on a custom-made belt buckle. But despite his wealth of aviation experience, he no longer flew; and he looked back on his career as a professional airline pilot with anger. The Russell family's finances were tight. Sally, Dick's wife of more than 30 years, began working outside the home after Braniff's 1982 bankruptcy—something she never did while Dick was flying the line.

Dick Russell *blamed* ALPA for this state of affairs.

Frank Robert "Bob" Harper, with his thinning hair and sober appearance, might easily be mistaken for a lawyer or accountant. Instead, he was a Boeing 767 captain for United Airlines. After graduating from Albion College, a prestigious private liberal arts school in Michigan, he too became a Naval aviator. Bob Harper and his wife were living well in a fine suburban home near Seattle, which commanded a sweeping view of Puget Sound. Life for Bob Harper had been good, and he was looking back on his time as an airline pilot with fondness. The few years he had remaining before retirement were secure, and he was looking forward to upgrading to the left seat of the Boeing 747. One day soon, he hoped to return to flying the Pacific routes to Japan and the rest of Asia, just as he had during his Navy tour. Under the terms of United's most recent contract, Bob Harper would earn more than $200,000 per year as a B-747 captain, should he choose to give up his domestic B-767 captaincy. Katie Harper, Bob's wife of more than 30 years, had no need to work outside the home.

Bob Harper *credits* ALPA for this state of affairs.

Louis R. "Lou" Squillante, a slender and laconic man who was living in the waterfront Maryland community of Leonardtown, spent 23 years with TWA before finally achieving his DC-9 captaincy in 1990. At the age of 54, this former Navy pilot and zoology graduate of the University of Maryland faced an uncertain future. TWA was teetering on the edge of bankruptcy, and *Time* magazine had listed TWA's pension fund (along with Pan American's) as one of the 10 most insecure in the United States. Lou Squillante and his fellow TWA pilots were finding themselves dealing with Carl Icahn, who once joked about "outlawyering" them, after subverting their good faith efforts to save TWA through salary and work rules "givebacks." Lou Squillante in 1990 feared that each paycheck might be his last. Luckily for Lou, his wife of more than 30 years, Sarah, is a successful businesswoman.

Lou Squillante, who was intending to retire as soon as possible, saw ALPA as *irrelevant* to his professional life.

Dick Russell, Bob Harper, and Lou Squillante, all of whom were ex-Naval aviators, went through flight training at Pensacola at the *same* time, served together in the *same* Navy squadron, and subsequently went to work as airline pilots at about the *same* time in the mid-1960s. By a process that lies beyond the parameters of rational analysis—out there somewhere in the twilight zone of existential fate, Dick Russell had the bad luck to choose a doomed airline; Lou Squillante hired on with an airline whose prospects in 1990 were dim; and only Bob Harper had the good fortune to pick a winner. *At the time of their hiring, none of them could have foreseen the fates of their airlines.*

Was ALPA responsible for the state of affairs in which these three professional airline pilots found themselves in 1990?

History is made up of many discrete facts, stories, and events, each distinct, some unique and original, others recurrent and part of a tapestry. The historians' duty is to take this welter of historical circumstance, sort out the merely nice to know from what really *must* be known, and distill those truths that *persist over time* into a "usable past." This "usable past" must necessarily be selective, a careful weeding of events that conveys enough of the substantive details, the flavor of the times, and the reasons behind human actions to allow people living in the present to understand the choices that people very much like themselves—people like Russell, Harper, and Squillante—made in the past. In the last analysis, those choices will be made by people who actually walk on history's stage—not by historians who merely chronicle their passage across it. History is not a roadmap that governs choices—it is a catalog of possibilities— past, present, and future.

Every work of history has its own audience. Every historian must select from the vast web of the past those telling moments that illuminate for that audience the present in which they live.

But which story tells it best? Is it the "success" story, like Bob Harper's? the cloudy story, like Lou Squillante's? or the "tragic" story, like Dick Russell's? Count Leo Tolstoy, the great Russian novelist who wrote *War and Peace*, once said that the stories of "happy" families are all the same. By inference, the tragic stories are the ones from which we learn. Consequently, historians have more often relied on misfortune to provide the "shock of recognition" that carries historical narrative toward truth.

So we must know the story of Dick Russell, whose story will stand as the surrogate for many thousands of stories like his.

From the cold perspective of official analysis, Dick Russell would be described as "a highly specialized middle-aged technocrat whose skills are in oversupply." Until May 1982, he ranked near the top of the American economic pyramid, easily able to afford his comfortable Miami home and 35-foot sailboat. Then, in what seemed the flick of an eyelid, Dick Russell and 1,100 other Braniff pilots lost their careers—Braniff went bankrupt, the first "major" airline to do so in modern history. Dick Russell, then 46 years old, began doing odd jobs on other people's sailboats while worrying about the legacy of fixed expenses from his vanished $70,000 salary.

"I used to help friends at the yacht club for free," Russell remembered in 1990. "They understood when I started charging a fee to put down a teak deck or something; and after a while, I had more business than I could handle. But it wasn't flying. That's what I do, what I am, a pilot."

When the air transport industry peaked in 1979, a year after the first rush of deregulation, nearly 40,000 men (and a few women) earned their livelihoods as pilots for U.S. airlines, 2,200 for Braniff, Dick Russell's airline. By April 1982, a month before Braniff's bankruptcy swelled the total, 4,525 airline pilots were already on indefinite "furlough." When the sharp economic recession of 1982–83 reached bottom, the overall jobless rate for airline pilots approached 20 percent. By Department of Labor reckoning, airline pilots suffered from unemployment at nearly double the national average for all workers.

Surprisingly, nobody felt much sympathy for either airline pilots in general or for their union, ALPA. If the overall unemployment rate for ordinary workers had been that high, Congress would have taken action and the President would have reacted. But owing to the prevailing opinion that airline pilots were "overpaid and underworked," this holocaust of jobs in the nation's airline cockpits evoked only yawns. Indeed, many people believed that airline pilots, whose reputation for haughtiness and self-assurance approached the legendary, were deserving of the comeuppance that the Airline Deregulation Act of 1978 had visited upon them.

For 40 years, from the passage of the Civil Aeronautics Act of 1938 to congressional enactment of the Airline Deregulation Act of 1978, professional airline pilots had lived charmed lives at the heart of an industry that was, perhaps, America's finest technological achievement. Airline pilots became, in their lifestyles, income levels, and technical expertise, the subject of almost universal admiration or envy. They were the critical few who dominated the apex of the airline industry, and from this position, through a combination of toughness, canniness, and hard-nosed unionism, airline pilots created for themselves, out of nearly nothing, all the trappings of "professionalism."

But if the truth be known, more than a little good luck also aided the pilots who lived through the four golden decades. Historically, most airline pilots were either unaware of this good luck or unwilling to acknowledge it.

Although they became perhaps the best examples of how skill, personal discipline, and unsentimental adherence to unionism can result in rich personal rewards and high professional status, far too many airline pilots complacently took their situation for granted—the way things currently were, they believed, is the way things would always be.

As the era of direct government regulation of the airline industry neared its "sunset," the salary and benefit packages of U.S. airline pilots were among the highest in the world. The captain of a jumbo jet flying prime North Atlantic runs approached $150,000 in annual earnings. Even a run-of-the-mill Boeing 727 captain flying domestic routes might take home $100,000. Airline pilots clearly owed their privileged position to government regulation and unionization. No purely economic justification existed for high airline pilot salaries. Airline operators have always been able to find plenty of pilots willing to work for less-than-union rates. But so long as the Civil Aeronautics Board regulated the industry, and friendly politicians presided over the web of labor laws that controlled the relationship between management and workers, unionized airline pilots lived in the best of all possible worlds.

In this environment, strikes tended (with some major exceptions) to be short, almost symbolic. Airline managers preferred to pass high pilot salaries along to the traveling public rather than engage in protracted fights. On those occasions when strikes and other unpleasantries occurred during the four golden decades, ALPA won far more often than it lost. Many airline pilots lapsed into complacency, shrugging off the legacy of hard struggle that had made their lives so enviable.

Of course, ALPA had to occasionally demonstrate its toughness and political clout against a few hard cases (notably Southern Airways in 1960–1962); but on the whole, labor relations between pilots and management became comfortable, almost ritualized, or so it seemed.

General Counsel Henry Weiss, who has fought ALPA's legal battles since the days of Dave Behncke, watched the slow, steady lapse into complacency of airline pilots with alarm.[1] More and more, Weiss feared, airline pilots were taking for granted the benefits of government regulation while they concentrated on issues that were obviously important, like skyjacking and air safety, but peripheral to their basic interests *as employees working within a labor union environment.*

"Quite candidly, what went on during these forty years of government regulation that I personally observed," Weiss says, "was the tendency of pilots to pour their energy into interstitial things. Meanwhile, the character of the people the pilots were confronting was changing, from pilot-oriented management to professional management. These new professional managers explicitly designed deregulation to reduce pilot wages."

By the late 1960s, most airline pilots flying the line believed they had seen the last of predatory managers who might threaten their livelihoods. ALPA had won repeated victories at the bargaining table and had beaten back challenges to its status as the preeminent voice of professional airline pilots. A certain mythology emerged, which found far too many pilots willing to believe that the tough, disciplined Old Guys who had created ALPA during the era of wooden wings had won all the wars and that only tranquillity stretched ahead for their legatees in modern jet cockpits. Far too many airline pilots contented themselves with running businesses on the side, polishing their golf games, or simply relishing the good life they lived.

By the beginning of the 1970s, the fateful decade of deregulation, most working airline pilots had forgotten one of the most fundamental axioms of history: "No victory ever stays won." When they looked at history, modern airline pilots saw only the victories the Old Guys had won. They did not see how close some of those calls had been—even under benign government regulation. For example, Henry Weiss believes that the Southern Airways strike of 1960, the last time an employer tried to destroy ALPA (until deregulation), should have provided an object lesson to airline pilots.[2]

"I must tell you that there were times when I thought the Southern pilots were gone," Weiss admitted during a 1990 interview.

The kinds of pilots who involved themselves in ALPA's active affairs generally did not share the complacency that riddled the rank-and-file. But because these active pilots were "political," they necessarily had to keep a low profile or lose their ability to represent ALPA. When airline deregulation first began to make headway in Congress, most ordinary airline pilots paid little attention. ALPA's leaders opposed it, as did most of the major airlines for which they worked. ALPA's presidents and national officers, who have always tended to be more politically aware than the rank-and-file, saw clearly that deregulation posed dangers for their union. But by the early 1970s, the typical airline pilot, like military officers who extol free enterprise while living in a cocoon of government benefits, had become a reflexive political conservative who seemed oblivious to the benefits derived from unionization and government regulation. Consequently, ALPA's officers took considerable flack from rank-and-file pilots for opposing "free enterprise."

"I often marveled at the utter ignorance of my colleagues," says Bill Himmelreich, a retired Northwest Airlines captain. "Sometimes I had to sit there and listen to a kid copilot making sixty grand a year say, 'What good is ALPA? We're professionals! Why do we need a labor union?' The little jerk actually thought he was worth his salary. He wasn't! What he was really worth was what Frank Lorenzo would pay him on New York Air, about $16 an hour. All the rest was gravy, courtesy of our union."

Perhaps if airline pilots had bothered to read Milton Friedman's *Free to Choose*, it would have tempered their enthusiasm for deregulation. Friedman, the Nobel laureate from the University of Chicago who was the leader of the "Chicago School" of conservative, free market economists, exercised enormous influence over Republican policy-makers during the Nixon and Ford Administrations. In *Free to Choose*, Friedman chose as *his prime example* of the evils of government regulation, *the high salaries paid to airline pilots!* Friedman argued that curbing airline pilot salaries would lead to better service and lower fares. By the mid-1970s, with full backing from the Ford Administration, legislation that would end federal economic regulation of the airlines emerged.

Jimmy Carter, perhaps the most conservative Democrat to occupy the White House in the 20th century, adopted Gerald Ford's airline deregulation policies as his own. Surprisingly, liberals like Edward M. Kennedy, whose Senate Judiciary Committee was instrumental in the process, joined forces with conservative, free-marketeers to make airline deregulation a reality by 1978.

Although impossible to prove, it seems likely that pro-labor liberals were sufficiently put off by airline labor's "gold plated" image to allow the deregulation experiment to begin with them. After all, when one thinks about unions and airline pilots during that era, the legacy of Charley Ruby pops readily to mind. On more than one occasion during the 1960s, Charley Ruby made his distaste for associating with other labor unions clear, and he all but boycotted the AFL-CIO. Ruby's attitudes would leave a lot of wreckage, in a purely *ideological* sense, for J. J. O'Donnell to repair when he became ALPA's president in 1970. But we must remember that Charley Ruby was merely reflecting the dominant attitudes of rank-and-file ALPA members, and also that many ALPA members were cordial supporters of politicians who were overtly hostile to other labor unions. Gordon J. Humphrey of New Hampshire was not only one of the most conservative, antilabor members of the U. S. Senate, he was also a former airline pilot.

By the early 1980s, as deregulation began to hit home, the absurdity of a group of trade unionists mouthing the platitudes of free market ideology was obvious. What was not so apparent to an airline pilot living in a snug Republican suburb during the 1970s, was painfully clear by the early 1980s. But in fairness to ALPA's leadership during the 1970s, we must remember that they *did not pull their punches in denouncing airline deregulation.* The problem was that the rank-and-file ALPA member simply wasn't listening. J. J. O'Donnell never ceased evangelizing against deregulation, despite considerable flack from his rank-and-file.

"We are a trade labor movement," O'Donnell constantly warned skeptical pilots during the 1970s. "When we forget that, we start getting dumped on."

Later, O'Donnell reminisced: "I was just stunned at the way some of our guys never wanted to use the word 'union.' Here's a guy drawing down a hundred grand a year—he's all for 'free enterprise.' We had to keep pounding it in: 'We are workers, we are union!' They don't know that their salaries are the result of our unionism. We put it out in writing, but it almost appeared that our guys *couldn't read*!"

Until tragedy hits home, few individuals are ever willing to believe it can happen to them. Pilots going into combat *must* believe that the SAM launched skyward has somebody else's name on it. The "Titanic syndrome" affects everybody—not just airline pilots. "Hey, my end of the boat's not in the water! It's those guys at the other end who have a problem!"

This attitude sorely tested one primary article of faith in the professional airline pilots' creed—the notion of unity across company lines. The storied "brotherhood" of the air, which had been a fixture of the pilot's mentality since the 1920s, began to erode in the late 1950s with the passing of the pioneer airmen who founded ALPA. As elite technocrats, airline pilots during the late 1960s felt less kinship with these notions. Then in the late 1970s and early 1980s, as the twin blows of deregulation and economic recession slammed into the profession, the ancient notion of aerial brotherhood faced its most serious challenge. The crisis at Braniff brought it about.

Among the Braniff pilots, as among no other group, the ideal of a community of interests among professional airline pilots would face its moment of truth. Their colleagues at Eastern Airlines would test their adherence to this ancient precept by plunging them into stark conflict. The specific cause was Eastern's purchase of Braniff's Latin American routes.

"If our Latin American Division was such a loser," asks Len Morgan, the retired Braniff captain whose considerable writing talents earned him a regular column in *Flying* magazine, "why were Eastern and Pan American falling all over themselves to grab it?"

For Dick Russell and his fellow Latin American Division pilots at Braniff, the primary question was *why didn't ALPA do something to save their jobs!*

When Braniff, lurching ever more desperately into debt, sold off its South American routes to Eastern shortly before bankruptcy, the faltering airline's pilots, counting on ALPA help, assumed that the provisions of ALPA's merger mechanism, or some other aspect of ALPA policy, would provide them a safe haven. When Braniff actually declared bankruptcy in May 1982, the South American routes were sold to Eastern. Bilateral agreements required Eastern to serve the former Braniff route structure in South America. Eastern hired nearly 1,000 former Braniff personnel—but no pilots.

Didn't some ALPA policy, perhaps on "fragmentation," or their contract's "scope" clause, or simple necessity (not to mention decency) dictate that Eastern should *take at least a token number of pilots* with the airplanes? After all, weren't they "brother pilots?" Didn't their Eastern brothers owe them something?

Naturally Eastern's management opposed the expense of indoctrinating new pilots into their corporate culture, and the Braniff pilots didn't expect much help from that direction. But when Eastern's pilots turned their backs and sustained their management's position by failing to offer any jobs to Braniff's pilots, their anger and sense of betrayal knew no bounds. Wasn't J. J. O'Donnell, ALPA's president, an Eastern pilot, they raged? Didn't this mean an ALPA–Eastern conspiracy existed, that ALPA was favoring another pilot group at their expense? This was *all* ALPA's fault, they stormed. Otherwise, why didn't J. J. O'Donnell do something?

Former ALPA president J. J. O'Donnell, fit and tanned from his retirement-developed passion for tennis, scowled when asked this question during a 1990 interview.

"Braniff got sold down the river by the Eastern MEC, not by ALPA, and certainly not by the Eastern pilots," O'Donnell says hotly. "In all fairness, it was really only a portion of the MEC, about four guys who dominated the other twenty-four and took them right off the cliff. God knows I tried to get Eastern to take some Braniff pilots, even if it was only a token number, but they wouldn't budge. They didn't want me down there. My relationship with Augie Gorse [Eastern's MEC chairman] was so bad I had to send Jack Bavis [ALPA's executive administrator] down to protect ALPA's policies. He couldn't get in the meeting! Some solid citizens were on that MEC, and I asked them, 'How could you let that happen? If ALPA's merger policy is ignored by one airline, what's to prevent every other airline from ignoring it also?'"

Although rank-and-file Braniff pilots might have been unaware of the strained relations between O'Donnell and his former mates on Eastern, Braniff's MEC understood the problem. Throughout the 1970s, some of O'Donnell's most vociferous critics within ALPA had been his own former colleagues on Eastern. When Hank Duffy defeated O'Donnell in 1982, the Eastern councils would provide an important part of Duffy's winning margin. O'Donnell maintains that Braniff's MEC understood that his personal intervention with the Eastern MEC would have been counterproductive, and he speaks favorably of Braniff's pilot leaders, particularly Joe Baranowski, Howard Cole, and Mike Ferraro.

"The Braniff MEC was a good one; they depended upon us for leadership; they wanted our assistance," O'Donnell said in his 1990 interview. "We had two lawyers down there in Miami working with the Braniff and Eastern MECs. But the opportunities for promotion washed out the Eastern pilots' loyalty to ALPA. There's no question that their behavior was a mistake."

Hank Duffy, who would not come to ALPA's presidency until after the Braniff tragedy played out, remembers O'Donnell's trials sympathetically.

"O'Donnell had two problems at that time," Duffy remembers. "First, some companies don't want to take on any of the cultural problems that come with another company's pilot group, particularly if they're grouped together. Then you have the pilot problem. I think the pilot problem really depends on if the airline's doing well or not."

If Duffy's analysis is correct, the first problem was that Eastern's management did not want the Braniff pilots *as a cohesive group* and coerced its pilots into supporting this policy. Good evidence exists that Frank Borman, Eastern's CEO, told MEC Chairman Augie Gorse that he would not proceed with the Latin American acquisition if the Eastern MEC did not agree to exclude the Braniff pilots. Given the sad fate of Eastern today, it is easy to see that the second of Duffy's conditions applied as well—the Eastern pilots had *not* done well recently, lagging behind their contemporaries on other airlines in almost every category.

While these factors do not excuse the behavior of Eastern's MEC, they do make it understandable. Eastern's purchase of Braniff's Latin American routes was, arguably, outside the *technical* scope of ALPA merger policy, but the issue clearly had a *moral* dimension. J. J. O'Donnell argued vehemently with the leaders of Eastern's MEC that ALPA merger policy applied to their airline's acquisition of Braniff's routes in Latin America. The Eastern MEC's reading of the policy, obviously affected by naked self-interest, differed.

"We didn't even know the meetings were going on between Frank Borman and Augie Gorse," O'Donnell declared in his 1990 interview. "When it became known that Eastern was purchasing Braniff's South American routes, Eastern and Braniff were put on notice that we were implementing the merger policy."

So, further complicating O'Donnell's problem, at a time when he *might* have been able to influence the "solid citizens" on the Eastern MEC, the MEC *leadership* kept him completely out of the loop. Because the MEC *leadership* and

Eastern's management colluded to keep him uninformed, O'Donnell insists that he was almost helpless to affect events. By the time O'Donnell became aware of just how far off the ALPA reservation Eastern's MEC had roamed, his only alternative would have been to refuse to sign the necessary contract amendments that the new Eastern routes would require. If he had done so, at a time when so many pilots were out of work, the Eastern pilots would probably have bolted ALPA, just like the American pilots had done in 1963. O'Donnell could have asserted the raw power of his office to remove Eastern's MEC or to implement a trusteeship, something that no ALPA president had ever dared to do before to a *major* carrier. He had placed the Frontier MEC in trusteeship over the crew complement issue in the 1970s, but it was a small pilot group.[3] Hank Duffy would impose trusteeship on a small-airline pilot group, the one at Air Wisconsin, after the airline merged with Mississippi Valley in 1985. But to impose trusteeship on one of ALPA's "elephants," O'Donnell believes, would have been catastrophic.

"I was on the Eastern MEC for six years and on the Negotiating Committee for fourteen years, and I know they would have said, 'Screw you! Don't tell us how to run our business,'" O'Donnell said flatly in his 1990 interview.

Which was cold comfort to Braniff's pilots. Like hundreds of other Braniff pilots who came back to fly the line until "Bankruptcy II," Dick Russell balked at paying the Eastern strike assessment during their hour of need and resigned from ALPA with an angry letter to Hank Duffy. Given the circumstances of his professional life since "Bankruptcy I," few could have blamed him.

During the interval between the two Braniff bankruptcies, Russell dusted off his Naval Academy degree and sought work as a mechanical engineer. After a year of unsuccessful job hunting, he discovered two sad truths—his piloting skills were largely untransferable, and no other job he could get would pay him nearly as well as flying. Some aviation jobs he was not sure he wanted. Russell was not anxious to live out of a suitcase while chasing the dregs of aviation employment in undesirable and often dangerous parts of the world. Some new airlines like Air Florida shunned Russell because of the fear that he would leave them the minute Braniff resumed operations. That Air Florida could have used Russell seems obvious. The passengers aboard the Air Florida Boeing 737 that crashed into the 14th Street Bridge in Washington, D. C., might be alive today had their captain been Dick Russell, with his vast flying experience, instead of a 34-year-old captain who had never flown in winter conditions before.

But the truth is that the new post-deregulation airlines were not eager to hire pilots accustomed to ALPA pay scales and working conditions. The industry's traditional age discrimination also worked against Russell. Although recent court decisions have changed this state of affairs, at the time Dick Russell most needed a job, age discrimination was a fact of life. In 1983, *Aviation Week & Space Technology* reported that the major airlines had hired only one pilot over the age of 38 since 1976!

For a while, many former Braniff pilots looked with hope toward the labor protective provisions (LPPs) of the Airline Deregulation Act. Democratic politicians with their traditional pro-labor bias had supported deregulation only on condition that workers of any airline bankrupted by it would have first call on available job openings on surviving carriers. Dick Russell and his fellow Braniff pilots needed the LPPs desperately, and therein lies a supreme irony.

In one of his first actions as U. S. President, Ronald Reagan fulfilled his campaign promise to "get the government off the backs of the American people" by *canceling* the LPPs that the outgoing Carter Administration had implemented. Although Congress had written in the LPPs for a situation *exactly* like Braniff's, and President Carter had signed the LPP regulations, Reagan used the administrative power of his office to rescind them. Calling the LPPs "unnecessary" and an "unwarranted government interference" in private industry, Reagan left Braniff's pilots naked just when they needed one final dash of government regulation most.

"We had an immediate need for first-right-of-hire in 1983 when I became ALPA's president," Hank Duffy recalls. "We needed a Department of Transportation [DOT] determination that deregulation was the cause of Braniff's bankruptcy. We weren't able to move that on the DOT side. So we got Ray Donovan [Secretary of Labor] to publish the regulations; and as soon as he did, the companies challenged it in court. We eventually took it to the Supreme Court and won on a 9-0 decision in a Reagan Court, which was amazing, and got first-right-of-hire put in. But they fought the damn thing until 1988, and it was just a frustration that we couldn't get it out when we needed it in 1983 through 1985, when we had a big surplus of pilots."

"I voted for Reagan," Dick Russell admits. "I'm a political conservative, I believe in free enterprise. I'm just like most airline pilots. But unemployment sure does change your perspective."

Working for something called Carnival Airlines after "Bankruptcy II" also changed Russell's perspective on ALPA. The gambling junkets Russell flew on Boeing 727s out of Ft. Lauderdale to the Caribbean were poorly paid and had no benefits, just flat hourly pay—block to block. Russell confesses that he and his fellow Carnival pilots needed an ALPA contract badly. Working conditions were so bad on Carnival that Russell eventually quit in 1990.

Deregulation of the airline industry, while it lies at the vital center of every airline pilots' career concerns, is by no means the only problem complicating the lives of the people who fly the line professionally. The traditional problems—pay, working conditions, safety—haven't gone away. ALPA still must deal with these meat-and-potatoes issues. But deregulation made the job that much harder, and J. J. O'Donnell would find his leadership tested repeatedly by events that his predecessors never experienced.

The O'Donnell years would see no shortage of tribulation and trial. ✦

NOTES
[1]See "Pilots, Republicans, and Labor," Chapter 12.
[2]For a full account, see *Flying the Line,* Ch. 18.
[3]See "Dodging Bullets," Ch. 4.

CHAPTER 3

THE TRIALS OF J.J. O'DONNELL
SOS Theory and Practice

If airline pilots as a professional group were doing well during the four golden decades of government regulation, the same cannot be said of ALPA *as an organization.* While ALPA has always been a "clean" union, free of the anti-democratic corruption and financial malfeasance one associates with the Teamsters, it was nevertheless quite troubled internally throughout much of the period. Some careful observers of ALPA's history believe that an *excess* of democracy (if such a thing is possible) lies at the root of the problem. Stewart W. Hopkins, the Delta pilot who played a prominent role in ALPA's national politics as first vice-president during the 1960s, once summed the situation up nicely: "In ALPA, the only thing that cuts off debate is exhaustion."

For most of the four golden decades, ALPA's history at the national level bore witness to a steady subset of disputes among its leaders. Airline pilots have tended toward gentlemanly, almost polite confrontations; but these repetitive quarrels wracked ALPA's administrative functions and detracted from its effectiveness as a labor union. Some quarrels originated in policy differences, but a great many were purely personal, the product of individual quirks and dislikes, idiosyncratic feuds, and all too often, naked ambition.

Intramural skirmishing has always plagued ALPA's presidents. Dave Behncke, ALPA's founder, although an erratic administrator who was quite capable of petty vengefulness against those he regarded as "bad eggs," nevertheless suffered from these attacks. Although his ouster in 1951 was necessary, who is to say that Behncke's struggle to hold onto power against his internal rivals did not contribute to his deterioration as a leader?

Clarence N. "Clancy" Sayen, Behncke's successor, sick of the constant sniping at his leadership, resigned under pressure in 1962, midway through his term. Charles H. "Charley" Ruby, Sayen's successor, had a terrible time in office, once surviving a 1968 recall effort by dint of a tie vote, *which he himself cast* in the Executive Committee! So, these internal quarrels clearly meet two of the tests of historical significance—they persisted over time and they led to major changes.

Throughout the four decades of regulation, ALPA's leaders were aware of this problem and wrestled with it intermittently. Perhaps the best example of this internal effort to rationalize ALPA's administration and immunize it from "politics" (a term that has a peculiar resonance in ALPA's history) is the collective history of the various Organizational Structure Study Committees (OSSCs). The first OSSC, founded in 1951 during the Behncke ouster, has had several incarnations over the years and has employed many celebrated outside consultants (probably the most famous being George P. Schultz, then dean of the University of Chicago School of Business and later Ronald Reagan's Secretary of State). That ALPA heavyweights frequently served on the various OSSCs proves the Committee's importance and the gravity of the problem.

Put simply, that problem was "internal politics" and the effect politics had on ALPA's administrative functions and other *routine* services. The culminating crisis of ALPA's administrative chaos followed the defection the American Airlines pilots from ALPA in 1963. Then, a bitter power struggle between President Ruby and his opponents on the Executive Committee, notably the regional vice-presidents (which we will discuss later), all but deadlocked ALPA.

While the word "politics" generally elicits a negative response, and "politician" is often a term of contempt, ALPA's presidency is essentially a "political" job. Nobody can lead ALPA without being a "politician." The person who lacks political skills, who has no knack for influencing others to adopt policy in their mutual interest, who cannot master the essential art of representing the opinions and sympathies of those who entrust decision-making for them, cannot long survive at the top of ALPA.

John Joseph O'Donnell survived for 12 years at ALPA's top. As a practitioner of the political arts, he was no slouch. The mere fact of his emergence from the relative obscurity of local executive council chairman to ALPA's presidency is sufficient proof of his political gifts. In fact, O'Donnell's internal opponents would often use his skill at politics against him, arguing that possession of these skills was sufficient proof that he was unsuited to hold ALPA's presidency!

"I see history repeating itself," former ALPA president O'Donnell said darkly in a 1990 interview. "There was this constant politics between one airline and the other, Delta off on its own, United out in left field, Eastern in some other part of the ball park, nobody really working together, efforts to cut Hank Duffy's throat. The same thing happened to me."

John J. O'Donnell (usually referred to as "J.J." by his contemporaries, but known as "John" to his intimates) has seen more ALPA history *from the top* than anybody except Dave Behncke. From his election in 1970 to his narrow and bitter defeat at the hands of Hank Duffy in 1982, O'Donnell survived at the top of ALPA's political world. Politics, by one ancient definition, is how people in any society decide "who gets what." By almost any definition, ALPA's particular brand of politics could be as treacherous as a Byzantine court's. As we shall see, this tendency toward intramural skirmishing permeated ALPA politics down to the local level.[1]

Benjamin Disreali, the 19th century British prime minister, once described politics as the art of "climbing the greasy pole." J.J. O'Donnell would have understood Disreali's point, for he had to struggle mightily to remain atop ALPA's "greasy pole." He faced bitter opposition and serious efforts to recall him from office, all of which left wounds that still cause pain.

"A bitterness still lingers," O'Donnell admitted. While living in Florida retirement, O'Donnell sat for a long interview in January 1991—*after* Hank Duffy's term ended. In the interest of fairness, he had refused to go "on the record" with his recollections until Duffy, the man who wrested ALPA from him in 1982, also retired. As we shall see, relations between Duffy and O'Donnell, influenced not only by the 1982 presidential election, but also by the difficult transition of power which followed it, were never close. That is not to say that O'Donnell failed to express sympathy for Duffy. Like former U.S. presidents, ex-presidents of ALPA belong to an exclusive club and, hence, pay each other a certain respect—regardless of their past differences.

"I wasn't really welcome at ALPA functions during Hank's presidency," O'Donnell said. "I invited Charley Ruby to every convention we had. Duffy didn't do that with me [something Duffy disputes and which probably requires a semantic interpretation of the term "invitation"], but I respected his right to run ALPA's politics the way he wanted to. He was the president."

With ALPA's internal and external wars behind him, O'Donnell became passionate about tennis and physical fitness, pursuing them with the same intensity that characterized his presidency. But time and retirement had mellowed him only slightly.

"It's a terrible thing to say, the analogy I'm going to use," said O'Donnell of one old adversary, "but he was like Saddam Hussein, absolutely ruthless. Every airline's MEC has got about a third who are wild radicals. Another third are dedicated, intelligent guys, but not forceful. The final third wouldn't open their mouths if their lives depended on it."

The bitterness that O'Donnell still harbored in 1991 from the myriad battles of his presidency emerged clearly in his rapid-fire Boston syntax. His conversation overflowed with tales of the intricate deals, misunderstandings, plots and counterplots that were the political reality of his 12 years as ALPA's president. O'Donnell's capacity to shrewdly sum up both friend and foe was evident in the series of finely drawn portraits (sometimes in acid) he sketched. The defeat that Hank Duffy inflicted in 1982 still rankled, although O'Donnell tried to pass it off with a show of philosophical detachment. Boston Irish are not known for accepting political defeat with equanimity.

"I was the big winner by losing," O'Donnell declared in 1991.

From O'Donnell's perspective, most of his troubles as ALPA's president came about because the "radical third" made life miserable for him. His recollections ring with denunciations of men who are, for the most part, now retired or dead. O'Donnell's list of "incompetent destructionists" is a long one: Rich Flournoy, the TWA captain who nearly succeeded in recalling Charley Ruby and subsequently became a thorn in O'Donnell's side; Robert G. "Bob" Rubens, the North Central (later Republic) captain who as a regional vice-president harassed O'Donnell mercilessly, until the 1974 BOD abolished that office; Augie Gorse, the Eastern MEC chairman who bitterly criticized O'Donnell during his presidency; Nick Gentile and Bill Brown, the Delta leaders who were the gray eminencies behind Hank Duffy's upset victory over O'Donnell in 1982.

But at the top of O'Donnell's "enemies list" was Bill Arsenault, the stolid United MEC chairman whom he defeated for ALPA's presidency in 1974. Arsenault plagued O'Donnell until February 1975, when the United MEC (for internal reasons having nothing to do with national politics), recalled Arsenault as MEC chairman. Gerry Pryde replaced Arsenault as United MEC Chairman and developed a close political alliance with O'Donnell. Arsenault never returned to power on United after 1975, but the difficulties he caused O'Donnell during his first five years in office made a lasting impression. O'Donnell visibly stiffened, the ghosts of dozens of old, mean-spirited political battles instantly materializing, when Bill Arsenault's name was mentioned in 1991.

Arsenault came to United in the 1961 merger with Capital Airlines.[2] Despite the minority position of the old Capital pilots once they became part of United, Arsenault rapidly became a factor in ALPA politics at the MEC level. He challenged and ultimately displaced from leadership positions the old United elite, men like Chuck Woods and Bill Davis. Until Arsenault undid himself with the United rank-and-file over contract negotiations in the mid 1970s, he was a fierce O'Donnell critic and a potent adversary.

O'Donnell explains Arsenault's rise at United as being the result of apathy, and his view finds some support in the observations of Charles J. "Chuck" Pierce, who after a long career of service on United's MEC, would become ALPA secretary during Duffy's first term.

"The rise to power of the Capital pilots within the United MEC after the merger was a very touchy subject until the late 1960s," Pierce says. "Even into the 1970s, a certain amount of resentment was directed at Bill Arsenault, because the ex-Capital pilots wielded power disproportionate to their size. They would work for and support one another in voting situations."

Gerry Pryde, who replaced Arsenault as United MEC chairman in February 1975, discounts the "ex-Capital" factor as an issue in the internal politics that led to Arsenault's recall.

"I'm quite sure that resentments directed at the ex-Capital pilots played some part in the recall of John Ferg [whom we will meet later] as MEC chairman during the late 1960s," Pryde observes. "But by 1975, when Bill Arsenault got recalled, all of us—the old Capital pilots and the old United group—were minorities. New hires who had no recollection of the merger swamped us."

Arsenault looked, talked, and acted like an old-fashioned labor boss, catering not at all to the sleek, sophisticated image most airline pilots preferred. If there is truth in the old notions that politics makes strange bedfellows, that opposites attract and equals repel, then perhaps that explains why Arsenault and O'Donnell were instantly at loggerheads—they were very much alike! But don't try to tell J.J. O'Donnell that!

"He threatened to physically beat me up at least a dozen times," O'Donnell declared in 1991. He insisted that the only civilized conversations he ever had with Arsenault were in social situations with ladies present. "When we were with our wives, Bill was always very nice, out of character. The next morning, he's pushing me to the edge again. Arsenault always stood behind me, I could always feel him there, and he was big, husky, like a guy in an old 1930s labor movie."

Politically, O'Donnell sounds and acts like a guy out of 1950s labor movie.

Street-smart, tough, quick-witted as Rod Steiger in *On the Waterfront*, O'Donnell built his ALPA career on the bones of political opponents who took him lightly, or who thought his grammatical lapses indicated a lack of native shrewdness. To assess O'Donnell during his 12-year stewardship of ALPA, a review of a few critical episodes is necessary.

O'Donnell had won the ALPA presidency in 1970, after a successful but relatively unremarkable 20-year career at Eastern. Although he had served on the Eastern pilots' Negotiating Committee for 14 years, O'Donnell was best known as a Charley Ruby loyalist who had displayed a high degree of doggedness in carrying out tasks assigned to him. O'Donnell had won a reputation as an expert in retirement and insurance (R&I) matters, and his willingness to help other ALPA groups restructure their R&I programs made him well-known to the pilots who specialized in this arcane area. But O'Donnell's was certainly no "household" name to pilots flying the line. His reputation was nothing like a W.T. "Slim" Babbitt's or a Jerry Wood's, even among his fellow Eastern pilots.

"He was a just 'boom,' out of nowhere," recalls former ALPA President J. Randolph "Randy" Babbitt, from his perspective as having been a junior second officer in 1970. "We heard of this R&I guy who seemed to be doing a good job and that everybody liked up in Boston, a small domicile that always had people active in ALPA work."

Eastern's Boston base, from which O'Donnell emerged, had provided more than its share of "inside players" who distinguished themselves behind the scenes in the "nuts and bolts" committees. Pilots like Vic Tully and Roy Anderson, both from the relatively small Boston base, fell into this category. Over the years, a characteristic of ALPA's history was that small domiciles, where everybody knew everybody else, tended to elect and re-elect the same pilots to local office until their faces became quite familiar within ALPA's inner circle. In a larger pilot base, relations between individual pilots were more impersonal, largely because of the constant coming and going. O'Donnell benefited from the "focused minority" aspect of his small pilot base in Boston and from the fact that his willingness to take on extra tasks had distinguished him as a "bear for work."

"I was on the BOD when Charley Ruby got elected in 1962, and I was violently opposed to him," O'Donnell recalled in 1991. "But once he was elected, I did my best to make him look like a hero. I had my problems with Charley, but I tried to be constructive. His enemies, including some guys on my own airline, held that against me; but I figure when you elect a guy president, you ought to get behind him. A lot of people spent all their energy attacking Charley and never gave him a chance to do the job as president."

As we have seen, the internal politics at ALPA's top have always been complex, riven by arcane rivalries that often had more to do with *personal* differences than policy matters. This personal factor was no less true of O'Donnell than it was of Clancy Sayen or Charley Ruby during their presidencies, but in O'Donnell's case, critical *policy* issues had a large bearing on the political equation.

One prederegulation issue, skyjacking, deserves special attention, because it led to the 1972 Suspension of Service (SOS), an episode that almost made O'Donnell a one-term president. It also tells us something about him as a political leader and about ALPA as an organization.

Skyjacking was perhaps the most dangerous and prolonged crisis of the O'Donnell era. To deal with it, ALPA necessarily had to step on some powerful toes in government and management, thus permanently affecting both internal and external relationships. O'Donnell's presidency began with the skyjacking crisis already full-blown. It was, second only to deregulation, the most immediate and personal crisis to confront professional airline pilots since the 1930s.[3] In terms of their personal safety, the physical threat of bodily harm, skyjacking menaced every pilot everywhere, a hazard unrivaled in modern times.

Broadly speaking, skyjacking could be subdivided into several categories based on the *purpose* of the skyjacker. Some skyjackers were simply deranged individuals whose motives were obscure. Others were common criminals. The extortionist using the name "D.B. Cooper," who parachuted from the rear ramp of a skyjacked Northwest B-727 on Nov. 24, 1971, after collecting a large cash ransom, was one of several such felons. Many U.S. skyjackers sought transportation to destinations denied to them for various reasons, usually political; individuals seeking to get to (or leave) Cuba after Fidel Castro seized power in 1959 made up the bulk of this category. But by far the most troublesome skyjackers were political terrorists, who most often sprang from the snake's nest of trouble that is the modern Middle East.

Terrorism is the last gasp of a political movement that has exhausted all other means of effectiveness. This act of desperation has political roots, hence the solution, in a long-term *strategic* sense, can only be political. But in the short term, skyjacking, whatever category of causation it falls into, can have *tactical* solutions.

Almost from the beginning of O'Donnell's tenure as ALPA's president, the skyjacking issue and the search for a *tactical* solution to it dominated his attention. Any number of the people O'Donnell brought into ALPA work, men who would later be regarded as his protégés (like Tom Ashwood of TWA), owed their rise to the skyjacking problem and ALPA's search for a solution to it.

Technical solutions, however imperfect, eventually would be found for the problem. The details of the kind of airport security familiar to passengers all over the world today owe much to the technical contributions of ALPA and International Federation of Air Line Pilots Associations committees and the hundreds of individual pilots from many nations who worked so hard on them. But the fundamental problem in advancing a solution to the skyjacking problem lay in the realm of politics. J.J. O'Donnell's whole presidency was, to some extent, colored by his response to skyjacking and the extraordinarily direct method many pilots favored to dramatize the seriousness of the skyjacking problem— the Suspension of Service, or SOS, concept.

A series of skyjacking incidents, several of them desperate and dramatic, forced O'Donnell's hand. Aware that something as radical as grounding an airliner to make a political point would be controversial with airline pilots, O'Donnell prepared for it in unusual ways. One innovative step, which Charles Dent (United) suggested to O'Donnell, was a celebrated B-747 ride ALPA sponsored for nearly 300 United Nations personnel on Nov. 6, 1971.

The short flight from New York to Montreal in the rented Pan Am B-747 (piloted by Stan Doepke of Pan Am) had as its purpose to intensively lobby influential politicians from all over the world to pass ALPA's "T-Plus" antiskyjacking program. Put simply, T-Plus was a comprehensive set of laws, penalties, and procedures for dealing with skyjacking. Among those being lobbied was future U.S. President George Bush, then U.S. ambassador to the U.N. Placing these world political leaders in a controlled and dramatic situation where they could hear the stories of more than 30 crewmembers who had been skyjacked (including pilots from recently defected American Airlines—with full approval of their ALPA-clone, the Allied Pilots Association)—won unanimous support among rank-and-file pilots.

Everybody who participated in the U.N. flight thought it went well. The roster of ALPA topsiders and MEC heavyweights aboard (including O'Donnell's nemesis Bill Arsenault of United) was impressive. Tom Ashwood of TWA, who would later come within an eyelash of unseating Hank Duffy from ALPA's presidency in 1986, acted as master of ceremonies. Ashwood functioned at top form, his cultivated British accent wowing the assembled politicos.

Former Executive Vice-President Merle C. "Skip" Eglet of Northwest, although no fan of Ashwood's politically, remembers that he made a marvelous first impression: "Ashwood used the Queen's English extremely well."

All the international politicians who accepted ALPA's hospitality on the Montreal excursion went home vowing immediate action by their countries. And nothing happened! Despite rave reviews in the press, heavy television news coverage, and all the back-slapping support, nothing happened! Terrorism slackened not at all, and skyjackings continued. The international community, for all the oral assurances that their U.N. representatives gave during the joyride to Montreal (complete with lavish meals at ALPA's expense), resisted a coordinated attack on skyjacking.

Even such traditional agencies as the International Civil Aviation Organization (ICAO), headquartered in Montreal, offered no help in quelling the skyjacking problem. ICAO, founded in 1944 in a far-sighted attempt to give structure to what was obviously going to be a major post-World War II expansion of international aviation, would repeatedly fail to take effective action against skyjacking. Because ICAO required a two/thirds majority to pass rules, African and Arab nations were able to block the anti-skyjacking efforts of the international community. Despite massive lobbying efforts by IFALPA, with ALPA members spearheading the campaign, African and Arab nations generally continued to see skyjackers as "freedom fighters," rather than as criminals.

While not as hamstrung as the ICAO, international political leaders were also divided and hesitant about how to handle skyjacking. ALPA, IFALPA, and professional airmen everywhere (including the Soviet Union and the Eastern Bloc countries), were united and determined to do *something* about it. Even the Israeli version of ALPA joined with IFALPA delegates to protest the skyjacking *by their own government* of an Arab airliner suspected of carrying guerrilla leaders. Israeli ALPA leader Y. Sheked flew to Washington, D.C., to support O'Donnell's denunciation of Israel—a courageous act. So pilots *everywhere* were determined take action jointly to end skyjacking once and for all.

But what should the pilots do? How could they get the *serious* attention of political leaders? J.J. O'Donnell, who was by nature a cautious and conservative man, listened with increasing alarm as rank-and-file airline pilots demanded *drastic* action. One idea, emanating from the European pilot groups in IFALPA, began to pick up momentum in the U.S. pilot community in the early 1970s. The idea that gained increasing support was for a symbolic temporary shut-down of *all* airline service for a short period.

Because the suspension of service, or SOS, tactic bore some resemblance to a traditional strike, it had obvious and immediate legal problems. American labor law, and particularly the Railway Labor Act of 1926 (including the "Pilots' Amendment" of 1936),[4] was designed precisely to *prevent* such "wildcat" actions as an SOS. Hence, any resort to the SOS tactic would need a careful and innovative legal approach, one that could be fully substantiated in both constitutional and statute law.

ALPA General Counsel Henry Weiss would eventually craft a defensible *constitutional* rationale for an SOS in 1981. By refusing to fly during a 24-hour shutdown (which was not a strike against their employers), airline pilots would, in effect, be petitioning Congress (and other governments around the world), for relief from skyjacking. The legal validity of this argument, which Henry Weiss devised almost entirely, would later be recognized by the Supreme Court when it upheld flag burning as "symbolic speech" and hence constitutionally protected.

But all that was in the future. In 1972 Weiss faced an immediate problem of justifying the skyjacking SOS in *statute* law. From his great breadth of experience in labor law, Weiss adapted the closest parallel cases he could find to serve ALPA's purpose.

"I remembered that in the 1950s the Longshoremen's Union refused to load ships with grain for Russia," Weiss says. "They did so on the proposition that they were protesting *not* against their employers, but against *government policy*. That case eventuated in a Supreme Court decision that upheld the action. That gave legal foundation to the ill-arranged skyjacking SOS. I say ill-arranged because ALPA's officers simply had not prepared the membership for the SOS."

Regardless of its legal validity, the SOS idea spooked average line pilots, not only because it could get them fired, but because it ran counter to every tenet of their personal code. Airline pilots are not people who defy authority. Their whole ethos revolves around the concept of order, duty, and steadiness of purpose, all carried out within the framework of legitimate authority. To ask people bred in this environment to act like aerial "hippie protesters" was dangerous. Why then, did the SOS concept develop such momentum?

J.J. O'Donnell in 1991 thought he knew.

"You go to a meeting of the largest council in ALPA, which is United Council 12 in Chicago with twelve-hundred members [during the early 1970s], and you had thirty people there," O'Donnell said hotly. "Twenty-seven of them are likely to be militants who want to carry sidearms in the cockpit!"

So O'Donnell concluded that the SOS concept, which he maintained was a bad idea, growing like the proverbial "Topsy," resulted from the apathy of ALPA's general membership and the activism of a militant few. Since the subsequent history of the SOS movement supports O'Donnell's thesis, why did he agree to it?Barely three weeks after the expensive, ALPA-sponsored "Montreal Joyride," the U.N. failed to take action on even the most elemental of the "T-Plus" proposals, one that would boycott nations giving asylum to skyjackers. The outrage of the international pilot community was such that the "crazies" won support for an SOS action, according to O'Donnell's view. But regardless of his personal misgivings, O'Donnell would have to lead the charge for a world-wide shutdown, a "Global Suspension of Service." On June 6, 1972, a special emergency meeting of the Executive Board approved the SOS, setting a date of June 19 for the action if the U.N. had not responded by then. IFALPA approved a coordinated SOS action on June 8, 1972, two days after ALPA's decision.

"The stupid idiots called for a shutdown, *policy as set by the BOD* called for a shutdown, *I didn't call for a shutdown*!" O'Donnell insisted in 1991. "Goddam it, they shouldn't pass hairy-chested resolutions they don't intend to implement, because if the BOD passes it, I'm going to try my darndest to implement it."

O'Donnell was still learning his job in 1972, and no doubt uncertain of himself owing to the closeness of his victory in 1970. But it is still an indictment of his leadership *at the time*, that he would permit an SOS movement to get out of hand, if indeed he thought it wouldn't work.

"I seriously believed that I could have shut it down..." O'Donnell said in the 1991 interview, his voice trailing off as he recalled the disaster that nearly made him a one-term president. "Certainly we had legitimate grievances, but...."

If in fact O'Donnell did oppose the SOS privately, his public activities gave no hint of it. Perhaps his reminiscences are more strongly molded by hindsight than remembrance, for as we shall see, the animosities that the failed 1972 SOS generated would haunt him for years. Certainly there is not the slightest hint of reluctance in O'Donnell's *public* posture of support for the SOS at the time of the crisis, and many contemporaries do not remember events the way he does.

John Gratz of TWA, many times an MEC chairman (and recalled from office by his fellow TWA pilots almost as often), found himself in the thick of the 1972 SOS controversy almost by accident.

"I was elected MEC chairman on April 7, 1972, and it was one of the proudest moments of my life," Gratz recalls. "I come from a union family. I remember my father once going to jail briefly over a strike, so I was confident that an SOS was the right thing to do. When I came to Washington, it was my first Executive Board meeting. My airline had been hit pretty hard by skyjacking, but I didn't know anybody at the meeting so I tried to keep my mouth shut. Well O'Donnell made his spiel, and he said we needed an SOS resolution that the president would call with the concurrence of the Board if, in his opinion, it was warranted. Everybody kind of slumped down in their chairs. O'Donnell said, 'Maybe you didn't hear me too well,' and he went through the whole thing again. Well, I rose to the bait and moved that we shut the world down. Everybody cheered, they moved to recess, and they whisked me away and told me to put it in writing, but I had a whole bunch of people helping me."

To John Gratz and many of his contemporaries at the meeting that authorized the SOS, O'Donnell seemed four-square in favor of it. But regardless of any misgivings he might have privately harbored, we must remember that for purely tactical reasons O'Donnell would have to put up a brave front to give the SOS credibility.

During a nationwide live telecast of "Face the Nation" on the eve of the SOS, O'Donnell did just that. He appeared committed, militant, and willing to defy a court injunction, which the Air Transport Association (ATA), representing 18 airlines, had obtained on June 17, 1972, which seemed, on first reading, to bar ALPA from the action.

"I don't know anything about the courts," O'Donnell said in response to a question. "I'm not a lawyer. All I know is there's no way I'm going to order my people to go to work tomorrow. The airlines are going to be shut down."

O'Donnell appeared at the time to be willing to defy the courts and risk going to jail. His remarks induced a near state of panic in Bruce Simon, Henry Weiss's law partner, who was monitoring the telecast in the studio. Simon, assuming that the telecast was being taped and could be altered, told O'Donnell they had to get the broadcast stopped or changed. But it was a *live* program.

"Bruce was standing right behind the camera," O'Donnell recalls. "About 22 minutes past the hour, I get this question, and I say, 'We're not going to work,' and Bruce stands up and says, 'Oh my God!'"

Simon, aware of the grave consequences of *announcing in advance* that he would defy a court injunction, hustled O'Donnell out the studio's back door immediately after the telecast and into hiding.

"I said, 'What the hell's the matter with you,'" O'Donnell remembered later. "He says, 'I've got to get you out of here before the sheriff throws handcuffs on you.' We did not go back to the ALPA office. It was *the most emotional experience I've had in my life*. I didn't make the policy, but that's what the members wanted, that's what the BOD said, and I didn't have the luxury of choosing which policies to implement."

John Gratz, the author of the SOS resolution, also went into hiding: "When O'Donnell disappeared, on the advice of friends I did, too. We went out to a motel, and we were all making jokes about the movie *The Godfather*. We 'hit the mattresses.'"

Although Gratz laughs about the episode now, in 1972 the possibility of going to jail was not funny. Nor was the subsequent SOS fiasco an occasion for humor. The outcome of the 1972 SOS was at best disappointing, despite some isolated successes. Eastern, which had lost one of its own (First Officer Chuck Hartley, after whom Eastern would name its Miami training center) to a skyjacker's bullet, shut down completely. Likewise the pilots of Northeast Airlines (who would later merge with Delta), managed a good shutdown. But faced with court injunctions against the SOS, other ALPA groups complied only spottily. United's Bill Davis, who was an ALPA national officer, walked off a loaded B-747 just before pushback, and a few other brave individuals did likewise.

Eastern's pilots came away from the 1972 SOS affair aggrieved at the lack of support from other ALPA pilot groups, resolved to vent their anger and frustration somewhere, *somehow* in the future—a dangerous matter for ALPA's internal unity. But the Eastern pilots were operating without the threat of punishment, for Frank Borman, Eastern's CEO, had approved their participation in the SOS and was willing to see his airline shut down. Other pilot groups faced a far different situation.

"I went in to see the president of TWA and said, 'We're having this SOS, I'm sure you've heard about it, so we'll be shutting you down Sunday at midnight,'" John Gratz remembers matter-of-factly. "He started hollering and calling me a mad dog union fool. I told him there was no way to stop it, but my guys were getting scared and trying to wiggle out, and my MEC was raising hell. So I learned that when you say you can lick anybody in the house, you damn well better be able to do it! It was bloody awful."

With TWA wavering in its support for the SOS, other pilot groups looking for leadership also began weakening. The MEC chairmen of Braniff, Northwest, Pan American, Seaboard World, and Western Air Lines all called Gratz, informing him that if the TWA pilots, who were identified in the public mind most heavily with the action because of Gratz's authorship of the SOS resolution, did not honor the SOS, neither would they. Gratz, with his own MEC crumbling, tried to tough it out. He bluffed and cajoled, bullied and begged his MEC, appearing outwardly confident of success. It was all to no avail. Gratz's gamble fell apart during a disastrous telephone conference call among his 18 MEC members just preceding the SOS.

"I told them they were cowardly, yellow-bellied whiners. I said, 'Man your battle stations,' and slammed the phone receiver down," Gratz recalls. "Pretty soon the phone rings, and it's my best buddy, and he says, 'John, nobody hung up when you hung up. They ain't gonna to do it.'"

Not only did Gratz's MEC pull out of the SOS, they recalled him as MEC chairman—and not for the last time! With the collapse on TWA, the other airlines looking to it for leadership also folded.

J.J. O'Donnell was not a slow learner. By the time the aborted 1981 SOS, titled "Operation USA" (the acronym standing for "Unity for Safe Air Travel), rolled around, he was older, wiser, and much cagier. In one sense, O'Donnell would handle Operation USA brilliantly, like a concert violinist handles a Stradivarius. He never intended that Operation USA should ever *actually* take place. Having learned his lesson about the dangers of the SOS concept in 1972, O'Donnell would use Operation USA as a Machiavellian ploy to extort concessions from the new Reagan Administration. The only problem with O'Donnell's brilliantly conceived strategy and performance during the 1981 SOS was that its political effect *inside* ALPA was not what he expected.

Operation USA was thus a simultaneous exercise in *external* and *internal* politics.[5] O'Donnell frankly admitted in 1991 that Operation USA was a "grab bag" approach to settling issues that had arisen as the result of deregulation, plus some other long-standing grievances ALPA had with the way the FAA enforced certain rules.

Thus, Operation USA was a purely tactical ploy on which O'Donnell spent money lavishly. He hired consultants, expanded communications within ALPA, and generally succeeded in getting everyone "in the loop" by holding "pep rally" type meetings at various crew bases around the country. All this was necessary to convince the incoming Reagan administration that ALPA was serious, that the nation's airlines really were going to shut down. O'Donnell's problem was that to convince the Reagan people of ALPA's seriousness, he first had to convince rank-and-file ALPA members. That required subterfuge, and it would lead to political problems.

"We got the nation's attention in 1972, that we had worldwide concerns about skyjacking," O'Donnell says. "But with the 1981 SOS, let's be honest, it was about self-interest. We were trying to solve a lot of different problems. We spent millions of dollars whipping up the troops, getting them emotionally ready to walk out of their airplanes."

In O'Donnell's judgment, which he based not only on the failed 1972 SOS, but also on the recent history of ALPA's strikes, if he had unleashed Operation USA it would have been, in his words "an absolute catastrophe." So, O'Donnell's game plan was to call off Operation USA when he thought he had extracted the maximum he could from it. He had no idea it would generate so much political heat inside ALPA.

In November 1980, shortly after the election of Ronald Reagan, the BOD once again authorized the Executive Board to call an SOS if the incoming Republican administration did not respond to ALPA's concerns.

The timing was deliberate. O'Donnell, who had contacts with high-ranking members of Reagan's campaign staff, knew that his best chance of influencing new Secretary of Transportation Drew Lewis was during the first weeks of his term in office.

Despite repeated campaigning against the Carter administration's policies as they affected aviation, ALPA had been unable to secure any relief. The object of this pressure on the Carter administration (as it would later be on the Reagan administration) was to secure a Presidential Emergency Board (PEB) to adjudicate the most divisive of the several issues—crew complement.

Even a highly publicized day-long picketing of the White House in October 1980, just before the election (when it was most damaging to the Democrats), had not secured the PEB. But O'Donnell was almost certain (to the extent that any deal involving "politics" can be) that the incoming Republicans would accommodate ALPA.

"Because I was an Irish Catholic from Boston," O'Donnell says, "everybody thought I was a Democrat. I have a lot of liberal views, but I was a registered Republican for many years. I was a strong supporter of Ronald Reagan, and I think 75 percent of airline pilots were, too. I thought it was in ALPA's best interests *not* to endorse him, but I had good 'ins' with the Reagan people, particularly the White House staff, on both a working and a social basis."

During the campaign, O'Donnell worked quietly for Reagan, one of the few labor union presidents to do so. The Reagan people were glad to have O'Donnell's support. The *quid pro quo* for this work, O'Donnell was given to understand, would be speedy action on ALPA's request for a PEB to decide, once and for all, the crew complement issue. So O'Donnell *knew*, long before the BOD meeting in November 1980 that he would *not* have to implement an SOS. O'Donnell had cleverly insured ALPA against the "catastrophe" he was sure an SOS would cause.

On Feb. 11, 1980, ALPA's Executive Board canceled the SOS at O'Donnell's urging. Two weeks later, living up to the bargain his subordinates had made with O'Donnell, Ronald Reagan announced the appointment of a PEB.

When the PEB met in early May 1981, ALPA got its day in court. But put simply, it was a foregone conclusion that the PEB that Reagan appointed would hand ALPA its head on a platter. Aside from window dressing, that's exactly what happened, with consequences for O'Donnell's political standing within ALPA that were to prove quite damaging. On every substantive issue, particularly the third-crewman concept, the PEB ruled against ALPA's position. The only positive aspect of the Reagan Board was that it finally ended the long internal wrangle over crew complement. Henceforward, the third crew member, with whatever safety edge that extra set of eyes provided, would fade away as technology improved productivity in the cockpit. The long battle was lost, but at least it would no longer trouble ALPA internally.

For J.J. O'Donnell, political problems, compounded by the devastating impact of airline deregulation, were multiplying. O'Donnell could point to the "window dressing" successes of Operation USA: a voice in aircraft certification, new channels of communication with the FAA, the quashing of that agency's attempt to use the cockpit voice recorder (CVR) as an enforcement tool, a function for which it had never been intended. But as the presidential election year of 1982 dawned, these benefits seemed trivial, and disaffection with O'Donnell spread. Part of this disaffection was simply that he had been in office long enough for a backlog of separate grievances to build up against him. The Northwest pilots, for example, felt that O'Donnell had not been sufficiently supportive of their 105-day strike in 1978, although when pressed for details, they generally admit that most of their complaints were more psychological than material.

Gerry Pryde of United puts it another way: "I was a close student of that strike, and what went wrong there had everything to do with the pilots of Northwest and little to do with J.J. O'Donnell. Kay MacMurray [the federal mediator assigned to the Northwest strike and, incidentally, former United pilot who had quit flying to become Sayen's executive administrator during the mid-1950s] confirmed my judgment."

Thus grievances emanating from separate airlines, and for varied reasons, nagged at O'Donnell. Many ALPA members traced their discontent to his handling of the SOS—some pilots disliked O'Donnell because they opposed the SOS concept, others denounced him for not carrying it through to completion.

The SOS idea has had a troubling history. Three times, in 1972, 1981, and as we shall see, during the Eastern strike of 1989, the SOS concept fractured ALPA's internal unity. While preparation for the aborted 1981 SOS, Operation USA, was much better than for the skyjacking SOS of 1972, rank-and-file ALPA members (had O'Donnell permitted it to go forward) probably would not have adhered to it any better. When Eastern's pilots, desperately at war with Frank Lorenzo during the 1989 strike, appealed to Hank Duffy for a nationwide SOS, he would make the same judgment as O'Donnell—that the basic SOS concept was unworkable.

In a sense, the SOS is ALPA's nuclear weapon. Before any ALPA president dares launch it, he must be certain that the issue necessitating its use is of such paramount importance that the vast majority of airline pilots *on every airline* will unhesitatingly risk not only the loss of their careers, *but also jail!* Given the unfriendly structure of the federal court system since 1980, American labor law has been transformed. An SOS (even a local one) would almost certainly bring an injunctive crackdown. A *nationwide* SOS would almost certainly entail prison time for ALPA's leaders. The antilabor proclivities of judges whom Ronald Reagan and George Bush appointed, and who by 1991 constituted over 80 percent of the federal bench, would almost certainly land ALPA leaders *down to the local level* in jail.

The abortive 1981 SOS would have serious political consequences for O'Donnell. His opponents believed he was vulnerable because of it, and they were determined that the 1982 BOD meeting would not see a repeat of the 1978 meeting. In 1978, O'Donnell's opponents failed to unite on a candidate, and he won a surprisingly easy reelection. Only Bob Shipner, one of the chronically disaffected Eastern pilots, challenged O'Donnell. Shipner had no following outside his own airline and negotiated a withdrawal (in return for a chance to address the delegates) on the eve of balloting in 1978.

O'Donnell by 1991 still fumed at the Shipner episode of 1978, because Shipner, in return for being allowed access to the rostrum before withdrawing from the race (which was, technically, a violation of the rules), agreed to say nothing derogatory about O'Donnell. Angelo "Angie" Marcione of TWA, chairman of the Nominating Committee, at first refused Shipner's request as improper. But O'Donnell encouraged Marcione, who was a strong supporter, to bend the rules in the interest of saving money and time.

"Running a Board of Directors meeting was expensive as hell," O'Donnell recalled. "I didn't want to appear anxious to have Shipner withdraw. But he starts this terrible cutting up of me, about no leadership. Then he withdrew. My friends were just totally bulgy-eyed. There was no applause for him—total silence. Shipner had only a few crazies. I had 95 percent of the votes."

Many ALPA insiders had expected the 1978 election to be a repeat of the extremely close 1974 election, which O'Donnell, still smarting from the failed 1972 SOS crisis, had won by an eyelash. Skip Eglet of Northwest, a close student of ALPA's political dynamics who has held a variety of important ALPA offices, including executive vice-president, cites O'Donnell's skillful pre-BOD maneuvers in explaining this lack of opposition in 1978.

"There's a certain anomaly in the 1978 election, because nobody was terribly pleased with O'Donnell," Eglet says. "In 1978 we had a 105-day strike on Northwest, and I was disappointed in the support we got from O'Donnell. So I made a pilgrimage to Seattle to visit Gerry Pryde of United to try to convince him to run against O'Donnell."

Pryde, the former United MEC chairman who had replaced Bill Arsenault after his recall, was an authentic "mover and shaker" in ALPA politics. If anybody had the clout, in terms of respect and name recognition, to unseat O'Donnell in 1978, it would have been Pryde. But Pryde's candidacy had a problem.

"I felt O'Donnell had done a good job," Pryde says frankly. "I had worked with him very closely as MEC chairman, and I thought that while he started out making a lot of mistakes, he grew into the job and became a well-respected leader within labor. He didn't make the same mistakes twice."

So Gerry Pryde would not challenge O'Donnell. He told Eglet and others who were urging him to run for ALPA's presidency that he was unwilling to live in Washington, D.C., which was, in effect true, but still something of a subterfuge. Imagine the anti-O'Donnell faction's embarrassment when they discovered, barely a month later, that Pryde had, in effect, joined O'Donnell's slate and was running, unopposed, for first vice-president.

"I don't know whether a deal was previously made or if O'Donnell found out that people were out actively recruiting people to run against him and decided to head them off," Eglet muses. "I picked the right guy [the widely respected Pryde], I just didn't offer him the right job."

Pryde denies that he was in any way _consciously_ a part of an O'Donnell slate in 1978. But _in effect_ he was. The true mark of a clever and effective politician is when he rules through others, with his unseen hand motivating others to take actions _without their being aware of it._ By every standard of measurement available, O'Donnell fit that definition.

For J.J. O'Donnell, the 1978 BOD meeting was the high-water mark of his political control of ALPA. But the tumultuous events of the post-1978 period would offer the anti-O'Donnell forces new opportunities. Next time, they vowed, it would be a different story. They would be organized and ready in 1982. ✦

NOTES

[1] See "Blue Skies and MEC Wars," Ch. 15.
[2] For a full account of the Capital–United merger and the stresses it generated internally among the combined pilot group, see "Jets and Thin Ice" _Flying the Line,_ Ch. 23.
[3] For a full account, see "Skyjacking," _Flying the Line,_ Ch. 24.
[4] See George E. Hopkins, _The Airline Pilots: A Study in Elite Unionization_ (Boston: Harvard University Press, 1971), pp. 178-182, for a full discussion.
[5] For further details, see _Flying the Line,_ Ch. 25.

CHAPTER 4

DODGING BULLETS
Crew Complement, Politics, and the Wien Strike

Charles J. "Chuck" Huttinger nursed a long-standing political grudge against J.J. O'Donnell. Slightly built with a pronounced limp (from a backyard fall that ended his aviation career), Huttinger had flown for a variety of small carriers during his 26 years as an airline pilot. He finally ended up as a BAC-111 captain with TACA, the Central American airline based in El Salvador. In 1967, Huttinger successfully organized his fellow pilots for ALPA, overcoming the fierce opposition of TACA's management, which had a well-deserved reputation for parsimony. In 1971, Huttinger became something of a legend when he masterminded the "kidnapping" of several TACA airplanes until his pilots got an industry-standard contract!

"When they can't find their airplanes, they've pretty much *got* to talk to you," Huttinger says wryly.

Huttinger's success as TACA's organizer and long-time MEC chairman made him a natural leader of the "Group V" airlines. Historically, pilots from small airlines have made few ripples in ALPA's political pond. Huttinger, well aware that he stood no chance of challenging J.J. O'Donnell for the presidency of ALPA himself, was dedicated to finding a candidate who could.

From Huttinger's vantage point as an MEC chairman of one of ALPA's smallest pilot groups, he was ideally situated to act as a political catalyst. Had he been a pilot from one of the large airlines (the so-called "elephants"), Huttinger's motives might have been suspect. But as a leader of the "ants" (the Group V airlines), Huttinger (who was based in New Orleans) bore no taint of personal ambition. In ALPA politics, pilots from small airlines have historically had to content themselves with fringe roles—the exception to this rule being genial Jack Magee of Ozark, who served as ALPA's treasurer for what seemed forever, from 1975 to 1991, beating back every attempt by pilots of larger airlines to unseat him during that 16-year period.

In 1974, the BOD changed the vice-presidencies from "regional" to the new "executive" status. In a technical sense, the new executive vice-presidency (EVP) was designed to accomplish two things: first, the BOD wanted to curb the power of the regional vice-presidents (RVPs); and second, the BOD wanted to *guarantee* that pilots like Chuck Huttinger, who flew for small airlines, would have more voice in national affairs. The tendency toward *tribalism*, which characterized the voting behavior of airline pilots, gravely hampered the pilots of small airlines seeking election to a major ALPA office. Many of these pilots were men of exceptional ability whose voice in ALPA's national affairs was needed.

But primarily, the BOD adopted the 1974 changes to put an end to the independent power bases some RVPs had built. From their regional bases, these RVPs often challenged the _purely administrative_ prerogatives of BOD-elected national officers.

Before 1974, the RVPs won office independently of the BOD, and many of them viewed their mandate to advise and monitor the president as a power derived directly from the membership _of their region_ and thus theoretically co-equal (collectively) to the president's. Operating from this perspective, several RVPs (notably Rich Flournoy of TWA during the Ruby era and Bob Rubens of North Central—later of Northwest via its merger with Republic) exercised more power and influence than some BOD-elected officers.

Before 1974, the popular vote of _all_ pilots living within a designated region directly elected each RVP. RVPs "campaigned" primarily by direct mail to the membership, which often meant that money, rather than merit, dictated victory. This system also meant that the individual with a flair for "dramatic rhetoric" (or demagoguery) had an unfair advantage over more-responsible candidates. After 1974, the BOD elected the new EVPs, and hence they were technically a subcommittee of the BOD. This was a far more rational (if somewhat less "democratic") system, and it eliminated much confusion about the vice-presidency's mandate, role, and function.

The new office of EVP effectively laid to rest another troubling aspect of the old system. Before 1974, the "ants" seldom had a representative on ALPA's Executive Committee. Although the MEC chairmen of the "ants" attended Executive Board meetings every six months, many thoughtful observers believed that their exclusion from the Executive Committee, which met at least every three months (and usually more often) was potentially dangerous.

Henceforth under the new EVP system, all ALPA's airlines would be subdivided into five groups, and each group would be represented on the Executive Committee. Ideally, each group should also have been roughly co-equal in total voting strength, but that presupposed an aviation industry stability, which deregulation would destroy. Initially, the "elephants" segmented in the top groups would far outweigh the "ants" (like Chuck Huttinger's TACA) in total voting strength. But the latter at least had hope that someday the elephants and the ants would find some balance in ALPA's politics.

Owing to the discrepancy in pay scales and consequent disparity in the amount of money the elephants contributed to ALPA's treasury in dues, however, the idea of _real_ equality between large and small pilot groups was hopelessly visionary. The elephants paid money in; the ants took it out. So when crucial matters arose, ALPA's presidents necessarily paid heed to the elephants and ignored the ants, formal structures like the Executive Committee notwithstanding.[1]

"I was frankly against the EVP concept," says Robert A. Holden of Eastern, who was elected Group I EVP at the 1974 BOD, a time when Eastern and United were paired elephants. "I didn't see the necessity for it. J.J. wanted it for political reasons. I went along with it because I liked the guy. He was a little too political for me, always responding to the power groups with the most votes. But that was his job."

Indeed, O'Donnell's mastery of ALPA's politics through 1978 owed much to his skill at counting votes. What this meant, in practice, was that O'Donnell always kept the elephants happy. Then, if he could, he would tend to the needs of the ants.

Or at least that's the way Chuck Huttinger saw it.

"John never listened to anybody but the big MEC chairmen," Huttinger says. "If you were from a small airline and you voted against him, you didn't get any money for your projects. That's the way he kept us in his pocket politically."

John Erikson of Delta (by way of merger with Western), who served until January 1985 as Hank Duffy's first executive administrator, echoes Huttinger's complaint.

"O'Donnell quite explicitly used money in a very political way," Erikson says. "The MECs of the big airlines, like United, could spend money like drunken sailors, and O'Donnell would accept it. But those of us on small airlines were very dependent upon money from ALPA national to run our operation, and O'Donnell used this leverage ruthlessly. It backfired on him at the 1982 BOD, when he warned us that if we voted for Duffy, he would cut us off if he won. We went for Duffy anyway."

In early 1982, Huttinger wrote to a select group of ALPA activists he knew were hostile to O'Donnell, suggesting that they begin coordinating their strategy for the 1982 BOD meeting. He reminded them of their failure to come up with a suitable challenger to O'Donnell in 1978 and suggested that they meet for discussions in New Orleans to begin advance planning. Huttinger included in his anti-O'Donnell circular a lengthy bill of indictment, detailing what he saw as failures of the O'Donnell years. Huttinger delved deeply into the past, dredging up the failed 1972 skyjacking SOS ("one of the most embarrassing disasters in ALPA history") and ranged forward into recent events. He described O'Donnell's handling of the 1980 BOD meeting in Los Angeles (at which the United pilots under MEC Chairman John Ferg had walked out, threatening to secede from ALPA in protest over the crew complement issue), as "chaotic and disgraceful."[2] Huttinger described the O'Donnell years in language that was far from temperate, repeated charges of doubtful substance, and detailed the abortive move to recall O'Donnell in 1981.[3] Huttinger finished by accusing O'Donnell of violating the most sacred of ALPA's covenants.

"Over the past twelve years," Huttinger wrote, "the most basic concept of ALPA—strength through unity—has been ignored."

Strong words from an "ant." But they served the purposes of some "elephants" who wanted very much to get rid of O'Donnell.

Huttinger's New Orleans meeting drew a gallery of ALPA political activists. Skip Eglet of Northwest, who had unsuccessfully tried to recruit Gerry Pryde of United to run against O'Donnell in 1978, although invited, did not attend. But Hank Duffy, the MEC chairman of Delta was there, quietly observing. So was Nick Gentile, the former Delta MEC chairman whom many people regarded as the driving force behind Duffy's recently announced presidential candidacy.

"We called ourselves the dragon slayers," Huttinger laughs. "Nobody could believe that with my little 35 votes I could get all those guys to come down to New Orleans, John Gratz of TWA, Tom Beedem of Northwest, Augie Gorse of Eastern, Hank. I chaired the meeting because it came down on my nickel, I paid for the rooms. My pitch was that in 1974 at Kansas City we had 65 percent of the vote against J.J. and we lost. I said we're going to do it again if we're not careful."

Huttinger came away from the New Orleans meeting discouraged. He had hoped that they would unite behind a presidential candidate, but neither Hank Duffy nor John Gratz, the two announced candidates, would defer to the other. Although various ideas and strategies for cooperation at the BOD meeting surfaced, the only concrete development was that Tom Beedem agreed to forego his presidential ambitions in the interest of narrowing the field. Beedem, the widely respected MEC chairman of Northwest, thus secured the support of the New Orleans group for his candidacy for first vice-president (which he would lose, coincidentally, to Tom Ashwood of TWA). Huttinger won no promises from anybody else beyond an agreement that they would sponsor debates for all announced presidential candidates.

"It was a basis, we all talked," Huttinger says. "But I could not put the rest of it together. My guesstimate was that we could not defeat J.J."

"Huttinger was just a front," said O'Donnell later. He had found out about the meeting in New Orleans after it was held. The cast of characters, many of whom were previous candidates like John Gratz of TWA, caused him little worry.

"I liked John Gratz, but he would screw up a one-car funeral," O'Donnell laughed in 1991. "He looked, acted, and talked like a gorilla; but he was a decent guy. He didn't want people to know it, and he was offended if you found out."

J.J. O'Donnell's political enemies were gathering for the kill in 1982, but they were by no means assured of toppling him. Since the last BOD meeting in 1980, things had gotten very dicey for O'Donnell politically. The aborted 1981 SOS over crew complement, the PATCO strike, the onslaught of deregulation, the terrible economic downturn in late 1981, Braniff's bankruptcy, and widespread pilot furloughs all combined to erode O'Donnell's political base. But he was a resilient and resourceful practitioner of the political arts, and he had turned defeat into victory before. His handling of the divisive crew complement issue, which had a long and troubled history, provides an object lesson in the perils of taking J.J. O'Donnell lightly.

The crew complement issue, in its first incarnation, dealt with the nature of the third crewmember's qualifications and *who* should do the job—a pilot or a mechanic.[4] This battle roiled ALPA's waters for years, finally culminating in a victory that was almost as bad as defeat. It led to terrible difficulties with the rest of organized labor and exacerbated the preexisting cancer that would later take the American Airlines pilot group out of ALPA in 1963.

In the mid-1950s, ALPA came within an eyelash of getting expelled from the American Federation of Labor (AFL), over the *qualifications* aspect of the first crew complement dispute. A motion by the International Brotherhood of Teamsters (this was before they were kicked out of the AFL-CIO for corruption), calling for ALPA's expulsion for "raiding" the jobs of fellow workers, reached the floor for action during the 1955 convention. The Teamsters acted on behalf of the professional nonpilot flight engineers represented by the Flight Engineers International Association (FEIA).

"Matters looked very bad in terms of probable expulsion, or at least suspension, of ALPA," recalled ALPA General Counsel Henry Weiss during a 1990 interview. "We were called upon to make a formal floor response the next day. Clancy Sayen and the entire Executive Committee were there, and we caucused by walking around the streets of New York City at midnight. They decided to show their scorn for the whole thing by not responding. I was very much opposed to that, but I didn't have very much luck persuading them until I got hold of Dave Cole, who was a man of great stature in the AFL who also had great standing with the pilots. I called him in the middle of the night, and Dave said, 'I'll be there in the morning.'"

Cole, the arbitrator who had formed warm relationships with many pilots dating back to the Behncke era, arrived in New York and went to work on ALPA's behalf. By dint of his influence with the AFL, Cole got the Teamsters' expulsion resolution shunted off to a committee, where the resolution could be studied to death.

"We were given to understand that the committee would take no action," Weiss recalls of ALPA's persistent troubles. "Our relationship with the AFL was not an active one for many years. Then, with the incumbency of J.J. O'Donnell, it took a more viable tone, as he actively participated in AFL-CIO affairs. J.J. had an instinctive sense of the meaning of trade unions, and he was quite concerned that ALPA not fall into more trouble over Article Twenty."

Article XX of the ALPA Constitution and By-Laws, as revised through several BOD meetings, was the intractable burr under the saddle of the crew complement issue. Once ALPA had won the war with the FEIA over the *qualifications* of the third crewmember, the issue of whether a cockpit should *have* a third crewmember still remained.

Article XX explicitly *mandated* the three-pilot cockpit for certain categories of large aircraft. This policy dated from the days when the Douglas DC-6 originally emerged from the factory as a two-pilot aircraft.

ALPA won the first round of this struggle in the 1950s because it had allies. Lockheed, maker of the famed "Constellations," favored the three-crewmember configuration because its aircraft could not be flown without a third crewmember. The "Connie" had an elaborate flight engineer's panel, and the crewmember who sat there had *real* duties. If Douglas was allowed to take advantage of improved technology and build a two-pilot aircraft (such as the DC-6) equal to the Constellation in capacity, it would obtain a decisive competitive advantage in the marketplace. So Lockheed, for purely economic reasons, sided with ALPA. This aspect of the dispute eerily foreshadowed the B-737/DC-9 crew complement problem in the 1970s.

The government, for reasons specific to the piston era, had mandated a three-pilot crew in "overwater" operations *and* when the gross weight of an aircraft exceeded 80,000 pounds. Largely owing to ALPA's political connections and skill at equating the three-pilot crew with safety, the government would continue this policy into the turbojet era. So the government also wound up as an ally of Article XX policy during the first round, and ALPA won jobs for a whole generation of pilots in the 1960s because of it.

The three-crewmember era lasted until the emergence of the first significant jet airliners designed for two pilots, the B-737 and the DC-9, both of which exceeded the old 80,000-pound gross takeoff weight limit. By then, the government had dropped the requirement for a third crewmember at that weight anyway, adding a curious twist to the weight-limit/third-crewmember history. The first DC-9, the "dash 10" model, was deliberately kept *under* the 80,000-pound limit specifically to avoid exceeding the limit. A contemporary Douglas Company newsletter, designed to circulate only among employees, listed the "ramp weight" of the aircraft at 78,500 pounds. By the time Delta received its first production model DC-9-10, however, the "ramp weight" had soared well over 80,000 pounds. The truth of Douglas's motivation will probably never be known for sure, but the initial design weight of the prototype DC-9-10 appears to have been a sham designed to circumvent both government and ALPA policy. In any case, all this deception, if that's what it was, proved unnecessary, because the government discarded the 80,000-pound policy shortly before the prototype DC-9 received certification. Thus the modern crew complement problem began with a confusing struggle over the DC-9, sharpened into a bitter squabble over the B-737, and left ALPA with serious internal divisions. By the time it was over, ALPA would have no allies in either government or industry.

The first DC-9, the "Dash 10" series, entered service with Delta in February 1965. Because the DC-9 was a turbojet, it fell under ALPA's three-pilot policy, and its crewing would set the precedent for the next generation of similar aircraft. Braniff had already ordered a comparable aircraft, the BAC 1-11, and would begin operating it in April 1965, shortly after Delta's DC-9-10 went on the line. American Airlines, whose pilots had recently left ALPA, had also ordered the BAC 1-11. Whether ALPA made any *sub rosa* attempt to coordinate its crew complement bargaining with the newly formed Allied Pilots Association, the ALPA clone, is unclear. In any case, the breakup was so rancorous that even if coordination had been attempted, it probably would have failed. So the initial contract to fly the DC-9-10 was a pivotal event.

In 1964, after Delta had already ordered the DC-9-10, the Delta MEC appointed a special committee to evaluate the aircraft, with special emphasis on its crewing, and sent it to the West Coast. This committee, composed of Roy Ferguson, Joe Meek, and Bud Watson (who would later die in a DC-8 crash in New Orleans), enjoyed great respect among the Delta pilots. Whatever they decided on crew complement for the DC-9 would have enormous implications for ALPA's crew complement policy. Should they find in favor of a two-pilot operation, the camel would have its nose under the tent.

We must remember that this pivotal event occurred at a time of enormous stress for ALPA, barely a year after the American pilots' defection and while Charley Ruby, who never wanted the job, was still feeling his way as ALPA's president. One would think that somebody at ALPA national would have lobbied the Delta Evaluation Committee in favor of the three-pilot cockpit—*no-*

body did! Nor is there evidence that Charley Ruby contacted Delta's MEC chairman at the time, Curtis L. Kennedy, and the question is unanswerable now, since both men are dead.

"Charley Ruby exerted no pressure on us at all on the DC-9-10," says C.A. "Snake" Smith, who served on the Delta pilots' Negotiating Committee at the time and would later become MEC chairman.

The Delta pilots' Evaluation Committee, which had a heavy background in aviation safety matters, recommended the two-pilot cockpit for the DC-9-10, and the MEC went along. They signed a basic agreement (not a "side letter," so no one can accuse the Delta pilots of not being "up front" on this issue), with the company on April 16, 1964. The language was specific: "It is hereby agreed that the pilots of Delta...will fly the DC-9 with a two-man crew."

Charley Ruby approved Delta's two-pilot operation without argument. Perhaps he was repaying a political debt to the Delta pilots, whose support had been crucial in getting him elected in 1962. Chuck Woods, the United MEC chairman, was furious at Ruby for signing the Delta two-pilot agreement.

"We later had a knock-down, drag-out fight with Woods over the issue," Smith remembers. "But we thought we were fat as far as ALPA policy went, and our experience with the aircraft was that it was a totally safe operation."

United's MEC would historically stress the safety aspects of the crew complement issue, but the Delta pilots were prepared for that.

"Joe Meek, who chaired the DC-9 Evaluation Committee, personally polled every pilot flying the DC-9 after the first year of line operations," Smith remembers. "Two out of 75 pilots said they thought it should be three pilots. So when we went up to Chicago for this meeting with Charley and Chuck Woods, we just hauled out these letters. Charley looked at them and said 'You can't argue with the pilots actually flying the line.' That was it."

In 1966, Douglas stretched the DC-9 into the "dash-30," which was 15 feet longer than the "dash-10." The FAA approved the "dash-30" as a two-pilot aircraft under the same type certificate as the "dash 10." Another "nine" was already on the drawing boards, the "dash-50," which the FAA had already promised to certificate as a two-pilot aircraft. Because the DC-9-50 was comparable in every way to the Boeing 737, a crisis was afoot.

When Piedmont Airlines' pilot group signed a "side letter" in its 1967 contract to fly the B-737 with a two-pilot crew, the crisis had arrived. Charley Ruby at first refused to approve the Piedmont contract. United had flown the B-737 as a three-pilot airplane since it had come on their property. Beset with other troubles, Ruby could not buck the powerful United pilot group. But how could he force the Piedmont pilots to fly with a third crewmember? ALPA's Article XX policy, now without any external allies and facing internal rejection by several pilot groups, clearly needed re-thinking.

"The practical reality was that the pilots were going to fly that airplane with two crewmembers, or management was going to be in a position to force them to fly it," says Hank Duffy, who as cochair of ALPA's National Crew Complement Committee in 1980 (along with Dick Cosgrave of United) made a careful study of the issue's history.

Management could entice pilots to fly these new aircraft with blandishments that were almost irresistible, and they weren't always *just money*. At Wien, for example, management tried unsuccessfully to lure its pilots into giving up the third crewmember on the B-737 by offering to buy a local service carrier and make the B-737 second officers into captains on Twin Otters. This offer was attractive because, while sitting on the jumpseat of one of these new aircraft was a job, it was a lousy one. The third crewmember had nothing to do, and ALPA would find itself waging a long struggle, contractually, to get management to give these pilots "meaningful duties." But all this aside, if ALPA could not tie the third crewmember concept to something concrete (and the safety aspect would eventually emerge as the most viable), then the whole thing would smack of "featherbedding."

The 1968 BOD attempted a fix. The United pilots, under pressure from their management to operate with two pilots to meet the challenge of the airline's competitors, wanted a strong Article XX that would *force* all B-737 operators to use three pilots. Bill Davis, United MEC chairman, knew that junior pilots who were then flying the B-727 would undergo massive furloughs once the B-737 replaced it on many routes. But he wanted somebody else to propose the new Article XX so that it would not appear to be just a United power play. Capt. Gerald Goss of Frontier agreed to draft the new crew complement policy. Ironically, the new Article XX would, a decade later, get Goss's Frontier pilots placed into ALPA trusteeship when they broke ranks and agreed to fly the B-737 with two pilots.

"Bill Davis and the United pilots really didn't have the courage to go it alone on the B-737," Goss recalls. "Management was stonewalling them, and he wanted ALPA's help. But he couldn't get the vote from ALPA the way he was drafting the resolution, so I rewrote it. The way I worded the new Article Twenty was that 'all new aircraft must be *considered* for three pilots.' The policy wasn't set in stone."

The Ruby era ended with gaping holes in ALPA's crew complement policy. Officially, no ALPA pilot group was supposed to be flying with fewer than three pilots on any "new" aircraft, like the B-737. But what about the new DC-9-50? Was it "new," or just "stretched?"

When J.J. O'Donnell became ALPA's fourth president in January 1971, he tried to defuse the issue through diplomacy. He personally went to the Douglas factory, talked to Donald Douglas himself, and received what he was sure was a promise that the next generation of DC-9s, the "dash-80," would be a three-pilot jetliner. The United pilots wanted to draw the line at the *nose* of the DC-9-50, the Delta pilots insisted on drawing it at the *tail*. As for the B-737, O'Donnell, hewing close to official ALPA policy, intended to draw the line at its nose, no matter that the FAA had certified it for two-pilot operations. From the government's viewpoint, the matter of crewing was simply a labor dispute.

Two major aircraft corporations were now involved, and if ALPA could not force them into crewing two essentially similar aircraft with three pilots, its crew complement policy would clearly damage the commercial prospects of one of them. Having an external enemy like Boeing was bad enough, but now serious internal divisions among pilot groups over the policy arose.

With management offering lucrative new contracts to the pilots of several airlines if they would agree to fly the B-737 or the DC-9-50 with two crewmembers, something had to give. To appreciate the ramifications of this dispute, we must remember that a pilot already flying the "Nine" could not tell from the cockpit whether it was a "dash 30" or a "dash 50!"

The BOD meeting held at Kansas City in 1974 lasted an interminable 10 days. The closely contested presidential election that O'Donnell won accounted for part of its length, but the bitter internal struggle over crew complement accounted for the rest. For two full days, the delegates fought over it. Finally, they approved what appeared, at first glance, to be a policy *set in stone*. But was it?

The reaffirmed and reworded Article XX required three crewmembers for all "new turbine-powered or jet aircraft certificated after January 1, 1975" (other than short-haul aircraft certificated for commuter and air taxi operations). It then listed the aircraft likely to fit the three-crewmember category, including such speculative ventures as the "swing panel" B-727. The policy included the B-737; but on the DC-9-50, the policy waffled. Aware that Delta's pilots were unalterably opposed to the third crewmember on their DC-9-50s, the BOD permitted that model to fall under an imprecise definition. Essentially, the language required that O'Donnell fight hard for its inclusion in the same category as all other "new" aircraft but, in effect, recognized that he would fail.

"There was no doubt that we were drawing the line at the tail of the DC-9-50," Hank Duffy recalls of the 1974 BOD. "To require otherwise would have forced several pilot groups out of ALPA."

On all other aircraft, *including* the B-737, ALPA would nail the flag to the mast and go down with guns firing. Proof of this intention lay in the BOD's approval of drastic measures should any airline try to fly the B-737 as a two-pilot aircraft. ALPA would pay full strike benefits to any pilot group that walked out over crewing the B-737. The Association would consider the possibility of a nationwide SOS (ALPA's "nuke") should any airline force its pilots to fly the B-737 with two pilots. And ALPA explicitly threatened to impose a trusteeship on any pilot group that broke the policy, either through a direct contract or a "side letter" of agreement.

As we know, ALPA would eventually lose this war, when the Presidential Emergency "Fact Finding" Board appointed by Ronald Reagan in 1981 ruled in favor of two-pilot crews for any aircraft *designed* that way. But did ALPA have a realistic chance of winning this struggle, and did J.J. O'Donnell do everything he could to salvage the third crewmember?

An answer, of sorts, to these questions might be found in the experience of the pilots of Texas International (TXI). We will meet them later in their capacity as the first pilot group to face Frank Lorenzo, but for now, let us consider their response to the crew complement issue. How did it play out at the "grass roots?"

"When Frank Lorenzo arrived on the property in 1973," recalls former TXI MEC chairman Dennis Higgins, "he wanted a commitment from the pilots that we would fly *any* new-generation airplane with two pilots, not three. We already had the DC-9, he was looking at the DC-9-50, but they weren't even cutting tin on that airplane yet. We had never flown anything but two-man airplanes, we knew that our pilots absolutely would not fight him on that issue, and even our MEC was divided. As leaders, we wanted to uphold ALPA policy, but we also wanted to do what was good for TXI."

While they sought to resolve this dilemma, TXI's pilot leaders, consisting of four local council officers plus the MEC chairman, stalled Lorenzo for several months. But when the first DC-9-50 rolled off the assembly line, the issue came to a head. Seeking to break the deadlock, Lorenzo arranged for the entire TXI MEC to travel to California for a look at the new jetliner.

"We had to keep it from becoming a public issue with our pilots as long as we possibly could," Higgins remembers. "But then the company, to put pressure on the MEC, invited us—Floyd Carpenter, Buddy Benedict, Gordon Darnell, and me—out to look at the first -50 being fabricated, Buddy was saying, 'What a gorgeous airplane, I sure would like to fly it, I bet I could make a lot of money on that airplane.'"

With his MEC eroding, Higgins and Carpenter, who had been an ALPA stalwart on TXI since the early 1950s, tried to hold the line.

"I remember Floyd arguing, 'The very last thing we need to do in facing Lorenzo is to piss off ALPA,'" Higgins says. "But the other guys on the MEC were saying, 'Well, ALPA's constitution doesn't really apply'—stuff like that."

Higgins called O'Donnell from California, asking for help. O'Donnell invited Higgins to fly with the entire MEC directly to Washington, D.C., instead of going back to Texas.

"We had been out there for two days, but we changed planes, got on TWA, and flew nonstop to Washington," Higgins says. "O'Donnell had a car and driver pick us up and take us to Congressional Country Club, where we met him for dinner. He did three hours, nonstop, telling us we were 'on point,' what the crew complement issue was about. Buddy Benedict was just dazzled by O'Donnell. He went back to Texas and says, 'I'll never fly that goddamn plane unless it has three seats on it!'"

So it is foolish to think that J.J. O'Donnell didn't give ALPA's crew complement policy his full support and best effort. Had he been president in 1964 at the time the Delta pilots were evaluating the DC-9, he would have insisted on upholding ALPA policy. O'Donnell, as we have seen, was adamant about that. But evidence shows that he did not think the issue was winnable. Two of his closest associates in ALPA, Executive Administrator Jack Bavis and Secretary Tom Ashwood, corroborate this.

"The funny part is that O'Donnell didn't really believe the DC-9 should have a third crewman on it," Jack Bavis asserts. "But since it was in the Constitution and By-Laws, he would move hell and high water to make sure that it either didn't get certificated or that each pilot group would live up to the policy. As long as the big airlines were holding the lines on crew complement, management couldn't afford to take them on in a strike. But when it got to the smaller groups whose pilots could be replaced in a strike, and if the rest of ALPA refused to call a strike in support of them, there was just no way to sustain it. The third crewman was just a thorn in our side, eroding us through pilot groups electing not to join ALPA and through internal dissension."

Tom Ashwood faults O'Donnell for not showing more resolve, and he views the loss of the third crewmember as "the biggest mistake we made." Ashwood believed the crew complement issue was winnable on its merits.

"Crew complement was an issue I wasn't really concerned with until I began to realize its industrial implications," says Ashwood, a dapper, articulate man. "As a result, I became an ardent three-pilot–crew supporter. I recognized what it was doing to ALPA, because people had strong beliefs both ways. Delta was making threats about pulling out, United was muscling everybody. United was the 300-pound gorilla, but right behind them was Delta at about 230, and of course O'Donnell's between a rock and a hard place. I argued vigorously with O'Donnell that we could win it, that Delta would not leave ALPA and would toe the line. I never went public with our disagreement out of a sense of loyalty toward him. He took a way out that I didn't approve. Frankly, it was a set-up with his friend Drew Lewis [Reagan's Secretary of Transportation]. I mean, the results of that Emergency Board on crew complement were known beforehand. But I recognized the dilemma O'Donnell faced. Opportunists were using crew complement against him for political purposes."

In fact, O'Donnell remains convinced that the entire crew complement issue was a political ploy from the beginning. We must remember that in 1974, when the BOD's actions sharpened the dispute and severely limited O'Donnell's flexibility, his arch-rival Bill Arsenault of United orchestrated the dispute. Clearly, Arsenault had to worry about massive furloughs on United if the B-737 reverted to a two-pilot aircraft. O'Donnell thinks Arsenault not only had a secret crew complement agenda, but that he also outsmarted himself.

"Arsenault may deny it, but I have it on good authority that he said to his MEC, 'We're going to milk this crew complement thing for everything its worth,'" O'Donnell declared in 1991. "He was going to sell the third man off the B-737. But it got away from him! He convinced the United pilots that the third man was necessary for safety, and the safety people weren't about to give him up."

John LeRoy of United in the late 1970s chaired a specially appointed national committee on crew complement for O'Donnell. The focus of LeRoy's committee was safety. By studying the whole range of FAA incident and accident reports, his committee found that the three-crewmember cockpit was safer than the two.

"This report incensed the Delta pilots," LeRoy recalls. "Because the DC-9-50 was coming on the line, we argued that it was a new airplane. Douglas executives were so worried about it that they came to the 1974 BOD meeting and assured us that they had absolutely no intention of trying to stretch the DC-9 beyond the -50. We put on a seminar for the pilots of airlines that had antipathy for the safety argument, and we *convinced* those guys."

Which leaves us with the question of O'Donnell's commitment to the third crewmember. Answers to this question can be found in the history of the Wien strike, the first practical test of ALPA's post-1974 crew complement policy.

The Wien Air Alaska strike of 1977 lasted 22 months. J.J. O'Donnell would fight the good fight over crew complement at Wien, whatever his private doubts. As has so often happened in ALPA's history, developments on small airlines would have large consequences. It happened on little Long & Harmon Airlines in 1934, which Dave Behncke used as a test case for enforcing the pilot pay scales and working conditions dictated by "Decision 83" of the National Labor Board.[5] It would now happen on Wien, where a long strike on small airline with fewer than 200 pilots would not only be the first step in laying the crew complement issue to rest, it would also provide a powerful example of O'Donnell's ability to handle a political dilemma.

The pilots of Wien Air Alaska prided themselves on being the best foul-weather fliers in the world. Many of them had come up as bush pilots under the nearly legendary Noel Wien, the airline's founder. Until Wien lost control of his airline in the 1960s, it was, by all accounts, a good place to work—a real pilots' airline. ALPA made Noel Wien an honorary member in 1974, shortly before his death. Two of his sons and a grandson flew the line for Wien and were ALPA members. They would walk out with their fellow pilots when the strike occurred on May 8, 1977.

The strike followed a brief period of ownership by a conglomerate called Household Finance and a leveraged buyout engineered by an entrepreneur named Jim Flood. Flood then became Wien's CEO and confronted the enormous problem all such financial manipulators must solve—how to pay off the debt incurred by acquiring the company. Flood proceeded to give ALPA its first taste of what deregulation would be like. The Wien strike, which lasted for 653 days before ending on March 1, 1979, was thus only partially about ALPA's crew complement policy. Certainly Wien's management wanted to get rid of the third crewmember on the B-737, but the device employed to do it was almost more of an issue than the substance of the crew complement issue itself.

"It was like a throwback to the 1930s," says F.C. "Chip" Mull of US Airways, who flew helicopters in Vietnam before hiring on with Wien in 1974. "We had a constant problem with out-of-seniority flying, which the company would not negotiate with us. They were just union-busters."

The aspect of Wien's operation that directly provoked the strike was the so-called "hire/fire" system. A pilot assigned to the second officer position on B-737s simply could not survive his probationary year. Wien routinely fired and then rehired each pilot on the anniversary of his hiring!

"The only way you could get off probation was to get on the Sky Van or the F-27," says Mull. "Until you could, you were forever at the bottom of the seniority list, because they'd issue you a new number each time they fired and rehired you. Some people stayed five years and never got off probation."

Adding to the problem of rotating pilots at the bottom of the seniority list (which meant that only luck got you off the B-737 jumpseat), Flood used a technique that would later be identified with corporate raiders like Carl Icahn and Frank Lorenzo—he began selling off assets to service the airline's debt. Confronted with an intractable labor situation and strong fears that management was jeopardizing their jobs by selling off vital infrastructure (an early form of what Eastern pilots would later call "upstreaming"), the Wien pilots, under the leadership of MEC chairman Ron Wood, walked out.

Flood promptly advertised for *permanent replacements*. Eventually, he managed a feat familiar to the Old Guys who lived through the National Airlines strike of 1948. Using a dozen Wien pilots who crossed the picket line (the "in-house scabs") and another 69 hired off the street (the "out-house scabs"), Flood completely "scabbed out" the Wien pilots and maintained a reduced schedule.

But this did not mean that the Wien strikers failed. They managed a good strike. Using the financial support of ALPA, the 132 Wien strikers maintained picket lines, traveled to New Zealand and Ireland to shut down (by appealing to sympathetic socialist and labor government officials) training operations that Wien was using, and won support from organized labor. But as the strike dragged on and no settlement appeared in sight, once again, like the Southern Airways strike of 1960, the Wien pilots obviously could not win without some form of overt political intervention.[6]

"That was the most difficult strike I dealt with," said O'Donnell in 1991. "I won't say the Wien pilots were sacrificial lambs to our crew complement policy, because we got them all back to work. But Jim Flood had hired a couple of ex-scabs in management who were just union-breakers who wanted to destroy ALPA. Ron Wood provided super leadership and kept his pilots together. He was dedicated to ALPA, and he believed in the third crewmember; and let me tell you, if I ever get into a war, I'd want those Wien pilots with me. They hung tough."

The Wien pilots, whose strike benefits were hardly lavish (B-737 second officers, for example, received a flat $1,000 per month, about a third of their prestrike pay), uniformly praise O'Donnell's support, emotional and otherwise. He made four separate trips to Anchorage, and Jack Bavis made more. But as the strike dragged on, the Wien strikers came to know all the highs and lows that only people who have been through such an ordeal can appreciate. J.J. O'Donnell was the focal point of all their hopes.

"There was a real question as to whether the Wien pilots would ever get back on the job," says ALPA General Counsel Henry Weiss. "My sense was that the issue of crew complement was no longer a live one for ALPA."

The Wien strike would ultimately be settled by a Presidential Emergency Board (PEB) appointed by Jimmy Carter. As a condition for their support of the Airline Deregulation Act of 1978, Democrats in Congress required the PEB. While the PEB ruled against Flood's "permanent replacement" scabs and assigned them to the bottom of the seniority list (which effectively ended their careers at Wien), it also "found" that the Wien pilots should fly the B-737 *with only two pilots*. While specifically disavowing that its finding was in any way a statement on either side of the safety argument, the PEB nevertheless dealt ALPA's crew complement policy a serious blow.

"O'Donnell's words said he was committed to the three-crewmember concept," John LeRoy believes. "But he was beginning to see political weaknesses in his own position; and the real arguments aside, I believe he came to the conclusion that this was going to be so divisive that ALPA couldn't survive it."

Nor would the Wien story have a happy ending. Flood's operation gave the illusion of health almost until the end, and the pilot group even expanded slightly. But in November 1984, Wien "temporarily suspended" service and went bankrupt shortly thereafter. The long, proud history of Wien Air Alaska, which dated back to the era of wooden wings, was over.

ALPA would remain publicly committed to the third crewmember, but the long Wien strike eroded support inside ALPA. The Frontier pilots, their carrier stressed by the adverse effect of deregulation and wary of the fate that the Wien pilots had suffered, had agreed, before the Wien strike, to give up the third crewmember on their B-737s. Their open defiance of Article XX was something O'Donnell would could not tolerate. On Feb. 19, 1976, O'Donnell took an unprecedented action—he placed the Frontier MEC in "trusteeship." The practical effect of ALPA's imposition of trusteeship on the Frontier pilots was nil—they flew as a two-pilot operation right through the Wien strike and went on as if nothing had happened. At the conclusion of the Wien strike, O'Donnell quietly withdrew the trusteeship, and he would never move to impose it again on any other pilot group because of an Article XX violation.

With a whole new generation of two-pilot aircraft, such as the Airbus A310 and the Boeing 757/767, arriving on the scene, ALPA was outgunned. By 1980, ALPA's crew complement policy had virtually no support aside from the International Federation of Air Line Pilots Associations, which promised to boycott all two-pilot airliners. Nobody took IFALPA's threat seriously.

The safety argument appeared to wane, as the public grew tired of hearing about it. Even the death by heart attack of Capt. Lloyd Wilcox at the controls of his Braniff B-747 enroute from Honolulu to Dallas in March 1979, which seemed tailor-made to prove ALPA's point, evoked only yawns. As luck would have it, First Officer Jim Cunningham had previously captained B-727s, _and_ an FAA check airman who was fully qualified to fly the B-747 was aboard riding as a passenger. One can only imagine the new life ALPA's safety argument would have acquired had this incident played out like the American Flyers crash. In April 1966, after the captain of a Lockheed Electra died of a heart attack at the controls during a military charter flight, the first officer could not handle the emergency. All 72 people aboard died near Ardmore, Okla. Braniff's Jim Cunningham saved the day in 1979, but his feat of airmanship stirred no widespread demand from the public in favor of the third crewmember as a safety factor.

J.J. O'Donnell, whose handling of ALPA's politics had reached a plateau in 1978, found himself increasingly on the defensive. His supple handling of the Wien strike indicated he was far from finished politically, but he was damaged by it nevertheless. The Wien strikers won nothing except self-respect and their jobs back—as a two-pilot operation.

Perhaps the Braniff pilot's death was an omen.

NOTES

[1] Of course, Group V had many "ants," while Group I might have only two "elephants," or conceivably only _one_, should deregulation result in a "super carrier." An airline's position would shift according to its fortunes, with successful expanding carriers rising, while weak, declining carriers fell. The first group alignment after 1974 was as follows: Group I— Eastern and United; Group II—Delta and TWA; Group III— Northwest and Pan Am; Group IV—Allegheny, Braniff, Continental, and Western; Group V—24 "ants," including airlines like Texas International, which had 400 pilots in 1974.

[2] See "Blue Skies and MEC Wars," Ch. 15, for a full treatment of the walkout.

[3] Which will be covered later—see "The End of the O'Donnell Era," Ch. 7.

[4] For a full discussion see "Safety and Crew Complement in the 1950s," _Flying the Line,_ Ch. 17.

[5] See "Flying for a Rogue Airline," _Flying the Line,_ Ch. 8.

[6] See "The Southern Airways Strike of 1960," _Flying the Line,_ Ch. 18.

LEFT: A weary Charley Ruby hands over ALPA to an almost visibly eager J.J. O'Donnell in 1970.

ABOVE: O'Donnell addresses the attendees at the AFL-CIO convention while AFL-CIO Executive Administrator Tom Donohue and President George Meany look on.
RIGHT: O'Donnell with AFL-CIO Vice-President Lane Kirkland and Capt. Mike Lyon, Pan Am's MEC chairman. Under O'Donnell, ALPA's relations with organized labor warmed considerably from the deep freeze under Ruby.

ABOVE: "Skyjackings": men with guns and bombs from Beirut to Cairo to Las Vegas demonstrated the potential for violence directed at airline pilots that characterized the 1970s.
BELOW: Approaching the deadline to "hit the mattresses" during the abortive 1972 skyjacking SOS, ALPA general counsel, Henry Weiss, and J.J. O'Donnell leave the United States Court House in Washington, D.C., after an injunction hearing following O'Donnell's "Meet the Press" television appearance.

ABOVE: UAL MEC Chairman John Ferg, center, at SOS meeting in Atlanta. Years later, he would gain infamy when he crosses the picket line to fly during the United pilots' strike.

LEFT: Capt. J.J. "Bud" Ruddy (UAL), air safety coordinator for Washington, D.C., converses with television reporters about safety issues during ALPA's Oct. 21, 1972, SOS picket of the White House.

RIGHT: O'Donnell's rise within the ranks of organized labor led him to become, in effect, a trouble-shooter for George Meany to other airline unions. The AFL-CIO looked to O'Donnell to be a mediating influence with PATCO because of his long friendship with PATCO's then president, John Leyden.

TOP LEFT: Capt. Richard Flournoy (Trans World), one of O'Donnell's most persistent critics in the early 1970s.
ABOVE RIGHT: TWA's John Gratz, typically assertive, makes a point on behalf of Rich Flournoy at the 1974 BOD meeting.
ABOVE LEFT: Eastern's Bob Tully, first vice-president under Ruby, was a significant force in inter-ALPA affairs. He was seen by many as the pilot who should have been ALPA's president in 1970 instead of O'Donnell.
BELOW: Capt. Lee Higman (United), center, was one of many who took O'Donnell lightly—and paid the price. O'Donnell easily defeated Higman in 1974.

Northwest pilots were forced to strike their airline for 3 months in 1972. Carrier management had the use of a Mutual Aid Pact with other carriers to pool their financial reserves as a hedge against the pilots' job action. The MAP survived for 20 years before its demise in 1978 as a casualty of deregulation and an intense ALPA lobbying campaign.

When the Wien Air Alaska pilots were forced to strike from May 8, 1977, to March 1, 1979, the dispute was partially about ALPA's crew compliment policy. The airline's CEO wanted to shed the third crewmember on the B-737. He routinely "fired" a pilot assigned as a B-737 second officer and then "rehired" him on the pilot's anniversary date, thereby never allowing the pilot to complete probation. When the CEO began selling off assets to pay off debt incurred from acquiring the airline, the pilots hit the bricks.

ABOVE: F/O John LeRoy (United) nearly won the internal fight over the third crewmember on the B-737. His persuasive approach and a fierce competitiveness nearly sank the deal O'Donnell had worked behind-the-scenes with the incoming Reagan Administration. Shown are the newly elected Executive Presidents in 1976. They include, from left, F/O Harry Hoglander (Trans World), LeRoy, Capt. Don McLennan (Pan Am), Capt. Gary Thomas (Continental), and F/O Stan Poynor (Texas International).

ABOVE: Capt. Joe Meek (Delta) doomed ALPA's "Article XX" policy mandating a third crewman in the cockpit of the DC-9 and its variants. A decade earlier he had headed an evaluation team at Delta that agreed to fly the DC-9 with only two pilots.
LEFT: Bob Rubens (NCA), left, almost single-handedly caused revision of the regional vice-presidency system. Using his office as an independent power base, he was a constant thorn in O'Donnell's side during the early 1970s.

ABOVE: Braniff had famed painter/sculptor Alexander Calder design paint schemes for it's aircraft.
LEFT: In June 1982 Braniff employees auctioned off personal items at Dallas's Love Field to help raise cash until they could find new jobs. One Braniff family sold its pet dog. Other items that went on the block were cars, boats, and real estate.
BELOW: Two Braniff pilots prepare to end this leg of their journey.

FAR LEFT: Group II Executive Vice-President and Eastern MEC Chairman August H. "Augie" Gorse dealt O'Donnell a serious setback in the Braniff Latin America route acquisition in 1983.
LEFT: Real estate salesman, Bud Cebell, a Braniff 727 pilot, shows off the miniature house his new employer uses to promote the agency. Cebell helped numerous Braniff pilots find work.

CHAPTER 5

THE BRANIFF DEBACLE
Deregulation Hits Home

Like the phoenix, that mythological bird that rose from the ashes with new life at each death, Braniff rose from the ashes of its first bankruptcy in 1982, only to fall victim, again, to a second bankruptcy in 1989. General questions concerning ALPA's role in the double debacle of "Bankruptcy I and II" linger in the minds of most airline pilots. What could (or should) ALPA have done? This question will forever be etched in acid for the Braniff pilots who lived through the bankruptcies.

The story of Braniff's life, rebirth, and death touches the very core of every working airline pilot's experience. Every pilot remembers each intimate detail of that first job search, from the initial idea of being an airline pilot (usually during some adolescent fantasy), to that first source of information about a possible job (perhaps during military service, when it dawns on a pilot that there are easier ways to make a living than landing on a carrier in mid-Pacific), to the letters of inquiry written (*many* letters), to the first return contact from an airline (*any* airline). Furthermore, the airline pilot who cannot recall the most minute details of the interview process that brought that first job offer from an airline—the challenging written tests, the "friendly" chats with austere Chief Pilots, those conversations in hallways with other equally nervous applicants, the long wait for the verdict of those mysterious corporate decision-makers in personnel departments—is rare indeed.

While all pilots who ever thought they *might* like to become an airline pilot probably had an idea of *which* airline he would like to work for, the truth is that *most* pilots have always taken the first job offered—by *any* airline.

On May 12, 1982, when Braniff became the first major airline to go bankrupt, throwing 1,200 airline pilots out of work, an almost audible shudder shook through the ranks of the profession. Among airline pilots everywhere, the universal reaction was "There but for the grace of God go I."

How many pilots working for other airlines had flirted with Braniff during their job search? How many would have taken a job with Braniff, had another airline not called sooner? How many pilots (like young Hank Duffy, a future ALPA president, when he first began contemplating an airline pilot's career) were admirers of Braniff's dash, verve, and sleek, sophisticated image?

As the first casualties of the Airline Deregulation Act of 1978, the Braniff pilots are entitled to a special and unenviable place in this history. While other airlines have technically gone bankrupt since the passage of the Civil Aeronautics Act of 1938 (notably Capital Airlines in 1961), the effect of these failures on pilots was minimal. Because the airline industry was a regulated public utility, with management *guaranteed* a certain fixed return on invested capital, poor management decisions seldom resulted in the total failure of a company. Under the leavening hand of government regulation, managers who proved themselves incompetent to manage found themselves forced out by government regulators, but the airlines *themselves* survived. Before financial collapse destroyed an airline's credibility with travel agents and the public, the regulators would intervene. Either by direct subsidy of federal dollars coupled with "crisis supervision" of errant mangers, or (if the failures of management were too egregious) by forced merger with another carrier, the old system of direct government regulation preserved the integrity of the air transportation system. The government, after all, had created the system, so the government was responsible for seeing that it survived.

The "shotgun marriages" of forced mergers were seldom pleasant under the pre-1978 system of direct government regulation, but they were a lot better than the fate awaiting Braniff's pilots. In 1961, the Capital pilots, accustomed to a more relaxed corporate culture, found the transition to United *very* trying.[1] But at least they had jobs. The Braniff pilots would be left with nothing, enmeshed in the first great test flight of the unproven vehicle called deregulation. For the first time since 1938, airline pilots would find themselves almost completely at the mercy of free market economics.

What happened at Braniff? When the airline abruptly quit flying in May 1982, the Braniff pilots (including ALPA's leaders) were as bewildered as everybody else. In fact, the MEC chairman at Braniff, Joe Baranowski, admitted at the time that lack of information, aside from "rah, rah stuff from management," nearly drove to distraction MEC members trying to track the company's real situation. All that Braniff's pilots really knew was that the company was sending mixed signals, saying things were bad one day, only to announce later that they were pretty good.

The general uncertainty about Braniff's economic viability caused pilot-room bulletin boards to blossom with offers to do whatever was necessary to keep the airline flying. Many pilots openly offered to fly *free* for one month. But the company had to come to the pilots with straight facts and requests for help *first*! Lacking full cooperation from management, the pilots of Braniff had no way of knowing just how bad the situation was, or what they could do to help.

"Everything we knew, we got from the newspapers," Baranowski declared.

This information deficit confirmed an ancient gripe among Braniff's "Old Guys." Braniff never told line pilots anything, and middle managers at the point of operational contact seemed to take perverse pleasure in ignoring any suggestion for improvement, particularly if it came from a pilot! Former Braniff pilot John Nance, whose book *Splash of Colors* chronicles the airline's downfall, attributes many of the airline's problems to these managers, whom he calls "empty suits," who were "confused, ill-trained," and working in a corporate atmosphere that was "disastrously ineffective."

John Giberson, the veteran ALPA activist and former IFALPA vice-president whose service dates back to 1947, agrees with Nance. A World War II Marine pilot, Giberson came to Braniff via merger with Kansas City-based Mid-Continent Airlines in 1952. Having gone through it all with Braniff, including the initial 1982 bankruptcy, Giberson returned to line flying and retired in 1984, before what came to be called "Bankruptcy II" in 1989.

"The vast majority of our middle management were idiots," Giberson says bluntly. "It was often said that Harding Lawrence had a drinking problem. Well, if so, it was those idiots who drove him to drink."

In fact, one lesson pilots would learn, collectively, from the Braniff debacle was that corporate incompetence was something that they could not ignore. ALPA would have to develop its own sources of information about events transpiring in corporate suites. To do otherwise, when jobs and careers were at stake, would mean that ALPA would enter the brave new world of deregulation blind. Because of Braniff, most MECs would begin learning how to track the business side of their airlines, acting almost as "shadow" managements. Corporate analysis done at ALPA National in support of these "shadow managements" would grow steadily during the 1980s. Pilots on many airlines, particularly those whose situation was most precarious, like TWA and Eastern, would spend their days anxiously monitoring corporate decisions instead of flying. After all, the pilots of an airline had infinitely more at stake than the managers running the airlines, what with "golden parachutes" guaranteeing these executives a soft landing, no matter how poorly they performed.

If history teaches any lessons at all, it is that surface explanations for great events seldom reveal the real truth. But in Braniff's case, the surface explanations are plausible enough. If fuel prices hadn't skyrocketed in 1979, just as Harding Lawrence, Braniff's president, began his spectacular postderegulation expansion plan, maybe Braniff today would be one of the "megacarriers." If rising fuel prices and economic recession had not ravaged the airline industry in 1982, maybe we would today think of Braniff the same way we think of Delta, which in some respects was Braniff's historical twin. If Harding Lawrence had not agreed to finance his rapid fleet expansion with a sickening burden of debt (at 2 percent over the prime rate, *whatever it was*!), Braniff might have *become* Delta.

Are rising fuel prices, unmanageable debt, and drastic reduction in passenger traffic owing to the worst economic recession since the Great Depression of 1929, sufficient to explain Braniff's failure? Other airlines survived under similar circumstances. Why didn't Braniff?

Braniff was an historical anomaly from the start, with a weak route structure and a powerful direct competitor, American Airlines. The reasons for Braniff's weakness lay in the circumstances of its birth. Two Oklahoma brothers, Paul and Tom Braniff, founded the first incarnation of Braniff in 1928, primarily to serve oilmen who needed rapid transportation. Of the two brothers, Paul Braniff was the flyer, Tom the businessman. Beginning with four Stinson "Detroiter" aircraft, they eventually served a route that included Tulsa and Oklahoma City, Okla., and Wichita Falls and Dallas/Ft. Worth, Texas. In 1929, shortly before the great Wall Street crash, they sold out to Universal Airlines.

The Braniff brothers' real business was insurance, not aviation, but their brief experience with running an airline had intrigued them. After the Great Depression began, airplanes were cheap and pilots plentiful. So, using two six-passenger Lockheed Vegas, the Braniffs promptly got back into the business in 1930, christening the second version of their airline "Braniff Airways." But they were surprised to learn that the Post Office had already awarded all the airmail contracts to large corporations at a conference held in Washington, D.C., in 1930. These conferences, while not exactly secret, were certainly low profile and restricted to selected inside bidders, among whom the Braniffs weren't included.

The Airline Deregulation Act of 1978 ended a statutory system embodied in the Civil Aeronautics Act of 1938. However, the idea of regulation began not with Franklin D. Roosevelt's New Deal, but with his predecessor, Herbert Hoover. As Secretary of Commerce in the Harding and Coolidge administrations, Hoover worried that the same fragmented system that bedeviled rail transportation would cripple the new airlines. Owing to the lack of planning, the nation's rail system was inefficient and irrational. In fact, to cope with the emergency mobilization of World War I, President Woodrow Wilson had to nationalize the railroads to introduce some order among them.

Hoover, a noted efficiency expert, seized control of the budding airlines through his Department of Commerce in the 1920s and set out to build them into a system that would be efficient, safe, and self-sustaining without government subsidy. Once Hoover became president, he ordered his postmaster general, Walter Folger Brown, a Toledo, Ohio, lawyer, to use airmail contracts to force the gaggle of fiercely competing airlines into a series of mergers that would turn their operation into a real "system" serving the whole nation.

From the beginning, Brown intended to force the small fry (like the Braniff brothers) out of the airline business. Brown's reasoning was that only large, well-financed corporations could afford the initial capital outlays that would make passenger operations successful. Brown figured that, eventually, passenger service would subsidize mail operations—and the government could get out of the business altogether. But before this could happen, the airlines would need a good, heavy dose of old-fashioned cartelization—under government guidance.

Angry at being excluded from this system, Tom Braniff, who was well-connected politically, led a public assault on Brown's policies. The Braniff brothers, to prove they could fly more cheaply, extended their airline to serve Kansas City and Chicago—which, with grave portents for the future, put them directly at odds with powerful American.

Sensing that he might yet come out of this business with a hefty profit, Tom Braniff used his resources and the venture capital of wealthy Oklahoma oilmen to keep Paul's airline alive while waiting for political fortune to smile. He made much of the greater speed of Braniff's Vegas, which could whisk deal-making oilmen from Tulsa to Ft. Worth more quickly than the subsidized competition's lumbering Fords and Fokkers.

Ultimately, Brown would be fully vindicated. The courts found that he had done nothing improper in laying the groundwork for the regulated mail and passenger system that FDR and the New Dealers copied almost totally. But at first, when they swept into power on March 3, 1933, they tried to dismantle Brown's national airline system. A series of spectacular Senate hearings chaired by an Alabama Democrat named Hugo A. Black, whom Roosevelt would soon appoint to the Supreme Court, offered the Braniff brothers a forum. Senators bought their tales of fraud and chicanery in the awarding of the 1930 airmail routes. In February 1934, Roosevelt canceled the contracts and ordered the Army to fly the mail. This experiment lasted only a few months, whereupon the new postmaster general, James A. Farley (an old style New York politician who knew how to reward friends and punish enemies) reopened the mail contracts for bidding. The Braniff brothers snatched away American's prime Chicago-to-Dallas/Ft. Worth route. Thus, almost from the beginning, Braniff faced a powerful enemy nursing an ancient grudge.

Between 1934 and 1965, when Harding Lawrence took over, Braniff was a steady, unspectacular performer. As one of the smallest "majors," Braniff cultivated an intense "family" feeling, promoted its executives from within, and did reasonably well in the competition with American for the Texas trade. Profiting from its identification with the Lone Star state (which American would negate when it moved its corporate offices there from New York in the early 1970s), Braniff pioneered the "hub and spoke" concept at its Dallas base, much as Delta (its historical cousin) had done at Atlanta. This approach was a necessity at Braniff and Delta, because neither could compete with the more prestigious "Big Four" (American, Eastern, TWA, and United). When the nature of the business shifted in the 1960s, the older "transcontinentals" would have to adapt to the hub-and-spoke system pioneered by Delta and Braniff, but they also had their lucrative and extensive old "city pair" markets to fall back on. Aside from its Chicago–Dallas city pair, Braniff was a poor relation in this arena.

Why did Delta make it work so well at Atlanta, and Braniff fail so miserably at Dallas? Much of the answer lies in the character of the strange, contradictory, and occasionally brilliant man who took over Braniff in 1965. Harding L. Lawrence learned his trade under the tutelage of Bob Six at Continental. Lawrence was a splendid deputy—bright, adventurous, constantly enthusiastic, hard working. Yet, something about Lawrence bothered people who worked with him—a certain imperiousness, a wild, sometimes irrational streak that identified him as a man who might lose his moorings in the game of high-stakes poker that was the airline business. As Bob Six's No. 2 man at Continental, Lawrence was the kind of guy who had a dozen ideas a day, one of which might be good, the rest disasters.

John Giberson, a close friend of Braniff's MEC chairman, Butch Poole, concedes that these criticisms of Braniff's new boss have some justification.

"I watched the way Harding Lawrence ran the company," Giberson says, "and when you're talking to me about him, you're talking to the choir. He was brilliant, astute, and completely open about where he wanted to take Braniff.

"His basic problem," Giberson says, "was that his middle managers were so incompetent they couldn't carry out his plans, and he was incapable of firing these idiots. Instead, he kicked them upstairs."

Although Lawrence had undeniable gifts and charm, there was something cranky about him. What can you say about a man who would name his son in honor of an outworn political slogan with racist overtones? *States Rights* Lawrence! One might logically conclude that any father, no matter how brilliant, who would stick a kid with a name like that had a cog missing.

Howard Cole, a Braniff pilot since 1958, served as MEC chairman during and just after Bankruptcy I. Like Giberson and many other pilots who had dealings with Lawrence during these years, Cole remains an admirer.

"If it weren't for the alcohol," Cole believes, "Mr. Lawrence would never have allowed himself to be run off, more or less in the middle of the night. If he had stayed and fought, I will always believe he could have flown Braniff through bankruptcy. One thing is for sure, he would never have parked those airplanes in 1982. He would have kept them and us flying."

Another view of Harding Lawrence is that he was a living embodiment of the "Peter Principle." A success until he reached the final rung of the corporate ladder, Lawrence would reach his level of "creative incompetence" as Braniff's president. At Continental, he had Bob Six's steady hand to keep him on track— at Braniff, nobody was there to rein him in.

But in the beginning, things were fine between Braniff's pilots and Harding Lawrence. His aggressive expansion of routes and purchase of new equipment put money in pilots' pockets. Eschewing the traditional distance from the pilot group that old Tom Braniff had left as his managerial legacy, Lawrence sought out MEC chairmen for "insider" chats.

Howard Cole, who served (along with Chuck Goduti and Charles Bohanon) as "custodial representative" in holding the Braniff pilots together during the difficult days between Bankruptcy I and the airline's rebirth in 1984, remembers how shocking it was to see Lawrence buddying up to Butch Poole, the MEC chairman in 1965–66.

"He really won the pilot group over," Cole remembers. "I'd see Mr. Lawrence and Butch with their heads together, and I'd think we really had it going."

John Giberson likewise remembers the early Lawrence days fondly.

"I can still remember personally seeing Mr. Lawrence take charge, like a breath of fresh air," Giberson says. "We pilots would see things wrong and complain, but those idiots who were in charge would simply ignore us and nothing would be done. Mr. Lawrence, if he'd had more people like himself, instead of the people he inherited, would have succeeded. But handicapped as he was by inferior middle managers, it was a struggle. I think eventually, they just wore him down."

"Harding Lawrence was one of the better communicators among airline management people," said J.J. O'Donnell in his 1991 interview. "I was like a lot of the Braniff people, a fan of his. I knew he was in trouble about a year before Braniff went bankrupt, because he called me and we talked about it. I remember he told me that his interest costs, just on the two Boeing 747s he had running back and forth to Honolulu, required each plane to have 280 people on it. He said, 'We're averaging 160, and that's not counting you pilots, labor, repair, maintenance, depreciation. That's just my interest costs.'"

But other, much earlier signs that something might be amiss with Harding Lawrence's stewardship at Braniff had appeared. His choice of members for the Board of Directors, for example, raised eyebrows among many close observers. Lawrence liked to select Board members less for their business acumen than for the impression they made. Several were Texas oilmen whose principal claim to fame was that they had been lucky at picking spots to sink wells. Others were "nice ladies" who met the Texas definition of "class" and circulated well at cocktail parties among the Dallas business elite. Politicians and bankers rounded out the Boards Lawrence helped to choose through the years. Some of them were incompetent, a few were drunks, and none of them knew beans about the airline business.

Maybe that was the way Lawrence wanted it. He had big ideas that were going to take Braniff on a wild ride, and he didn't want a Board that might exercise a restraining influence upon him, which Bob Six had done at Continental. Suave, debonair Harding Lawrence, he of the expensive silk suits and carefully coiffed hair, would charm the socks of these well-heeled rubes while he launched Braniff into the stratosphere and they rubber-stamped his every move.

To begin, Lawrence hired a classy New York advertising agency headed by blonde, beautiful Mary Wells, whom he subsequently married (after divorcing his wife of 37 years). Under his new wife's stylish tutelage, Lawrence completely reshaped Braniff's image. First, he outfitted Braniff's flight attendants, who were predominantly female and referred to as "stewardesses" in those days, in wild, high-fashion outfits. (He would have had the pilots don similar garb; but except for new double-breasted uniform coats, they successfully resisted Lawrence's wilder wardrobe renovations. In any case, the idea of Butch Poole, a heavy-set bear of a man, in an Italian designer airline pilot uniform, inspired more hilarity than outrage.)

Lawrence hired internationally famous artist Alexander Calder to paint the exterior of a Braniff DC-8. Calder's unique, _avant-garde_ paint schemes made Braniff instantly recognizable, even famous, an airline curiosity, situated at the cutting edge of style and fashion. Lawrence inaugurated "ultra service," which took first-class passengers into the realm of chef-prepared French cuisine and fine wines, all served in high style, supposedly, although critics scoffed that this wing-ding pampering was more hype than performance. Lawrence's ideas about luxury service were geared to the Texas elite's notions of that concept, which Mary Wells deftly adapted into an advertising blitz featuring slick, internationalist themes. At her urging, Lawrence had the interiors of Braniff's aircraft redesigned, featuring first-class seats of soft leather.

The corporate headquarters at "Braniff Place," just outside Dallas, featured an indoor-outdoor swimming pool, tennis courts, a miniature lake, and a hotel. Most striking of all, through an interchange agreement with Air France and British Airways, Braniff flew the supersonic Concorde—the ultimate "statement" about where Harding Lawrence was taking his airline.

And Braniff grew—prodigiously. Under the old system of direct government regulation, Lawrence could expand his airline only by acquiring another carrier or by competing for new route awards from the CAB. He was successful at both. Braniff had acquired the "international," which allowed it to use the initials "BI," in 1948, when it began limited DC-6 service to South America. Lawrence sought expansion with a vengeance. Like the born plunger he was, he gambled heavily in 1967, engineering the acquisition of Panagra. This bold movement into the Latin American market, which gave Braniff about half of all U.S. service to the region, mainly through its Miami base, only whetted Lawrence's appetite. Braniff pilots from those heady days remember Lawrence boasting that they would soon be flying into every European capital, and they even heard talk that the airline would absorb Pan American!

For the pilots, those were the best of times. The rapid expansion of the 1970s, and especially the postderegulation period following 1978, made Braniff a wonderland of rapid promotion. A pilot who hired on just before the boom in 1964 would attain the left seat in a scant five years. Junior captains were common in the cockpits of the airline's "fastback" BAC 1-11 jets, and Braniff's pilot force grew to levels that left veterans of the old, stodgy pre-Lawrentian era stunned.

"I caught a little bow wave on promotion," says Duane Woerth (elected ALPA's first vice-president beginning in 1990 and president in 1999), who hired on at Braniff in 1977. He would later catch on at Northwest after the first Braniff bankruptcy. "At the Kansas City base," Woerth says, "the pilots of every airline would ride the crew buses, and it was embarrassing. By the time of our first furlough, in 1981, I was a first officer only about 150 numbers away from holding a captain bid. Sitting right across from me on the crew bus would be guys from TWA who'd been second officers for 18 years!"

Braniff, at its peak strength in 1979, employed more than 2,700 pilots, 125 of whom were captains who were flying B-747s. Harding Lawrence had applied for almost every route in sight, and he bought new equipment and hired new pilots with what seemed reckless abandon. Braniff's logo became familiar on several continents.

In a regulated environment, as a mid-level carrier, Braniff got just the touch of panache from Lawrence it needed and dominated the Dallas/Ft. Worth "metroplex." But Lawrence was no fool; and he knew that, once the Airline Deregulation Act of 1978 took effect, Braniff could not survive unless it expanded. Wiser heads figured that Lawrence was overdoing it, that this massive expansion would lead to trouble unless all the breaks went Braniff's way.

But there was a certain method to Harding Lawrence's madness. Probably because he misunderstood history, Lawrence plunged. He knew that the last time the government flirted with deregulation, after the 1934 airmail cancellations crisis, those entrepreneurs bold enough to expand their operations to serve unprofitable routes had come out on top. Deregulation hadn't worked, so when the government reregulated the system, the airlines actually serving routes had an advantage over the competition. Many of them were, in effect, "grandfathered in."

Harding Lawrence, studying this episode from aviation's past, probably concluded that the future would belong to the bold. So he rushed to serve unprofitable routes, hoping that he could hang on long enough for reregulation to save him. Lawrence made no secret of his plans—he told dozens of people when he began his rapid expansion that within a couple of years Braniff would be either "as big as United or gone."[2]

"During the first phase of deregulation, we could pick up only routes that other airlines had abandoned," recalls Jack Morton, a retired Braniff captain. "Pan American gave up Seattle–Honolulu, and Mr. Lawrence rushed to pick it up. He should have been asking, 'Why did they give it up?' They must have had a reason. We began flying every place and no place, with no way to feed those routes. So we were flying half empty a lot of the time."

History is a tricky teacher, and Lawrence got its lessons badly wrong. Many people, including ALPA's leadership, opposed deregulation. Lawrence, like ALPA President J.J. O'Donnell, figured that an unregulated airline industry would never make sense and that eventually the government would have to reregulate to preserve safety standards. But in the interim, while the government was coming to its senses, rapid expansion made sense. If the banks were willing to lend him the money to expand, Lawrence was willing to take the gamble. From his point of view, he really had no choice. In the deregulated environment, only two kinds of airlines would survive—very large and very small. Braniff would either become a "megacarrier" or be merged out of existence—a fate worse than death to a man with Harding Lawrence's towering ego.

There were problems with this analysis, as we can see through hindsight. First, the political climate, conservative and free-market in orientation, was running against the concept of government regulation. Ronald Reagan, who would win election in 1980, believed passionately that government was the problem, not the solution. Reagan's promise to "get the government off the backs of the American people" meant that reregulation would not be an option during the 1980s.

Secondly, the banks urging Lawrence toward ever greater indebtedness to finance his expansion were themselves engaged in some dubious lending practices. Loan officers received promotion and bonuses not for making *good* loans, but for the *volume* of loans they engineered. The banks, flush with "petro dollars" deposited by price-gouging OPEC nations (the oil embargoes of 1973 and 1979 had made them rich beyond imagining), had to lend money out—they couldn't eat the deposits. So the banks encouraged young loan officers to pressure applicants to "over borrow."

Farmers in the Midwest, Third World nations, and Harding Lawrence were among the notable takers of this bait. Loans gone sour to Latin American nations would be made whole by U.S. taxpayers (the government's conception of "national interest" would dictate this outcome, since the days of sending in the Marines to collect debts were over). But the farmers and Braniff, whose assets were mostly in land and airplanes, not only *could* be foreclosed, they would almost *have* to be foreclosed, partly to appease angry taxpayers, but mostly as a symbolic gesture. In short, somebody was going to have to go down the drain to serve as an object "lesson" about "traditional values." And no help would come from the government.

In the wave of deregulation that swept the country, beginning during the

1970s and culminating with the excesses of the 1980s, the government was willing to let the big banks loan themselves silly. A bank as big as Continental Illinois, up to its eyebrows in "nonperforming loans" to Third World countries, was (like Lockheed and Chrysler) too big and important to be allowed to fail. Such a catastrophe might pull down the entire financial and banking structure. But Braniff was small potatoes. No significant national interest would be affected if Braniff failed. Massive failure of a really big company might warrant government intervention, but Braniff's tragedy would affect only its own employees, not the nation at large. In fact, half the existing airlines could go out of business without significantly affecting the nation's economic health. And in truth, the deregulators, like Alfred Kahn, believed that a certain number of airline failures were a necessary "corrective" on the road to a free market airline system.

Braniff was the Christmas turkey at this particular banquet. The banks, which had so blatantly overexpanded loans to unworthy borrowers, played a role in the accumulating troubles that engulfed Harding Lawrence. In an impossible conflict of interest, one of the banks that had loaned Braniff money also had one of its officers on the airline's Board. This Board member, who was in a position to second-guess Lawrence, essentially had veto power over management decisions. By threatening to deny an extension of credit unless things were done the way the bank thought proper, Braniff's management was thus denied its basic prerogatives. Put simply, when the airplanes securing the loans became more valuable to the bank on the open market than the interest they earned on the airline's loan, the bank could force a sale—regardless of the effect upon Braniff's operations.

Under these circumstances, Harding Lawrence did what any self-respecting executive would do—he resigned. But Braniff's floundering only got worse. Under John Casey, who had served as Lawrence's chief of operations, boardroom skirmishing reached new heights. The Board members, increasingly worried about their fiduciary responsibility (the possibility of stockholder lawsuits), cut ever more deeply into managerial functions. They didn't want Casey in any case, because they figured Braniff's problems were in the marketing area, and they wanted a slick salesman instead of an old-fashioned operations guy.

At this point, things were serious but not desperate. As usual, the pilots were told little or nothing of the Board's infighting. But the Braniff pilots' respect for Casey was strong, and they stood ready to provide whatever contract concessions were necessary to help him succeed.

"John Casey knew his stuff, and he was a man of absolute integrity," John Giberson remembers. "The problem was getting them to *ask* us for help, to tell us what they wanted."

In retrospect, Casey's hands were clearly tied. The Board wanted somebody else, and they would shortly get him in the person of Howard Putnam. In a surprising move that Braniff's pilots could only watch helplessly, the Board lured Putnam away from Southwest Airlines, a non-ALPA carrier. The Board's thinking was that Braniff's future under deregulation was as a low-budget carrier, and Putnam, having worked at the prototype cheap airline, was the man to ramrod that transition. Closer analysis by the Board would surely have revealed that Putnam's career at Southwest hardly suited him to cope with Braniff's problems.

Southwest Airlines was something of a freak. It originated in the forced merger of the Dallas and Ft. Worth airports. The authorities extracted written promises from all existing airlines that they would discontinue scheduled service to Dallas Love Field and Ft. Worth Amon Carter airport once the FAA-mandated construction of new combined Dallas/Ft. Worth International Airport (DFW) was complete. Because passengers prefer close-in fields, any airline that continued to serve the old airports, instead of the new one being built miles away out in the boonies between the two cities, would beat the pants off any competitors who moved. The FAA did its part by forbidding any interstate carrier from serving the old airports, which were supposed to become general aviation fields. Furthermore, in what came to be known as the "Love Field Compact," all the existing carriers agreed that they would not serve the "Metroplex" at the old airports (eventually, only Dallas' Love Field would stay open) on their *intrastate* routes, over which the FAA had no control. Because Texas has 3 of the 10 largest U.S. cities within its borders (Dallas, Houston, and San Antonio), an intrastate commuter airline modeled on California's Pacific Southwest Airlines (PSA), could do the established carriers (and DFW) considerable damage. Hence the "Love Field Compact."

Despite these precautions, some savvy operators with plenty of money were determined to skim the cream off the Texas commuter trade, specifically the Dallas–Houston market. They were definitely not "little guys" competing against the corporate barons, although Rollin W. King, who originally conceived of Southwest, might fit that description. The airline began flying in June 1971, backed by Murchison money and several influential Texas politicians, among them Herbert D. Kelleher (an associate of Governor John C. Connally), and future Democratic Party National Chairman Robert Strauss. This kind of backing caused one editorial observer to comment during the company' formative stage: "Southwest Airlines won't use aviation fuel—just political power."

Because Southwest had not existed at the time of the "Love Field Compact," it was not bound by it. Following extensive legal challenges, the airline took to the air, complicating life for every airline that served the Texas market from brand-new DFW. Although it would be an overstatement to say that Southwest did Braniff irreparable harm, nevertheless the damage was substantial (as it was to other ALPA carriers).

So it didn't take a genius to make money at Southwest, and anyway, Howard Putnam had nothing to do with it. During the airline's formative stage, tough, curmudgeonly old T. Lamar Muse, who had learned the business at American, made Southwest a success. Muse, figuring that anybody smart enough to pay pilots half the going wage could make money, eventually left Southwest to form his own airline, MuseAir, thus opening the way to Putnam.[3]

Putnam, whose career had been unremarkable to this point, found himself, inexplicably, tapped as Braniff's savior. It was a poor choice. No Braniff pilot who lived though this era has a good word to say about Putnam; and in fact, a majority of them suspect deep conspiratorial involvement of other airlines in his choice. Put bluntly, they believe that Putnam never had any intention of making a success at Braniff. They sneer at his idea, which ultimately proved unworkable, of converting Braniff into a cheap, jumbo-sized version of Southwest. Many Braniff pilots also believed that Putnam was hired by somebody (a shadowy, illusive "them") to be the airline's undertaker. Putnam himself, by his own admission, couldn't understand why Braniff's Board wanted him, but since they were offering big money and a no-risk challenge (he had a "golden parachute"), Putnam left his comfortable berth at Southwest for the listing deck at Braniff. Upon arriving, Putnam said publicly that he doubted Braniff's ability to survive! It was hardly a Churchillian moment.

So Putnam, who took over Braniff in September 1981, cut fares as the "Reagan Recession" deepened. Braniff's cash-flow problems only got worse, as American matched fares in a deepening spiral. Only one thing would have saved Braniff—some sort of direct federal assistance. The most obvious regulatory move would have been for the CAB (then approaching "sunset" itself and quite incapable of taking action) to guarantee Braniff's tickets. Travel agents, who were crucial to any airline's success, could then have sold Braniff tickets without fear of getting burned. More important, American, Braniff's chief competitor, would have had less incentive to put the airline under. A federal edict requiring other airlines to honor a failed Braniff's tickets (and American would have had to redeem more of them than any other airline) would have been a powerful incentive to help Braniff survive.

In the last analysis, American *did* offer to help. American's CEO, Robert Crandall, impetuously telephoned Howard Putnam, hoping to put an end to the ruinous price war. On some routes, Braniff and American were *both* losing money flying airplanes with full loads of passengers. Incredibly, Putnam resisted the efforts to reach an accommodation. Instead of grasping at this last life preserver American was throwing Braniff's way, Putnam secretly tape-recorded the conversations with Crandall, hoping to prove a violation of anti-trust law. These putative "criminal" conversations, even had they resulted in stiff jail sentences and fines for every last American executive, would not have saved Braniff.

On May 12, 1982, a teary-eyed Howard Putnam, still barely familiar with his job, announced that Braniff was shutting down. The Braniff pilots faced a crisis no other pilot group had ever confronted. The first hatchlings of the deregulation chicken had come home to roost squarely upon them.

All eyes were now upon ALPA.

NOTES

[1] See George Hopkins, *Flying the Line*, Ch. 23, "Jets and Thin Ice."

[2] In 1967, when Braniff was growing rapidly, I interviewed Harding Lawrence about making Braniff the subject of my doctoral dissertation in history. While he delayed making a decision, ALPA offered to cooperate fully in my project, thus leading me to write *The Airline Pilots: A Study in Elite Unionization* (Harvard university Press, 1971).

[3] I interviewed Muse in 1975. Those interviews became the basis of "The Texas Airline War," *The Washington Monthly* (March 1976).

CHAPTER 6

O'DONNELL'S DILEMMAS
The PATCO Strike, Braniff, and Furloughs

In 1970, at the final BOD meeting Charley Ruby would preside over as ALPA's president, he made a farewell address that was oddly predictive of his successor's downfall a dozen years later. After eight embattled years, Ruby could have selected from a wide array of troublesome issues as the focus of his remarks. He chose pilot furloughs.

"We have a fairly large income for a small union, but you cannot dip both arms in that pot and come out in the black," Ruby warned the delegates.

Furloughs, Ruby told the BOD, created a "crisis of sympathy" for the pilots losing their jobs and had the potential to threaten ALPA's financial stability. Ruby, whose professional career began in the days of seasonal layoffs, saw furloughs as a normal *but temporary* aspect of the professional pilot's experience. In fact, he expressed great sympathy for managers who had to make these furlough decisions, and he spoke out strongly for cooperation with the airline industry in such matters. Ruby's expression of a "managerial mentality," while not totally lacking concern for the plight of furloughed pilots and their families, was at least a bit old-fashioned. It was also symptomatic of the "You ain't a *real* airline pilot 'till you've been furloughed" syndrome so typical of his era.

But signs of change were appearing. During the heady expansion of the 1960s, a new generation of airline pilots, mostly hired owing to the government's support of ALPA's three-crewmember policy, had come to see furloughs as anything but routine. Consequently, Ruby's warning that ALPA's finances would suffer if the delegates tried to do too much to help furloughed pilots stirred mutterings among some delegates. Talk about fiscal restraint was all well and good for Charley Ruby, as he rode off into the sunset with a comfortable retirement package; but the larger question remained unanswered. What *was* ALPA's responsibility to members of the profession who lost their jobs?

Of all the headaches O'Donnell would inherit from Ruby, furloughs were the most debilitating. For Ruby, this problem would require only a couple of aspirins and the stern warning he left as his legacy in 1970. But for O'Donnell, furloughs would become a full-fledged migraine. The problem with furloughs wasn't just the lost dues revenue to ALPA, as some cynics suggested. The problem went much deeper, to the very core of the professional airline pilot's image of himself as a stable, respected, and prosperous member of the upper middle class. Take away the profession from which most airline pilots derived their sense of self-worth, and ALPA would inevitably become a tempting target for blame and criticism, as would whoever happened to be ALPA's president at the time.

"The guy who loses his job or is being furloughed doesn't think rationally," J.J. O'Donnell sighed in his 1991 interview. "He says 'Goddamn it, why didn't *you*, why didn't *ALPA*, do something to protect my job!'"

The furlough issue would trouble ALPA well into the postderegulation era, and it would attain new significance as the great merger crisis of the 1980s unfolded. But in 1970, at a time when questions of "fragmentation policy" and "scope clauses" were mostly abstractions, the furlough issue seems, in retrospect, relatively trivial. But it struck contemporary observers as quite serious. While ALPA membership had doubled from 14,000 in 1965 to 28,000 in 1970, the number of pilots on furlough by then had increased 10-fold, to 880. Even in an era when being furloughed was looked upon as a routine part of the airline business, these numbers alarmed many pilots.

Imagine the crisis O'Donnell faced in 1982, when the number of airline pilots out of work jumped by more than 2,000 from the Braniff collapse alone! And these pilots weren't just furloughed—they were part of a mass "termination" unlike anything in ALPA's history. What did ALPA owe the Braniff pilots, and how could O'Donnell dodge *this* bullet?

As we have seen, O'Donnell had coped successfully with political crises before. If he chose to run for an unprecedented fourth term as ALPA's president in 1982, he would, as an incumbent, have enormous resources to counterbalance the negative baggage he had accumulated over the previous 12 years. Coming less than a year before he would have to face reelection, O'Donnell knew that the Braniff bankruptcy would be a political problem, but he did not think it an insurmountable one. At the time of Braniff's bankruptcy, he had not yet formally declared his candidacy, and he kept his intentions to himself.

With his usual flair, O'Donnell pacified a majority of the Braniff MEC by the kind of "hands on" personal touch at which he was a master. Friends and foes alike agree that in dealing with small groups, O'Donnell was a formidable operator. But with larger groups, particularly at one step removed from personal contact, O'Donnell often appeared stiff and brusque. The volume of angry letters from rank-and-file Braniff pilots indicated that he was vulnerable on this count.

Part of the hostility Braniff's line pilots displayed toward O'Donnell stemmed from the fact that he kept a relatively low profile. This shying away caused more than one Braniff pilot to express the feeling that O'Donnell and ALPA were abandoning them to their fate.

"The Braniff pilots were like all rank-and-file pilots, in that they did not understand that the president of ALPA doesn't have the muscle they think he has," says Howard Cole, who as Braniff MEC chairman after Joe Baranowski, almost singlehandedly kept ALPA alive during the nearly two years after 1982. "Our pilots felt put upon, cannibalized by our brethren at Eastern; and that left a very bitter taste. Because O'Donnell was an Eastern pilot, he got a lot of the blame. When I took over as master chairman, the Braniff membership in good standing was less than 20 percent."

O'Donnell's financial support for the Braniff MEC was never in doubt. At the May 1982 Executive Board, the Braniff MEC received an emergency grant of $50,000 to continue routine representational activities. Subsequently, the Executive Committee authorized nearly $500,000 to support the Braniff MEC in its various activities, which included an 800 number "hot line" that kept the airline's pilots abreast of the latest developments.

But the fate of Braniff's pilots was only one of several contentious issues nagging at O'Donnell, and with an election coming, minimizing their plight and distancing himself from it was good politics. But more to the point, O'Donnell believed that Braniff would emerge from bankruptcy, resume operations, and the crisis would solve itself. Consequently, he saw no need to rush into unfamiliar terrain. To implement the kind of "crash program" of employment assistance many Braniff pilots were urging upon him was *precisely* the kind of thing Charley Ruby had warned about. That things would pan out, at least temporarily, just the way O'Donnell predicted earned him little credit among unemployed Braniff pilots at the time.

When Hank Duffy took over ALPA's presidency in January 1983, he would find a bulging file of letters from Braniff pilots asking for assistance. Many of these letters were rife with the personal tragedy of divorce, lost homes, and shattered lives. Unemployed Braniff pilots wanted many things from ALPA, among them "strike benefits." These letters repeated a familiar refrain—loyal dues-paying members who had never asked for anything from ALPA before needed help. What about a loan equal to the dues they had paid in over the years? But Braniff wasn't on strike, and ALPA's Constitution and By-Laws had no way to help them financially with loans.

"When people can't get jobs, when they have everything on the line and they see it all going down the drain, they want some place to vent their emotions," says Dick Goduti, who would become Braniff's "custodial representative" following "Bankruptcy II" in 1989. "ALPA was an easy target when they got to the point where there was nobody else to blame."

But the Braniff pilots *did* have one legitimate complaint. Above all else, they wanted ALPA to *somehow* force the government into complying with the "first right of hire" provisions of the Airline Deregulation Act of 1978. While O'Donnell had indeed *quietly* supported the Braniff MEC financially, to ordinary line pilots this form of aid was almost invisible. What they really wanted was new jobs, which seemed to be their right under the law. In this critical area, which involved directly pressuring the Reagan administration for first-right-of-hire, O'Donnell was strangely silent.

"I don't know if J.J. had some understanding with Ray Donovan [Reagan's Secretary of Labor], but for some reason he never pushed the Labor Department to post its [first-right-of-hire] regulations," Duffy insists. "Until they issued the regulations, we could do nothing. We had to start from scratch, trying to get the Secretary of Labor to post the regulations."

As we have seen, the "Reagan Revolution" began with a crusade to "get the government off the backs of the American People." To this end, President Reagan announced that he was canceling all "unnecessary government regulations."The first-right-of-hire regulations issued by his predecessor, Jimmy Carter, under the terms of the Airline Deregulation act of 1978, fell victim to the Reagan cancellations. In the March 1981 issue, *Air Line Pilot* reported that the cancellation was "to give the new Reagan administration a chance to make any changes it might deem necessary."

First-right-of-hire regulations spelled out the implementation procedures governing the labor protective provisions (LPPs) of the Airline Deregulation Act of 1978. Government intervention in situations like this, historically called employee protective provisions (EPPs), typically applied to businesses over which the government had regulatory or oversight authority. As ALPA had experienced them previously, these regulatory activities applied mostly to mergers, like the Allegheny–Mohawk union of 1972.

The deregulation LPPs were new in that they required an existing airline to hire, on a *preferential* basis, pilots who had lost their jobs *because* of deregulation. The problem with this legislation was that it first required the President, through his administrative subordinates, to "find" that deregulation was the cause of the airline's bankruptcy and *then* to issue a set of administrative guidelines *implementing* procedures for first-right-of-hire. An airline was not obligated to hire pilots it didn't need under the 1978 act, but any pilot who couldn't get a job within a 10-year limit that Congress imposed had the right to compensatory payments from the federal government.

All this sounds like a double-barreled safety net—either the Braniff pilots would get new jobs with another airline or they would get compensation. But it held a "Catch 22." Any President who philosophically opposed the concept could thwart it simply by doing nothing—which is exactly what Reagan did. Secretary of Labor Ray Donovan, the Reagan Administration official directly charged with action under the 1978 deregulation act, mindful that LPPs were the kind of direct government intervention in business that the President had built his political career by opposing, refused to act.

"It took years for the Department of Labor to implement first-right-of-hire because the companies fought it like hell, they thought it was going to cost them millions," O'Donnell explained in 1991 about the long LPP delay. "Congress wrote a law that was in my opinion watered down, almost worthless, and worded in such a way that the Department of Labor was the scapegoat."

In the 1991 interview, O'Donnell blamed the utter failure of the LPPs as a job-protection device on congressional Democrats, particularly Senators Howard Cannon and Edward M. Kennedy, who chaired the committees that drafted the legislation. He also criticized airline management for thwarting the LPPs. O'Donnell offered no criticism of either Ronald Reagan or Ray Donovan. Because O'Donnell would later serve as Under Secretary of Labor under Reagan, his disclaimers are at best disingenuous, and many of O'Donnell's critics believed at the time he was "playing politics" with the LPP issue.

"I have no doubt that John O'Donnell was job hunting with the Reagan people almost from the moment they took office," says Merle C. "Skip" Eglet of Northwest, who served as an ALPA executive vice-president at the time. "I have no direct knowledge that he was delaying the LPPs for that purpose, but it would not surprise me. There wouldn't have been any negative political fallout within ALPA, because at the time, in 1981, the LPPs just weren't an issue. After Braniff's bankruptcy in 1982, of course, they would be."

As we have seen, by the time of "Operation USA" in 1981, O'Donnell had become very close to the new Republican administration. He obviously wanted to maintain that relationship and build upon it. Had O'Donnell pushed aggressively for implementation of the LPPs, his action probably would have alienated Reagan topsiders and almost certainly would have damaged his standing with them. So, out of either personal ambition and political expediency, or conversely, a sincere belief that "staying on the right side" of the Reagan administration best served ALPA's interests, O'Donnell opted for a low-key approach to implementation of LPPs.

No one but O'Donnell himself knows *for sure* what his motivation was, and in all fairness, we must remember that the LPPs that Braniff's pilots would shortly need so much were not an issue until later. At the time of the Reagan administration's sidelining of the LPPs, few airline pilots had any interest in them. During the months leading up to the Braniff bankruptcy, only two relatively small airlines, Air New England and Airlift International, whose pilot groups totaled barely 100, would theoretically have benefited from the LPPs. But when Hank Duffy took over from O'Donnell in January 1983, the LPPs regulations were still in administrative limbo.

"We started working on Ray Donovan pretty hard," says Hank Duffy of his first months in office. "We finally got him to post the LPP regulations, but then the airlines tied it up in court. We eventually won it, but it took years."

After nearly three years of delay, the Reagan administration finally succumbed to ALPA's pressure and published the LPP regulations. Fifteen airlines promptly sued to halt their implementation. In May 1984, a federal court further delayed implementation of the LPPs because the Airline Deregulation Act of 1978 contained a "legislative veto" designed to oversee and limit the President's administration of the law. The Supreme Court had previously ruled that such limitations were unconstitutional, but Congress believed that its LPP wording in Section 43 of the deregulation act would pass muster. This provision was in the law because congressional Democrats feared the adverse effect of deregulation on their labor constituents and distrusted the labor policies of the current Carter administration, not to mention of future Republican administration.

This attempt to protect labor from the effects of deregulation backfired, much to the dismay of airline pilots, who stood to benefit from it more than any other occupational group. But the original prolabor intentions of Section 43 were clear. In the absence of Reagan's support for the LPPs, all ALPA could tell pilots who lost their jobs because of deregulation was to continue asking employers for "special consideration" under first-right-of-hire provisions. Meanwhile, ALPA appealed the court decision and eventually prevailed, but not until 1987. It was a hollow triumph—the statutory 10-year limit on the LPPs associated with the Airline Deregulation Act of 1978 had run out.

"I am not sure anybody ever got hired because of first-right-of-hire," says Hank Duffy frankly. "But it was a fight worth making."

As for the compensation due to pilots who lost their jobs because of deregulation, not one Braniff pilot (or any other airline pilot, for that matter) has ever received a penny.

The Department of Labor's long delay in issuing the regulations meant that it would be years before Congress could appropriate money for that purpose. By 1987, when the administrative and legal systems had finally finished with the LPPs, the federal budget was deeply in deficit and had no money to spare. Congress and the President had mutually agreed to understate the deficit by the sham of refusing to spend money in federal "trust funds"; among these were taxes that passengers paid for the specific purpose of airport improvements. In this financial environment, neither Congress nor the President showed interest in appropriating money to compensate airline pilots.

Ironically, in several lawsuits that Braniff pilots brought, judges would later rule that Braniff had indeed failed because of deregulation. So the Braniff pilots were entitled to compensation under the LPPs, but no money was available to pay them—the final "Catch 22."

As for O'Donnell, he was playing his political cards very close to the vest in early 1982, emphasizing his "connections" with political leaders and his "quiet clout" with them. So in fairness to him, the decision to soft-peddle the Braniff collapse was consistent and intellectually defensible. While many Braniff pilots pilloried O'Donnell and all his works, an influential segment, particularly among the Braniff MEC, worked hard to counter their attacks, thus insulating him from damage somewhat.

In any case, the *direct* political impact of the Braniff pilots at the BOD meeting in 1982 would be minimal, because owing to their unique situation, they were granted only "observer" status, which meant they were not permitted to vote. In addition, the fact that the Braniff pilots had high hopes of getting their airline back into the air further ameliorated the tension. But Braniff's pilots were the ghost at the banquet in 1982, and their presence as "observers" was a visible reminder to every delegate that the unthinkable was now possible—airline pilot furloughs might *not* be just temporary, after all.

"We didn't even debate Braniff that much," recalls Hank Duffy. "At that point, everybody thought it was an isolated thing, not the trend for the future."

And in fact, Braniff would revive, metamorphosing into "New Braniff" (or Braniff II), on March 1, 1984. This rebirth was largely the work of two retired Braniff pilots, Jack Morton and Glen Shoop, plus one active pilot, Jack Murdoch.

A more overtly political problem, the PATCO strike of 1981, provides another view of just how tricky the furlough issue could be. When the Professional Air Traffic Controllers Organization went on strike against the federal government in August 1981, many pilots were so incensed at O'Donnell's handling of it that they mounted a serious effort to recall him from office.

Because of the profound dislocations the PATCO strike might cause in the working environment of airline pilots, O'Donnell necessarily had to involve himself in it. The restrictions on airline operations that the PATCO strike generated almost certainly played a role in the bankruptcy of some small carriers, notably Air New England, and might well have aggravated the troubles of others, including Braniff. For O'Donnell, the PATCO strike was almost a match for Braniff—neither crisis, no matter what he did, was likely to win him many friends.

ALPA and PATCO had a symbiotic relationship in that both worked inside a mutually dependent system. Like most such relationships, it had deep internal tensions that often erupted into outright fissures. Many airline pilots saw PATCO as irresponsibly aggressive, while many PATCO members viewed pilots as pampered prima donnas. This friction often showed in the verbal mannerisms of pilots and controllers when they dealt with each other. "On the frequency" conversations were often characterized by brusqueness, sarcasm, and even outright nastiness. As a committed trade unionist, O'Donnell tried mightily to create an atmosphere of mutual cooperation between PATCO and ALPA. His efforts generated an irate reaction from many airline pilots.

"Some pilots gave the controllers fits," O'Donnell reflected sadly in 1991. "We had pilots who just continually rubbed salt in the controllers' wounds and ridiculed them for wanting a starting pay equivalent to a pilot's. By the same token, we had some controllers who didn't treat pilots right. We tried every way in the world to build a positive relationship with PATCO, running articles in *Air Line Pilot* about them, because a lot of them are good people."

A valid professional conflict underlay the hostility between airline pilots and air traffic controllers. Put simply, it came down to the question of authority. Pilots have historically disliked giving up their "command authority" to anybody. The nature of the modern ATC system meant that as the airline industry developed, air traffic controllers would inevitably assume *de facto* "command authority" in many situations. PATCO owed its origins *partly* to the feeling of many controllers that their "job" did not receive the same respect as airline pilots' "profession."

But in another sense, a purely psychological rift existed between pilots and controllers, one that was primarily sociological in origin. Typically, controllers learned their trade in the military as enlisted personnel who were under the command of pilot officers. When PATCO began stressing the similarity of their responsibilities, even going so far as to suggest that controllers should receive "equal pay for equal work," many airline pilots heartily disagreed. Who did these ex-enlisted men think they were?

During the long buildup to the PATCO strike, the controllers' tactics against the federal government earned them the enmity of a clear majority of airline pilots. While many airline pilots, particularly those "nuts and bolts" types who specialized in ATC problems, felt the controllers had legitimate grievances, these sympathies did not extend to PATCO, its leadership, or most importantly, its tactics.

On at least two occasions before 1981, PATCO members demonstrated their unhappiness with the FAA and its administrator, Langhorne Bond, by "working to the book." This tactic, which airline pilots had occasionally used themselves, might at first glance seem to fall within acceptable parameters. But PATCO's case was different. When pilots used the "slowdown" as a tactic, it was against their private employers and affected nobody else. When PATCO engaged in a slowdown, it was against the U.S. government—an inappropriate and unpatriotic action, in the opinion of many airline pilots. But far worse, a PATCO slowdown damaged other people, most directly the airlines that pilots depended on for a living. For example, during a one-day slowdown in August 1980 at a single airport, Chicago's O'Hare, PATCO cost the airlines almost a million dollars in excess fuel alone. And pilots had one more reason to be unlikely to support a walkout by PATCO—strikes by federal employees were *illegal!*

Questions of legality aside, strikes are traditionally about muscle—politically, economically, and morally. An element within PATCO believed that if it could hold its 13,000 members on the picket line, they could shut down the nation's air transportation system and force the government to meet their demands. FAA Administrator Langhorne Bond, the Carter appointee with whom ALPA also had differences, warned PATCO's leaders that their demands were excessive and that he would crack down hard on them if they went on strike.

In January 1981, shortly before the Reagan administration took office, Bond explicitly told PATCO that the FAA had a contingency plan in place to break a controllers' strike. Bond warned PATCO that the FAA's plan involved using military personnel, hiring "permanent replacements," and engaging in aggressive criminal prosecution designed to force strikers to cross the picket line. Bond also warned PATCO's leaders that despite their endorsement of Ronald Reagan in the 1980 campaign, they should not expect more lenient treatment from incoming Secretary of Transportation Drew Lewis. Bond's warning was prophetic, and his disgust with PATCO's leadership was one of the few things he and J.J. O'Donnell agreed upon.

By early 1981, a more radical element had replaced much of PATCO's original leadership. Barely a week before the strike, Robert Poli displaced John Leyden, a man O'Donnell had known and respected since before assuming ALPA's presidency. In fact, O'Donnell's relationship with PATCO had become quite close during John Leyden's tenure. When Poli tricked Leyden into resigning, the nature of O'Donnell's relationship with PATCO changed.

"I had ten years of excellent relationships with PATCO through John Leyden," O'Donnell said in 1991. "I knew him very well socially, we were on TV together, and we filed several joint lawsuits. I brought him to every ALPA convention. But Bob Poli and his radicals, who wanted to jump controllers' pay from $23,000 to $55,000, replaced Leyden in July because he was a peacemaker who opposed striking in violation of federal law."

Owing to O'Donnell's rise within the ranks of organized labor to a vice-presidency of the Executive Council of the AFL-CIO, he became, in effect, George Meany's troubleshooter and ambassador plenipotentiary to other airline unions. He enjoyed a similar relationship with Lane Kirkland, Meany's successor. The AFL-CIO looked to O'Donnell as a mediating influence on PATCO because of his long friendship with John Leyden. On one occasion, Leyden had invited O'Donnell to address the PATCO convention in Honolulu. But Bob Poli was not John Leyden.

"In February 1981, John Leyden warned me that Bob Poli and the radicals were planning an illegal strike," O'Donnell recalled 1991. "I told John not to expect airline pilots to honor PATCO's picket line because the great majority of pilots were angry at the controllers. I said, 'If you have a strike, my guys will run over you; they'll fly every damned flight.'"

During a May 1981 meeting between Poli, Leyden, and O'Donnell, with Jack Bavis present, Poli announced that PATCO would have a strike that was a "set up," in that it would have the silent support of the Reagan administration, which would use it as cover to meet their demands. Poli insisted that he had a commitment from Reagan owing to PATCO's endorsement of his candidacy in 1980 and that the strike would be short.

"I said, 'Bob, you're smoking a pipe,'" O'Donnell recalled later. "I believe some of Reagan's people said they'd do that, I really do; but a commitment like that would never have come from him. And I don't think they ever said they'd give in or were going to solve PATCO's problems. They said they were going to look into them, see what they could do. Stupid leadership—that was Bob Poli."

Ben Cleveland, a former Marine fighter pilot who helped found PATCO before moving into FAA management, confirms that ordinary PATCO members were tricked into going on strike by Poli's misrepresentation of Ronald Reagan's position: "I attended a meeting at Phoenix just before the strike at which a regional vice-president of PATCO assured us that the strike was an 'inside deal,' that it would be short and just for show, theater really, to give Reagan the excuse to cave in to us.

" I was already a supervisor at the time," Cleveland recalls, "and I *knew* it *had* to be another pile of Bob Poli's bullshit. The word was out in management that if those guys went out on strike, they were going to be fired, and no kidding! By then I was not in PATCO, just a friendly observer. I warned—nobody listened."

O'Donnell, because of his close contacts with the Reagan people, also knew that Poli was either lying or a fool. Ronald Reagan came to the White House committed to a radical restructuring of American society, and one of his targets was organized labor. He clearly meant to dismantle what he called "the welfare state," because he saw it as a drag on economic growth. Reagan had noble goals, best summed up in his cheery slogan, "A rising tide lifts all boats," to explain how he believed economic growth would cure America's ills. But implicit in the "supply side" economics that Reagan espoused was the notion that any institution that hampered the free flow of market economics was counterproductive. Traditionally, conservatives have viewed labor unions as a drag on economic growth, a dead weight carried on entrepreneurial backs. Furthermore, conservatives have long believed that governmental favoritism was the base upon which organized labor's power rested. In short, organized labor would clearly be one target of the Reagan Revolution. Bob Poli completely misunderstood this fact.

But J. J. O'Donnell did not. In late July, at a national meeting of PATCO's Executive Board, the radicals and their opponents fought it out. With the strike issue hanging in the balance, Bob Poli engineered an internal coup that ousted John Leyden. O'Donnell followed these events with great interest.

"As they were flying to Chicago for a special meeting of the PATCO Executive Board and their Negotiating Committee, Poli says to John Leyden, 'Let's you and I resign in protest and say we're not going to strike.'" O'Donnell recounts. "This Executive Board wanted to strike. So Poli convinced Leyden to resign as president, but then Poli didn't!"

When PATCO's Executive Board named Poli to replace Leyden, Poli then proceeded to set the strike date for the first week of August 1981.With O'Donnell warning him that ALPA would not support the strike, Poli agreed to delay it until after a meeting with the AFL-CIO Executive Council in Chicago on August 2. PATCO, ignoring the advice of the AFL-CIO to rethink their strike plans, on the following day, Aug. 3, 1981, walked out and threw up picket lines at O'Hare. Lane Kirkland was unhappy about it, but he would not cross PATCO's picket line. He canceled his return flight, rented a car, and drove to his home in Washington, D.C.

"They had picket lines set up at the base of the control tower at O'Hare, but not at the airport," O'Donnell says. "I got on an airplane and came back to Washington. I was trying to stop this stupid strike."

O'Donnell had been talking to Drew Lewis regularly for months and knew that the Reagan administration would give PATCO no quarter. O'Donnell also knew that rank-and-file airline pilots would cheer PATCO's destruction, no matter that it might do some damage to themselves in the process. This fact left O'Donnell with a classic dilemma. Getting the PATCO strike settled as soon as possible was in everybody's interest. But to mediate the strike, to act as an effective go-between, O'Donnell would have to appear conciliatory to both sides. His private sympathies were, of course, entirely opposed to PATCO, and particularly Bob Poli, whom he considered an unreliable radical. But O'Donnell couldn't let his distaste show.

Had O'Donnell been left alone, he might well have engineered a compromise that would have settled the strike and salvaged the professional careers of thousands of hapless PATCO members.As we have seen, O'Donnell was a gifted negotiator and conciliator whose contacts with all parties were intimate. He spoke with the authority of his AFL-CIO vice-presidency and his friendship with John Leyden (whom he would later offer an ALPA job, after Poli had engineered his ouster from PATCO). O'Donnell had access to the top levels of PATCO, while simultaneously remaining on close terms with Drew Lewis, the Reagan administration's point man in the PATCO strike.

But circumstances and bad luck prevented O'Donnell from stopping the PATCO strike.A hostile reaction developed among many ALPA members, who saw O'Donnell's efforts at conciliation as favorable to PATCO. Put simply, most ALPA members wanted PATCO figuratively strung up by its heels. Should O'Donnell persist in his efforts, the political fallout within ALPA would be costly. Although August was far too early to announce his candidacy for reelection to a fourth term as ALPA's president, O'Donnell's political antennae were nevertheless up. He had no intention of suffering political damage within ALPA because of the stupidity of PATCO's leaders.

"I'd say 70 percent of ALPA members were ultraconservative Republicans," O'Donnell said in 1991. "But I also knew that the PATCO strike had the potential of losing large numbers of them their jobs for a period of six months or a year, as they hired and trained new controllers. The only thing I wanted was to make sure I didn't lose people to layoffs. I was scared of losing 20 percent of our members to layoffs—then there would be big trouble because we didn't do something to stop the strike."

On Aug. 5, 1981, just two days into the PATCO strike, at *precisely* the moment when O'Donnell could have been most effective at mediating an end to it, his enemies inside ALPA struck. The Eastern MEC, at the urging of his archenemy of many years' standing, Augie Gorse, passed a resolution condemning O'Donnell's activities in the PATCO strike. The resolution accused O'Donnell of "favoring" PATCO and called for his resignation. O'Donnell, sensing the mischief his enemies could make for him politically with such charges, withdrew from active involvement in the effort to end the PATCO strike. Even a direct appeal from Drew Lewis, who had come to rely on O'Donnell, failed to get him back into the fray.

"That Eastern MEC resolution criticizing me for supporting the controllers was a beauty," O'Donnell said angrily in his 1991 interview. "I had done just the opposite."

Shortly thereafter, Secretary of Transportation Drew Lewis, with whom O'Donnell had conferred repeatedly on the PATCO strike, called to ask for help. Lewis particularly wanted to know Bob Poli's whereabouts, since he had gone into hiding.

"Drew Lewis asked me to communicate with Poli," O'Donnell says. "I told him I was not a mediator, that I was not a friend of Poli's, and I suggested that he call John Leyden and gave him the phone number. But John was still so angry at that double-cross by Poli that he wouldn't help. So Lewis called back and asked if I had any suggestions. I says 'Yeah, I got a suggestion. Let's all go fishing.'"

O'Donnell was now under dire political stress within ALPA, and he dared not take any further active role in the attempt to settle the PATCO strike. But he did delegate full authority to Jack Bavis and sent him into battle. This approach, although politically expedient, also made sense, because Bavis had developed something of a friendship with Bob Poli.

"O'Donnell *did* get involved in the PATCO Strike, even though the Executive Council hadn't approved it," Jack Bavis says of his mission to Poli. "He sent me to be his personal intermediary with Bob Poli. J.J. did this because he had developed a friendship with Drew Lewis, who needed to know what was taking place inside PATCO and under what conditions Poli would take the strike down. Lewis trusted O'Donnell to communicate with PATCO back and forth. For example, I carried the message to Poli that if he would resign and say that he made a mistake, Lewis would take all his people back. Poli refused. It was the worst case we saw of a union leader who sacrificed his troops even when he knew they were going to be defeated and replaced."

And so the PATCO tragedy played itself out. Using a combination of military controllers, crossovers, and supervisory personnel, the ATC system limped along while "permanent replacements" were hired and trained to take over for the PATCO strikers. The FAA drastically reduced access to the ATC system for many months; and while the hardship on general aviation was enormous, the airlines came out better than anyone had hoped. The mass layoffs that O'Donnell had feared did not materialize.

Once the Reagan administration decided to break PATCO, only one thing could have saved it—ALPA's direct intervention. The only rubric under which ALPA would have honored PATCO's picket lines was safety. On Aug. 19, 1981, O'Donnell laid that possibility to rest. At a press conference in Washington, D.C., he refuted charges made by striking PATCO members that the system was unsafe. Armed with an Executive Board resolution affirming that the ATC system was functioning safely "under reduced capacity," O'Donnell explained to a large gathering of news media that ALPA's Air Traffic Control Committee was closely monitoring the situation.

"I have 33,000 members flying the system, reporting from all over the country at all major traffic hubs," O'Donnell said. "I can say without equivocation that the ATC system is safe." O'Donnell went on to blast Poli, thus giving the Reagan administration public assurance that ALPA would not rescue PATCO. Actually, O'Donnell had already privately assured Drew Lewis that ALPA would not step into the fight.

"On the tenth of August, Drew Lewis called me about rumors that we were going to start honoring PATCO's picket lines," O'Donnell recalled later. "I told Drew very candidly that if I told my people to honor those picket lines, they'd run over *me*!"

Despite O'Donnell's best efforts, his handling of the PATCO strike was very damaging to him. With Eastern's MEC savagely denouncing him, O'Donnell felt under more pressure than he had ever been before. In the autumn 1981 Executive Board, O'Donnell would face a formidable recall movement, spearheaded by his own Eastern MEC. To forestall it, O'Donnell gave what many observers took to be a promise that if they would reject Eastern's recall resolution, he would not stand for reelection in 1982.

The O'Donnell era seemed to be over. But it wasn't—not quite.

CHAPTER 7

THE END OF THE O'DONNELL ERA
The Election of 1982

J.J. O'Donnell's last campaign for the presidency of ALPA ended in defeat, frustration, and a welter of bad feelings. Multiple allegations of deal-making skullduggery came from all sides—standard fare for ALPA's politics, historically. Because he carried the accumulated baggage of 12 years in office, J.J. O'Donnell knew he faced an uphill fight. Still, he was a known factor—which counted for something in uncertain times. In any close election, small factors, any one of which might merit the definition "decisive," come into play. But almost certainly, O'Donnell would not have lost to Hank Duffy in 1982 had it not been for the emergence of the "Delta Machine."

Delta's pilots had always been relatively low key in their ALPA activities. On one occasion, at the 1976 BOD meeting, their general quiescence was such that they failed to exercise their right even to *nominate* a candidate for executive vice-president (EVP). Two pilots from TWA wound up fighting it out with each other for the EVP post! As for ALPA's national offices, since the days of First Vice-President Stewart W. Hopkins (who, we must remember, was not a *real* Delta pilot, having come over in the Chicago & Southern merger in 1953), the Delta pilot group had generally not bothered to compete.

"Delta wasn't a national player in the 1970s, but they had my grudging admiration at BODs because they had an extremely well-disciplined MEC," says Merle C. "Skip" Eglet of Northwest. "They were knowledgeable, conversant with the issues important to them, and capable in debating their position. They were far from the mainstream of ALPA in the 1970s, but they did an outstanding job of getting their position heard—seldom passed, but always heard."

Until Hank Duffy's campaign in 1982, only two Delta pilots, Al Bonner and George Berg, had mounted campaigns for ALPA's presidency before, both feeble, and oddly enough, both in competition with each other at the same BOD meeting in 1974. In the early 1970s, Bonner, already ill and no longer flying the line owing to the heart condition that would eventually kill him, had briefly made himself a factor at the national level as an O'Donnell supporter. But generally, until the emergence of Hank Duffy as a visible presence in ALPA's national councils owing to the crew complement controversy, most airline pilots regarded the Delta pilot group as only minimally "in" ALPA, and certainly not "of" it—at least in the sense of being hard-nosed unionists.

All that was about to change. Beginning in 1980, a dynamic group of Delta

73

pilots whose leader was MEC Chairman Nick Gentile (pronounced "Gentilly"), began to remake that image, and they would shortly burst upon ALPA's national political scene. This group of Delta pilots, whose political skills (in the ALPA context) matched in "professionalism" anything available to Democrats and Republicans nationally, would unseat an incumbent seeking reelection—an unprecedented event in ALPA's 51-year history.

Both admirers and detractors alike would call their disciplined operation the "Delta Machine." Nick Gentile's lieutenants, Bill Brown, L.C. "Les" Hale, and Cameron W. "Cam" Foster, would finetune the Delta Machine into a formidable political weapon and use it to win a stunning first-ballot victory for Hank Duffy. Delta had become to ALPA what Napoleon feared China would one day be to the world. "Let China sleep," Napoleon said, "for when it wakes the world will tremble."

August H. "Augie" Gorse, who won election as Eastern's MEC chairman in 1980, believes the genesis of the Delta Machine lay in Nick Gentile's staunch unionism—an unusual trait for a Delta pilot. According to the "conventional wisdom," Delta pilots were historically the kids born with silver spoons in their mouths, beneficiaries of a benign management they never had to fight. This view of Delta pilots was particularly prevalent among the Eastern pilot group. But Augie Gorse knew it wasn't true of all Delta pilots.

"The first person I heard from after getting elected MEC chairman in 1980 was Nick Gentile," Gorse recalls. "He said, 'It's time for Eastern and Delta to bury the hatchet.' Nick was a damn good union man—he acted, talked, and thought like a union man."

Among the things Gorse and Gentile agreed upon was that TWA and United, under their respective MEC chairmen, Harry Hoglander and John Ferg, had become the proverbial bullies on ALPA's block. Gorse and Gentile both believed that O'Donnell deferred far too much to these "elephants," and they feared that John Ferg in particular, largely owing to United's recent "Blue Skies" contract (which we will discuss later) was setting a precedent in contract negotiations that would prove ruinous to ALPA in the long run. Gorse and Gentile also agreed that the major reason for the dominance of the United–TWA alliance was the rivalry between their own two airlines. Reflecting the pressures inherent in their competitive route structures, Delta and Eastern often canceled each other out in ALPA affairs.

"We both agreed that it was time we stopped fighting each other and did something about the sorry state of ALPA," Gorse recalls.

From Augie Gorse's point of view, that meant doing something about J.J. O'Donnell. Gorse, an engineering graduate of Clemson University who speaks with an authentic southern accent, retired on a medical disability from Eastern in 1988. He believes that the bad blood between himself and O'Donnell (which many people saw as a "given" in Eastern's internal affairs) has been overblown, largely because they seemed such polar opposites in terms of their sectional backgrounds.

"We were in the same class as new hires in 1956, and to this day, I admire and respect J.J. O'Donnell," Gorse insists. "I think that through his first two terms, he

74

did a damn fine job as ALPA president. The problem I had with him was just that he stayed in office a mite too long."

Gorse, well aware that O'Donnell saw him as an archenemy at the time of his election as Eastern's MEC chairman in 1980, was capable of joking about it. At the spring 1982 Executive Board, Gorse bantered publicly about his rocky relationship with O'Donnell.

"John, set your fears at ease," Gorse said lightly as he addressed the chair during a routine session. "I know I sometimes have a tendency to inflame your fears."

Actually, this levity between O'Donnell and Gorse came at a time when everybody thought O'Donnell's ALPA career was over and might have accounted for it. In the spring of 1982, nobody expected O'Donnell to run again for a fourth term that fall. He had seemed to foreclose that possibility at the previous Executive Board meeting.

In his opening remarks to the assembled MEC chairmen and national officers at the 38th Regular Executive Board in November 1981, O'Donnell dropped his bombshell. After recounting the woes besetting ALPA, all of which he described as having their origin in the Airline Deregulation Act of 1978, O'Donnell launched into a discourse on the effect of these troubles internally. As everyone at the meeting knew, the Eastern pilots under the leadership of Augie Gorse were seriously considering a formal campaign advocating O'Donnell's immediate recall, largely owing to their dissatisfaction with his handling of the PATCO strike.

"There are some who are deliberately exploiting these difficult times," O'Donnell said, as he struggled to control himself. "I have been a target of this for some time. I am frank to admit my anger at these tactics. I fully intend to complete this term of office through 1982. *However, I shall not seek another term as president.*" (Emphasis added.)

As we have seen, long-standing animosities had existed between O'Donnell and his own pilot group. The root of these disputes lay deep in the tangled past of Eastern's internal politics at the MEC level. A messy conflict between O'Donnell and Eastern's Retirement and Insurance (R&I) Committee Chairman Charles "Chuck" Dyer over basic investment philosophy, particularly as it applied to real estate, had further inflamed the situation. By the time of the PATCO strike, these animosities had festered into a formal resolution that the Eastern MEC passed denouncing O'Donnell—clearly an indication that the Eastern pilot group wanted O'Donnell to resign *immediately*.

"A very strong movement was afoot among his own MEC to circulate recall ballots among the general membership," says Skip Eglet of Northwest, who was an EVP at the time. Eglet, an ex-Marine aviator who was at one time an Eastern pilot (before a furlough in the early 1960s sent him job-hunting to Northwest), was a perceptive observer of Eastern's internal dynamics.

"I was violently opposed to recalling John," Eglet says. "But a lot of influential players at Eastern were really upset with him over a lot of little things."

As Delta's MEC chairman at the time, Hank Duffy actively involved himself in *stopping* Eastern's effort to recall O'Donnell. Arguing that the repeated efforts to recall ALPA presidents historically had been counterproductive, Duffy was instrumental in persuading Augie Gorse to drop the matter before it came to the floor of the Executive Board meeting "officially."

O'Donnell's announcement that he would "not seek" another term as ALPA's president was almost certainly related to the recall movement. O'Donnell, a proud, disciplined, and self-contained man, would not admit that, of course. But in an oral history interview in January 1991, he came close to it.

"To be very honest with you, I thought I wouldn't get through the summer of 1981," O'Donnell conceded, as he expressed his continuing belief that a "conspiracy" existed between Gentile and Gorse. "I had no problem with people constantly criticizing, if they came in and grabbed an oar and helped us pull this thing through the water. Nick Gentile was not involved in that [kind of criticism], but the people [who were] were considered his fronts. Jack Bavis pursued Nick on this, and he denied that he was part of that conspiracy."

Clearly, O'Donnell believed at the time that a conspiracy to force his resignation was building up in the summer of 1981. He almost certainly chose to defuse it by announcing his intention to step down from ALPA's presidency at the end of his term in December 1982. What this meant, so far as most ALPA officers were concerned, was that the 1982 BOD would see an open presidential election with no incumbent.

Almost immediately, speculation about who would fill O'Donnell's shoes became the hot topic at the Executive Board. Almost nobody noticed what should have been an obvious fact about O'Donnell's announcement—it had left some semantic wiggle room. Unlike Lyndon B. Johnson, who said "I shall not seek and I *will not accept*" another term in his withdrawal announcement following the 1968 Tet Offensive in Vietnam, O'Donnell did not rule out a draft. But *at the time*, nearly everybody understood O'Donnell's announcement as definitive. They certainly did not see it as a Machiavellian ploy.

Skip Eglet, whose relationship with O'Donnell went back to the time when Eglet had flown as a probationary copilot with O'Donnell at Eastern, had gotten to know O'Donnell very well during his tenure as EVP. Eglet saw nothing suspicious in O'Donnell phraseology. Like almost everybody present during O'Donnell's speech, Eglet shares the perception that O'Donnell's withdrawal from the upcoming presidential race in 1982 was sincere. Augie Gorse, who had more reason than most to be suspicious of O'Donnell, agrees.

"There is no question in my mind that when he said he was quitting after 1982 he meant it," says Gorse. "I certainly didn't see it as just some kind of political maneuver."

But some O'Donnell supporters, like Jack Bavis and Tom Ashwood, more attuned to the nuances of O'Donnell's psyche, were less certain. They believed that O'Donnell's decision to retire from ALPA was much more tentative and conditional, and that it was motivated primarily by personal matters that were specific to that particular time of his life. They understood that if certain personal conditions in O'Donnell's life changed, then his political plans might change, too. But for the moment, both Ashwood and Bavis, who harbored ambitions of their own, had no alternative but to accept O'Donnell's announcement as genuine. It seems, in retrospect, that O'Donnell was afflicted with the same kind of midlife restlessness that in 1962 caused Clancy Sayen to leave ALPA's presidency in mid-term.

"I would say, at that point, I was 60 percent in favor of running again," O'Donnell said in 1991 of his thinking at the time of his "withdrawal" announcement 10 years earlier. But he emphasized and reemphasized that his decision had nothing to do with ALPA politics. "For solely personal reasons, *solely personal reasons*, I was concerned whether I was going to finish 1982."

O'Donnell's after-the-fact recollections are at variance with what he was saying *at the time* about his reasons for withdrawal, which cited internal political dissension exclusively as the source of his decision. But O'Donnell clearly was open to new challenges and a career change. He had alluded to this just before his withdrawal statement.

"I want to advise you that I have recently had an offer of an attractive position with a major airline," O'Donnell told the delegates just before announcing his unwillingness to run another presidential race. His friends understood that he wanted to get on with the next phase of his life, which some observers thought might include government service or even a run for political office. The only question in their minds was whether he would serve out his full ALPA term. But O'Donnell put their speculations to rest.

"After much inner searching," O'Donnell told the delegates of his job offer, "I have decided that my principal obligation is to ALPA. I cannot turn my back on my responsibilities to our members' interests."

Although O'Donnell did not tell the delegates anything further, the job he alluded to was as vice-president for government relations at Eastern Airlines. Frank Borman, Eastern's CEO, formally offered O'Donnell the job when a routine retirement left that Washington, D.C., position vacant. Borman called Augie Gorse to, in effect, "clear" it with the Eastern pilot group. Gorse gave O'Donnell his approval, possibly seeing it as a convenient way to ease him out of ALPA's presidency by "kicking him upstairs."

Staring directly at Augie Gorse and the other Eastern pilot representatives as he made the announcement that he would not "seek" another term, O'Donnell concluded: "It is my sincere hope that those who are enjoying destructive sharpshooting at various officers, myself included, would work constructively toward our common goals in 1982."

Aside from his personal needs, O'Donnell's motivation in taking himself out of the 1982 race owed much to another undeniable political fact—he had totally lost control of his own MEC. An ALPA president who cannot control his own MEC stands on shaky ground. Once elected, of course, he can continue in office with minimal support from his own MEC. Indeed, O'Donnell had done so earlier. But on the eve of a national campaign, the lack of a stable MEC base upon which to stand while seeking reelection was a formidable handicap.

Historically, some very strong candidates for national office had fallen victim to the politics of their own MECs. O'Donnell's political career in ALPA had been unique in that he had survived at the top with a divided MEC behind him; but as the 1982 election approached, it was no longer merely "divided." A clear majority of the Eastern MEC opposed O'Donnell's continuation in office. A true "elephant" at the time, Eastern weighed in with a total of 3,452 votes in 1982. Of that number, O'Donnell would eventually receive a mere 493—fewer than the 532 votes John Gratz of TWA got! Hank Duffy, heavily backed by Augie Gorse, would get the lion's share of the Eastern vote—a total of 2,427.

In general, a pilot seeking national office without the support of his own MEC has had virtually no chance of succeeding. Even candidates who possessed substantial credentials, long ALPA service, and rank-and-file appeal faced impossible odds. For example, Lee Higman of United, whose service dated from the days when he was a Boeing 247 copilot, would fail despite a list of credentials that was almost unrivaled in ALPA's history. Higman had served on a stunning array of blue ribbon committees, had written the first administrative policy manual for ALPA Field Offices, and commanded rank-and-file appeal as a directly elected regional vice-president. But he got nowhere when he challenged O'Donnell in 1974. The reason for Higman's failure was that United's MEC, committed to their chairman Bill Arsenault and under his tight control, refused to endorse Higman's candidacy. Rank-and-file appeal counts for nothing in an ALPA presidential election—only MEC members vote.

Assuming that O'Donnell's decision to retire from ALPA's presidency at the end of his third term in December 1982 was genuine (or at a minimum "40 percent" genuine, as he insists), what happened in the interim to change his mind? At the time of the spring 1982 Executive Board meeting, O'Donnell had still not reversed his noncandidate status. But strangely, he *sounded* like a candidate.

The bankruptcy of Braniff, which happened less than two weeks before the meeting convened on May 25, 1982, sent a seismic shock through the assembled Executive Board. Braniff's fate and the misfortune of its pilot group absolutely dominated conversation in the hospitality suites, hallways, and the meeting room itself. At first glance, one might think that Braniff's failure would be the final nail in O'Donnell's political coffin. But ironically, it opened several political avenues to him. By reminding the delegates that he had predicted "major bankruptcies" would result from deregulation and reprising portions of his previous speeches opposing it, O'Donnell was, in effect, saying, "I told you so" to his internal critics while warning of a grim future.

"The Braniff situation would not have occurred in a regulated environment," O'Donnell told the delegates. "One does not need much imagination to realize the problems of the past were insignificant compared to those we face today. Some of us do not have to worry, it seems; but five years ago, the Braniff pilots didn't have to worry either."

As O'Donnell cited a long list of crises looming in ALPA's future, from "cabotage" to "the deficiencies of airline managements," he not so subtly reminded Executive Board members that having friends in high places was the best insurance against future catastrophe.

"Our objectives cannot be achieved solely through collective bargaining," O'Donnell declared. "Our relations with the Reagan administration are a vital link—perhaps more influential than any other avenue available to us today. It is critical that we do not lose these assets."

Because O'Donnell missed no opportunity to remind the delegates of his closeness to and influence with the Reagan White House, it all sounded very much like a campaign speech. His approach, demeanor, and emphasis were not at all those of a man whose political sun was setting. But strangely, most of the assembled delegates, taking O'Donnell firmly at his earlier word that he would not "seek" another term, did not interpret it that way.

With O'Donnell seemingly out the picture, several candidates had begun testing the waters. The May Executive Board served as a sounding board for people with presidential ambitions. As they took the pulse of their contemporaries, none of them paid much attention to O'Donnell. Jack Bavis, O'Donnell's executive administrator, and Tom Ashwood, ALPA's secretary, were among those considering presidential runs who could logically expect to receive O'Donnell's blessing. Ashwood's comments to the Executive Board indicated that O'Donnell had not yet reversed his noncandidacy position and that everything was still wide open. Likewise, Jack Bavis was busily lining up support before announcing his candidacy. If anybody should have been privy to O'Donnell's intention to get back into the race, it would have been Ashwood and Bavis.

Normally, ALPA's political season would not open until *after* the May Executive Board. Both Ashwood and Bavis had tested the waters and liked the results. Each planned to formally launch his campaign in June. Likewise, John Gratz of TWA and Tom Beedem of Northwest planned to announce their candidacies. Hank Duffy, who also intended to enter the race, was so sure that O'Donnell was out of the picture that he even went so far as to consult with him about strategy and tactics. In fact, Duffy insists to this day that if he had known that O'Donnell intended to run again, he probably would not have entered the race himself.

Sometime in either late May or early June 1982 (the exact date is uncertain), O'Donnell surprised everybody by announcing that he had changed his mind and would be a candidate for reelection to ALPA's presidency once again—this time for an unprecedented fourth term. In retrospect, Tom Ashwood admits he should have seen it coming.

"John did not consult me about the withdrawal announcement, and my jaw dropped when I found out afterward that Henry Weiss had drafted it," says Ashwood.

"In 1981, John was vacillating," Ashwood says. "He was playing the game of 'Will he run or won't he.' I was anxious for John to make a decision because I thought I had a chance to win. But there was no way I would have run against him. On a number of occasions during 1981, John said, 'I have earned the right to run unopposed.' He believed the Association should recognize this by not putting up any candidates against him. I warned him that this was dangerous and unrealistic."

In Ashwood's opinion, the announcement that he would "not seek" another term never amounted to anything more than a misguided attempt to elicit a "Draft O'Donnell" movement. But Ashwood admits that it didn't register on him immediately. Ashwood says he would have seen through this ploy earlier had he known that ALPA's general counsel, Henry Weiss, of whom he was deeply suspicious, had consulted with O'Donnell and drafted the "withdrawal" announcement for him. Put simply, had Ashwood known that Weiss was involved, he would have been more sensitive to the dodges that lawyers so often put language.

Jack Bavis, who was closer to O'Donnell than anybody else in ALPA, was even slower than Ashwood to realize that O'Donnell's plan was to encourage a "draft" movement. Any number of ALPA "movers and shakers" believe that Bavis would have been the most formidable candidate to carry the O'Donnell faction's banner. Bavis was a respected administrator who had wide contacts within ALPA, he was a skilled negotiator, and his personality lacked O'Donnell's sharp edges. Bavis was in the midst of planning his own announcement when O'Donnell pulled the rug out from under him.

"I confess I was deeply hurt by O'Donnell's turnabout," Bavis says. "I had served John loyally for more than a decade, he knew I wanted to run, and he let me think I would have his support. I guess there's no other word for it—he deceived me."

Skip Eglet was among the first to find out that O'Donnell would be returning to the political fray. Only days after the May 1982 Executive Board ended, Eglet was conferring with O'Donnell in the latter's eighth floor office at the ALPA building in downtown Washington, D.C. O'Donnell startled Eglet by suddenly announcing that he had changed his mind about running for reelection.

"By the fall of 1981, John was in so much trouble that it never occurred to me that his phraseology in withdrawing was meant to leave the door open to a draft," Eglet recalls. "In retrospect, I guess I should have been more sensitive to the nuances. When I asked him why he was changing his mind, he said, 'There are some people out there that I simply cannot leave this union in the hands of.'"

Augie Gorse clearly topped the list of "some people" to whom O'Donnell could not entrust ALPA. John Gratz of TWA, who had been among the first to announce that he would be a candidate, did not worry O'Donnell because he did not think Gratz could win. Hank Duffy of Delta was someone with whom O'Donnell had always enjoyed good relations and, under different circumstances, might have secured something approaching his blessings, if not an outright endorsement. But the budding alliance between Delta's leadership and Augie Gorse absolutely enraged O'Donnell and almost certainly was the key factor in his decision to reenter the race. In short, O'Donnell feared that Augie Gorse would wind up running ALPA through his alliance with Delta.

"Things changed substantially at the May Executive Board in 1982," O'Donnell said in 1991 of his 1982 decision to reenter the race. "With Augie Gorse talking to Nick Gentile and Bill Brown, I felt like I had to get back into it. But not because of Hank Duffy's candidacy. Frankly, I liked Hank. I just didn't like the guys supporting him."

O'Donnell based his 11th-hour attempt to recover his political fortunes on his ties to Ronald Reagan. Although the evidence is anecdotal, the consensus of opinion is that the typical ALPA member supported Ronald Reagan's candidacy in 1980. As we have seen, O'Donnell began building ties with the Reagan campaign staff in 1980 and would later capitalize on those contacts during the

1981 "Operation USA" affair. All evidence indicates that O'Donnell believed that he could rekindle his political spark within ALPA by claiming that his ties with the Reagan administration would be ALPA's salvation. When coupled with the truly disturbing effects of Braniff's bankruptcy, this influence could be the winning factor for him in 1982. If he could convince members of the BOD that he could better serve ALPA as a go-between with the Reagan administration than any other candidate, then his chances were good.

In O'Donnell's opening address to the May 1982 Executive Board, he made certain that the delegates knew of his pro-Reagan leanings, and he wasted no time in depicting himself as ALPA's best hope for putting these connections to use. But this approach held hazards for O'Donnell. He had no sooner launched upon his campaign to hitch a ride on the Reagan bandwagon, when he fell afoul of the LPP issue. Augie Gorse made sure that O'Donnell would stub his toe on the LPPs.

As we have seen, Reagan canceled the Carter administration's LPP regulations upon taking office in January 1981. Because the Braniff bankruptcy had focused attention on the fact that the LPPs specified in the Airline Deregulation Act of 1978 had never been "revised" as promised by the Reagan administration, O'Donnell confronted an obvious problem.

"Our objective must be combined legislative and contractual LPPs," O'Donnell declared to the Executive Board members. "The Carter administration did not send its draft LPP regulations until January 18, 1981, three days before President Reagan was inaugurated. For the past year, we've been fighting the industry to get new regulations. The industry is fighting us tooth and nail. Last Wednesday I met with [Secretary of Labor] Ray Donovan on the question of acting immediately on the provisions of Section 43 of the Airline Deregulation Act."

Clearly, O'Donnell was doing his utmost to shield the Reagan administration (and himself) from any blame on the LPP issue. His attempt to link the LPP delay to the Carter administration made little sense, and his repeated denunciations of Jimmy Carter, who was in no way responsible for the long delay, struck a note of blatant political pandering. O'Donnell would later insist that Carter's LPPs "as written" were worthless. But unemployed pilots clearly preferred flawed LPPs to none at all.

"I'm very upset over the long delay that has taken place since the law was enacted in 1978," O'Donnell said to the Executive Board. "But I do agree that additional time was necessary to rewrite the terrible rules that were put forth by President Carter."

For O'Donnell to beat on the dead horse of Jimmy Carter and blame him for the absence of deregulation LPPs more than a year after he had left office struck many Board members as disingenuous at best and downright shifty at worst. Focusing additional blame on airline management, which opposed the LPPs from the beginning, simply restated the obvious and only compounded the problem.

"You can be sure that the airlines are aggressively opposing Donovan's efforts," O'Donnell said. "In the meantime, we must give high priority to obtaining LPPs in our contracts. We'd like you all to go back to your airlines and say, 'Hey look, we need the LPPs.'"

O'Donnell's critics were quick to pick up on these weaknesses, particularly his contention that LPPs should be achieved through collective bargaining rather than by federal legislation. To make clear that O'Donnell had failed in his efforts to get the Reagan administration to issue the LPPs, Augie Gorse introduced a formal resolution that began: "WHEREAS the long-awaited LPPs have not been forthcoming, and WHEREAS there exist today three separate ALPA pilot groups on the street…," and concluded by urging O'Donnell to "continue his efforts in the *legislative arena* to secure LPPs, including 'First Right of Hire.'"

Gorse's resolution set off a long floor debate that put O'Donnell thoroughly on the defensive. With the Braniff bankruptcy on every Executive Board member's mind, Joe Baranowski, Braniff's MEC chairman, pointed out the obvious: "Our salvation is going to be in the *legislative arena* [emphasis added], with the deregulation act LPPs."

Amidst angry cries for action, Wes Davis of Frontier said, "I don't mean to be disparaging toward President O'Donnell, but is that the best we can do, just keep pushing? This is the most serious situation facing us right now, and it seems a bit ineffective."

Obviously discomfited by the furor Augie Gorse's LPP resolution had stirred up, O'Donnell sought to defend himself and shift blame from Ronald Reagan. He praised Nancy Kassebaum, the Republican Senator from Kansas, for her help in putting "pressure on the Department of Labor." Then, perhaps realizing that he had inadvertently called attention to the fact that it was Reagan's appointees who were delaying the LPPs, O'Donnell shifted to an attack on the Democrat-controlled House of Representatives. "We think that the regulations are going to face trouble in the House of Representatives."

But this approach also called attention to Reagan's failure to issue the LPPs—Congress had *already* sent up LPPs once. O'Donnell, in obvious frustration, finally resorted to a blatant appeal to what he saw as rank-and-file ALPA members' pro-Reagan views, obviously hoping that by going "over the heads" of delegates attending the Executive Board, he could score political points.

"We sure as hell can't correct the mistakes of the last thirty years by the U.S. Congress, and that's what we're living with right now," O'Donnell said angrily. "They like to blame it on President Reagan. I'm talking about the U.S. House of Representatives."

O'Donnell's emergence as a champion of the "Reagan Revolution" struck many observers as forced. Although O'Donnell insisted that he had always been a registered Republican, many close associates were surprised when he came "out of the closet," so to speak. A long list of ALPA heavyweights, foes like Northwest's Tom Beedem and Skip Eglet, as well as friends like TWA's Tom Ashwood, thought O'Donnell was a staunch, Boston-Irish Democrat!

"I always accepted the fact that O'Donnell was a Democrat," Ashwood says. "It came as a surprise when I discovered he was a fairly strong Republican, but John managed to conceal it very well until Reagan ran in 1980. He really was sincerely, terribly, genuinely smitten with Ronald Reagan."

O'Donnell certainly wasn't concealing it by 1982. "He waved the Reagan Republican banner pretty hard during the 1982 campaign," Skip Eglet recalls. "It was a surprise, because everybody thought he was a Democrat—maybe a Reagan Democrat, but still a Democrat."

Bob Bonitatti, whom O'Donnell had hired as ALPA's Legislative Affairs Director in 1975, could have disabused Eglet and Ashwood of their illusions. As a Republican operative who had served in the Ford Administration and would drop ALPA immediately to return to the White House as a special assistant to President Reagan in 1981, Bonitatti knew that O'Donnell was a Republican.

"Why did he keep it a secret?" Bonitatti asks rhetorically. "If you were the president of a labor union and you had ambitions within organized labor, as O'Donnell did, would you broadcast your Republican leanings?"

In the final analysis, O'Donnell's emphasis on his connections with the Republican administration might have backfired. With Hank Duffy as his opponent, a man whose established Republican credentials as a county chairman were beyond question, that issue could be neutralized. But even more damaging, by 1982 a good many MEC members were having second thoughts about the Reagan administration. Historically, pilots who are actively involved in ALPA affairs have been much more attuned to the political realities of organized labor's existence than ordinary pilots flying the line. What this meant was that they often aligned themselves with the Democratic Party out of sheer self-interest— emotional Republicanism aside. The people who were actually going to cast votes for or against O'Donnell at the BOD meeting in 1982 were therefore more likely than rank-and-file pilots to view Reaganism skeptically.[1]

O'Donnell argued that "the quality of our professional life is increasingly affected by what goes on in the White House," and he insisted that "we have been well-received and listened to at the White House." But in the final analysis, this argument was unlikely to sway delegates who were disaffected by the Reagan mystique. Similarly, delegates who admired Reagan might just as likely conclude that Hank Duffy's unforced Republicanism would carry ALPA farther than O'Donnell's highly suspect brand. So, how O'Donnell thought he could capitalize on this issue is difficult to see.

In any case, when news of O'Donnell's turnaround candidacy became common knowledge, many BOD delegates would regard it as evidence of bad faith. O'Donnell's age further inflamed the "bad faith" factor. He would exceed age 60 before his fourth term ended, should he win reelection. ALPA's official policy firmly opposed *any* flight deck crewmembers over the age of 60. Since ALPA's president had historically been accorded the rank and status, in terms of pay and prestige, that a captain earning the highest pay on the most favored equipment received, how could O'Donnell justify continuing in office once he reached age 60? Theoretically, he could continue as a flight engineer to age 65, but as an ex-pilot, that would violate ALPA policy. ALPA was at that time engaged in multiple lawsuits as a defendant in cases filed by ex-pilots who wanted to revert to second officer status at age 60. O'Donnell's reelection would set a damaging precedent.

"John's age was not a small issue during the election campaign," Skip Eglet believes.

The campaign that followed was a curious one. Formal debates at various pilot domiciles featured the three candidates—O'Donnell, John Gratz, and Hank Duffy. Although both Gratz and Duffy had attended the anti-O'Donnell "unity" meeting in New Orleans sponsored by Chuck Huttinger in July, they were in no sense a "slate." But Gratz's candidacy worked to Duffy's advantage because as a "favorite son" he would neutralize the TWA bloc. Had it come to a second ballot, the TWA vote would almost certainly have gone to O'Donnell by unit rule.

Football games and wars, it is said, are won in the trenches. That's pretty much where the "Delta Machine" won Hank Duffy's election. The Delta pilots, who had historically been very disciplined at BOD meetings, raised the art of ALPA campaigning to new heights. They brought a large contingent of nondelegate volunteers to the convention, and they used this manpower to "hold hands" with practically every delegate who might support Duffy. Wavering delegates, whether they represented only a few votes from an "ant" council, or several *thousand* votes from an "elephant" council, received special attention. Delta's hospitality suite, which featured elaborate Cajun cuisine personally prepared by New Orleans LEC Chairman Jack Saux, undoubtedly helped. In a close election, little things count. Some political pundits say that Tom Dewey lost the 1948 election to Harry Truman because of his mustache, which reminded too many people of "the little man on the wedding cake!"

But more importantly, the technical efficiency of the Delta Machine built momentum for Duffy. The Delta pilots' "war room" was a technological marvel. It bristled with computers, delegate count boards, phone banks, and the like. From this "war room" (which some astonished observers described as "like a Combat Information Center on an aircraft carrier"), the "Delta Machine" tracked every delegate's vote on an almost hourly basis once the BOD meeting began in Bal Harbour, Fla. If a previously committed Duffy voter showed signs of wavering, the Delta Machine knew it almost instantaneously and dispatched a well-briefed volunteer to shepherd the apostate home. The Delta Machine was to ALPA's politics what steroids were to bodybuilding!

But the Delta Machine was by no means a strictly Delta operation. Chuck Huttinger of TACA would prove to be a crucial player, because he used his influence with the Group V airlines to siphon away from "ant" councils nearly 250 critical votes that O'Donnell believed were safely in his column.

"John O'Donnell was the most able politician I ever came across in ALPA," says Tom Ashwood of TWA. "I mean the guy could have been Tip O'Neill [the legendary Boston politician who served as speaker of the U.S. House of Representatives]. But he had a weakness—he tended to treat his enemies better than his friends. If you were a supporter of his and he knew it, O.K., he would forget about it and spend a great deal of time trying to convert an enemy. I watched it happen. I saw friends turn against him because of neglect."

Something like this happened among the "ants" at the 1982 BOD. The disciplined Delta Machine assiduously courted the Group V airlines. Many of them were supposed to be safe for O'Donnell, but the chink that Tom Ashwood saw in O'Donnell's political armor became glaringly apparent among them. The Delta Machine was quick to remind these "ant" voters that O'Donnell had "kowtowed" to United, the mightiest of "elephants" at the 1980 BOD meeting in Los

Angeles. The United group had staged a three-day walkout at the instigation of John Ferg, primarily over the crew complement issue. For "ant" airline pilots, putting a third crewmember in their cockpits was almost a guarantee of bankruptcy and unemployment. O'Donnell, seriously worried that the United group would go the way of American Airlines in 1963 and bolt ALPA, had been quite lenient with the United pilot group—humiliatingly so, many "ant" delegates believed.[2]

But in reality, once the heavy politicking began at the BOD meeting, O'Donnell's lack of attention to his friends was not what proved fatal. Rather, it was something quite strange, particularly for a man who in 1970 had pioneered sophisticated campaign techniques. O'Donnell's three previous winning campaigns had featured buttons, posters, and brochures. In 1982 he had *nothing*! In effect, he had *no O'Donnell campaign*!

Jack Bavis, O'Donnell's campaign manager, still hurt and disappointed at O'Donnell's supplanting of his own candidacy, seemed to lack heart, according to several witnesses. O'Donnell himself, who should have been out in the hallways and hospitality suites doing what he did best, pressing the flesh and personally stroking undecided delegates, instead sat in his suite atop the Sheraton Hotel, seemingly disinterested. When his presence was necessary to seal a bargain or make a deal, O'Donnell was unavailable. And not because John O'Donnell didn't know how to make deals.

"When it came to sensing what people needed and wanted to cut a deal, John was the best," Tom Ashwood asserts.

Certainly the Delta Machine did not shrink from "cutting a deal." Realizing that victory or defeat hung in the balance, the Duffy forces used their ultimate weapon—promise of the coveted job of executive administrator to sew up victory. With their sophisticated intelligence network telling them that their vote count was still below what was needed for a first-ballot victory, Duffy offered the job to John Erikson of Western Airlines, a mid-sized pilot group with 1,223 votes. The night before voting began, when the "elephants danced" in the hallways and hospitality suites of the Sheraton Hotel, Duffy's campaign manager struck the deal.

The Western pilot group was under severe stress. Western was everybody's next candidate to follow Braniff into bankruptcy. Under John Erikson's leadership, the Western pilot group had, in 1981, engineered a careful series of concessions that not only saved the airline, but incredibly enough, avoided furloughs, too. Erikson's extraordinary handling of this crisis allowed Western to live on until 1986, when a merger with Delta saved it. Had Erikson not provided the necessary leadership, Western clearly would not have been a viable airline and hence not a merger candidate.

So Duffy had good reasons for wanting Erikson as his executive administrator, not the least of which was that he was an early Duffy booster who had committed months earlier. But the problem was Erikson's fellow Western pilots. O'Donnell's pitch, that Western was in deep trouble and that only he had the political connections in Washington, D.C., to save the airline, had considerable appeal for them. But ultimately, the prospect of seeing one of their own at the elbow of power in Washington struck the Western pilots as better job insurance than O'Donnell's claims of political influence with Ronald Reagan.

O'Donnell played the Reagan card on the first day of the convention. Not only would Drew Lewis personally address the BOD, but Ronald Reagan himself made a short videotape address. Reagan's video speech tacked an obvious endorsement of O'Donnell onto some standard political boilerplate: "I have been working closely with your president, J.J. O'Donnell, and I want you to know that his input and your support have been a real help in forwarding our recovery program."

Drew Lewis's endorsement of O'Donnell was more personal but no less vague on specifics than Reagan's. "J.J., I am extremely indebted to you because without your support we would not have been able to come through that problem [the PATCO strike]," the Secretary of Transportation told the BOD delegates. "I think with the concerns you have, and I sensed them last night as I walked around the reception, we have to keep the right perspective."

On election day, the pattern that had characterized the various debates at pilot domiciles around the country repeated itself. Hank Duffy took the high road, pledging improved communications and better control of ALPA's finances, and promising unity across company lines. O'Donnell's brief speech was curiously muted, tired, almost subdued. Only John Gratz, a stocky, well-built bear of a man, seemed to enjoy himself on the rostrum. During the various debates, Gratz had taken considerable pleasure in blasting O'Donnell.

"I am convinced that there will be a new president of ALPA," Gratz told the BOD members. "That is the mood of this convention. We in ALPA are caught in the middle of a time when we were never so ill-prepared, when the indecisive handling of basic issues by those at the top has created overwhelming feelings of disunity, disappointment, and even depression."

Gratz's remarks were directed at United's "Blue Skies" contract and the rash of concessionary contract demands that were ravaging ALPA. He played on the general resentment many pilots felt over O'Donnell's kid-glove handling of the United pilot group during the 1980 BOD in Los Angeles. Whatever negative baggage O'Donnell owned, Gratz made sure it didn't get lost.

In his seconding speech for O'Donnell, Bob Gould of Pan Am urged the delegates to ignore the baggage.

"All right, along the way J.J. has taken some hits," Gould admitted. "He has even been sacked a few times. But by God, he has always gotten up. This is the time to stay with an old pro."

At last it was over. All the speeches had been made, all the deals cut. The "elephants had danced," and the moment of decision was at hand. Skip Eglet, who held the rostrum during the actual election, notified the delegates of the rules and acted as chairman of the convention.

O'Donnell's supporters knew they couldn't win on the first ballot, but they had good reason to suppose that Duffy would fall short of the 13,644 votes necessary to elect. John Gratz harbored some vain hopes that a deadlocked convention might turn to him as a compromise. Duffy's managers were certain that if their man did not win on the first ballot, O'Donnell's legendary deal-making skills would find room to maneuver and that would spell doom on the second ballot.

The vote went exactly as the Delta Machine had planned. Among the elephants, Northwest, Delta, and most of Eastern fell to Duffy; O'Donnell got United and PanAm; Gratz got TWA and a bigger chunk of Eastern than O'Donnell. Among the mid-sized airlines, Duffy got Continental, Piedmont, Republic, and Western; O'Donnell took only half of USAir. But among the Group IV and V airlines, the Ozarks and the Frontiers, O'Donnell swept the board. So, the "ants" went mostly to O'Donnell, except for the 250 votes from the likes of Air North, Aspen, Reeve Aleutian, and Ross, which Chuck Huttinger of TACA siphoned away to Duffy.

Duffy needed 13,624 to win. He got 13,753—a slender 129 votes more than necessary.

And so, with breathtaking suddenness, the roster was called, the votes were cast and counted. There were calls for Duffy to come forward, but he was away from the floor. He appeared within a few minutes and made gracious, healing remarks. O'Donnell, concealing his bitter disappointment well, resumed the rostrum and went on with his duties.

"O.K., gentlemen," O'Donnell said with business-like detachment, "we've had a good fight. Now in our own best interests, our own _selfish best interests_, let's get behind the new president and support him. It's a lonely, hard road, and he needs your support. He has mine, without question."

The O'Donnell era was over.

NOTES
[1] See "Pilots, Republicans, and Labor," Ch. 12.
[2] See "Blue Skies and MEC Wars," Ch. 15.

CHAPTER 8

HANK DUFFY'S DESTINY
The Making of an ALPA President

Henry A. "Hank" Duffy, a 20-year Delta Air Lines pilot, became the fifth president of ALPA at a time when a man with the gift of prophecy might have passed it up. Trouble of unimagined intensity, unlike anything ALPA had ever experienced, was lurking just over the horizon. By January 1983, when Duffy took office, the full impact of this trouble, the stepchild of deregulation, was about to descend on the profession with sledgehammer force.

The 1982 bankruptcy of Braniff, the first failure of a "major" carrier since the passage of the landmark Civil Aeronautics Act of 1938, was the first blow. But perceptive rank-and-file ALPA members were realizing that Braniff's demise would not be the last. The cold reality of free market economics, which had spurred ALPA's creation in 1931, was about to play a return engagement. However belatedly, ordinary rank-and-file ALPA members were beginning to realize that their leaders were not just crying "wolf." As we have seen, Hank Duffy's election stemmed, in large part, from the feeling that he would deal more effectively with the transition to an unregulated system than had J.J. O'Donnell.

The task confronting Duffy was daunting, but with the optimism and self-confidence that were the natural by-products of his long and productive career as an ALPA leader at Delta, he eagerly accepted the mantle of Behncke, Sayen, Ruby, and the vanquished J.J. O'Donnell. The fissures that Duffy's quest for the presidency, the first successful challenge to an incumbent in ALPA's history, had opened would have to be healed, and harmony would have to be restored in relationships with O'Donnell's wounded supporters. But Duffy, displaying the aplomb that was so typical of Delta pilots, was confident of his ability to repair the breach.

Being with Delta contributed to Duffy's trademark optimism. Owing to the airline's traditional labor harmony, Delta pilots who were active in ALPA affairs were accustomed to success. Being a Delta pilot and being confident were almost two sides of the same coin.

"ALPA's leaders expected to bring home good things to the membership," Duffy remembers of the general tone of labor/management relations during the years since Delta hired him in 1962. "Delta's management wasn't hard to bargain with, but for people to think they just slide the money across the table is a misunderstanding. But management always dealt with an integrity level you never questioned."

Whether the kind of consensus-building, cooperative approach that characterized the Delta pilots' experience with management could be extended to the industry at large was an open question. For the long term, "Delta-izing" ALPA's national structure would obviously be Hank Duffy's goal. But for the short term, Duffy's job was to become familiar with ALPA's Washington, D.C., operation, while the rest of ALPA got to know him.

Who was Hank Duffy, anyway?

Born in Norfolk, Va., on Sept. 27, 1934, the youngest son of garage owner who specialized in automotive body repairs, Duffy grew up in a world of machinery, fascinated more with cars than airplanes. An older brother had tried to become a military pilot during World War II but had washed out of flight training. Perhaps his brother's failure discouraged young Hank from pursuing aviation with the intensity that so often characterizes little boys who grow up to be airline pilots. In any case, he was much more interested in a purely military career than one in aviation.

"I grew up on the seaplane lane in Norfolk," Duffy says, "and I was a great airplane watcher. But there wasn't any fascination. I was fascinated with cars and mechanical things because of the garage, but not flying."

Duffy did not fly until after beginning what he thought would be a career in the U.S. Army. An accomplished horn player who attended the University of Miami (Florida) on a music scholarship, Duffy majored in business and earned an Army commission through the Reserve Officers Training Corps (ROTC) program. Upon graduating in 1956, he wound up in an artillery unit on active duty and entered upon his aviation career almost by accident.

In the aftermath of World War II, military aviation became the object of a fierce intraservice tug-of-war. Initially, the newly independent Air Force was supposed to have control of *all* flying activities. For a time, there was even discussion of abolishing the Navy's air arm—the admirals would still run the carriers, but an Air Force general would be on the bridge, commanding flight operations. The celebrated "Revolt of the Admirals" saved Naval and Marine aviation, but the Army found itself with virtually no aviation after 1948.

The Korean War proved this concept unworkable. The Air Force preferred to concentrate on *serious* flying—Strategic Air Command (SAC), North American Aerospace Defense Command (NORAD), glamorous high-frontier stuff—not the kind of mud-on-the-wings flying that the Army needed for close air support. Tactical aviation directly connected with field operations (a stepchild even before the creation of an independent Air Force—winged artillery, if you will) was never a priority, even during the old Air Corps days. As for logistical and support aviation, the new independent Air Force made no secret of its disdain for this kind of flying, although the parochial need to protect its "turf" meant that it would grudgingly serve the Army's needs.

Where helicopters were concerned, the Air Force was so doubtful of this emerging technology that it voluntarily surrendered it to the Army. After a few years of half-hearted haggling over the helicopter question, the two services agreed that fixed-wing flying would generally remain the Air Force's prerogative, while the Army would be free without hindrance to develop rotary-winged aviation. Owing to the needs of the service and the Air Force's indifference, however, over time the Army regained a fixed-wing capability, which was mostly single-engine.

What these shifting military priorities meant for young Second Lieutenant Duffy was personal opportunity. Eager to succeed as a career Army officer, Duffy volunteered for flight training in the newly reconstituted Army aviation branch, which appeared (as the new "air mobile" concept took shape) to be in line for a tremendous spurt of growth. The artillery units to which Duffy was assigned had a few L-19 spotter aircraft, in which he hitched backseat rides, but he never touched the controls of an airplane until he actually got to primary flight training.

"They made you do a year of ground duty before they let you go to flight school, just like the Marines," Duffy remembers. So he spent a year as a "grunt" and then entered Army flight training at Camp Gary, San Marcos, Texas, in 1957.

Duffy won his Army aviator's wings in 1958 and shortly thereafter became qualified in both helicopters and conventional aircraft. Having married his college sweetheart, Cordelia Ann Brockway, Duffy was already a settled family man well positioned to begin climbing the Army's career ladder. The potential of Army aviation promised benefits to young officers who caught the first flush of growth, Duffy had all the right educational qualifications, and his prospects were bright. He won routine promotion to first lieutenant and captain and, upon completion of his three-year tour of duty as a reserve officer in 1959, accepted a regular commission, obligating himself for additional years of service. At the time, Duffy fully expected to remain in the Army until retirement.

But many twists and turns lie on the road to any man's final career choice. In the military, these twists and turns are sometimes bizarre. The military calling has a certain distortion of reality, and lengthy periods of schooling only exacerbate this problem. For example, while a young officer undergoes training in a technical specialty, he gets all the excitement of growth and newness, with developing skills providing a sense of limitless self-confidence and potential. Then, when the period of schooling ends and the hard reality of the military life sets in, the young officer invariably feels a letdown. In short, "becoming" is always more exciting than "being." Becoming an Army aviator was an exciting experience for young Hank Duffy—being an Army aviator was something else entirely.

The undisguised reality of Army life hit Duffy very soon after he launched upon his tour of duty as a regular commissioned officer. It involved a good deal of personal hardship, dreary routine, and uninspiring duty, coupled with a long series of absences from his family, which now consisted not only of his wife, but three small daughters as well.

"About the first year after getting out of flight training," Duffy declares, "we had a long separation. I went to Greenland, then down to Panama and into the jungle. I decided that this is the life for somebody else."

Like many other young potential career officers, Hank Duffy discovered that the promise of military life did not measure up to its reality. So how did he come to the profession of airline piloting?

"I had done all the South American flying in the Army, and I had always ridden down there and back on Braniff, and I thought I would really like to do that," Duffy remembers. "I had a romance with Braniff, and because of my southern upbringing, I also applied to Delta—those were my one-two choices. Of course, I applied to everybody, like everybody else did, but nobody was hiring at the time."

So firm was Duffy's decision to leave the military in 1962 that he dusted off his college business degree and secured a job with the Internal Revenue Service as an accountant. That would have to await his formal release from active duty, but owing to the IRS's needs for people with his kind of college background, Duffy's prospective employer was willing to hold the position open for him. In short, Duffy's future held no unemployment.

"You don't want to have any gaps in there," Duffy laughs, citing the responsibility of supporting a family.

By a quirk of fate, Duffy got what he wanted—he would become an airline pilot instead of a government bureaucrat. It wasn't easy, because as a regular instead of a reserve officer, the timing of his departure from the Army was beyond his control.

An officer who accepts a regular commission technically serves "at the pleasure of the President," with no _guaranteed_ date of release from active duty. Reserve officers, on the other hand, serve for specified periods of time, like enlisted men. Once young Hank Duffy had applied for and accepted a regular commission, the Army could take its own sweet time releasing him to civilian life—there was no _warranted_ release from active duty date (or "RAD" date, as it was known colloquially). In fact, a regular officer did have a right to resign, but the timetable for this process was strictly dependent upon "needs of the service." More than one young military flier, anxious to become an airline pilot, has had trouble with this peculiarity of military service. How does one commit to an airline's training date with the threat of involuntary retention on active duty hanging over the process? Under normal circumstances, a young regular officer can put in his papers to leave the service, and a specified amount of time later (as defined by regulations—not statutory law), get out—depending upon the needs of the service.

None of this was bothering young Hank Duffy in early 1962, when he decided leave the Army. Despite rising Cold War tensions, things were still generally routine, and a peacetime mentality pervaded the military establishment. Vietnam was just a distant echo then, a billet only a few really "gung-ho" careerists sought to enhance their promotion potential. With that distant-jungle guerrilla war still a sideshow (which professionals wryly referred to as "the only war we've got"), the Army was actually encouraging young regular officers to get out, owing to an overstaffing problem. The simmering potential for conflict with the Russians in Europe was like a long-running serial at the old Saturday morning movies, as were recurrent crises over Berlin, which usually dissipated when the newspapers tired of it as a headline story and buried it in the back pages. Nothing here to delay young Hank's release from active duty and return to civilian life.

The IRS job was secure and waiting for him. The soon-to-be ex-Army pilot had pretty well given up on hearing from either Braniff or Delta, his preferred airlines. Then, at the last minute, Delta came through. The first great wave of mass expansion, brought on by the increasing popularity of jet travel among ordinary Americans, was upon the airline industry. Delta's managers were among the first to see this new boom as more than a temporary phenomenon, so they started culling through their pilot application file, looking for likely prospects. Hank Duffy's name popped up—he had all the qualifications Delta liked for its new hires: a college education, southern background, military training—though Air Force or Navy wings would have made him more desirable, in Delta's opinion. But offsetting this, young Hank Duffy had already secured his release from active duty—a "date certain" commitment from the Army to let him go—and thus could be assigned to a class. So, Delta hired Hank Duffy in the early fall of 1962, and he joyfully informed the IRS that they could find somebody else to audit tax returns—he was going flying!

But fate is a tricky master, often dependent upon great events not easily foreseen—as young Captain Duffy was about to discover. Hank Duffy and his career as an airline pilot were about to be caught in the web of the Cold War's greatest crisis. The "Missiles of October" brought the world to the brink of nuclear war in the fall of 1962, just as Hank Duffy was packing away his Army gear. For 13 days, the United States and Russia came "eyeball to eyeball" (in Secretary of State Dean Rusk's phrase) over nuclear-capable medium-range missiles the Russians had deployed in Fidel Castro's Cuba—just 90 miles from Florida. The career preferences of a young, soon-to-be ex-Army aviator clearly took lower priority than dealing with the prospect of nuclear annihilation. Hank Duffy's career at Delta was in jeopardy.

"I was supposed to get out a month and a half before I was hired," Duffy remembers of the careful plans he had laid for his transition to civilian life. "The Cuban missile crisis came along, and the military extended everybody."

Before Duffy could don Delta's uniform and begin flying the line, he would have to do his part in the big buildup of forces in the southeastern United States. His commercial aviation future now on hold, Hank Duffy became a small cog in what was the largest peacetime domestic mobilization in U.S. history—a massive invasion machine pointed directly at Cuba. Duffy, along with literally millions of others in the military, found himself preparing for combat—flying the line would have to wait.

A class date to begin training in an airline's program is a perishable commodity and comes with no guarantee that it will be honored once it has passed—national security and reasons of state notwithstanding. An airline's personnel needs are specific to a time and set of circumstances, and Hank Duffy could not be sure that the U.S.-Soviet duel of nerves that fall of 1962 did not spell the end of his career as an airline pilot—before it even began!

But almost as quickly as it erupted, the crisis ended—to all humanity's collective sigh of relief. One small story among millions in this giant drama was Hank Duffy's, which might seem insignificant by comparison, but of such small episodes are the lives of mice and men made up.

"I finally had to fly to the Pentagon, hand-carry my papers through, and fly back," Duffy remembers of the mad dash to make his Atlanta training class date in December 1962. "I got there the day before we started school. It was tight."

After making his class date, Hank Duffy faced the serious problem of competing with other young pilots who had far more experience in complex aircraft than he did. Delta, like most companies during that time, hired ex-military pilots whenever possible, and among those with military backgrounds, heavy-multiengine experience (preferably on piston-engine equipment—which the airlines still flew more of in 1962 than turbine aircraft) was important.

"The guys who came out of multiengine programs had an advantage," Duffy recalls. "Practically everything was propellers at the time, and everything we were going into was props."

Lacking the technical background of his peers, Duffy's success as an airline pilot was by no means assured. Almost all of his contemporaries in school had flown in either the Navy or the Air Force—Army pilots were comparatively rare, and most airlines viewed them strictly as rotary-wing pilots whose experience was unsuitable for airline purposes. Indeed, some old-fashioned chief pilots, who in those days had the final word on hiring a pilot, were known to scoff that helicopters were not really airplanes at all. The fact that *some* Army pilots (like Hank Duffy) were primarily fixed-wing pilots didn't impress them very much.

But Delta's hiring philosophy, which stressed potential and background, meant that a few Army pilots, despite their lack of experience in heavy multiengine aircraft, would be given a chance to compete. Offered the opportunity, Duffy made the most of it. Although he was apprehensive about what awaited him in Delta's training program, Hank Duffy soon found that he could more than hold his own.

"I was better than a lot of the people around me, guys that came out of multiengine programs," he recalls. "In the Army, we had no hydraulic systems or variable pitch props or any of that stuff. I had to work quite hard."

His diligence in training landed young Hank Duffy a second officer's slot on DC-6 equipment, thus beginning a rapid rise through various equipment that would culminate in an extraordinarily early captaincy, by traditional airline standards. Just five years after hiring on with Delta, Hank Duffy was a Convair 440 captain, and a year later he was commanding DC-9s. Like certain military academy classes, which happen to come along in just the right zone to benefit from a wave of war-induced promotions (those fabled "classes the stars fell on"), Duffy's training class caught the first wave of Delta's explosive growth. Assigned seniority number 860 when he began flying the line, Duffy remained a flight engineer for only a year.

"Delta advancement was very fast," Duffy recalls, "but we did multiple things. At one point, I was DC-6 and -7 engineer qualified, Convair 880 qualified, and Convair 440 copilot qualified, moving back and forth between all those airplanes, which is unbelievable in today's environment."

Just this predicament was what turned Hank Duffy into an ALPA militant—at least by Delta's standards. As Delta's rapid growth and Duffy's relatively low seniority elevated him out of the ranks of "plumbers," he found himself in a dispute with management over interpretation of the contract. The way Hank Duffy read the standard employment agreement between ALPA and Delta, his upgrading to first officer on smaller equipment (in this case the Convair 440), entitled him to first officer pay rates when the company assigned him to second officer duties on larger equipment.

"They needed to assign you downward because they didn't have enough Convair 880 second officers," Duffy recalls. "The contract said if you were a copilot and you were assigned to fly another airplane, you got copilot rates."

But management didn't see it that way, and when Hank Duffy, who was barely out of his probationary period, complained about the company's interpretation of the contract, ALPA's local officers in Atlanta refused to back him up. In short, what should have been a routine grievance at any other airline was looked upon as improper, even "uppity," behavior at Delta.

To understand why labor relations at Delta were so different from other airlines, we must delve a little deeper into the corporate culture and psychology of the airline and its pilots.

Duffy's election to the presidency of ALPA in 1982, at the age of 48, was in some respects a tribute to the corporate success of Delta Air Lines. Like the companies for which they fly, the various pilot groups that make up ALPA tend to exhibit a character that often reflects the corporate culture in which they live. Eastern Airlines pilots, for example, during the era of Captain Edward V. Rickenbacker, tended to be close-lipped "company men." Years later, as Eastern's corporate culture changed, the airline's pilots became equally close-lipped advocates of union solidarity. Some airline pilot groups have traditionally been more militant in their unionism than others. Northwest Airlines pilots, for example, have had more than their share of difficulty with management; consequently, they have more "bomb-throwers" than other airlines. Historically, United's pilots have occupied a kind of traditional middle ground, willing to fight management when provoked, but on the whole rather amenable to company policies. Each pilot group at each airline in ALPA is unique: Each group has been subject to discrete historical circumstances, peer group pressures, and the influences of strong individual leaders who were able to stamp their personalities on an MEC or LEC. Thus, generalizations about the nature of each pilot group are difficult to make.

But few ALPA members would dispute that Delta's pilots were traditionally the least militant and most company-oriented pilot group in ALPA. They had never had a strike, never suffered from seasonal layoffs, and had benefited from what was generally regarded, historically, as the most enlightened and efficient management in the industry. Thus, their almost apologetic approach to unionism was understandable. Delta's pilots had the only significant union on Delta's property. (The dispatchers, who direct company flight operations on a daily basis, are also unionized, but they are a very small group.)

In short, the conservative, "family" atmosphere at Delta made unionism weak, and of all the pilot groups that made up ALPA, the commitment of Delta pilots to the *concept* of union had always been regarded, rightly or wrongly, as the most suspect. The company's view of collective bargaining was a source of envy throughout ALPA—Delta's pilots got what all the other pilot groups got (and usually more), but without any of the messy disagreements. In fact, ALPA leadership had often been a stepping stone to management at Delta, a tradition dating back to the legendary Charles H. Dolson[1], the Delta captain who founded ALPA on the airline and later rose through the ranks of management to replace the equally legendary C.E. Woolman as president.

Dolson, who represented ALPA in the first contract negotiations with Delta, declared later: "I don't think Woolman ever forgave me for getting ALPA started on Delta." But regardless, relations were so typically smooth between Delta and its pilots that old Dave Behncke, who liked protracted negotiations because they enhanced his own sense of importance, was known to express irritation—if negotiations were *that* easy, Behncke figured, the company must be cheating the pilots. The "Old Man" was inveterately suspicious.

In fact, the generally enviable working conditions at Delta *were* purchased at a price, as young Hank Duffy, miffed at the company's refusal to grant him first officer pay, was about to discover. Both the company and ALPA's "Old Hands" at Delta expected young pilots to accept their superiors' decisions quietly, without complaining.

Pilots didn't file "many grievances at Delta," Duffy recalls wryly. "They usually intimidated you out of it. They didn't hassle you very much, but they expected you to do what they said."

But Duffy, displaying a steely determination that his genial exterior masked, refused to let the prevailing "go along to get along" culture of Delta deter him. Feeling thoroughly abused by both management and the local ALPA officers who were supposedly representing him, Hank Duffy not only pressed his own grievance, but he also talked several other junior second-officer/first-officer switch-hitters into joining him.

"Eventually there was a compromise settlement, and we got sold down the river," Duffy recalls sourly. "But a group of us stood up and said, 'This isn't right,' and I learned a lesson—the company wasn't to be trusted in all respects."

Of such things are union activists *and professional pilots* made. An old pilots' adage holds that a pilot has become a professional when he asks, "Who pays me?" By this definition, Duffy was well on his way to becoming a *real* professional. Similarly, most union activists are *made*—not born. Management at Delta seems to have understood this principle. Historically, the benign atmosphere that had so generally characterized relations between pilots and management at Delta, had probably deterred many young pilots from becoming hard-core union activists.

"I thought I needed to get involved in ALPA," Duffy declares of his early days at Delta. "I was doing outside stuff—Kiwanas Club and Republican politics— and I thought I ought to be doing something that is applicable to my profession. I ought to know the contract. So I got involved in grievance work."

Thus, Hank Duffy, unlike most young Delta pilots, was an active unionist almost from his first days with the airline.

Council 44 at Atlanta was, in 1963, like most LECs everywhere, chronically short of volunteers willing to do committee work. When Hank Duffy volunteered his services to the LEC, he set in chain a series of events that would eventually bring him to ALPA's presidency.

So while Hank Duffy was going through the experiences typical of any airline pilot during his first few years with Delta, he was also gaining a thorough grounding in ALPA work. The ancient prejudice in favor of captains in ALPA meant that his rapid promotion to that rank made him just that much more appealing as an ALPA "mover and shaker."

"It was fun, it was great!" Duffy remembers of his first few years of rapid advancement, both in the cockpit and doing ALPA work. "Flying the 440, and quickly the DC-9, and going back and forth between the two—I think that's always the most exhilarating time, when you are a new captain, flying all around the system, up in New England or down the Ohio and Mississippi valleys. Just a fun time."

During his 20 years as a line pilot, Duffy held several significant ALPA jobs, including the MEC chairmanship at Delta. But his most important early work was as Delta's Retirement and Insurance (R&I) Committee chairman. His performance in this technical "nuts and bolts" area (as opposed to the purely "political" side of ALPA activities) brought him favorable notice from the pilots of several other airlines.

Atlanta, Delta's home base, was at one time claimed by Eastern as a principal territory. The city's rapid growth since the 1950s, from comfortable regional center to world-class metropolis, paralleled Duffy's years with Delta. So desirable did the city's location become as an airline hub that ever-increasing numbers of airlines, large and small, sought a place in the Atlanta sun. By the late 1960s, Atlanta began to rival places like Chicago and New York as a pilot domicile. With the pilots of several airlines often in direct contact with each other, and a major ALPA Field Office as a focal point for that interaction, Hank Duffy's reputation among the pilots of other airlines in Atlanta began to spread.

Duffy, who was developing a keen sense of the problems of other airlines during this period, saw the airline community in Atlanta as a microcosm of the larger ALPA community.

"Everybody is a product of what they experience from their own management," Duffy believes. "It's not the people who fly for an airline, because if you exchange the total pilot population on the airline for another, they would be just the same."

The insights Duffy gained into the history and specific conditions of the various pilot groups domiciled in Atlanta has permitted him to view the old issue of intra-airline rivalry, which has dogged ALPA for generations, from a long perspective.

"If I had gone to work for Northwest," Duffy notes, "I would have been a militant, too. I understand the selfishness that crops up. It's frustrating, because I came to see that we have a lot more uniting us than separating us."

In addition, the fact that Duffy was active in Republican Party politics in Georgia as a county chairman was helpful. The political mood of the country was swinging decidedly toward conservatism by the 1970s, and Duffy's political inclinations indicated that he fit the image that most pilots had of themselves as reluctant unionists with conservative sympathies.

So, beginning with that first assignment as a member of the LEC Grievance Committee, Duffy took on an ever-increasing load of ALPA work and began to attract notice among ALPA movers-and-shakers. Duffy's most important characteristic was his ability to focus his attention and master a technical subject while exhaustively serving the needs of fellow pilots who came to him for help. While grievance work was relatively undemanding at Delta, it nevertheless required close reading of the contract, which most pilots were not inclined to do—until they got into some specific difficulty.

"Most pilots don't read their contracts, so they need somebody to *tell* them what's in it, which I enjoyed doing," Duffy laughs, echoing the lament of many other ALPA leaders over the years. "I enjoyed understanding the contracts—it really fostered my own understanding of the job."

In 1970, still just a junior captain, Hank Duffy served on the crucial bargaining committee, where he played a major role in negotiating a new retirement plan. Ironically, this interest in retirement and insurance was precisely the route to power that J.J. O'Donnell had followed in the 1960s. In fact, a preview of the 1982 election contest, which saw Duffy unseat O'Donnell, occurred at the 1973 Executive Board meeting over R&I matters.

"There were a lot of holes in the company's funding," Duffy remembers, "and we insisted on much stricter standards. For instance, loss of license was always a major problem for us, and we got the first company-paid guaranteed 50 percent average of the final five years' earnings. O'Donnell was vehemently opposed to it. He came from this retirement background and was so proud of the retirement plan that he had built, and he saw this as a threat to it. But it was really short-sighted, because we escalated the retirement benefit tremendously."

Despite O'Donnell's opposition, Duffy's plan carried. On this matter, the Delta pilots were independent of ALPA national's control; and by setting a higher standard in the R&I area, they led the industry toward more generous benefits for all ALPA groups. But these R&I activities nevertheless stirred up "a lot of tension, back and forth," as Duffy remembers of his first dealings with O'Donnell. Duffy attracted favorable notice from others, however, and it was apparent that he would soon play a leading role on the Delta MEC.

"I'm sure these guys were grooming me to be the next MEC chairman," Duffy says of George Berg, Nick Gentile, and Al Bonner, who preceded him as MEC chairmen.

Duffy's next challenge came in 1973, during the celebrated Arab oil embargo of that year. Delta pilot group leaders, notably Al Bonner and George Berg, suspecting management of using the embargo as an excuse to cut the number of flights and thereby reduce pilot employment, assigned Duffy as the ALPA watchdog, or "fuel czar."

"We were suspicious, probably wrongly so," Duffy remembers, "that it was just a downturn economically, and they were using the fuel allocation as a reason not to be flying everything the company could be flying."

By 1974, Hank Duffy was Delta's MEC chairman and a presence at the ALPA

Board of Directors meeting in Kansas City that year, where the twin issues of crew complement and suspension of service (SOS) were paramount. ALPA's policy was to require three pilots on all new turbine-powered or jet equipment. As we have seen, this nettlesome issue was causing ALPA severe internal stress, because some pilot groups disagreed vehemently with the three-pilot crew complement for *some* aircraft. Hank Duffy, speaking for the Delta pilots, argued that the two-pilot cockpit was a technological inevitability and that ALPA would have to bow to it. The United pilots, led by John LeRoy (chairman of ALPA's national crew complement study committee), championed the three-pilot cockpit. The only way ALPA could maintain even a facade of internal unity on the crew complement issue was by papering it over. Although this parallel might seem overdrawn, the crew complement issue was to ALPA what slavery was to the pre-Civil War union.

"We got drawn into the crew complement debate," Duffy recalls, "because we were the main two-pilot operator. LeRoy, to make his argument work, had to attack the whole two-pilot operation. So we rose to the defense."

Hank Duffy was a burr under the saddle at the 1974 BOD meeting, because he would not submit to the verbal subterfuges that dogged the crew complement issue. The specific issue that year was the "stretched" version of the McDonnell-Douglas DC-9-50 model, which ALPA insisted was a *new* aircraft and therefore could not be flown with two pilots. Long-standing ALPA policy called for drawing a line in the sand *somewhere* on the crew complement issue, but each time it came up on a specific aircraft, the issue was so divisive that the only sensible way to handle it was to duck. The Delta pilot group favored flying the DC-9-50 the same way they flew the flew earlier models of the DC-9, the "dash 10" and "dash 30"—as a two-pilot airplane.

"It was bizarre," Duffy remembers of the crew complement debate at the 1974 BOD meeting. "This was the first time I had ever seen the operation. The USAir guys were getting the DC-9-50. We were the largest DC-9 operator, and United was bound and determined that they were going to draw the line at the nose of the DC-9-50. You couldn't tell the difference in the cockpit."

Complicating the cloudy crew-complement issue was the fact that *two* Delta pilots, Al Bonner and George Berg, were among the seven candidates challenging J.J. O'Donnell for the ALPA presidency. As we have seen, neither succeeded, and the press of other issues, such as improper handling of hazardous materials, the misuse of cockpit voice recorders, and the continuing mischief of the airlines' Mutual Aid Pact, detracted attention from the crew complement matter.

But one thing was certain—Hank Duffy had emerged as a major player in ALPA. Throughout the remainder of the 1970s, Duffy was an often-mentioned potential successor to J.J. O'Donnell. He had the experience, he had the solid backing of his own airline, and he was just the right age—10 years younger than O'Donnell—to provide the kind of gradualist succession that has been traditional in ALPA politics. But all that might not have been enough. The central thing that would catapult Duffy toward his destiny was the changing national political climate.

The election of Ronald Reagan in 1980 accelerated the pattern of ominous changes that airline pilots had been experiencing since the passage of the Airline Deregulation Act of 1978. While the conservative Republican revival of the Reagan years probably won support from most airline pilots owing to their economic status and social attitudes, Reagan's antiunion tendencies were nevertheless worrisome. Despite their ideological Republicanism, most pilots realized that they benefited from government regulation. Although airline deregulation was a product of the Carter Administration, Republicans strongly supported it. As we have seen, J.J. O'Donnell had aligned ALPA solidly against deregulation—with minimal results. Hence, when O'Donnell's term expired in 1982, the pilots logically sought a leader like Duffy, whose Republican credentials and background in Delta's successful corporate culture promised compatibility with the Reagan "revolution."

Duffy's qualification for ALPA's presidency was thus based upon long years of work in the union's technical infrastructure and the widely shared perception among airline pilots that he was likely to be effective in dealing with the Republican administration. O'Donnell's announcement that he would not stand for reelection prompted Duffy to announce his candidacy. Shortly after Duffy launched his campaign, however, O'Donnell changed his mind and entered the race, seeking a fourth four-year term. Planning an open campaign with no incumbent, Duffy readily admits that if O'Donnell had not hesitated in announcing for reelection, Duffy would not have run.

"A lot of people wanted to support me," Duffy declared in a 1990 interview, "but we couldn't convince them that anybody had a chance against a twelve-year incumbent."

But O'Donnell's temporary noncandidacy opened the door to Duffy, whose support snowballed. By the time O'Donnell entered the race, another candidate, John Gratz, the leader of TWA's pilots, had also announced for the presidency. Gratz, a Boeing 747 captain flying international routes out of New York, spearheaded the attack against O'Donnell, allowing Duffy to occupy the middle ground. In a close and bitterly contested election at the 1982 BOD, Duffy outpolled his two opponents and became the next ALPA president.

ALPA's destiny and Hank Duffy's were now intertwined. ✈

NOTE
[1] Charles Dolson died in 1992 at the age of 87.

CHAPTER 9

DUFFY TAKES CHARGE
A Troubled Transition

By the rules of "Woods' Law," named for Chuck Woods, the veteran United pilot leader during the 1950s and 1960s, J.J. O'Donnell should have known that he couldn't beat the odds in 1982.

"Working for a bunch of pilots and keeping them happy is impossible," Woods always advised newly elected ALPA officers. "You'll lose 20 percent of your support per year, so after five years, you'll have zero support."

Woods was only half joking. O'Donnell had worked a minor political miracle by surviving in office for so long. His 12 years were exceeded only by founder Dave Behncke's 21 years at the helm. O'Donnell, bitterly disappointed at his rejection by the organization he had served since 1971, was understandably sulky as he shelved his plans for molding the future. *The Washington Post* head-lined the story of his defeat by saying that ALPA had rejected a "Reagan adviser" and that it was a "surprise move."

Pleased as Duffy's supporters were about his win, they nevertheless had cause to worry. Aside from the presidency, the elections of other national offic-ers at the BOD meeting had not gone well. The "Delta Machine" seemed to lose a wheel in the other races. It recovered to score some victories in the executive vice-president races, but it lost important races for first vice-president and sec-retary. So Duffy's supporters had substantial reason to worry about the political balance in the new Executive Committee. Put simply, Duffy's supporters were worried that an obstructionist majority in the Executive Committee might wreck his presidency before it ever got started.

"There was a lot of anger and bitterness during the period between the election in November and when I took over," Duffy recalls, citing the peculiar political dance following his own election, which resulted in Tom Ashwood of TWA becoming first vice-president. "Tom was really disappointed because he thought he should have been running for president."

Ashwood's crushing victory over Tom Beedem of Northwest illustrates the chancy nature of "slate making" in ALPA politics. At Chuck Huttinger's New Or-leans "unity" meeting in June 1982, Beedem agreed to sacrifice his own presiden-tial ambitions in exchange for the coalition's backing for the first vice-presidency. Why couldn't the Delta Machine deliver the vote for Beedem against Ashwood?

Ashwood's ability as a campaigner, acknowledged by friend and foe alike, partially explains it. But playing a more important role was the feeling among many BOD members that, in the interests of internal unity, appeasing the O'Donnell's vanquished supporters, particularly the large United Airlines pilot group, would be wise. Despite all the symbolic expressions of support for internal unity across company lines that followed Duffy's razor-thin victory, many BOD members were uneasy about the United pilots. Rumors that they were contemplating leaving ALPA had been circulating ever since John Ferg led the three-day walkout at the 1980 BOD meeting in Los Angeles.[1] Unconfirmed but believable reports were circulating that Ferg had been talking to the Allied Pilots Association (APA), the company union American Airlines' pilots had cloned after leaving ALPA in 1963. Was there a chance that Hank Duffy would face the defection of the United pilot group from ALPA? Old Guys remembered the circumstances of Charley Ruby's accession to ALPA's presidency in 1962 and shuddered—the American pilots' defection began during his transition.

John Ferg, United's MEC chairman, was becoming a loose cannon on ALPA's deck. He had harbored presidential ambitions before 1982, but two things destroyed them—the Ferg-led boycott during the 1980 BOD meeting, which irritated almost everybody, and his role in masterminding the celebrated "Blue Skies" contract United's pilots agreed to in 1981.[2]

In some respects, the "Blue Skies" contract was the opening shot in the "B-Scale" furor that would ravage ALPA in the mid-1980s. It actually preceded the first formal, nonexpiring "B-scale" that American's pilots, who were no longer ALPA-represented, signed in 1983. Because the "Blue Skies" contract handed United's management broad concessions, particularly in work rules, it undercut the existing contracts of other ALPA carriers. The pilots of many of United's competitors saw the "Blue Skies" contract as an open invitation for United's management to take on their carriers in the deregulated marketplace. United was big and powerful, but its pilots' tough collective bargaining and Civil Aeronautics Board regulation had always held the airline's competitive advantages in check. The United pilots' contract, because it was so superior to all others, had historically provided a measure of protection to lesser airlines. When John Ferg took the wraps off these contractual restraints, it frightened and angered many smaller pilot groups who lived in the giant's shadow.

So to some extent, the pro-Duffy vote in 1982 had been an anti-United vote. But this sort of thing could be pushed too far, wiser heads warned. Perhaps that's why a consensus emerged in the BOD, hard on the heels of Duffy's victory, that the United pilot group had to be mollified. United was dangerous enough inside ALPA's tent—it would be even worse outside. The historically close relationship between TWA and United pilots, which rested on the fact that their airlines did not compete significantly with each other, also caused concern. But by electing Ashwood first vice-president and United's Chuck Pierce secretary, the BOD could appease *both* and thus balance the scales internally. Northwest's Tom Beedem became the sacrificial offering to internal unity.

In the election for first vice-president, Ashwood got more than 15,000 votes, *double* Beedem's total and 2,000 *more* than Duffy got in winning the presidency. This lopsided victory was even more impressive when one considers that Ashwood was running against three opponents—Beedem, Dan Affourtit of

Pan Am, and Gil Chase of Frontier. Ashwood's impressive showing was an ill omen for Hank Duffy, because it meant that he would have as his second-in-command somebody who could argue persuasively that he had shown more political strength than Duffy had.

The suspicion Duffy's supporters directed at Ashwood thus had a logical basis. Ashwood, an articulate Briton who had served in the Australian Air Force before wangling a job with TWA in 1966,[3] had risen rapidly in the ALPA hierarchy owing to the patronage of O'Donnell, who always referred to him as "that Limey." Ashwood won a national reputation with the public in the early 1970s through his role as ALPA's principal spokesman on the subject of terrorism and skyjacking. Ashwood also developed a considerable following internationally through his IFALPA service.

Following his election as first vice-president in 1982, Ashwood was clearly in a position to build an independent power base. With his extensive background as a national officer, and ALPA's history of electing leaders with a certain degree of continuity, Ashwood was a major player. The only mitigating factor, as the Duffy team saw it, was that Ashwood was miffed at O'Donnell for misleading him about his intentions before the 1982 election and therefore might be amenable to a truce. Ashwood insists that he was willing to work with Duffy, to defer his own political ambitions in the interests of harmony.

"My election was a devastating blow to Hank," Ashwood recalls. "As Duffy began his transition, I took him to dinner, which I figured was proper because I'd been in Washington for six years and was an old hand. I told him frankly that neither of us was sitting there with the person we wanted. I said, 'I won't play political games, I won't stab you in the back.' We looked deeply into each others' eyes, manfully shook hands, and it went downhill from there."

Ashwood's closest supporter on the Executive Committee, reflecting the strong alliance between TWA and United, was Charles J. "Chuck" Pierce (known to his friends as "C.J."), the new secretary. Pierce came to his office with a strong reputation as an administrator owing to his service as secretary/treasurer of the United MEC, ALPA's largest. He was also a moderate whose standing with other pilot groups had survived the Ferg blemish. Figuring that Ashwood's election might not be enough to appease the sullen United pilot group, the BOD also rolled over the Delta Machine and elected Pierce. Duffy's supporters, putting the best face on a bad situation, agreed to make it unanimous when Pierce's victory became inevitable, although they supported Larry West of Republic against him in the formal balloting. Duffy's supporters were under no illusions about Pierce, however. They knew he was Ashwood's friend, something Pierce never denied.

"I had done some national work for J.J., but Tom Ashwood was who raised the subject with me of running for national office," Pierce recalls. "I'm not so naive as not to understand that part of the motivation was to curry the vote of the United MEC. I decided to run, the idea being that it would be J.J., Ashwood, myself, and whoever got elected treasurer."

So the Delta Machine, although it had won the top spot, could not prevent the election of the remainder of the O'Donnell slate. This outcome called into question Duffy's basic political appeal, for it seemed to many observers that Duffy's victory was really a rejection of O'Donnell *personally*—not his policies.

About the remaining national officer, John J. "Jack" Magee, a quiet, genial Ozark pilot who had held the treasurer's post since 1974, the Duffy people had less reason to worry. Jack Magee's loyalty to ALPA always took precedence over his loyalty to any individual leader. Even the inveterately suspicious O'Donnell finally came to accept Magee at face value, although Magee admits it took several years: "O'Donnell to this day doesn't know how to take me. I could win office, although he did not understand how."

Magee's repeated reelections to the job of treasurer had survived O'Donnell's active opposition throughout the 1970s. At one point O'Donnell encouraged Tom Ashwood to run against Magee. So the Duffy transition team saw Magee as a potential ally, an assessment with which Magee would later agree.

"I am much closer to Hank than I ever was to J.J.," Magee declared in 1989. "Hank and I go back to 1974, when we became friends. The first time I broached the idea of running for national office to anybody was to Hank Duffy on St. Patrick's Day, 1974. I remember it was cold, we were both in Washington, and we went walking for about two hours that night, and Hank Duffy promised to support me. He said, 'We probably won't win, but you're not going to be a laughingstock.'"

In races for EVPs in 1982, the Delta Machine regrouped and did better, with favorable results for Hank Duffy. O'Donnell's nemesis, Augie Gorse of Eastern, won the Group II race. In consort with John Ellington, a Delta pilot who won the Group I EVP, and Chuck Huttinger, who won Group V, Duffy would have a strong nucleus of support. Dennis Duffy of Continental and Don Jefferson of Pan Am [later United, owing to the Pacific route acquisition] rounded out the EVP roster. Dennis Duffy would eventually become Hank Duffy's ally, but Jefferson more often sided with Ashwood. Thus Duffy had only a narrow and uncertain working majority on the Executive Committee.

The climate at ALPA national headquarters was uncertain as Hank Duffy and his transition team arrived in Washington, D.C. The potential harm an Ashwood-Pierce alliance could do was worrisome, as was the recent tendency of Delta and United pilot groups to square off on opposite sides of every issue.

"Ashwood came in not a friend," Duffy admitted, with uncharacteristic circumlocution in his 1989 interview. "Chuck Pierce quickly formed an alliance with Ashwood that was very difficult to break down. I never broke it down with Ashwood. Pierce, toward the end, changed considerably, and I felt like I had a good relationship with him. But Ashwood was building a case to run in 1986."

O'Donnell's role in the bad feelings that erupted between Ashwood and Duffy was indirect but substantial. He had done his best to persuade Duffy not to run, insisting that the social "cocktail circuit" in Washington would, among other things, not be to Duffy's wife's liking. O'Donnell's puzzling behavior continued into the transition period, manifesting itself in a kind of eerie detachment.

Duffy needed help from O'Donnell to become comfortable with ALPA's existing operation, to sort it out, to discard what would hamper his program to make ALPA more effective, and to preserve those aspects of ALPA operations that could further the "Duffy New Beginning." O'Donnell was an unenthusiastic onlooker.

"J.J. left me in a kind of a hole," Duffy confirmed later. "I was up here with a transition team, and he just stonewalled us. He did not introduce me to one person. No making of the way, no passing of the torch. None of that."

Shortly after his victory at the 1982 BOD meeting, Duffy telephoned O'Donnell to set up the transition process. Because of the strained situation, Duffy thought it best to commit to writing, in a formal memorandum, the points he believed O'Donnell had agreed to. Duffy appointed a transition team of five pilots. Three of them were from Delta—Les Hale, Cam Foster, and Nick Gentile (who had managed the just-completed campaign) as chairman of the group. Bob Tully of Eastern and John Erikson of Western (who would be Duffy's executive administrator) rounded out Duffy's transition team.

Duffy hoped that by formalizing the transition process he would eliminate ambiguities and possible misunderstandings. He outlined three broad areas his transition team would be looking into: first, chain of command "so that [the team] can make recommendations to me on changes that suit my style of operation"; second, national officers and the executive administrator, so that he would have their "recommendations as to the most efficient and practical use of the new national officer team"; and third, "to begin the planning for the first round of membership meetings (regional receptions) to be held in early spring, 1983. This task will require the use of an *independent* [emphasis added] public relations firm."

Although Duffy tried to inject a note of collegiality into the letter announcing the goals of his transition team, using phrases such as "with your concurrence," nothing could hide the fact that the transition team would be questioning every aspect of O'Donnell's stewardship.

O'Donnell took the letter badly, as a rebuke and a not-so-subtle insinuation that he might try to sabotage Duffy's transition.

From Duffy's viewpoint, it made sense to have independent experts examine areas that he had made key targets during his campaign. As we have seen, allegations of public relations and management failures struck a resonant chord among the many ALPA members who believed that O'Donnell was too remote from the membership. Duffy wondered how else could he fairly assess ALPA's performance in these areas.

But to O'Donnell, this insistence on outside experts intruding into what had formerly been *his* private preserve, seemed a brazen announcement that *his* chosen ALPA staffers were incompetent and possibly disloyal! The effect on the staff of Duffy's sweeping investigation of their performance was disquieting.

So O'Donnell, still smarting from his defeat, declined to smooth a path for Duffy's transition team during the remaining two months of his presidency, as he himself would later admit.

"What the hell, I never had a transition with Charley Ruby," O'Donnell said in his 1991 interview. "I got in there and met all the departments, by myself, and found out what was going on. When Hank came in, he tried to do everything in an organized way. They had this 'transition team,' which was BS to me. Hank thought I cold-shouldered him. I didn't, but there was nothing I could do with his transition team."

Even more irritating to O'Donnell and frightening to the staff, Duffy's transition team seemed to threaten the principles of "Project Acceleration." Put simply, this operating concept was meant to insulate the professional staff from direct contact with, and hence interference by, pilots.

"The eighth floor was almost funereal during the transition because the staff were devastated," says Tom Ashwood, who as secretary had come to know them well. "They had been with O'Donnell for 12 years, and here's this stranger coming in. It wasn't Duffy's fault really, just the fear of the unknown. But rumors of a slash in staff were circulating, so to say the atmosphere during the transition was strained would be an understatement."

Skip Eglet, who had served as EVP during the latter part of O'Donnell's administration, agrees with Tom Ashwood that the ALPA professional staff was "scared stiff." As a Duffy ally, Eglet tried to mitigate these fears.

"I had reason to be in contact with several national staffers," Eglet recalls. "These people were absolutely petrified that Hank was going to come in like Attila the Hun. I understood their concerns; I mean after all, they had worked with John for so long, most of them had been hired by him, in fact. I think I helped put a lot of their fears to rest. Hank was much too decent a guy to do something like that."

Ashwood confirms Eglet's judgment: "Despite all my difficulties with Duffy, *I know* he was absolutely incapable of vindictive action like that against the staff. It just wasn't in his nature."

O'Donnell's strained relationship with Duffy probably lay at the root of the national staff's apprehension. Perhaps by "body language," inference, or inadvertence, O'Donnell frightened them about their future with Duffy.

"Project Acceleration meant that the departments ran themselves, which they should do," says O'Donnell. "These were professional people, and some of them felt that Hank's people were know-it-alls, that they were going to straighten the home office out."

Aside from directing Jack Bavis to cooperate with Duffy's transition team, O'Donnell did little to accommodate them. As a result, the transition team saw itself as entering unfriendly territory upon arriving in Washington, and consequently it harbored deep suspicions about several members of the ALPA staff, whom they believed capable of pursuing a separate agenda that might damage Duffy.

Because of the strained relations that the election campaign had generated, the new ALPA president came to office with an immediate need to repair the internal schism. But he also needed to hit the ground running. A number of serious difficulties, all directly connected to the growing adverse effect of deregulation of the airline industry, demanded attention. Duffy's education in the intricacies of ALPA's ways would have to proceed simultaneously with his attack on these problems. Furthermore, Duffy would have to educate the ALPA rank-and-file membership as to the seriousness of these problems.

"The Association was ready for change," Duffy said in 1989 of his ouster of

O'Donnell,"but the typical pilot really did not understand deregulation at that point."

Things were moving very fast in early 1983, and Duffy realized he had a narrow envelope of time in which to demonstrate his effectiveness to the membership. With the wounds of the Braniff debacle still fresh, and more potential disasters looming, Duffy knew time was short, and he was under no illusions about a prolonged "honeymoon" with ALPA's membership should things turn sour.

In January 1983, shortly after his election, Duffy launched his campaign to educate ALPA rank-and-file members about the threats they faced. To shake the complacency that still characterized most line pilots (despite the Braniff debacle), Duffy chose as his forum the widely read publication *Aviation Daily*. Declaring that the gravest threat facing ALPA was the use that unscrupulous employers could make of the bankruptcy laws, Duffy anticipated Frank Lorenzo's favorite union-busting tactic months before it became a reality. Braniff had already shown the way by asking the courts to eliminate almost all the bankrupt airline's existing labor contracts, among them ALPA's. But all this seemed terribly remote to *most* ALPA members. After all, Braniff was a special case, most line pilots believed. Their end of the Titanic was doing fine—those guys on the other end were the ones in the water!

In the aftermath of the rigorous campaign that had brought him the presidency and unseated O'Donnell, Duffy necessarily had to ration his cries of alarm, lest he exhaust his credibility. Rank-and-file opinion among ALPA members would have to be educated so that it could withstand the assaults that Duffy knew were in the offing. And Hank Duffy would have to buy some time for himself as well—time to seize control of the instrumentalities of ALPA and bend them to his will. Transitions of power between hostile and opposed political factions are notoriously difficult under the best of circumstances. Unfortunately for ALPA, the transition between O'Donnell and Duffy would take place during the worst of times.

"It was probably after the first half of 1983 before I really started feeling comfortable in the office," Duffy remembered in 1989. "Then Frontier hit us that summer, and Continental in September."

Historically, ALPA members have been subject to long periods of complacency, interspersed with periods of intense alarm about developments at their airline or in the industry. But the pace of change and the shocking rapidity of the events in Duffy's first year in office were without precedent. The startling fact of Braniff's bankruptcy, Frontier's clumsy attempt to void its ALPA contract by creating a nonunion subsidiary modeled upon Frank Lorenzo's "alter-ego" airline, New York Air, and Lorenzo's multiple machinations elsewhere would shortly engage Duffy's attention to the exclusion of all other issues. Lorenzo's use of bankruptcy laws to break his ALPA contract at Continental[4] meant that, in the future, pilots would feel more continuously threatened than they ever had before. Worried and apprehensive, ordinary rank-and-file ALPA members, who had historically been so uninvolved, would now anxiously and hypercritically survey every action of their national leadership.

Duffy, because he had run against O'Donnell by accusing him of not being sufficiently available to the rank-and-file membership, planned to make communicating with himself easier for ordinary members. Accordingly, Duffy and his transition team bubbled with ideas—Hank would begin writing a monthly column in *Air Line Pilot*; the team would introduce new methods of communicating, perhaps a postcard that a member could clip out of the magazine and mail in with various opinions on the state of the industry, or the world for that matter; plans for extensive use of computer "networking" among typically gadget-crazy pilots were afoot.

All this talk of change and "getting back to the grass roots" was a clear source of irritation to O'Donnell during the transition. Until Jan. 1, 1983, O'Donnell was *still* ALPA's president, and the enthusiasm and energy of the Duffy supporters who descended on ALPA Washington, D.C., office as a preliminary to their takeover struck him as pushy and premature. Furthermore, they reminded him of his galling defeat.

Among the problems Duffy faced, the need to prevent any more Braniff-type debacles loomed high, and political baggage lingering from the election campaign troubled this issue even more. This was particularly true of the situation at Western Airlines.

Following Braniff's failure, the Western pilots worried that their airline would be next. Western's troubles were almost a carbon copy of Braniff's, the pilot group had supported Duffy over O'Donnell, and Duffy owed them a political debt.

"The Western people were really scared," Duffy says. "One of the things I had to overcome was O'Donnell's going to them and saying, 'I've got twelve years of connections in Washington, I know people I can go to while Duffy is learning.'"

But the Western pilots had rejected O'Donnell. They knew that the best they could hope for was salvation through merger with a stronger carrier, and they liked their chances with Duffy at the helm better than they liked the prospect of O'Donnell managing their probable merger. The eventual merger of Western and Delta in 1986 played no role in these considerations, because at the time nobody had any idea which airline would absorb Western.

The Western pilots weren't the only group preparing for merger. Mergers among airlines, among the most difficult of all ALPA internal problems, crowded in on Duffy. He would have no honeymoon in this area; and owing to the deep recession of 1982–83, other dangers loomed. Thus, the need to restructure ALPA's intelligence-gathering apparatus was obvious, an imperative if ALPA was to serve its membership effectively and weather the industrywide near-collapse. If events outran ALPA's ability to deal with them, pilots would inevitably blame their own union, not the industry itself.

"This is Frank Mayne's axiom," Frank Mayne of Delta (executive vice-president elected in 1986) observes sardonically: "Whatever goes wrong, ALPA will get the blame. Whatever goes right, the company will get the credit."

From ALPA's earliest days, since its founding in 1931, "Frank Mayne's axiom" could have borne the name of several hundred ALPA activists, all of whom understood its fundamental truth. Hank Duffy understood it, too, and he was aware that the way his membership *perceived* his first actions as ALPA's president would weigh heavily on their assessment of his effectiveness. But because of the difficult transition, Duffy would begin his term as ALPA president laboring under multiple liabilities.

The underlying tension between Ashwood and Duffy was always there, palpable to close observers, particularly the other national officers. Duffy ruefully admitted in his 1989 interview that the lack of smooth transition between O'Donnell and himself meant that ALPA's membership was poorly served until he got acclimated to the Washington environment.

"The office itself is entrée to a lot of things, but I could have gotten off to a faster start," Duffy said later. "I was dependent upon the staff giving me instruction, and that probably set me back about six months."

Although the problems in the industry were not of Duffy's making, they were now his responsibility. Some problems were general, affecting the industry as a whole. For example, the escalating tendency of management to claim economic hardship and then approach each MEC for "givebacks" begged for a suitable national policy in response.

Some problems were specific to an airline. For example, the overriding issue so far as the Braniff pilots were concerned was getting their airline back in the air, an outcome ALPA was essentially powerless to assist, aside from cheerleading. During Duffy's first few months in office, the most promising merger partner for the bankrupt airline was Pacific Southwest Airlines (PSA), which had been negotiating for terms since the original bankruptcy. Although the matter rested entirely with the courts because of Braniff's legal status under Chapter 11 of the Bankruptcy code, Duffy necessarily had to involve himself in it, owing to the _expectation_ of rank-and-file members that he would adopt a high profile.

"The bottom line is that ALPA didn't serve the Braniff pilots well," Duffy said in his 1989 interview. "As a union, we didn't know how to deal with bankruptcies, and internally our failure to transfer pilots with a bankrupt carrier's routes was a mistake. Had we involved ourselves more at the corporate level of the transaction, I think we could have influenced it so that the Eastern pilots would have accepted some of the Braniff pilots. They were unwilling to do that, but if it had just come down to them that to get these routes, they had to take a hundred Braniff pilots, I think they would have accepted it. Of course, this is good old hindsight."

As we have seen, Augie Gorse, Eastern's MEC chairman at the time, was the focus of the Braniff pilots' anger over Eastern's purchase of Braniff's Latin American routes. Because Gorse was also an EVP and one of Duffy's strongest supporters, it is logical to suppose that had the Braniff pilots been allowed to vote during the 1982 BOD meeting, they almost certainly would have gone with O'Donnell—_not_ the candidate Augie Gorse supported. But owing to a ruling from ALPA General Counsel Henry Weiss in his capacity as parliamentarian, the Braniff pilots were denied the vote and granted only "observer" status at the BOD. Weiss's decision was critical, but then again, in an election won by a mere 129 votes, _all_ decisions are critical.

Augie Gorse, when questioned about his opposition to taking any Braniff pilots with the Braniff routes, is obviously discomfited. He pauses before answering, choosing his words carefully. "My MEC told me 'no aircraft, no pilots,'" he says. "We got no Braniff aircraft, only Braniff routes. Borman intimated strongly to me that if ALPA insisted on taking Braniff pilots, he would furlough. We had already taken wage cuts during PATCO so that we wouldn't have to furlough. We tried to get preferential hiring for Braniff pilots after the bankruptcy."

Clearly, Augie Gorse wants these words to be his last on the subject of Eastern's failure to save the jobs of Braniff pilots. For Hank Duffy, the issue would remain troubling, and as we shall see, a substantial number of Braniff pilots would complicate his life by acting as strikebreakers in the upcoming trouble at Continental. Had Gorse and the Eastern pilots had a crystal ball, they surely would have made another decision—one like the United pilot group made when their airline acquired Pan Am's Pacific routes.

The United pilot group's decision to take _all_ the Pan Am Pacific pilots, while not exactly comparable to the Eastern–Braniff case, worked to ALPA's benefit, not its detriment. Learning as he went, Hank Duffy worked well with the United pilot group in structuring the deal that rescued the Pan Am pilots' jobs. In mitigation, O'Donnell, as we have seen, for complex reasons lacked Duffy's access to the Eastern pilot group.

In a show of concern for their fellow pilots on Pan Am, which contrasted sharply with the Eastern pilots' rejection of Braniff's pilots, United integrated the Pan Am pilots directly into their seniority list. Of course, the United pilots were economically well off, while the Eastern pilots had endured years of economic stress; but the fundamental fact was that one group distinguished itself by its unselfish devotion to principle, while the other failed the test. By the time of the United–Pan Am Pacific route acquisition, the lessons learned at Braniff caused the corporate agreement between United and Pan Am to specify the job security rights of the Pan Am pilots.

The process by which lessons are learned is invariably costly. As Hank Duffy settled into office in 1983, burdened with external threats and harried by internal dissension, he would have to start learning the lessons of history on a crash basis. A crisis of unsettling proportions was about to burst upon ALPA and his fledgling presidency. The roots of this crisis lay deep in the tangled history of deregulation and the man who would be the first to use it ruthlessly.

ALPA was about to find out about Frank Lorenzo—just like the world found out about Adolph Hitler. ✈

NOTES
[1] See "Blue Skies and MEC Wars," Ch. 15.
[2] See "Blue Skies and MEC Wars," Ch. 15.
[3] Ashwood delights in the story of his hiring. After getting furloughed by Qantas, he immigrated to the United States. His many letters of application getting no response from any U.S. carrier, he simply showed up at TWA's Kansas City headquarters and faked his way into a job interview.
[4] See "The Continental Strike," Ch. 14.

CHAPTER 10

WHO ARE THESE GUYS?
Frank Lorenzo and His Kind

In the Hollywood classic *Butch Cassidy and the Sundance Kid*, the two train-robbing protagonists, played by Robert Redford and Paul Newman, find themselves pursued relentlessly by a new and mysterious group of lawmen they can only glimpse in the distance. The two outlaws try every trick in their considerable bag to throw these shadowy, deliberate trackers off their trail. As they flee, "Butch" and "Sundance" mutter repeatedly to themselves: "Who are those guys?"

In the modern era, airline pilots would find themselves in similar straits. But instead of a shadowy posse wearing straw boaters, airline pilots would find themselves pursued by a new band of corporate executives, intent upon making fundamental changes in pilot pay and working conditions. These new-breed airline managers were something different in the history of the industry. In the old days, managers tended to be, first and foremost, real airline people, as imbued with the mystique of aviation as any airline pilot. Indeed, many of them *were* pilots. Even some of the legendary old curmudgeons of management who were *not* originally airline men (like W.A. "Pat" Patterson of United, a Wells Fargo banker from San Francisco) eventually *became* real airline men.

The new corporate wheeler-dealers who began entering the airline business in the 1970s were quite different. Their natural milieu was the boardroom, not airline operations. Their pride was manipulating paper profits, not building something *real* out of muscle, sweat, and dreams. Their interest in aviation was nil— airplanes were just another "tangible asset" to them, something to manipulate, not admire. As for the working people who actually made the labor-intensive airline industry function, this new breed of corporate whiz kids seemed interested in them only as targets. For these "modern" airline executives, only the "bottom line" mattered.

Nothing was intrinsically wrong with managers who made profit and efficiency their watchwords. Historically, if management had not paid attention to these fundamental concerns, no airline pilot would have been secure in the profession. But the old breed of managers had established their *bonafides*, paid their dues, and earned the confidence (or grudging respect) of the men and women who worked for them. Owing to the prolabor political climate that marked most of these years, the old managerial elite also (with a few exceptions) generally played by the rules and honored the concept of equitable give-and-take when dealing with their employees.

110

The new breed held these old standards in contempt. Their attitude toward unionized employees was not something the Old Guys who built ALPA hadn't experienced in their time. Pioneer airline managers were often mean "bottom liners," too, but pilots never had any doubts about those managers' ability to run an airline. What worried pilots most about this new breed of managers was their basic *incompetence*. Who were these guys, and where did they came from?

As the era of deregulation dawned, this new managerial breed was positioned to assume a dominant role in the airline industry. Many of them were only in their 30s, often recently graduated from prestigious Master of Business Administration (MBA) degree programs and without *practical* experience in the airline industry. As they began percolating into top airline management in the 1970s, these new "whiz kids" often seemed to believe that the airline industry began with them and that the lessons of the past and its accumulated wisdom had no relevance.

By the early 1980s, as the country slipped into recession and large numbers of airline pilots found themselves either furloughed or in danger of losing their jobs through bankruptcy, this managerial trend became an issue for ALPA. It was so worrisome that it repeatedly surfaced in formal meetings as a topic of discussion. At the May 1982 Executive Board meeting in Washington, D.C., J.J. O'Donnell stated the problem clearly: "Unlike most American unions, airline pilots have historically participated in traditional management areas. We cannot afford to bury our heads and later cry 'poor management,'" O'Donnell told the delegates.

Following up on O'Donnell's remarks, ALPA Secretary Tom Ashwood declared: "It stretches credibility that management makes decisions that place the very existence of our airlines in jeopardy. They act like wildcat oil drillers, either boom or bust, with expensive idiocies and 'brilliant innovations' from which *they* seldom suffer. We have to stop them from doing foolish things. Our industry and our careers are far too important to leave solely in the hands of management."

Even worse, these new managers were awfully sure of themselves, full of the kind of cocky self-confidence that showed in the series of changes, both financial and operational, that they instituted and that left many grizzled old veterans (both in management and in cockpits) uneasy. Arrogance and ignorance, volatile and dangerous when mixed, marked many of their decisions, particularly in the ruinous price wars and fare-cutting that marked the immediate post deregulation period. But for pilots actually flying the line, the worst thing about the new breed of airline managers was that whenever they could conveniently break the long-established rules of labor/management relations, they did so—gleefully!

As these new "go-go" corporate manipulators began to dominate airline boardrooms, questions would arise about their intentions, abilities, and background. Many of them came out of nowhere, with absolutely no experience in airline operations. The old idea that corporate executives should work their way up in an industry, "learning the ropes," seemed to disappear, as airline chiefs suddenly began to emerge from obscure backgrounds, schools of "hotel management," shadowy Wall Street "consulting firms," and increasingly, from the graduate schools of business administration.

One thing the Icahns, Lorenzos, and Ferrises all shared in common, however, was the conviction that airline pilots were "overpaid and underworked." The same went for ground support personnel and flight attendants.

Phil Nash, who went to work for Continental in 1966 after serving in the U.S. Air Force, and later became an ALPA EVP in 1980–82, will never forget his first encounter with Frank Lorenzo. Above all others, Lorenzo typified this new managerial breed. At a special meeting in Denver, Nash asked Lorenzo (who was in the process of taking over Continental at the time) why he was so intent on reducing the pay of flight attendants. Didn't he know, Phil Nash asked, that many of them were single parents who couldn't afford to own homes at the pay rates he was proposing? Lorenzo looked at Nash as if he were crazy.

"Quite frankly, I don't believe flight attendants ought to make enough money so they can own houses," Lorenzo told a flabbergasted Nash. "Maybe they should find another job that pays better."

When Frank Lorenzo captured Continental in 1982, he clearly saw pilots as the most tempting target for establishing the "cost advantage" he worshiped like a religion. Lorenzo was by no means alone in this new faith. At American Airlines (no longer part of ALPA), pilots in the Allied Pilots Association had already submitted to a humiliating "B-Scale" forced upon them by Robert Crandall. The United pilots, under pressure from Dick Ferris, had acquiesced in the infamous "Blue Skies" contract of 1981 (which we will deal with later). Small wonder that professional airline pilots began looking back over their shoulders at people like Ferris and Lorenzo, wondering, as had Butch and Sundance: "Who are these guys?"

The question was more than an idle one, for as deregulation became a reality after 1978, the future of the profession rested in the hands of this new managerial class. Did the United pilots really deserve to have their fate decided by somebody like Dick Ferris? "Who was this guy?"

After graduating from high school in the 1950s, Dick Ferris joined the Army. Today, contemporary advertisements urging young people to "Be All You Can Be" usually stress the challenges, both physical and moral, that result from exposure to combat arms. To think that Dick Ferris spent time in the military learning to function in this most rigorous school of human experience—commanding (and being commanded) in an arena where life and death literally hang in the balance—would be nice.

But Dick Ferris didn't command an armored personnel carrier or maintain complicated electronic gear aboard a ship. Ferris didn't ramrod a heavy weapons squad or master the intricacies of military aviation. Dick Ferris ran an enlisted servicemen's club! After mustering out of the Army in 1962, Ferris entered Cornell University, one of the most prestigious institutions in the nation. But Cornell serves a curious role as a "quasi-governmental" university. In addition to the traditional colleges in the university, whose academic rigor leaves no doubt about their graduates' ability, Cornell also contains certain "contract"

Capt. O'Donnell's strong character and very vocal opinions always created a lasting impression, but never more so than when he faced a microphone before the news media or a congressional comittee. As ALPA president and leading spokesman, O'Donnell greatly increased the public's and airline industry's awareness of ALPA's goals and pilots' concerns.

A new team of officers was elected in October 1980. Here they pose between sessions of the BOD: seated, from left, Capt. Ashwood, reelected secretary; President O'Donnell; First Vice-President Pryde; and Capt. Magee, reelected treasurer. Newly elected Executive Vice-Presidents, from left, S/O Oliver, Capts. Tully, Nash, Eglet, and Brown.

CLOCKWISE FROM TOP LEFT:
Bill Arsenault (United), O'Donnell's
nemisis. The man who brought
down O'Donnell, TACA's Chuck
Huttinger, happy about Hank Duffy's
1982 victory. Jerry Pryde. Capt. Al
Bonner (Delta) took the first steps
toward making Delta a "player" in
ALPA's national affairs by losing to
O'Donnell in 1974. Merle C. "Skip"
Eglet (Northwest), who deferred
his first vice presidency for
internal unity in 1986.

Capt. Sam O'Daniel (United).

Capt. Robert H. Strauss became MEC chairman for the
Continental Airlines pilots in 1977, shortly after ALPA
concluded a 25-day strike against the carrier.

ABOVE: Frontier crew members still smile before their carrier threatens to create an alter-ego, nonunion airline, Frontier Horizion. The threat remained until the carrier folded in 1985.
RIGHT: The last scheduled trip for Air New England was Flight 53 from Burlington, Vt., to Boston (with a stop in Lebanon, N.H.), piloted by Capt. Paul Johnson, left, and F/O Kenneth Hughbanks in a Fairchild FH-227C. The flight touched down at Boston about 6 p.m., Oct. 31, 1981, bringing to a close Air New England's troubled career of 6 years as a certified carrier.

LEFT: Capt. Tom Ashwood (Trans World), doing what even his opponents agreed he was brilliant at—using the "Queen's English."

ABOVE: Capt. O'Donnell testifies before Congress against FAA's decision in 1979 to withdraw immunity against enforcement action for pilots who file reports with the Aviation Safety Reporting System.

ABOVE: Capt. O'Donnell and Sen. Abe Ribicoff press for economic sanctions against countries that aid skyjackers.
RIGHT: Capt. O'Donnell and ALPA experts testify before a House committee in 1978 on aircraft certification. ALPA warned that the process is outdated by a generation or more and has been "pockmarked by catastrophic failure...."

BELOW: Capt. O'Donnell calls a press conference in 1980 to challenge the FAA's certification process for the MD-80/Super, including the question of crew complement. **BOTTOM:** Capt. O'Donnell tells news reporters in 1981 that pilot reports did not support striking air traffic controllers' reports that the nation's airways were unsafe.

Capt. O'Donnell and president-elect, Capt. Henry A. Duffy, greet the 1982 ALPA BOD.

FIRST VICE PRESIDENT

ABOVE: Capt. Duffy addresses the Spring 1985 Executive Board with First Vice-President Tom Ashwood (TWA) and Secretary Chuck Pierce (United), looking on.
RIGHT: Pilots, flight attendants, and flight enginers of Transamerica Airlines and some of their supporters demonstrate, in 1985, at the California State capitol in Sacramento.

ABOVE: Capt. Duffy speaks to informational picketers in front of the FAA headquarters in support of Machinists protesting overseas aircraft repair shops.

LEFT: Capt. Duffy speaks to the Chicago Association of Commerce and Industry in 1983. He discussed the state of the airline industry and the concerns facing airline pilots.

RIGHT: Capt. Duffy congratulates Capt. Robert Schornstheimer and then F/O Mimi Tompkins for their heroic efforts, in April 1988, to fly and land an Aloha B-737 that had lost a large portion of the top of its fuselage.

ABOVE: Demolition workers, in December 1987, tear apart the foundation of ALPA's former headquarters building at Midway Airport to uncover a time capsule buried in the front steps.

ABOVE: Capt. Duffy and Capt. Jerry Mugerditchian, then Midway MEC chairman, open the sealed time capsule.
RIGHT: ALPA's original mail drop door is displayed. It now hangs on a wall in the union's Herndon, Va., offices.

schools operated under special auspices. To report that Dick Ferris earned a degree in engineering, business, or one of the traditional liberal arts at Cornell would be nice. But he didn't. Dick Ferris studied in the school of "hotel management." In addition, his early biographical PR sheets indicate that he merely "attended," which is a coded way of saying he never earned a formal degree.

By 1966, when Ferris was 29, he had become the manager of a hotel in Chicago. Again to report that Ferris's rise in the hotel business was the result of his own drive, ambition, energy and talent would be nice. Perhaps he had all these qualities, but the truth is that his rapid rise owed more to his "close friendship" with Edward Carlson, then CEO of the Western Hotels chain (later renamed Westin Hotels). The downside of the "Horatio Alger" myth—that any young person can rise from rags to riches—is that insider connections (marrying the boss's daughter, as it were) often have been an easier and more certain path to success. Maybe Dick Ferris was the most competent 29-year-old hotel desk clerk in the world. Then again, maybe he was just good at "sucking up."

When United bought the Westin Hotels in 1970, the vagaries of boardroom politics brought Carlson to the top of United itself. Dick Ferris trailed in his wake, at first managing the airline's food service operations. He must have been good at it. Within four years, he was *president* of the airline! In 1976, Ferris replaced Carlson and became CEO of the whole of United. It was quite a rise. In barely six years, Ferris had gone from supervising in-flight meals to running the entire corporation!

But Dick Ferris's rapid rise (and as we shall see, equally rapid demise) was by no means unique. The 1980s saw the emergence of any number of young hotshots whose qualifications were minimal. The one thing they had in common was that they were all excellent "talkers" who could, as the saying goes, "sell refrigerators to Eskimos." Dick Ferris, for one, certainly sold the United pilots the equivalent of an Eskimo's refrigerator when he persuaded them to buy "Blue Skies" in 1981, as we shall see.

But the man who defined this new class of managers, the one whose verbal abilities outstripped all the others and earned him the nickname "Frankie Smooth Talk," was Francisco A. "Frank" Lorenzo.

Who was Frank Lorenzo? The Texas International pilots would be the first to find out—rather like Czechoslovakia found out about Hitler.

Texas International Airlines began life as Trans-Texas Airways (TTA) in October 1947, flying DC-3s over the Houston–San Antonio–Dallas triangle, with stops at intermediate cities. TTA also had route extensions to several smaller Texas cities feeding Braniff, but Braniff, which feared *all* competition in its home Texas market, bitterly objected to its birth. TTA was thus one of the original batch of "second level" airlines that the Civil Aeronautics Board had permitted to develop with a dual purpose—they provided limited competition for the "trunks," while also being "feeders" for them.

But TTA promised to become more than a mere "feeder." It had a coherent route structure within the only state to contain 3 of the 10 largest U.S. cities (Dallas–Ft. Worth, Houston, and San Antonio), each separated by enough distance to make airline operations feasible. The other post-World War II "regionals" were, for the most part, heavily dependent upon "flow through" traffic destined for the trunk carriers—rather like modern "code sharing" airlines.

By the mid-1950s, when regional airlines had became known officially as "local service carriers" (LSCs), the United States had 13 of them. The LSCs joined the 11 "trunks" as the stable basis for the old integrated system of government-regulated airlines. TTA, along with Mohawk (which would eventually serve all four major New York population centers), came closest among LSCs to being able to survive without the CAB subsidy. But none of them was really self-sustaining economically, nor were they intended to be. The LSCs operated as regulated public utilities, serving mostly smaller cities.

Although LSC pilots began as second-class citizens in the airline industry, they were caught in the great post-World War II job crunch and thus were grateful for *any* flying job. Initially, ALPA acquiesced in substandard pay for them to establish their right to collectively bargain in the future. But ALPA explicitly promised to bring them up to "industry standards" once the lean years were over and their airlines became successful. By the late 1960s, ALPA had fulfilled this pledge.

Life for LSC pilots was thus good, and many "trunk" pilots who signed on temporarily during a furlough chose to remain with them, rather than trade a copilot's job for a return to the "plumber" slot upon recall. Because ALPA had cooperated with the LSCs to get union representation established, pay parity with the "trunks," generally speaking, became a reality by the late 1960s. LSC pilots still made less money, on average, than "trunk" pilots, but only because they flew lower-paying equipment. Economically, they were doing fine, with their pay scales and working conditions benefiting from ALPA's ancient policy (supported by government regulators) that all pilot pay, regardless of the airline, should be roughly the same for flying comparable aircraft. Since the days of Dave Behncke, the golden spike that held together the cherished concept of unity across company lines was ALPA's determination that *all* airlines, regardless of size or equipment, should consider pilot pay as the one fixed expense shared in common.

As LSCs acquired turbojet equipment, something very curious happened. The CAB, under increasing pressure because of federal budget deficits caused by the Vietnam War, adopted a policy of weaning LSCs from the subsidy. The original purpose of LSCs was to serve markets which were, *by their nature*, unable to sustain airline operations profitably. To make them self-sustaining, the CAB had no alternative but to grant LSCs "route authority" to serve "city pair" markets that had heretofore been reserved for the trunks. LSCs would thus become "profitable" by tapping into the trunks' market share. In the late 1960s, the CAB began allowing LSCs to serve selected city-pair markets; the CAB would deduct their profits from the subsidy paid to support their old unprofitable routes.

In November 1967, Frontier Airlines reduced the LSC concept to ultimate absurdity when it applied for a trans-continental route! TTA went Frontier one better in 1968, winning the right to serve a route into Mexico. TTA thus became Texas International (TXI). By 1970, the distinction between "locals" and "trunks" had vanished. The old LSCs would henceforth be known, colloquially, as "regional" airlines, but in fact they were simply smaller versions of the "trunks."

Along with their new status, regional airlines like TXI also faced new problems. The old TTA pilots, men like Floyd Carpenter, a World War II B-17 pilot who had grown up with the airline, saw their group's numbers increase to more than 400 as DC-9s came on the line in the late 1960s. Their route structure expanded accordingly. Carpenter and his fellow "Old Guys" had organized TTA for ALPA in 1949 and, despite occasional problems with the owner of the airline, a classic Texas-type "good ole' boy" named R.E. McKaughan, had lived in reasonable harmony with him. The TTA pilots had never had a strike; but on one memorable Christmas Eve in 1959, when contract negotiations were going badly, they came close. McKaughan sent *every* pilot a termination notice! Then he hired them all back on Christmas Day.

"Some people in senior management were extremely close to the pilots and smoothed that mess over," remembers Dennis Higgins, who went to work for TXI in 1966 and would later become MEC chairman. "They spent time in pilots' homes, went to kids' graduations. It was very much a family atmosphere."

But into this Texas version of a labor-relations Eden, a snake crawled. The CAB's new policy of turning the former LSCs loose to live or die in competition with the big boys caused trouble. Frankly, old man McKaughan and his family were not equal to the challenge. As airline entrepreneurs, they were like bugs in amber—fixed in the past, incapable of changing their ways of doing business. By late 1969, TXI was in deep trouble, teetering on the edge of insolvency.

"The airline started out as a little family operation, and the McKaughans had reached the top of their ability to run it," Dennis Higgins believes. "They just couldn't transition into the jet age. I once heard old man McKaughan say, 'You know, when they start charging more than $25,000 for an airplane, the airline business doesn't make sense anymore.'"

The McKaughans sold out in 1969 to a consortium of investors called Minnesota Enterprises, among whom was Carl Pohlad, later famous as the owner of the Minnesota Twins baseball team. The investment quickly went sour. Pohlad and his associates paid $25 per share. Within a year, TXI stock was trading for less than $2 per share. Minnesota Enterprises needed help! They went through a series of managerial gyrations while frantically beating the bushes trying to find someone who could run an airline.

Enter Frank Lorenzo.

In 1971, at the behest of Chase Manhattan Bank, which had money of its own tied up in TXI, 31 year-old Frank Lorenzo and his partner, Robert J. Carney, both recently graduated from Harvard University's MBA program, were sent down from New York as "consultants" to advise Minnesota Enterprises on how to right this listing ship called TXI. Previously, Lorenzo had worked as a financial analyst for both TWA and Eastern, which seemed innocuous enough. The chickens, in short, had no way of knowing that they had just invited the fox into their coop.

By 1972, after a year on the property as shadowy figures unknown to most of the pilots, Lorenzo and Carney completed their "consultancy" at TXI (they were paid $15,000 per month) and delivered their recommendations. Minnesota Enterprises should, Lorenzo and his Harvard business school chum Carney said, let *them* buy the airline. Since TXI was sliding into financial ruin anyway, Pohlad and his associates agreed to a deal that allowed Jet Capital (a company Lorenzo had put together in 1969 with a total capitalization of $50,000) to use money borrowed from the owners to acquire the airline. Frank Lorenzo was off and running in the airline game, playing it with other people's money. But he had a plan to pay the money back, a plan of such brilliant simplicity that Lorenzo was amazed nobody had thought of it before. The unionized employees of TXI would pay off the debt!

"From beginning to end, Lorenzo knew only one way to produce profits," Dennis Higgins declares. "That was by manipulating the employees' pay downward and their productivity upward."

Lorenzo, for all his faults, made no secret of his plans, but he deviously led various employee groups believe that he was after concessions only from *other* unions. At the time of his takeover, Lorenzo hosted a cocktail reception for TXI's pilots at Houston's Intercontinental Hotel. Lorenzo flatly declared that *except for pilots*, he intended to take the airline back to the employment levels of 1967.

" 'There are profits to be made here,' " Dennis Higgins recalls Lorenzo saying. "We are going to continue operating the same number of trips, but we are going to get rid of some ground folks."

Since TXI's "ground folks" were unionized, this strategy meant that the airline was in for a long bout of old-fashioned labor strife. Lorenzo seemed eager to take on his unions. He proposed turning many of TXI's baggage handlers and ticket agents into "temporary" employees—the bane of organized labor. He argued that many of TXI's outlying cities, which often had only one or two flights per day, had no need of full-time employees. He intended to hire part-timers, college students and the like, to work only during those times when a flight was arriving and departing. Lorenzo straightforwardly told the pilots that TXI could not survive if the profits earned by their labors continued being siphoned off by employees who spent most of their time sitting around doing nothing. He was persuasive. Not for nothing was Lorenzo known, as far back as his Harvard MBA days, as "Frankie Smooth Talk."

Some pilots at the Intercontinental Hotel meeting argued, rather feebly, that Lorenzo ought to try offering a better product instead of changing the character of TXI's workforce. He was having none of that.

"Lorenzo was openly against the better-product concept," Dennis Higgins recalls. "He said, 'The traveling public looks for the dollar sign. What they are interested in is a cheap seat. The ones who don't like our service can go pay higher prices on another carrier.' He was very cynical about the public."

TXI's pilots, fully committed to their airline's success, wanted to be as supportive of Lorenzo as possible. They understood that his approach would stir resistance among ground employees, but they really were in no position to challenge Lorenzo until the ground unions, his first target, tested his strength.

TXI's ground personnel were represented by the Air Line Employees Association (ALEA). Dave Behncke had helped create ALEA in the early 1940s, when he was trying to put together an "umbrella of airline unions" (as he put it) with himself at the head. ALEA was a relatively quiet union with a peaceful reputation. Lorenzo, confident that ALEA was the weakest link in the union chain at TXI, at first focused his demands on only one category of ALEA workers—the ticket agents.

Lorenzo's labor-relations style and bargaining technique were honed in the ALEA strike of 1974–75. Basically, his plan was to divide and conquer, to negotiate endlessly, but to never agree to anything concrete. These tactics, which would become familiar, served to keep the ALEA-represented agents in a state of constant nervous turmoil and emotional distress. TXI's pilots could only watch with anxiety, grateful that ALPA wasn't under assault.

But Lorenzo's war on his ticket agents put TXI's pilot group under pressure nevertheless. Some pilots actually supported Lorenzo's demand for massive part-time working provisions from the agents, which would, of course, reduce TXI's expenses and make the airline more profitable, largely by eliminating such things as retirement and health benefits.

"If you looked at it strictly from a management point-of-view, it was not a bad idea," Dennis Higgins concedes.

In December 1974, ALEA, pressed beyond limits, went on strike. ALPA and the International Association of Machinists (IAM), the other two major unionized groups on TXI, did nothing at first. Five days into the strike, Lorenzo ratcheted up the pressure when he began hiring "permanent replacements" for the striking ALEA members. Although badly divided about what to do, TXI's pilots decided that Lorenzo's decision to hire scabs *permanently* was a direct threat to all unionized workers at TXI. After an intense debate, TXI's pilots joined the IAM and other unionized workers in announcing they would honor ALEA's picket lines. Lorenzo promptly sued ALPA for $3 million, while simultaneously asking the court for an injunction forcing pilots to cross ALEA's picket lines.

Lorenzo would lose the legal battle, but win the war. In the 1970s, the legacy of previous liberal Democratic presidential appointments to the federal bench meant that the courts were at least neutral, if not slightly prolabor, ideologically. On Feb. 12, 1975, a federal judge in Dallas ruled that ALPA could legally honor ALEA's picket lines without violating its contract with TXI. Lorenzo, who had already announced that TXI would resume operations on Feb. 13, 1975, had to hastily cancel. Had he won the injunction, he was fully prepared to begin hiring permanent replacements for pilots who refused to return to work.[1] Lorenzo's actions would undoubtedly have triggered the kind of "crossover" crisis among TXI's pilots in 1975 that the combined TXI–Continental pilots would later experience in 1983.

Meanwhile, with his plan to fly through the ALEA strike stymied by the courts and with his airline shut down, Lorenzo coolly took advantage of the airline industry's Mutual Aid Pact (MAP) to keep TXI's coffers full. The MAP was actually the key to Lorenzo's strategy and eventual victory. Created in October 1958 by six "trunk" airlines (others would join later), the MAP was the airline industry's direct response to a series of successful strikes by ALPA and other unions in the

1950s. Under terms of the original MAP, a struck carrier would refer its customers to one of the other pact members and then receive back from those carriers, *through* the MAP, payment equal to the increase in their revenues. The CAB later forced technical, cosmetic changes in the original MAP plan, but basically it functioned like a "capital strike" slush fund.

During the MAP's 20-year history (it would be a casualty of airline deregulation in 1978 *and* an intensive ALPA lobbying campaign), this antistrike profitsharing arrangement was at best a mixed blessing for the airline industry. Responsible managers who negotiated fairly with their employees avoided strikes, paid vast sums into the MAP "contingency fund," and got nothing back from it. But irresponsible managers could goad their employees into strikes and then take MAP money out, thus earning profits while not flying. The MAP system was therefore vulnerable to abuse. But until Lorenzo's emergence, no airline except Northwest had really misused the MAP. Lorenzo's actions during the ALEA strike of 1974–75, some careful observers of the airline industry believed, might have eventually caused the MAP to fall of its own weight.

To pilots who ask the age-old question, "What has ALPA done for me lately?" no better historical answer exists than the 1975–78 lobbying campaign against the MAP. Every airline pilot everywhere, whether represented by an ALPA contract or not, stood to suffer from the MAP. If each of these pilot groups, standing alone, had sent its MEC chairman down to Washington to lobby against the MAP as unaffiliated, local union leaders, the effort would in all probability have gotten nowhere. Every pilot flying the line today should always remember old Dave Behncke's ancient argument, first advanced in 1931 during his struggle to persuade his fellow pilots, that unionization was the only way to get their voice heard.

"If we go down to Washington as a weak, unaffiliated organization," Behncke told his fellow pilots, "about all we would get is, 'It's a nice day. How does it seem to fly?'"

During the 1960s, ALPA's *professional* lobbying staff had suffered from Charlie Ruby's disdain for politicians and consequent neglect. J.J. O'Donnell, in his first term, had begun to rebuild ALPA's lobbying capability by hiring a new Legislative Affairs director, a former member of Congress named Robert Gartland, whom everybody referred to as "the Judge." Gartland, a colorful southerner who reminded many pilots of an alcoholic character out of a Faulkner novel, was supposed to use his extensive personal contacts with politicians in Congress to open doors for O'Donnell, who intended to do most of the lobbying himself. In 1975, largely because Gartland had proven inept at running the anti-MAP campaign following the Northwest strike of 1972, O'Donnell eased him out in favor of a Bob Bonitati. Bonitati, a former Republican presidential aide who had a professional's healthy disdain for what he called "amateur pilot lobbyists," had worked as a congressional liaison for the Office of Management and Budget in the Nixon and Ford Administrations. He moved quickly, under no illusions that if he did not show results in the war on the MAP, he would suffer the same fate as "Judge" Gartland.

As ALPA's Legislative Affairs director, Bonitati began his anti-MAP strategy by establishing close contacts with several Democratic congressmen and senators who chaired key committees. It was a slow process, requiring a good deal of personal attention by O'Donnell—fund-raising dinners, helpful letters during political campaigns, and so on. O'Donnell was good at ingratiating himself with politicians, as even his strongest critics conceded. But lobbying was a skill that could not, by the very nature of politics, spring to maturity at once. In politics, nothing happens overnight.

Northwest's heavy use of the MAP in the bitter three month-strike of 1972 (June 30–October 2) had alerted O'Donnell and ALPA's national officers to the dangers of the MAP. At the time of the Northwest strike however, ALPA's lobbying capability, which O'Donnell had made a priority of his first term, was still not fully developed. When Lorenzo plunged TXI's pilots into crisis in 1975, it was obvious that the MAP (far more so than during the previous Northwest strike) was potentially very dangerous to ALPA.

"ALPA has always confronted the industry in the form of a particular carrier acting as the cutting edge for the entire industry," argues ALPA General Counsel Henry Weiss. "Once the Mutual Aid Pact was created, this was particularly true. Certain carriers would take provocative actions, then go happily to the bank at the expense of their fellow carriers, including those who had good labor relations. I personally had discussions with the top people of at least two such carriers. I asked, 'Why on earth do you want to subsidize a carrier that creates havoc in the industry?' They said, 'It's an insurance policy for us.'"

Until Frank Lorenzo came on the scene, the MAP "insurance policy" was probably worth its premiums. But Lorenzo's blatant exploitation of it to defeat his employees in a situation from which other carriers not only would *not* profit, but which would do them actual competitive harm, caused many airline managers to rethink the value of this "insurance policy."

"We did not turn a wheel for four months, and Frank Lorenzo made $10 million in pure profit from MAP payments!" Dennis Higgins asserts angrily. "I think his misuse of their money was the linchpin in his fellow owners' decision to get rid of the Mutual Aid Pact. They just couldn't afford this guy!"

ALPA certainly helped Lorenzo's fellow owners to arrive at this decision. All during the ALEA strike, J.J. O'Donnell lobbied furiously in Congress against the MAP. While the strike was in progress, O'Donnell persuaded 58 members of Congress to cosponsor Minnesota Rep. Joseph Karth's bill to outlaw the MAP. Rep. Glenn Anderson of California, chairman of the key Aviation Subcommittee of the House Public Works and Transportation Committee, signed on, as did Sen. Mike Gravel of Alaska, who agreed to enter the MAP abolition bill in his chamber. *All* of these lawmakers were Democrats.

Inasmuch as most airline pilots were probably Republicans, O'Donnell ironically had to struggle mightily to find at least a *few* Republicans who would sign on as cosponsors of ALPA's anti-MAP bill. Eventually he persuaded two Republican Senators, Clifford Case of New Jersey and Richard Schweiker of Pennsylvania, to join six liberal Democrats (among whom was former World War II bomber pilot George McGovern) to cosponsor ALPA's anti-MAP bill. Lining up two Republican Senate sponsors was no mean feat for O'Donnell, for as we shall see, the evolution of their party into an intensely antilabor posture was almost complete by the mid-1970s. In 1989, proof of the Republicans' antilabor position became clear. When both houses of Congress passed legislation requiring a Presidential Emergency Board (PEB) to resolve Frank Lorenzo's last antilabor spasm at Eastern, George Bush vetoed it. His fellow Republicans in Congress sustained the veto, thus dooming Eastern's pilots.[2]

"The Mutual Aid Pact was absolutely the complete answer to any attempt by a pilot group to strike or get its demands satisfied," says Henry Weiss angrily. "ALPA had to put up a tremendous battle to get rid of the MAP."

Whether Frank Lorenzo actually helped destroy the MAP by providing a textbook case of how to abuse it remains unclear. Certainly he used it to his own advantage during the four-month ALEA strike in 1974-75. After winning the strike, he would, owing to the cash reserves he had on hand from MAP, be in a position to undercut his competition. Lorenzo began offering "Peanut Fares," which were unprofitable even with a full planeload of passengers, but which nevertheless forced other airlines into a series of ruinous price wars that would spread with devastating effect throughout the industry during the early 1980s. This destructive chain of fare-cutting provided the rationale under which management pressured pilots and other unionized employees into contract "givebacks."

So the widening ripples in the airline industry's troubled pond began with Frank Lorenzo's war against ALEA in 1974-75. Had the MAP not existed, Lorenzo could not have caused such turmoil. Consequently, when airline deregulation finally killed the MAP in 1978 (as the result of congressional compromise made during its passage), few responsible airline managers shed tears for it.

The 1974-75 ALEA strike was ALPA's first exposure to Lorenzo's multifaceted approach to breaking a strike. It would not be the last. It left TXI's pilots angry, shell-shocked, and wary.

"Lorenzo got us out in the street, and he wasn't going to let us back on the property unless it was on his terms," Dennis Higgins remembers bitterly. "He got his part-time provisions from the ground personnel by beating up on all of us. He divided and conquered, and he won, absolutely whipped us, and *we were afraid of him*. The worst thing about the guy, though, was that while he was a corporate manipulator without peer, *he didn't know anything about running an airline*."

But regardless of whether he knew what he was doing, Lorenzo was on his way. In the late 1970s, Pan American, that magnificent cripple, during one of its recurrent crises inadvertently gave Lorenzo a boost. Pan Am needed regional domestic partner airlines to funnel passengers into its international route system. But before deregulation, the only way for Pan Am to get into the domestic market was to buy its way in. Not realizing the ruthlessness of the man they were dealing with, Pan Am's president, former U.S. Air Force General William T. Seawell, made a minor "hub and spoke" agreement with Lorenzo to feed his Latin American routes out of Houston. Meanwhile Seawell was trying to buy National Airlines.

George T. "Ted" Baker had built National from one inconsequential little airmail route linking St. Petersburg and Daytona Beach into a "trunk" carrier. Following the airmail crisis of 1934, Eastern's Eddie Rickenbacker had failed to bid on the route. Baker grabbed it, expanded National to Miami later, and eventually provided stiff competition for Eastern all up and down the Eastern seaboard. In 1962, Baker sold National to Lewis B. "Bud" Maytag, who had formerly owned Frontier. Maytag proved an inept manager, and National went through a series of revolving door managements into the 1970s, as rumors about its demise through merger swirled. The most-often mentioned merger partner was Pan Am.

Because of Lorenzo's working relationship with Pan Am, he observed this mating dance with great interest. In 1978, he quietly launched a program to purchase National stock, which, as Pan Am's merger with National approached, helped drive the price up. In 1979, Lorenzo cleared $40 million from this market operation, which was really little more than corporate "greenmail."

"I was in the CAB hearing room when they subpoened Lorenzo to testify on the Pan Am–National merger," former TXI MEC Chairman Dennis Higgins says. "The president of Pan Am, Bill Seawell, was there, and he told this little story. He said that during a luncheon meeting in New York he told Lorenzo that he was going to buy National, but that he might want Frank to serve spokes to feed his other hubs. About a month later, Seawell invited Lorenzo to London for a big party to celebrate the inaugural of Pan Am's service out of Houston. When Frank and his wife get over there, they go up to Seawell's hospitality suite, and Frank tells him, 'By the way, I recently purchased 17 percent of National's stock.' Seawell was so mad he nearly threw Frank off the top floor of the hotel."

According to Seawell's official CAB testimony, Lorenzo used "inside information" to profit from the Pan Am–National merger. Seawell claimed to be "seething mad" about it.

"I myself heard Frank say, 'I bought National stock for $17, and I'll sell it for $50.' I asked Frank who would pay that, and he said, 'Pan Am will—to get it back.' We didn't know where he was taking us," Dennis Higgins admits.

The airline industry and ALPA were about to find out. Lorenzo, because of his successful stock manipulations during the Pan Am–National merger (finally completed in October 1980), now had the money to put some really ambitious expansion plans into operation. These financial resources, plus his aggressive antiunionism, won the respect of some important Wall Street operators and brought more investment capital his way. By the late 1970s, Lorenzo had attracted the attention of Michael Milken, the "junk bond" and "leveraged buyout" (LBO) manipulator. Milken, a financial felon whose depredations would later earn him a 10-year federal prison sentence (minus his toupee), saw Lorenzo as an ideal investment vehicle. To finance Lorenzo's expansion plans, Milken would ultimately make available to Lorenzo more than *$1 billion!*

But these expansion plans did not include TXI's ALPA pilots. On Dec. 19, 1980, operating through Texas Air Corporation, the holding company that also owned TXI, Lorenzo launched New York Air, a wholly nonunion subsidiary, which would enter direct competition with Eastern's dominant East Coast shuttle service. He literally took TXI DC-9s off the line, repainted them with an apple logo on the tail (New York City was, of course, the "Big Apple"), and began operating them with nonunion crews he had trained at TXI's school in Houston. The little man from New York City, by way of the Harvard Business School and TXI, now stood a good chance of becoming deregulation's first nonunion major player—at the expense of both Eastern and ALPA.

New York Air, Lorenzo's nonunion "alter ego airline" operation, really got ALPA's attention! It illustrated clearly what everyone on TXI who lived through the bitter 1974–75 strike and its aftermath in the late 1970s already knew—that Lorenzo was a "one-trick pony." He knew nothing about the airline business, and he really didn't care about it. His only strategy was to squeeze labor hard, exploit his employees' vulnerabilities, and thus generate the cash flow necessary to pay off the crushing burden of debt that he had accumulated in acquiring his properties. Lorenzo was smart, tough, ruthless, and extremely ambitious. His victory over his employees at TXI only whetted his appetite and motivated him to get rid of his unions totally. To ALPA, New York Air (which used the ATC call sign "Apple") was rotten to the core.

Before deregulation, Lorenzo had to hold the full scope of his antiunion plans in check. The CAB, although it was approaching "sunset" in the dying days of the Carter Administration, still had some residual powers, particularly over "international" carriers like TXI. But with the election of Ronald Reagan in November 1980, Lorenzo expected no hindrance from ALPA's traditional government allies. It was no accident that Lorenzo set his start-up date for New York Air one month *after* Reagan's election. Politically, ALPA was now on its own.

Following the ALEA strike of 1974–75, TXI's pilots signed a contract that guaranteed labor peace until after the onset of deregulation. Once deregulation became a reality, Lorenzo began pressuring his pilots for a series of structural changes in their contract. At first, the TXI pilots had no inkling of what Lorenzo had in store for them. When they entered contract negotiations in 1979, Lorenzo's intentions were still unclear, but they realized immediately that Lorenzo was stonewalling them.

Negotiations began with the pilots extremely wary of Lorenzo because working conditions on TXI had deteriorated. Just as he had with the ticket agents represented by ALEA, Lorenzo would negotiate, but he would never agree to anything. Skirting the edge of the law in an effort to get a contract negotiated, the TXI pilots had tried a program that the United pilots would later call WOE— Withdrawal of Enthusiasm. This tactic involved working "to the book," availing themselves of every reason to take sick leave, and generally doing what they could, short of getting themselves fired, to express their displeasure with Lorenzo. The last thing TXI's pilots wanted, however, was another strike.

"We knew by then that *this guy breaks the rules!*" Dennis Higgins says. "We knew we had to be very, very careful with him because if he ever got us out of our cockpits again, we knew he wouldn't let us back in. He wanted all kinds of changes in our contract, the kinds of things that would force any pilot group to strike. The best legal advice we were getting was that he could not 'permanently' replace us, but we knew that he would try some cute trick and do it anyway."

By early 1981, with the emergence of New York Air, ALPA as a national organization focused its attention on the threat Lorenzo's tactics and style of management presented. Many ALPA pilot groups believed that the TXI pilots hadn't put up a stiff enough fight against Lorenzo, that they should have struck him immediately for violations of their "scope clause" when he launched New York Air. But the TXI pilots *had* fought. They had done everything they could short of striking. Leaving their cockpits, the TXI pilots were convinced, would be suicidal. Their resistance to Lorenzo before, during, and after the New York Air alter-ego airline affair eventually landed them in court, following a three-day "sick-in" during February 1980, which was largely over his demand for changes in their scope clause. Lorenzo was adept at filing lawsuits against his enemies, frequently under the RICO (Racketeer-Influenced Corrupt Organizations) statute, which was originally intended to combat the Mafia.

"I'll never forget the sight of a dozen of our DC-9s parked on the ramp at Houston," chuckles Dennis Higgins. "I had never seen so many of our airplanes together before. The 'sick-in' really was a spontaneous event. Our pilots had to show this guy that they were in support of their elected leadership. It wasn't a strike. Our pilots were just sick."

Lorenzo promptly served Higgins with a "cease and desist" order from a friendly Texas judge and sent teams of nurses around to all the sick pilots' homes to check on their "illness."

"The nurse would knock on the door and say, 'We are here to check on your vital signs,'" Higgins laughs. "We told the pilots to just throw them off their property. We also told them, 'If you are not sick, go to work.' The pilots felt like they had shown their strength, but Lorenzo sued us and ALPA national in federal court for damages, contending that we *ordered* the 'sick-in.'"

When Lorenzo's lawsuit alleging an illegal "sick-in" finally came to court in 1981, ALPA got lucky. By chance, the federal judge assigned to the case turned out to be a black woman whom Jimmy Carter had appointed and who had a labor law background.

"Judge McDonald called me into her chamber," Dennis Higgins remembers. "She said, 'I have to find ALPA guilty, but I want you to know I understand your frustration.' She then gave Lorenzo no legal fees and no damages and said everybody ought to get back to negotiating."

In the final throes of the 1980 contract negotiations, TXI's pilots, although legally bloodied, still fought Lorenzo's demand for changes in their scope clause down to the wire.

"The train never stopped with Lorenzo," Higgins says. "We would no sooner finish with an agreement than Lorenzo would draw back from it."

Just as Lorenzo had during the 1974 ALEA negotiations that led to the strike, he played cat-and-mouse with his pilots. Under National Mediation Board (NMB) auspices, the talks had moved to Oklahoma City, a neutral site. Lorenzo's negotiating team, headed by Don Breeding (whom the Continental pilots would later come to loathe) boarded a TXI DC-9 at Dallas. When he realized who was aboard, the captain (who now flies for another carrier and doesn't want his name published) refused to take off.

"The captain wanted to kick them off his plane," Higgins remembers with a twinkle. "When told he couldn't, he simply grounded the airplane by writing up a magnetic compass gripe—an absolute no-go item. Breeding appealed to me and said, 'There's nothing wrong with that magnetic compass.' I said, 'Don, if you've got a mechanic's license, you write off the gripe.' Which of course, he couldn't do."

The Oklahoma City negotiations of February 1980 finally produced a contract. Or so everyone thought.

"It was 2:30 in the morning, we called Lorenzo at home, woke him up, and told him we had finished," recalls Dennis Higgins. "He said, 'Great,' checked with his people that they had costed it out, and told them, 'Put it on the company teletype so all those mad crews out there know they have a contract.' We went back to Houston for the official signing, and at this official ceremony, they push a new proposal across the table to remove language from our contract that had to do with 'successors.'"

The TXI pilots absolutely refused to reopen negotiations, but Lorenzo was undeterred. Through legal maneuvers orchestrated by a newly hired consultant, Phil Bakes, who had until recently been an assistant to Professor Alfred Kahn, the guru of deregulation while he was a member of the CAB, Lorenzo moved ahead with his plans to launch New York Air—in clear defiance of the TXI "successor" clause language. Bakes, after leaving the CAB staff in 1977, signed on with the committee, chaired by Senator Edward M. Kennedy, that approved the Airline Deregulation Act of 1978. Bakes knew more about the inner workings of the new law and the possibilities it offered to Lorenzo than any other man alive. Bakes would use this knowledge to midwife New York Air into the world, as he artfully dodged TXI's "scope" language.

Dennis Higgins, TXI's MEC chairman, who had acted as a missionary to the rest of ALPA, warning pilots far and wide that Lorenzo was a formidable foe and a danger to all of them, had done about all he could do.

"We warned everybody that they had to stop this guy, that he does what he wants, that he beats you up," Higgins sighs. "Despite all our legal advice, the lawyers couldn't feed into it the really unorthodox things Lorenzo would do and the way the courts would react. I mean, we'd say, 'Nah, he wouldn't do that—he *couldn't* do that!' But he would, and he did. We were conventional in our thinking, Lorenzo wasn't. That was the message we took to the Continental pilots at the time of our merger."

The TXI pilots had played Czechoslovakia to Lorenzo's Hitler. The pilots of Continental were about to play Poland. ✈

NOTES
[1] A development we will cover later, see "Pilots and PACs, Republicans and Labor," Ch. 12.
[2] See "Pilots and PACs, Republicans and Labor," Ch. 12.

CHAPTER 11

BAD DUDE RISING
Frank Lorenzo Grabs Continental

John F. Kennedy, renowned phrase-maker that he was, will probably be remembered as much for some of his flippant utterances as for the stately
cadences of his more serious ones. His pithy observation that "life is not fair"
bears heavily on ALPA's history in the Duffy era. That Hank Duffy, the product of
Delta's peaceful world, should find himself presiding over ALPA during a time
of savage confrontations on Continental, United, and Eastern is a surpassing
historical irony. But life isn't fair and neither is history—Frank Lorenzo's emergence guaranteed it.

When last we left Francisco A. "Frank" Lorenzo, he had successfully gobbled
up little Texas International (TXI), stalemated J.J. O'Donnell, and converted himself from an industry lightweight into somebody who clearly had designs on
heavyweight status. In the process, this upstart flea who would be an elephant
had made himself thoroughly obnoxious to ALPA (as we have seen in the New
York Air episode) and established links to Michael Milken, the junk bond king
who would finance Lorenzo's ventures, which many observers saw as little
more than stock market "greenmail" at first. The pilots and other unionized
workers at TXI saw Lorenzo as the Devil Incarnate, but the rest of the airline
community regarded him as rather "cute"—a bit bug-eyed and overly ambitious, perhaps—but cute.

"We were still Tree Top Airlines [a play on the pre-TXI name of Trans Texas
Airways]," recalls former TXI Master Chairman Dennis Higgins of Lorenzo's heady,
early days. "Here is a guy who is doing things real fancy. We could hardly pick up
a newspaper without reading something about our company, and we wanted
to pat him on the back. But we were afraid he might bite our arm off."

Everybody loves a success story, and Frank Lorenzo seemed to personify the
genre, almost defining the myth of rags-to-riches in his workaholic personal
habits and aggressive style. J.J. O'Donnell, as we have seen, was worried about
Lorenzo, whom he saw as an amoral and potentially dangerous adversary, even
under the pre-1978 system of governmental regulation of the airline industry.
With the coming of deregulation, O'Donnell, fully supported by the TXI pilots,
raised alarms about Lorenzo's methods and the portents his negotiating tactics
raised for the future. But most rank-and-file ALPA members weren't overly concerned. To them, Frank Lorenzo was still just a small blip on the early-warning
radar. Although increasing numbers of informed ALPA members fretted about

him, far too many line pilots saw Lorenzo as slightly comical, particularly in his abortive efforts to outbid Pan Am for control of National, or barring that, muscle in on their markets with such things as "Peanut Fares." Many line pilots (including even a few who worked for him) actually saw Lorenzo as admirable, a "comer" who miraculously induced large financial networks to support his ventures and generally shook things up in the airline industry.

"Based on what we knew of him as a consultant, we looked forward to having him come aboard," Dennis Higgins recalls. "We wanted to be supportive because the McKaughans (the family who owned TXI) had reached the top of their ability to produce profits, and the carrier had teetered on the edge of bankruptcy a couple of times."

This favorable attitude evaporated rapidly, but some ALPA insiders thought that focusing too heavily on Lorenzo, in a personal sense, was a mistake. They saw this as giving him too much free publicity and distracting ALPA from other problems that were more serious. To turn Frank Lorenzo into the *bete noir* of the industry prematurely, they felt, would give him clout he didn't deserve and might hamper efforts to work with him in the future, a particularly important consideration should Lorenzo actually succeed in establishing himself and his holding companies (Jet Capital, and later Texas Air Corporation) as major players in the industry.

"We did everything but take out full-page ads calling his wife a whore," says Tom Ashwood, who held the offices of secretary under O'Donnell and first vice-president during the first Duffy administration. "Frank was just nastier and tougher than most airline executives, but by personalizing the attack on him, making him into Darth Vader, we reached the stage where doing business with him was impossible."

Ashwood's view of Lorenzo was logical enough, given the climate of labor relations during the long peace between management and pilots, which generally characterized the era of direct government regulation. After all, ALPA had not for a long time confronted a rapacious airline owner who sought domination rather than accommodation—occasional unpleasantries notwithstanding.

All that was about to change. The generation of professional airline pilots who matured in the 1970s had never dealt with an airline boss who manifested an instinct for the jugular. Behavior like that was *passé*. The whole experience of modern airline pilots was that their counterparts in management were reasonable technocrats who knew the limits of their power and understood that the airline business was, at base, a cooperative enterprise that required informed consent and mutual respect, particularly when in dealing with flight deck crews. Even the fabled curmudgeons of the early years who survived into the modern era, men like Bob Six of Continental Airlines, men who had once engaged in the airline equivalent of tong wars with their pilots, had eventually mellowed. A modern version of E.L. Cord was no longer possible. So most pilots believed.

The ghost of old Dave Behncke must have stirred uneasily somewhere, for historically, the airline bosses he dealt with wanted the heads of their unionized pilots on a platter—not some namby-pamby "working relationship" with them. In the brave new world of deregulation, no ALPA member should have been surprised that Frank Lorenzo would cast himself as an atavistic throwback to an earlier age—he had certainly given plenty of warning. When the crunch with Lorenzo came, many pilots would see him as the Adolph Hitler of the airline industry.

Historical analogies are tricky things. By comparing the story of ALPA's wars with Frank Lorenzo to the struggle against Adolph Hitler, we risk trivializing one of the great tragedies of history. Nevertheless, the analogy has a certain symmetry, wherein the pilots of Texas International become Czechoslovakia, the pilots of Continental Airlines become Poland, and (as we shall see in a later chapter) the pilots of Eastern become the Soviet Union—victorious, but at a terrible cost.[1] Similarly, many would say that comparing Frank Lorenzo to Hitler trivializes crimes of unimaginable dimension. Frank Lorenzo may have disrupted peoples' lives (and even caused a few psychologically shaky individuals to commit suicide), but he never sent anybody to the gas chamber. But then again, some professional historians argue that Hitler was really no different from any other European leader of his era—just "tougher and nastier" (to quote Tom Ashwood's comparison of Lorenzo to other airline bosses). And so the analogy comes full circle.

Continental Airlines, whose pilots would shortly take center stage in the struggle against Lorenzo, worked in a corporate culture as distinctive as any in the industry. Despite previous namesakes in the 1920s, the modern version of their airline dates only to 1937, when Robert F. Six parlayed his holdings in Varney Air Transport (a small feeder airline operating single-engine Lockheed Vegas in the mountainous West) into a merger with Wyoming Air Service. Six gave the combined airline its current name and, from the late 1930s through World War II, learned his business while benefiting from the cautious expansion that government regulators allowed. Bob Six inspired intense loyalty among his employees, developed a cadre of talented managerial subordinates (such as Harding L. Lawrence, who would later take Braniff to glory and grief), and eventually transformed Continental from what was no more than a regional airline into a "trunk" carrier (by the Civil Aeronautics Board's definition).

As one of the smallest of the 11 major airlines, Continental grew in the post-World War II period into a respectable operation, serving routes that stretched from Texas to the West Coast and beyond. In the 1950s, Continental acquired Pioneer Air Lines, won the right to serve Chicago, and began flying turbine equipment, the Vickers Viscount. During the 1960s, Continental's flight crews, through the airline's Air Micronesia (popularly known as "Air Mike") subsidiary, gained international experience and graduated to the same equipment that the major carriers were flying, mainly B-707s on Military Airlift Command contract operations in the Pacific.

During the long years of Bob Six's reign, Continental's pilot group developed a "Delta-ish" reputation, in that they were steady and quiet about their unionism, rather than militant. Continental pilots were more likely to be active in the professional and technical aspects of ALPA work (the "nuts and bolts" committees) than in the "political" side of ALPA, although there were exceptions, like Dennis Duffy, who became executive vice-president (EVP) at the same time

Hank Duffy became president—to the endless confusion of ALPA's mailroom. Continental's ALPA members could occasionally be hard-nosed when they thought management was persecuting a pilot, but that was a rare occurrence. In general, the Continental pilots' relative quiescence spared them the kind of rancor that scarred relations between other ALPA pilot groups and management.

The Continental pilots' relatively peaceful life was purchased at a price, however. Owing to the airline's semi-feeder status in the early days, Continental's pilots always lagged behind the national average in pay and benefits. They were so intensely proud of their airline that they were willing swallow these inequities, for many noneconomic compensations went with wearing a Continental uniform. Their special relationship with management and agreeable working conditions fostered a cohesive, close-knit sense of belonging, and they tended to live in "airline ghettoes" at the various domiciles (Denver, Los Angeles, Houston, and Honolulu), where they socialized together, both as individuals and families. Despite a brief strike in the late 1950s during the struggle with the Flight Engineers International Association over the qualifications of the third crewmember, peace and goodwill reigned at Continental for many years. Being a Continental pilot and being a "good company man" were almost synonymous.

But change was in the offing. The temper of these changes between the "old" Continental pilot group and the younger pilots hired during the 1960s emerged clearly in the 22-day strike of 1976 (October 24 to November 15). It began when the younger pilots' patience with Bob Six's promises of pie-in-the-sky finally ran out and ended in a three-way welter of bad feelings among ALPA's national officers, the Continental MEC, and the Continental pilots themselves. The strike also marked a watershed of sorts for the Continental pilots in their relations with management.

Although a majority of Continental's pilots still regarded themselves as "Bob Six's boys" and saw their airline as "family," an increasing number of junior pilots (the so-called "Young Turks") grew skeptical of both the company's intentions and the senior pilots' procompany bias. This problem came to a head over Continental's history of seasonal furloughs, which had historically been short. Senior pilots regarded these furloughs as a normal part of paying professional dues—the "You ain't a *real* airline pilot, kid, 'till you've been furloughed" syndrome. But to junior pilots, the furloughs were intolerable—a prime example of managerial incompetence. As the company's financial position became shakier in the waning years of Bob Six's tenure, two relatively long furloughs, in 1970 and again in 1974, affected a substantial number of junior Continental pilots.

Thus the younger pilots were the catalyst in the 1976 strike, which was strictly economic in origin. Put simply, the Young Turks were tired of living under the threat of furloughs and flying for 80 percent of the pay their professional colleagues at other airlines received. Two key players in this strike were Bob Strauss (a handsome and magnetic leader who bore a striking physical resemblance to the movie star Tom Selleck) and Larry Baxter, both of whom were members of the Negotiating Committee. As leaders of the Young Turks, Strauss and Baxter all but took the play away from Gary Thomas, the MEC chairman. With the assistance of Jim Rinella, the LEC chairman at Los Angeles,

Continental's largest domicile, the Young Turks seized effective control. Thomas was closely tied to a group of senior pilots, men like Don Ballard, Wes Coss, and Jack Daniels, who had dominated ALPA affairs on Continental through the 1960s. Larry Baxter, highly intelligent but abrasive, was generally regarded as the most militant of the Young Turks.

One startling aspect of the 1976 strike was a series of angry confrontations between J.J. O'Donnell and the Continental pilot leadership. For example, during an Aug. 17, 1976, meeting in Washington, D.C., the Continental Negotiating Committee (composed of Strauss, Baxter, and Dick Nelson) became so angry with O'Donnell's criticisms of their tactics, timing, and expenditures that they walked out *en masse* on him!

"I told Baxter he wasn't competent to conduct negotiations. I really laid into him," O'Donnell recalled in his 1991 interview of that stormy meeting in Washington. "I said, 'Larry, you're going to take the Continental pilots right off the cliff, and they're going to die, and you'll be responsible.' He stood up, said something to little Jim Rinella, who pretty much did what Baxter said at that time, and out the door they go."

O'Donnell, previously burned by an unsuccessful strike on Northwest, was increasingly skeptical of the effectiveness of strikes. He made no secret of his belief that Continental's pilot leaders were behaving unwisely, and he feared a strike would poison the well of "good-faith bargaining" that had previously existed at Continental. Even more alarming to O'Donnell was what he regarded as the Young Turks' unyielding negotiating stance, which he feared would force a strike that might drive the carrier into bankruptcy. O'Donnell was acutely aware that bankruptcy could lead to the abrogation of union contracts.

"I was absolutely skeptical of the strike as an effective weapon as early as 1972," O'Donnell said in 1991. "Every time we tried it, we lost. I told the Continental pilots in 1976 that they had other alternatives—take a look at sick days, stay within the Railway Labor Act, operate by the book, as long as you start that program a year before, show it's your normal delays, never use the term 'slowdown.'"

O'Donnell had good reason to fear that bankruptcy might lead to the abrogation of union contracts. In an eerie foreshadowing of Frank Lorenzo's later use of the bankruptcy laws in 1983 to terminate the Continental contract, Universal Airlines (which had previously been known as Zantop Air Transport), a cargo operation based in Michigan, had broken its ALPA contract in 1971 through the auspices of a bankruptcy judge. ALPA contested this contract abrogation, but before it could be resolved in the courts, Universal ceased operations in May 1972, putting 400 ALPA pilots on the street. O'Donnell had been forced to deal with the fallout from this obscure case during his first term as ALPA's president. Ed Nash, who got out of the U.S. Air Force in 1959, just in time to confront a very tight job market for pilots, went to work for Zantop before it merged into Universal. He flew Zantop's DC-3s and DC-6s for a flat 3 cents per mile, an experience that motivated him and his fellow Zantop pilots to explore union affiliation.

"ALPA wasn't particularly interested in us, so we approached Allied [the American Airlines pilots' union]," Nash recalls. "They didn't want anything to do with us, so we looked at the Teamsters. That got kind of ugly—forklifts through cars and so on. I was pushing for ALPA from day one."

By the time Nash left Zantop in 1967 for a job with Continental, Zantop had 400 pilots, and ALPA was definitely interested, largely owing to Ed Nash's skills as an organizer. In 1968, Universal (the renamed Zantop) signed an ALPA contract, but the victory was short-lived. After the "non-sked" airline declared bankruptcy in 1971, its pilots worked without a union contract until it shut down. O'Donnell, aware that bankruptcy could jeopardize an ALPA contract, worried that Continental's pilots were courting a similar disaster in 1976.

"Zantop pulled a maneuver similar to Frank's later one when it declared bankruptcy right after ALPA organized them," Ed Nash recalls. "I am convinced that Frank Lorenzo was aware of it."

Indeed he was. A very young Frank Lorenzo, fresh out of school with his MBA degree, was working for Universal (Zantop) as a financial analyst at the time! At the time of Continental's 1976 strike, O'Donnell was privately furious with Gary Thomas, the Continental MEC chairman in 1976, for letting things get so out of hand that a reprise of the Universal–Zantop bankruptcy might be possible.

"He made the mistake of letting that third, you know, that militant third, guys like Larry Baxter, get out of hand," O'Donnell declared later.

But an ALPA president interferes *directly* in the internal affairs of an MEC at his peril. O'Donnell could only watch with rising alarm and disapproval as the Continental Negotiating Committee, in the absence of firm control from a generationally divided MEC, allowed itself to be maneuvered into a strike the majority of Continental pilots did not want.

Ed Nash, who had gone to work for Continental in 1966 after leading the organizational effort among his fellow Zantop pilots for ALPA in the early 1960s, involved himself in ALPA service as a "water carrier" all through the 1970s. Nash, who was not an admirer of the Young Turks, saw Larry Baxter as the cause of the strike: "Larry was the kind of guy who, once given authority, would not take advice or direction. The 1976 strike was a bitter experience for us. Basically, it destroyed our good relationship with management."

So the 1976 strike occurred under circumstances that left everybody angry. During a brutally frank closed session shortly after the strike began, O'Donnell flayed the MEC for failing to control its bargainers, ripped Los Angeles LEC Chairman Jim Rinella for filing an unauthorized lawsuit, and denounced the Continental pilot leaders for tacitly condoning an illegal slowdown. Continental had promptly sued ALPA over these tactics.

"I was shocked at the violation of ALPA policy and the Constitution and By-Laws," a furious O'Donnell told a closed MEC meeting in Los Angeles shortly after the strike began. "You as an MEC and we as ALPA representatives are in one hell of a mess. You were repeatedly cautioned against any type of a slowdown, and under the law, you are charged to make certain you prevent it. There's not much we can do about the lawsuit now. We are trapped. The company now has all the ingredients to deny you an equitable agreement and tie up our key people and all of our legal resources in court."

Eventually, under this kind of pressure, the Continental MEC forced the Negotiating Committee to resign and installed a new one, chaired by Bill Kennedy, which agreed to a settlement the Young Turks did not like. Phil Nash (no relation to Ed Nash), who left the U.S. Air Force in 1965 for a job with Continental, described the mental state of the younger pilots during 1976 perfectly when he declared: "We made mistakes because we wanted to get well again real damn fast."

Too fast, as it turned out. The 1976 strike caused the Continental pilot group to enter the crucial late 1970s (the first years of deregulation) badly divided. The stresses of free market economics soon soured many more rank-and-file Continental pilots on the company's policies, enabling the Young Turks to repair relations with them and win control of the MEC. Larry Baxter dropped out of ALPA work temporarily, but Bob Strauss became MEC chairman, replacing Gary Thomas. The new leaders' resentment toward J.J. O'Donnell, whom they regarded as insufficiently militant, festered, but was kept under control owing to the fact that Strauss and O'Donnell began to form a personal friendship in the late 1970s. In fact, the friendship became so intense that it was widely assumed that O'Donnell was grooming Strauss as his replacement. But O'Donnell could barely tolerate most of the Young Turks, and he disliked Larry Baxter in particular.

The Continental pilots would later support Hank Duffy against O'Donnell at the 1982 BOD meeting, with the wounds of the 1976 strike and its aftermath still fresh in their minds. Larry Baxter, who O'Donnell thought was a dangerous radical, would emerge as the Continental MEC chairman following the death of Bob Strauss (from cancer) in March 1982. Although terminally ill, Strauss had clung to power until he was removed by the MEC—involuntarily. Baxter, partly because of his poisonously bad relationship with O'Donnell and partly because of his intense nature, inspired both considerable opposition and fervent admiration among the 15-member MEC. These internal stresses afflicting the Continental pilot group reached boiling point just at the time of Frank Lorenzo's advent.

So the unpleasantness of the 1976 strike, the substantial expansion of the pilot roster in the mid-1960s, and the first adverse effects of deregulation had left old Bob Six's peaceful kingdom in a shambles by the early 1980s. The building resentment of the pilots eventually included even Six himself, who cleverly used the Mutual Aid Pact to turn a $15 million profit during the 1976 strike, while his airline foundered operationally and his disillusioned employees fumed on the picket line.

Six's successor, Al Feldman, did his best to patch up morale and eventually became something of a hero to the Continental pilots through his resistance to Lorenzo. But nothing could replace the lost tradition of mutual trust, although Bob Strauss eventually became quite close to Feldman. Pride in the airline and the pilots' sense of personal identification with it did not entirely die, but the Continental pilots were deeply suspicious of management by the early 1980s.

Ironically, relations between the company and its pilots actually improved temporarily, because the conflict between Baxter and O'Donnell deflected some rank-and-file resentments from management to ALPA National, thus providing another good example of Frank Mayne's Axiom—"When things go wrong, ALPA gets the blame."The strike did give the Continental pilots a certain sense of pride and a psychological uplift through the solidarity they achieved, but this temporary internal harmony among the Continental pilots cost a considerable amount in intra-ALPA collegiality.

Instead of being angry at ALPA, the Continental pilots should have focused on other factors, among them the effect of the Nixon–Ford era economic policy, such as the "Presidential Pay Board" (the anti-inflationary device of the early 1970s), which exacerbated existing pay inequities between themselves and other pilot groups. Ironically, Richard Nixon would be the last U.S. President to resort the old expedient (used extensively during World War II) of wage and price controls.The Nixon-era wage restraints penalized unionized workers excessively, but rank-and-file ALPA members in the 1970s, predominantly Republican and conservative, were not yet ready to deal with national politics. Because of national political trends and the shape of the American economy, Continental's pilots would never achieve the dream of a "Delta-type" contract. But many Continental pilots viewed their 1976 "job action" as a victory, because they did win some gains that brought them closer to parity with other pilot groups, the stresses generated notwithstanding.

The Continental MEC behaved with increasing independence from ALPA National as their airline's situation deteriorated during the final years of the O'Donnell era. Deregulation had something to do with this, for as we shall see, it served to weaken the power of unions and, consequently, the power of union leaders to control their rank-and-file. Proof of this assertion lies in the Continental pilots' willingness to ignore O'Donnell's advice and cross the picket lines of other unions, notably those of the Association of Flight Attendants in 1980. When the Continental pilots believed the strikes of other unions jeopardized their carrier's future, they were capable of some very bad manners.

Although the MEC wanted to support the AFA in 1980, the rank-and-file angrily rejected any "sympathy action."This was particularly unfortunate for Bob Strauss, the MEC chairman. Strauss, handsome and divorced, fluttered more than a few hearts among Continental "stews."As he was crossing the girls' picket line one day, one of them shouted,"Did you hear that loud noise, Bob?" Strauss asked,"What loud noise?" She replied,"The sound of 2,000 [bleeps] snapping shut. Better get used to it—you'll hear it a lot from now on."

Then suddenly in February 1981, reality landed on Continental's pilots with a thud—after 38 years, the Bob Six era was over. The legendary old pioneer, tired and discouraged by the new deregulated system he didn't understand, announced his retirement. Six's hand-picked successor, Al Feldman, would have to deal with the effects of deregulation.

Pete Lappin, who learned flying in the USAF and went to work for Continental in 1969, served as MEC vice-chairman during 1983. He echoes the sentiments of many Continental pilots when he speaks of Al Feldman, who would later end his life with a single pistol shot on the eve of Frank Lorenzo's takeover of Continental.

"Under the old system of regulation," Lappin observes, "Al Feldman would have been superb. I think he realized that the future belonged to Frank Lorenzo, who would come in like Attila the Hun, and that the rank-and-file pilot, because of the legacy of Bob Six, was unprepared for him. I talked to Al Feldman on the morning he killed himself. He said that we were in a lot more serious shape than any of us allowed ourselves to believe. With hindsight, I see that he was very relaxed because he'd already made the decision to commit suicide, I think because he couldn't live with failure."

Against this dramatic backdrop and the failure of the Continental employees to buy their airline through an ESOP (which we will discuss later), the Frank Lorenzo era at Continental began. It was complicated by the necessity of merging the TXI and Continental pilot rosters, the crushing debt with which Lorenzo had saddled Continental to acquire it, and from ALPA's perspective, the fact that the transition between Hank Duffy and J.J. O'Donnell was a difficult one. Duffy and his new team were still learning the ropes and knew next to nothing about Lorenzo and his techniques when they took over.

Early in Duffy's administration, he had inaugurated a series of meetings with airline CEOs, both to get to know them and to let them understand his position. Because of Duffy's Delta background, most airline CEOs were curious about him and eager to meet him.

"People I had worked with in management at Delta went out of their way to tell everybody that I could be dealt with, that I was tough but fair," Duffy recalls. "I tried to get to know them all, the larger ones especially, but I did not meet Frank Lorenzo during the whole Continental strike."

Duffy was extremely busy during the first half of 1983, and Lorenzo's lack of a response to Duffy's request for a meeting went virtually unnoticed. But shortly before the explosion on Continental in August 1983, after Lorenzo had apparently already laid his plans to declare bankruptcy to break his unions, Don Breeding, Lorenzo's chief operations officer at TXI (a position he would shortly assume at Continental), contacted Duffy about a face-to-face meeting with Lorenzo. Breeding, whom the TXI pilots intensely disliked and who would shortly earn similar enmity from the Continental pilots, suggested Duffy and Lorenzo have breakfast together. He offered the opinion that Duffy and Lorenzo, because they were both serious long-distance runners, might find that they had enough in common to establish a working relationship of some sort. This offer of a meeting appealed to Duffy, who saw it as a way to establish an "eyeball-to-eyeball" feel for Continental's new boss.

"I was going to fly to Houston," Duffy remembers, "when an emergency came up on Eastern, and I had to go down there instead. This was just before the bankruptcy. I have often wondered if it would have diverted anything or not."

Probably not. By the time Continental's hierarchy approached Hank Duffy for a meeting, things had already deteriorated badly between the airline and its pilots, and what little goodwill remained from the days of Bob Six had evaporated. Additionally, an ALPA president, by the very nature of his position, must always be wary of management efforts to use him to undercut an MEC. Because of the history of difficult relations between the Continental MEC and ALPA National during the O'Donnell era, and Lorenzo's reputation for guile, Hank

Duffy thought an arm's-length approach prudent. In retrospect, Duffy believes it might have been wiser if he had met Lorenzo personally.

"When Lorenzo bought Eastern," Duffy said in a 1989 interview, "I told Borman I needed to meet Frank Lorenzo, I couldn't go through another whole cycle without at least sitting down and having that talk with him. Borman arranged breakfast, where we chatted. He was surprisingly informal and gracious. I have a strong belief that you always need to keep that communication going, despite the rhetoric, hype, and passion."

But a far more serious obstacle to resolving problems between Frank Lorenzo and the Continental pilot group existed—the pilot group itself. Because the TXI pilots (commonly referred to as the "Texas" pilots) and the Continental group were in the process of merging, a variety of internal factors badly divided them and hampered their effort to craft a united front against Lorenzo.

On June 29, 1983, TXI MEC Chairman Ron Waters wrote to Duffy complaining about a proposed joint meeting between the two MECs and Lorenzo, scheduled for June 9, which Baxter had sabotaged. Warning that Baxter was falling victim to a Lorenzo stratagem to divide the two pilot groups, Waters declared: "I don't have to tell you what a vicious labor antagonist Frank Lorenzo is. One can only imagine how a split in a group our size will help his game plan. Last week, I initiated an attempt to arrange a meeting between the MEC officers, TXI and Continental, to go as one solid group in the event we are faced with a strike. Larry [Baxter] emphatically indicated he didn't think there was any purpose in such a meeting."

At the separate June 9 meetings, Lorenzo and Stephen Wolf, the president of Continental, told the two MECs that they wanted concessions, that they intended to "take on" the International Association of Machinists, and that they expected the pilots to cross the IAM's picket lines.

"They informed us that they expected the IAM to strike around September 1," Waters told Duffy. "Sources within the company are now saying that the TXI pilots will cross the line but not the Continental pilots. I deem this a serious attempt by Lorenzo to split the two pilot groups."

As we have seen, the TXI pilots emerged from their baptism of fire during Frank Lorenzo's initial foray into the airline business badly burned. The Continental pilots regarded the TXI pilots as "defeatist" because of their horror stories about Lorenzo, while the TXI pilots saw the Continental pilots as insufficiently worried about the new Continental boss's rapacity.

The TXI pilots' irritation, aggravated by the normal stresses of integrating two pilot seniority lists, became more acute over what they saw as the Continental pilots' condescending attitude toward them. In a nutshell, the TXI pilots thought the Continental pilots viewed them as "bushleaguers" who had been unable to cope with Lorenzo. The TXI pilots also smarted from the Continental pilots' cocky insinuations (real or imagined) that the "big leaguers" would now bring skinny little Frank to heel.

The TXI pilot group, concurrently, tended to see their earlier battles with Frank Lorenzo, particularly over New York Air, as unappreciated. Many of these difficulties were probably unavoidable, owing to the normal stresses of merging the two seniority lists, but there is general agreement that Larry Baxter's leadership style made things worse.

"Larry Baxter was an intelligent, tough, hard-working guy," recalls Phil Nash, a member of the MEC during 1983 who counted himself among the Continental chairman's admirers. "But he could also be overzealous and caustic. For example, he got into the habit of calling Red Stuebens, one of the Operations VPs, 'Beet Face,' because of his complexion, and he did this to his face."

Pete Lappin, Baxter's MEC vice-chairman and a close personal friend, agrees: "Larry's approach *was* confrontational, and because of their styles, he and Lorenzo clashed. It was a very uncomfortable atmosphere."

By general agreement, Baxter was Lorenzo's equal when it came to rhetorical sparring and, on more than one occasion, made Lorenzo look bad in front of his executives. While most pilots approved of Baxter's ability to trade insults with Lorenzo, the problem was that Baxter had trouble turning off his abrasive style when it came to dealing with internal ALPA matters.

The election of the first combined Continental–TXI MEC provides a case in point. From the time of Lorenzo's merger of Continental and TXI in October 1982 to the eve of the strike in 1983, the TXI and Continental pilots were joined in name only. Although the airplanes had all been repainted with Continental's colors by early 1983, keeping the two pilot groups divided and suspicious of each other was to Lorenzo's advantage. Things would have been bad enough without Lorenzo's meddling (as anybody who has ever been through a merger understands), but Baxter made things worse by failing to control the tribal instincts of the Continental pilot group. The result was that, in the first election for officers of the merged airline, the TXI pilots were completely shut out.

"We had only two local councils in common, Denver and Houston," recalls Dennis Higgins, *de facto* leader of the TXI pilots. "We barely knew the Continental guys, and we were vastly outnumbered, but I told Baxter that the Texas pilots must not be disenfranchised. I told him to pick a position on the MEC, and we'll supply the candidate, and it was up to him to guarantee that our guy got elected. They elected all their own guys, no Texas faces anywhere."

Hank Duffy, watching the situation warily, also tried to intervene to ensure that the combined MEC, which would not begin functioning until September 1983—barely a month before the strike—contained at least some symbolic tokens of unity. The legacy of antagonism that existed from the days of J.J. O'Donnell's presidency had diminished, but Duffy was powerless to force the Continental rank-and-file to elect any TXI pilots at their local council meetings.

"We are, as a national organization, tied to the character of an MEC," Hank Duffy later recalled ruefully. "If you've got good, strong leadership, it's one thing; if you've got the other, it controls the situation. At Continental, we had a split MEC, this tug of war going on inside, at the same time we were trying to fight a really tough adversary."

In addition to the Continental–TXI split, there was also an intra-Continental split. Gary Thomas, who had been displaced from the MEC chairmanship by Baxter's ally (the deceased Bob Strauss) following the 1976 strike, led a significant anti-Baxter faction. Thomas (who would also die of cancer later, in 1989) was openly critical of what he called Baxter's "lack of people skills." Careful observers of the "all-Continental MEC fiasco" cite the episode as an example of Baxter's flawed leadership.

"Hank Duffy was there during the election of the new MEC chairman," Dennis Higgins remembers. "He backed me up when I warned that Frank would try to drive a wedge between us, and then he'd drive a truck through both of our houses. The Continental pilots thought I was being overly dramatic. They were basically confident that they could handle Frank Lorenzo."

Almost without exception, people who knew Larry Baxter, both friend and foe, testify that he felt equal to the challenge of dealing with Lorenzo, that he perhaps relished the confrontation. But he wasn't foolhardy. Baxter recognized that shutting out the TXI group on the new combined Continental MEC was impolitic, so he asked Dennis Higgins to join him as a sort of "Minister Without Portfolio" to foster unity. Higgins agreed and became quite visible on the MEC, despite not being officially a member.

Almost immediately, Continental's unionized workers found themselves at the point of Lorenzo's assault. They were the logical first target because Lorenzo was, in fact, a "one-trick pony" in a strictly business sense. He had no interest in the technical aspects of the airline business, nor was he an innovator or a motivator. He was as unlike Bob Six and the previous generation of airline industry pioneers as it was possible to be.

Phil Nash, who served as EVP under J.J. O'Donnell, recalls a conversation with a former Continental executive who (like so many others) had fallen afoul of Lorenzo and lost his job in the revolving door managerial system Lorenzo favored: "I bumped into Roy Rawls, comptroller under Al Feldman. We were standing in the King Super grocery store in Houston, and I'll always remember him telling me, 'Those young men around Lorenzo are not interested in running an airline at all—they're interested in making deals.'"

Lorenzo cared virtually nothing about the airline business as such—his _metier_ was, like Donald Trump's, _the deal_. He would have been as happy manipulating the affairs of a widget maker as an airline. But fiercely ambitious, possessed of a towering ego and a raging temper, Lorenzo also wanted to be _big_—whether in widgets or airlines, he wanted to run the biggest operation around.

By definition, in a heavily unionized labor-intensive industry, if Lorenzo were to zoom to the top, the most attractive avenue of attack, given the weak state of the economy owing to the 1982 recession and the initial dislocations of "Reaganomics," was to go after Continental's unions. Lorenzo would later argue that his financial predicament, brought on by the debt-leveraged process that bought him control of Continental, meant that he had to extract a lot of cash from somewhere in the company, _fast_, or he would be unable to service his debt. But at the time he declared bankruptcy, Continental had plenty of cash on hand and was not broke. Nobody should have been surprised at Lorenzo's disregard for the truth—he had earlier promised California legislators, _in writing_, that he would not move Continental's corporate headquarters to Houston. He took less than a month to break that promise.

In addition to his alleged financial predicament, Lorenzo also had another weapon with which to bludgeon his pilots—the fact that the non-ALPA pilots of American Airlines, through their union, the Allied Pilots Association, the clone with which they had replaced ALPA following their 1963 defection, had agreed to the industry's first nonexpiring "two-tier," or "B-scale," contract in 1982. Given the actively antilabor political climate of the early 1980s, American's competitors quickly moved toward B-scales themselves. We will deal more fully with the B-scale issue in another chapter; but generally, carriers represented by ALPA responded at first by asking their pilots for across-the-board concessions, typified by United's notorious "Blue Skies" contract of 1981.[2] Because this approach tended to create a united front between senior and junior pilots, how much management could extract from their pilots with it was limited. The B-scale concept played to shortsightedness and human greed (the "I'm all right Jack" syndrome), because it pitted pilots currently working against those who weren't even hired yet. So it was fiendishly clever.

Oddly, Frank Lorenzo didn't ask the merged pilots of Continental and TXI for a B-scale. He had in mind something far more sinister—a B-scale for all of them—*right now*! ✈

NOTES

[1] See "Lorenzo's Last Gamble" and "The Eastern Strike and the Fall of Lorenzo," Chs. 18 & 19.
[2] See "Blue skies and MEC Wars," Ch. 15.

CHAPTER 12

PILOTS AND PACS, REPUBLICANS AND LABOR
The "Reagan Revolution" Hits ALPA

"I wanted to take him by the scruff of his neck and throw him out of the room," said President Theodore Roosevelt.

Who was the President so mad at, some tinhorn Central American dictator? Some slick lawyer defending a cattle rustler whom Teddy had caught red-handed? Actually, he was a perfectly respectable member of the President's own class, a man named George F. Baer, who had come to the White House about the little matter of a nationwide coal strike.

"Teddy" Roosevelt, for whom the "teddy bear" was named, has come down through history with something of a "cuddly" image. Often seen as an eternally adolescent President, forever out hiking, camping, and exploring, Teddy's zest for life and concern for the "less fortunate" (as the poor were quaintly called in those days) made him a hero to millions.

But Teddy Roosevelt had another side. He was also noted for carrying a "big stick" (he hardly ever "walked softly"), which he used regularly on enemies—foreign and domestic. Overseas, Teddy laid into sleazy politicians in Latin America who dared stand in the way of his canal in Panama. At home, he took dead aim at the corporate greedheads who were known then as "robber barons." Teddy's pugnacity toward the "trusts" (or business monopolies) earned him enemies in corporate boardrooms and affection in the hearts of ordinary Americans. In short, working people loved Teddy Roosevelt for the enemies he made.

One such enemy was the aforementioned George F. Baer, a pompous, over-bearing labor-baiter who acted as principal spokesman for the nation's coal mine owners. Despite the fact that he and Teddy spoke the same language (in an upper-class accent barely distinguishable from that of the British aristocracy), Teddy found Baer immediately disagreeable. So disagreeable, in fact, that Teddy wanted to lay hands on Baer and throw him bodily out of the White House.

Teddy's angry remark about Baer came in 1902, following a meeting he had just sat through in the White House. Teddy had called the meeting between the coal mine operators and representatives of the United Mine Workers to help settle the strike. This unprecedented attempt by a sitting President to mediate a labor dispute (which the newspapers of the day were calling "The Great An-thracite Coal Strike") invites some obvious comparisons with the lack of action by George Bush during the Eastern Airlines strike of 1989.

Nothing like Roosevelt's intervention had ever happened before. Before Teddy

Roosevelt, Presidents (whether Democrat or Republican) had been uniformly hostile to labor unions and had sided with the courts in regarding them as "syndicalist conspiracies." Grover Cleveland (a Democrat, we must remember) had ordered federal troops to shoot down strikers during the Pullman Strike of 1894, on the totally spurious grounds that they were "interfering" with the mail.

Teddy Roosevelt was something new in the history of the American presidency and its relationship to organized labor. Despite his wealth, patrician upbringing, and privileged place in the American caste system of the 19th century, Teddy Roosevelt was a fair-minded man. Unlike most men in his social class, he had actually gotten to know the working people of America, first as a rancher in the Dakotas in the 1880s, where he became something of a cowboy. Later, during the Spanish-American War, Teddy got to know working men even better by sharing the unvarnished reality of combat.

So when privileged people like George Baer spouted "social Darwinism" at him, declaring that working men were lazy and irresponsible and deserved their lowly status because of "character flaws," Teddy knew better. He had seen men like these striking coal miners in action, and he knew that they were the same breed of men who had charged up San Juan Hill with him in Cuba. They weren't saints, but their character under fire was far from "flawed." So Teddy decided the miners deserved a hearing of their grievances against the mine owners.

The coal mine operators (several of whom had been Teddy's Harvard classmates) had ready access to political power and influence. Teddy had already heard their horror stories about the UMW's penchant for violence. But he wanted to find out for himself, firsthand, rather than have his information filtered through people who were hostile to unions. To get at the truth, Teddy Roosevelt created what was, in effect, the first Presidential Emergency Board in American history.

Let us flash forward from 1902 to 1989. The Eastern Airlines employees, stressed beyond endurance by their boss, Frank Lorenzo, and in the same position as the miners during the Great Anthracite Coal Strike of 1902, needed a forum to air their grievances. The sitting president in 1989, George Bush, was a man "born with a silver spoon in his mouth" into an ancient family of wealth, power, and political influence—just like Teddy Roosevelt. Roosevelt had gone west to the Dakotas in the 1880s to prove himself in the rough-and-tumble ranching business. George Bush also went west, to Texas after graduating from Yale, to make his bones in the oil business. Teddy fought in the Spanish-American War; Bush was the youngest Naval aviator in World War II. But that's where the similarity between Roosevelt and Bush stopped.

As an ex-Navy pilot, one might have expected George Bush to feel sympathy for men like those he had fought alongside during World War II. Although there is no evidence of any continuing interest in aviation by Bush after his military service, nor any record of his ever having piloted an airplane again, one might have logically expected him to give *at least a fair hearing* (which is what a Presidential Emergency Board is for) to the pilots of Eastern in their dispute with Frank Lorenzo. Teddy did as much for the coal miners who soldiered with him in Cuba.

But for the moment, let's put this speculation aside and return to the meeting Teddy chaired in October 1902. He was in a state of high irritation because winter was looming and the nation's principal source of home heat, the grade of coal called "anthracite," was in short supply because of the strike. The UMW delegation, led by John Mitchell, had already agreed to binding arbitration of their dispute with the coal operators. As working men, they had no desire to inflict hardship on people like themselves or to see women and children suffer in unheated homes and factories. The purely economic aspects of their strike were negotiable. *But the miners wanted the arbitrator to recognize their right to bargain collectively.*

In a leap of faith, UMW President John Mitchell (whose rapport with Roosevelt easily leaped across lines of class and social standing) gambled that he could trust the President to appoint an arbitrator who would judge this vital issue impartially. But the mine owners dug in their heels, emphatically rejecting arbitration of the UMW's right to bargain collectively for coal miners. They expected Teddy Roosevelt to support them. That labor unions were fundamentally illegitimate was, we must remember, an article of faith among people of their background. If need be, the mine owners argued, Teddy should call out the U.S. Army to dig coal. How dare the President even listen to this rabble, let alone invite them into the White House! Baer had argued forcefully that merely sitting down with the UMW leadership at the same table was a travesty. But when the President of the United States, against all expectations, agreed to sponsor the meeting, Baer and his fellow mine owners really had no choice but to attend.

Advance this scenario to 1989, and one might logically expect George Bush to *at least not veto* a congressional bill mandating an impartial fact-finding commission in the Eastern Strike. Owing to Bush's background in aviation, and the undeniable fact that a majority of the Eastern pilots had probably voted for him in the 1988 election, accepting such a bill would have been a painless way to handle the pilots' dispute with Frank Lorenzo, one that entailed no political risks. After all, Frank Lorenzo was unlikely to retaliate by becoming a major fund-raiser for the Democrats, as he had been for both Reagan and Bush. Not vetoing the bill would cost Bush nothing, and as a gesture, it might earn him political points with labor.

Back to 1902 for a moment and Teddy's relationship with the striking UMW and their employers. Teddy, like George Bush a blue-blooded aristocrat to his fingertips, never tried to hide his social status. He would never have stooped to publicly declaring pork rinds his favorite snack food, as George Bush did in 1988. Teddy's identification with the ruling class of America was obvious, and he never bothered with theatrical tricks to build a bogus sense of connection with working people. To build that sense of commonality, Teddy relied on fair play and an open mind, not cheap shots. In Teddy's moral universe, the price of political power was an honest stewardship of his office, and he was supremely confident that God had ordained his Presidency and the values by which his class lived.

And that's what got George Baer and his fellow mine owners in trouble with

Teddy Roosevelt. Baer's scornful attitude toward working people was bad enough, but what really irritated Teddy Roosevelt was Baer's belief that he spoke with the voice of God Almighty!

"The rights and interests of the laboring man," Baer said "will be protected not by the labor agitators, but by the Christian men to whom God in His infinite wisdom has given control of the property interests of this country."

As the reader will note, Baer said nothing about the role of the President of the United States in this process. Aside from the pure pomposity of Baer's remark, talking that way around Teddy was unwise for Baer. Roosevelt sincerely believed that *he*, not Baer, had the direct pipeline to God, and that if anybody spoke with the authority of The Almighty, it would be the President of the United States—not some pushy coal hustler!

Update the language used by Baer and the coal mine operators to our own time, and they sound a lot like Frank Lorenzo. Certainly the underlying assumptions that characterized Baer's attitudes toward labor unions harmonize nicely with the assumptions of the new breed that began appearing in airline management during the 1970s. Actually, modern greedheads might have been worse, in a philosophical sense, than the robber barons of Teddy's day. At least Baer and his ilk talked about their "Christian duty" and expressed a sense of *noblesse oblige*—the notion that by virtue of their privileged positions, the wealthy were responsible (in a general, or perhaps spiritual, sense) for their workers' welfare. Contrast Baer with Lorenzo, who once declared that his flight attendants *did not deserve a living wage*, and George Baer doesn't sound all that bad!

The underlying question that every airline pilot flying the line into the 1990s must ask is, *why was there such a difference between a president like Teddy Roosevelt and a president like George Bush?* Two men, both war heroes, both aristocrats, both Republicans—but so very different. Bush, under circumstances that were roughly comparable to the Great Anthracite Strike of 1902, *vetoed* the congressional bill that would have created a Presidential Emergency Board for Eastern's pilots in 1989. Teddy took the risk of *leading* the effort to settle the Great Anthracite Strike of 1902. George Bush sat on his hands.

Like his forebears in the coal industry, Lorenzo flatly rejected binding arbitration. Both George Baer and Frank Lorenzo believed they could win the fight with their employees, and they wanted no interference from politicians while doing so. But there was a big difference between the coal miners' strike of 1902 and the airline pilots' strike of 1989—the coal barons had to contend with a fair-minded President who would not bow to the antilabor shibboleths of his time, even though they constituted the "conventional wisdom." The striking Eastern pilots of 1989 would have no such luck with George Bush. How do we explain this set of historical circumstances, and what does it mean for professional airline pilots?

The Republican party was born out of the struggle against slavery. As the vehicle of middle-class idealism, the "Grand Old Party" (GOP) came into the political arena as the authentic voice of reform, speaking for the noblest ideals of which the U.S. system of government is capable. As the party that freed the slaves and saved the union, Republicanism was absolutely dominant for two generations. Between the election of James Buchanan in 1856 and Franklin D. Roosevelt in 1932, only two Democrats won the White House, and both on flukes. Grover Cleveland got lucky in 1884 and again in 1892 (the only split-term President in U.S. history), when the GOP nominated weak candidates; Woodrow Wilson won in 1912 because of a split within the GOP between Teddy's "Progressives" and the "Old Guard" conservatives.

The long dominance of the GOP in national politics came at a price, however. Gradually, the GOP evolved into the national conservative party, committed to the status quo on social and economic matters and identified with the idea that corporations should be seated first at the banquet of American life.

This political transition did not take place without a struggle. A fierce war for the soul of the Republican party broke out in the first two decades of the 20th century. This struggle illustrates a point that historian Arthur M. Schlesinger, Jr., has made about U.S. history. Schlesinger argued persuasively in *The Age of Jackson* and subsequently in his multi-volume *The Age of Roosevelt* that U.S. political history was really about the struggle between "businessmen" trying to use government power for their own purposes and "reformers" trying to limit the business community's power over government. Generally, businessmen used government power to line their own pockets; reformers sought to use it to serve "the general welfare."

In the early 20th century, this battle pitted Teddy Roosevelt and his "Progressives" against those Republicans who called themselves the "Old Guard." As the dominant party, the GOP had the power to mold the social, economic, and political landscape, so it was natural that the conflict over these issues should manifest itself as a factional dispute within the party. The Democrats were a minority party, strongest in the backward South and tainted with treason because of the old association with the Confederacy. The Democrats were, in short, nonplayers, powerless to mold events. Post-Civil-War Republicans dismissed the opposition by saying: "While not all Democrats were traitors, all traitors were Democrats!"

By the early 20th century, this old argument about who was loyal to the Union and who was a traitor, an emotional campaign technique called "waving the bloody shirt" (which was roughly comparable to George Bush's use of the Pledge of Allegiance in 1988) was losing its power to obscure the real issues confronting working Americans. The overriding issue between Teddy Roosevelt's "Progressives" and their "Old Guard" opponents was simple and stark: what should the limits of corporate power be? Should the men who controlled great corporations be free, unhindered by government, to seek profits at the expense of ordinary Americans? Or should government have the power to shape and control corporate power in the interests of the ordinary working people?

Teddy Roosevelt spoke for that segment of the GOP that wanted to control corporate power, to guide its creative and beneficial aspects into socially useful channels. He denounced the greedheads of his day as "malefactors of great wealth" and fiercely resisted the buccaneering aspects of *laissez-faire* capitalism. Did employers have the right to lock their employees into unsafe workplaces, to avoid spending money on fire safety equipment, simply to maximize profits? Following the Triangle Shirtwaist Factory fire in New York, few ordinary Americans thought so. Several hundred women workers, trapped hopelessly in the inferno because of their employers' greed, perished horribly.

Teddy was outraged! The answer to such malfeasance was obvious—laws *mandating* a safe workplace. The Old Guard thought this kind of interference in the marketplace was terrible. If the women who died in the blazing shirt factory didn't like their conditions of employment, they were free to quit! In a nutshell, the argument between liberals and conservatives in the 20th century has pretty much boiled down to the question of whether government should force businessmen to behave. Teddy Roosevelt was the first politician of stature to take the "liberal" position. He called it the "New Nationalism."

In 1912, Teddy Roosevelt split his party over this issue. His hand-picked successor, William Howard Taft, whom Teddy thought a Progressive like himself, had betrayed the cause and gone over to the Old Guard during his Presidency. After unsuccessfully seeking to regain the GOP nomination (Teddy had retired voluntarily from the White House in 1909), he entered the 1912 campaign at the head of his own party, the Progressives. In the three-way race that followed, Teddy came in second to the Democrat, Woodrow Wilson, but well ahead of Taft.

Teddy Roosevelt would die in 1919, while this war for the GOP's soul still raged. His opponents, who controlled the party's machinery, eventually outlasted Teddy's "Bull Moose" Progressives and became dominant. During the 1920s, the GOP's Old Guard consolidated power and elected three presidents—Harding, Coolidge, and Hoover—who were among the most conservative men ever to occupy the White House. The GOP increasingly became the party of "Big Business." Coolidge expressed this perfectly when he said: "The business of America is business. The man who builds a factory builds a temple. The man who works there, worships there." George Baer couldn't have said it better.

And this is where airline pilots enter into the political equation. Dave Behncke would use this remnant of Teddy Roosevelt's Bull Moose Progressivism (so-called because Teddy said he felt "fit as a bull moose" when he entered the 1912 election) to secure passage of the "Pilots' Amendment" to the Railway Labor Act in 1936. This "Title II" of the RLA is arguably the most significant, far-reaching piece of legislation in ALPA's history, in the sense that every pilot flying the line today still lives with it on an almost daily basis. Dave Behncke won the RLA's passage by adopting a cold-eyed view of politics. Can airline pilots in the next century learn anything from him?

Dave Behncke was a child of the 1920s. He bought the whole Republican world view. He believed the conventional wisdom of the day, which preached the values of individualism and hard work. Behncke scratched his way up from obscurity, became an "officer and a gentleman," founded his own business, went broke, and came up swinging again. John Wayne, in his finest Hollywood fantasy, couldn't have played Dave Behncke's life better than Behncke lived it. Behncke was the living embodiment of the Republican ethos in the 1920s.

But Behncke was not stupid. After repeated bashings by the corporate power structure that Teddy Roosevelt had failed to tame, Behncke came to the conclusion that only labor unions provided the simple justice that working men needed. So he became a trade unionist, learning his lessons at the elbows of giants of the old labor movement, men like William Green of the American Federation of Labor (AFL). The labor leaders of the 1920s, who guided Behncke as he formed ALPA, had in turn, learned from legendary activists like Samuel Gompers, the patron saint of 19th century unionism.

What fundamental truths did they learn? In a nutshell, labor leaders of the old AFL learned that without friends in politics, organized labor's position was almost hopeless. Samuel Gompers argued for "pure and simple unionism," but he also taught another cardinal lesson—"Reward your friends and punish your enemies."

But how can airline pilots at century's end learn from the past? What have Dave Behncke or Samuel Gompers got to say to contemporary airline pilots, whose unionized jobs involve a technology that neither could have imagined? Behncke surprised many pilots by taking ALPA into the political thicket during the 1930s.

"I am a strong Roosevelt man myself," Behncke habitually declared. "You can just take the simple facts and put them on the table. Had it not been for him, the picture would be pretty black today."

But Behncke also said, somewhat slyly: "It doesn't matter where the coal comes from, so long as it gets on the fire."

What Behncke meant can be seen clearly in his friendships with politicians of both parties, Democrat and Republican. A former Bull Moose Republican named Fiorello H. La Guardia was ALPA's strongest congressional supporter during Behncke's time. Behncke understood that unions need friends in politics; but by the 1930s, his fellow pilots were becoming skeptical. Behncke lined up with Franklin D. Roosevelt's New Deal at a time when many airline pilots were beginning to think of themselves as "professionals" who belonged in the GOP alongside doctors and lawyers. Owing to the high economic status that ALPA's successes had won them, many airline pilots began to lose sight of their roots in organized labor, and they flirted with a "conservatism" that was more emotional than practical. They forgot that most fundamental Machiavellian dictum: "My enemy's friend is my enemy."

Political parties, like nations, have no permanent friends, only shifting interests. When the interests change, so do the friends. Repeatedly, ALPA has relied upon its friends in politics to secure its goals. In practice, this has meant that ALPA's friends were Democrats, because that party has served the labor movement's interests better since Teddy Roosevelt's day. But it doesn't have to be that way.

In the scary world of deregulation, a time of turmoil and change that the Old Guys who formed ALPA could scarcely have imagined, political alliances may well prove as crucial as they were in Behncke's day. Because organized labor's friends have mostly been Democrats, and because ALPA depends so heavily on its friends in organized labor, it stands to reason that airline pilots should be *practical* Democrats. The awful truth is that if a Democratic President had been in the White House instead George Bush, he almost certainly would *not* have vetoed the Eastern bill that Congress passed in 1989. Under the white heat of a Presidential Emergency Board, Frank Lorenzo would undoubtedly have suffered the kind of damage that would have forced a settlement of the Eastern Strike on terms favorable to working people—that's what happened in 1902.

The kind of fact-finding commission that Teddy Roosevelt pioneered, which looked into the meat packing industry's unsavory history and brought about the passage of the Pure Food and Drug Act in 1905, would undoubtedly have sunk Frank Lorenzo in 1989. Harry Truman, following his reelection in 1948, paid his debt to organized labor by forcing George T. "Ted" Baker into a settlement of the National Airlines strike in 1948. Would Tom Dewey, the defeated Republican, have done so? John F. Kennedy appointed the Feinsinger Commission, which investigated the Southern Airways Strike of 1960. The result was a victory for ALPA. Would Richard Nixon have done so?[1]

In the modern "global village" of instantaneous communication, public opinion is a powerful tool. The most effective way to mobilize it, historically, has been the kind of fact-finding commission Teddy Roosevelt invented—the kind George Bush vetoed. Democratic Presidents have historically been willing to use this tool in support of organized labor, while Republicans have not. Teddy Roosevelt did not intend it to be that way.

In 1902, Teddy appointed a commission to study the miners' grievances. The commission met, investigated, and exposed the facts. The white heat of public scrutiny, once focused on the mine owners' abuses, was enough. Public opinion did the rest. It was the first great victory for organized labor.

While Teddy Roosevelt was not exactly a fan of labor unions, he knew a knave in a three-piece suit when he saw one, and George Baer fit the definition. Much to his surprise, Teddy rather liked the rough-hewn UMW leader, John Mitchell. His reasonableness and good humor contrasted favorably, in Teddy's mind, with the overbearing smugness of Baer.

Why didn't George Bush sit down across a table from Frank Lorenzo, with Jack Bavis or Skip Copeland and Hank Duffy alongside, so he could take the measure of the men? Why was Bush unwilling to judge for himself which among these men was the knave? Why wasn't George Bush like Teddy Roosevelt?

In the 1980s, ALPA finally got serious about using the only weapon guaranteed to get the attention of politicians—money. ALPA-PAC (for Political Action Committee), created by the BOD in November 1975, was the final vindication of Dave Behncke's hard-headed political realism. For all his lack of formal education, Behncke grasped the fundamental fact that only political pressure—intelligently applied—could mold events to ALPA's advantage. Money, Behncke knew, was "the mothers' milk of politics." He waged a long guerrilla war against pilots who just couldn't see the connection between politics, money, and ALPA's well-being. Behncke's vindication began with J.J. O'Donnell's creation of ALPA-PAC in 1975 and blossomed with Hank Duffy's cold-eyed use of it in the 1980s.

The PAC concept emerged as part of the reform package of campaign financing laws following the "Nixon scandals." In addition to Watergate, Nixon and his minions literally _extorted_ campaign contributions from businessmen who depended upon the favor of the federal government. A shamefaced series of powerful businessmen would later plead guilty to knowingly violating the law by diverting corporate funds to the 1972 Nixon campaign. Airline executives were particularly vulnerable to this kind of financial mugging, all questions of ideological kinship aside. Nixon's attempt to convert the regulatory agencies into political instruments was already well advanced by the time Watergate erupted. When Congress voted on Nixon's impeachment, "abuse of power," particularly his corruption of regulatory agencies like the CAB, was one of the charges that stuck.

"I was under pressure," Braniff's Harding Lawrence said when pleading guilty to making an illegal $40,000 contribution.

Indeed he was! Imagine the damage G. Gordon Liddy, John Dean, and assorted "plumbers" could have done Braniff as members of the Civil Aeronautics Board!

The PAC reform was designed primarily to permit ordinary people to make their political-financial muscle felt _collectively_. Simultaneously, the reform movement strengthened the prohibition on _direct_ corporate political contributions, a law that had been on the books since the 1920s, thanks to Teddy Roosevelt's Progressive supporters in Congress. Henceforth, people who wished to _voluntarily_ contribute to a PAC, whether organized by corporations or unions, would be free to do so. ALPA's leadership, after a fierce internal debate, created ALPA-PAC, which by the early 1990s was widely acknowledged as one of the most effective and well-financed in Washington, D.C. But because of internal conflicts brought on by the emotional Republicanism of many pilots, ALPA-PAC was relatively quiescent until Hank Duffy energized it in the mid-1980s, largely as a result of reverses such as the Continental strike.

"Jay was nervous about pressing for PAC contributions from the membership," Duffy said in his 1989 interview. "Pilots really do have a jaundiced view of the morality of the PAC, of making contributions for favors returned. I didn't have that shyness. O'Donnell was raising about $180,000 per year. I raised about $1.5 million per two-year election cycle. I believe in it. It's a great system for ALPA. We're not like the Teamsters, where we can affect an election through voting power. We have to do it through our contribution power. And it works!"

O'Donnell's reluctance to fully activate ALPA's financial power in politics through the PAC was understandable. Although O'Donnell lined up with Democrats for _practical_ reasons, he was a closet Republican and like most pilots, _emotionally_ attached to the conservative view. The hard realities of politics meant that ALPA-PAC's funds, to be effective, would have to go mostly to _Democrats_. Confronted with this conundrum, O'Donnell froze at the controls, figuratively speaking.

By the mid-1980s, as ALPA staggered under the adverse effect of deregulation, recession, and the Lorenzo wars, taking ALPA into the political thicket via the PAC was not only easier, but politically imperative for Duffy. No clearer evidence can be found of this changing mood, and the sense of betrayal that encouraged PAC contributions, than a letter that Republic Airlines MEC Chairman Richard A. Brown sent to Ronald Reagan in 1983.

"Most of the Republic pilot group supported you and the Republican Party with money and time in 1980," Brown wrote in this official letter sanctioned by ALPA national."What Mr. Lorenzo is doing may be legal under the bankruptcy laws, but to airline employees, it is certainly immoral. Mr. President, in your 1980 campaign, you exhibited pride in having been a union officer for the Screen Actors Guild. Are we naive in even hoping to gain your support? To permit your administration to support union-busting risks losing the few unions that have supported you in the past. Though it would be difficult for us as a group to switch our allegiance, it may be our only course of action to preserve our jobs."

Only money gave meaning to Brown's threat. Certainly Hank Duffy's long association with the GOP as a County Chairman hadn't paid off.

"The Reagan people just didn't care about labor," Duffy declares flatly. "They were so right-wing. That was not the Republican Party I had known. I thought we had a chance with Bush, but it was just shifting color, a shading, still right-wing. We got to him personally, and he did send a message back saying that his veto of the Eastern bill was not aimed at the pilots. We wouldn't have gotten that polite response from Reagan. He would have just said, 'Screw you, guys.'"

As professional airline pilots began flying the line into the 1990s, a new political awareness emerged. In the summer of 1990, ALPA-PAC's Steering Committee, which consisted of Hank Duffy and First Vice-President Roger Hall as ex-officio members, plus Pat Broderick of Eastern, Andy Brown of Delta, Harry Hoglander of TWA, Jamie Lindsay of United, and Pete Pettigrew of USAir, had a formidable weapon at their disposal—money. Average donations of just over $100 per year by ALPA-PAC supporters, who make up slightly more than 20 percent of ALPA's total membership, put a powerful war chest of nearly $1 million per year at the Steering Committee's disposal. While ALPA-PAC made contributions purely on a politician's stands on issues relevant to ALPA and was, thus, nonpartisan, Democrats got _most_ of the money because they most often supported ALPA's position. That was the reality of politics that professional airline pilots had been forced to accept by the 1990s.

As this century draws to a close, it is time for professional airline pilots to recognize some hard political facts. From the point of view of organized labor, Teddy Roosevelt was just about the last friendly Republican to occupy the Oval Office. By income, education, and social inclination, pilots are _emotional_ Republicans. But the circumstances of their workplace require pilots to be _practical_ Democrats. Airline pilots who call themselves Republicans should constantly remind their fellow Republicans that their party has betrayed its historic legacy of fair play for unions. This legacy, which dates from the days of Teddy Roosevelt and whose proudest moment was the invention of the impartial fact-finding commission to investigate conflicts between management and labor, has been all but forgotten by Republican Presidents since Teddy Roosevelt.

Unlike George Bush, who walked away from flying and never again showed the least interest in it, Teddy was fascinated with airplanes. At St. Louis in 1910, while on a political visit to supporters urging him to enter the Presidential contest upcoming in 1912, Teddy visited a commercial airshow at Kinloch Park. While running his hands over the fabric wing surface of a Wright pusher Model B, Teddy wondered aloud what it would be like to fly. As President, he had gone down in the Navy's first commissioned submarine, while the nation held its breath. Arch Hoxsey, the legendary "Birdman," acting as the ex-President's host, volunteered to take him aloft. Teddy could never refuse a dare. Impetuously, he accepted. The flight lasted three minutes. Thousands of spectators gasped as Teddy, strapped bravely alongside Hoxsey, rode this primordial Air Force One skyward. Teddy later said it was "bully."

Professional airline pilots were about to rediscover the importance of having a friend in the White House. Frank Lorenzo had plans for the pilots of Continental Airlines that only a President like Teddy Roosevelt could have stopped. ✈

NOTE
[1] See "The National Airlines Strike of 1948" and "The Southern Airways Strike of 1960," _Flying the Line_, Chs. 13 & 18.

CHAPTER 13

THE ORIGINS OF THE CONTINENTAL STRIKE
Lorenzo Prepares His Blitzkrieg

To say that the pilots of Continental Airlines entered the lists against Frank Lorenzo in 1983 under unfavorable circumstances understates the problem. The Reagan Administration encouraged an antilabor climate, internal divisions marred the Continental pilots' sense of community, and the national economy was still suffering from the steep economic slide of the early 1980s. An old axiom holds that when the economy catches cold, the airline industry gets pneumonia. Because of government regulation before 1978, airline employees had been less vulnerable to the consequences of hard times than workers in other industries, but Frank Lorenzo planned to change that. Until 1980, he had to proceed cautiously because Jimmy Carter, although not as friendly to organized labor as previous Democratic Presidents, might make trouble. Lorenzo also had to be wary of ALPA's influence with Congress and the regulatory agencies before 1980.

ALPA's 1980 campaign against Lorenzo's "alter ego" airline, New York Air, justified his caution. Although the precise costs cannot be known for certain, ALPA's resistance to New York Air (and to his 1981 takeover of Continental) forced Lorenzo to spend millions in legal fees. Thus Lorenzo, accustomed to easier victories in his fights against the smaller TXI pilot group, received unexpectedly rough handling from the Continental pilot group and bore them an obvious grudge because of it.

"We knew the seriousness of the problem, we knew the TXI pilots weren't just crying wolf," remembers Continental's Dennis Duffy, who served as an ALPA executive vice-president (EVP) between 1982 and 1984. "But we also felt that they were beaten so badly that they had lost their will to fight. We were determined to fight, and we probably delayed his timetable by at least a year."

Throughout 1981, Continental's pilots mounted a strenuous lobbying campaign in both the California legislature and in Congress to block Lorenzo. They sought unsuccessfully to have Congress outlaw the leveraged-buyout (LBO) financial technique Lorenzo used (with the help of his money man, Michael Milken, the "junk bond king") to launch New York Air and acquire Continental. During the 1980s, Lorenzo would circulate in the same rarefied financial atmosphere as Ivan Boesky, the Wall Street shark who would (like Milken) later go to prison for his crimes. Both Boesky and Lorenzo were special and honored guests at Michael Milken's 1986 celebration in Los Angeles of their creative use of "junk bonds."

New York Air owed its existence to this new form of financing expansion through debt. By injecting a nonunion airline into the geographic and professional heart of the America's most heavily unionized industry, Lorenzo whetted the appetites of Wall Street sharks who saw the newly deregulated industry as vulnerable. Put simply, if the assets of an airline were worth more, separately, than the cumulative value of its stock, this new breed of financial buccaneers would borrow to buy it (the LBO), then sell off its assets piecemeal, often to subcontractors who would not respect existing union contracts. These corporate raiders would then pay off their lenders and pocket the difference. The catastrophic effect of LBOs on employees bothered neither the Lorenzos of this era nor the pliant Reagan Administration. In the name of "maximizing shareholder value" (itself fraudulent), they would tolerate putting long-term employees on the street.

New York Air, with its "Apple" call sign and logo, was the first bitter fruit of deregulation and a harbinger of the LBO menace. It began flying on Dec. 19, 1980, barely a month after Ronald Reagan's election. New York Air had a long gestation, partly because ALPA and its allies in organized labor fought it so hard from the moment of its filing with the Civil Aeronautics Board in August 1980, and partly because other airline managements joined the legal challenge although not for the same reasons.

Because of the extensive controversy over his "runaway shop" airline, Lorenzo postponed its debut until *after* his friend Ronald Reagan (for whom he had been an active fund raiser) had won election in November 1980. We must remember that an *explicit* element of the "Reagan Revolution" was a promise to bring "special interests" like "big labor" to heel. Lorenzo saw himself as the point man for this aspect of *Reagan's* crusade.

New York Air was a straightforward attempt to skim the cream from Eastern's East Coast shuttle operation. The *only* innovation Lorenzo brought to this project was low wages—to be accomplished through a nonunion workforce. Because he assembled New York Air largely from the internal resources of TXI (with "leased," repainted TXI aircraft and borrowed training facilities for the non-ALPA pilots), Lorenzo knew he would encounter stringent opposition from the entire national apparatus of organized labor. But he also knew that an Achilles heel was present in all this—airline pilots themselves.

Put simply, Lorenzo had learned the same lesson about pilots that Ulysses S. Grant had learned about Southerners during the Vicksburg campaign—that they would not scorch their earth. In 1941, the Russians left Hitler's armies only desolation as they retreated while awaiting their traditional allies—General Cold, Field Marshal Snow, and Admiral Ice. But during the U.S. Civil War, ordinary Southerners' loyalty to the Confederacy did not extend to burning their barns and slaughtering their livestock. Thus, for short periods, Grant learned he could cut loose from his train of supply and operate while living off the land, returning to his logistical base only to replenish ammunition. General William Tecumseh Sherman, Grant's subordinate, would apply this tactic with devastating effect upon the Confederacy during his celebrated march from Atlanta to the sea in 1864.

In retrospect, many observers believe that the *only* chance the TXI pilots and

ALPA had to stop New York Air (and Lorenzo) was a version of the scorched earth policy. If in the beginning TXI's pilots had taken the dramatic and risky step of an *immediate* strike, *with ALPA paying their full salaries*, Lorenzo might have blinked. By going on strike, the pilots would have shut TXI down at a crucial stage and thus deprived Texas Air Corporation (TAC), the newly created parent of both TXI and New York Air, of the revenues that were the key to Lorenzo's ability to borrow. By fully supporting such a strike financially, ALPA *might* have sufficiently unnerved Lorenzo's financial backers to dry up the lending he needed to sustain New York Air's early operations. ALPA would later, during the Continental strike, pay strike wages equivalent to the salaries Lorenzo was offering scabs. Such a tactic applied early against New York Air would have unmistakably demonstrated ALPA's resolve.

The basis for the strike would have been that by peeling off DC-9 aircraft from the TXI fleet, repainting them with New York Air colors, and crewing them with non-ALPA pilots hired strictly for that purpose, Lorenzo was violating the TXI pilots' "scope" clause. From the beginning of his tenure at TXI, Lorenzo had made a mockery of his pilots' labor contract. He would routinely violate it, then challenge the pilots to file grievances. The grievance process is time-consuming and expensive. When applied vindictively to wear a small pilot group down, the cumulative effect can be devastating.

"We learned that this guy breaks the rules," says former MEC Chairman Dennis Higgins of Lorenzo. "He pulls some cute trick and then says 'sue me.'"

Because of such tactics, the TXI pilots were simply too battered to strike Lorenzo in 1980. Also, J.J. O'Donnell had come to the conclusion, following the Wien fiasco, that strikes were ineffective. He much preferred litigation to direct action, and TXI's pilots, shell-shocked from their repeated confrontations with Lorenzo in the late 1970s, readily agreed. So the pilots would wage no scorched-earth strike over New York Air.

Lorenzo had won his early confrontations with the TXI pilot group hands down, and he knew that with the weak economy, the Continental pilots were also unlikely to resort to the desperate expedient of a strike. Lorenzo knew how to manipulate pilots, using techniques that would have been familiar to the Old Guys who had built ALPA a generation earlier. Pioneer airline bosses understood their pilots' managerial mentality, and they knew that given the slightest evidence of good faith, pilots would quickly join forces to build an airline, sometimes quite literally working themselves to death in the process.

Lorenzo had little else in common with the pioneer airline founders, but he was an expert at faking "good faith," and he understood that people who fly the line *want* to believe in management. Lorenzo was a smooth practitioner of the "Lucy Syndrome." Lucy, the cartoon character in the comic strip "Peanuts," would invariably swear that she would not move the football just as Charlie Brown tried to placekick it. She kept promising, he kept believing, and she kept jerking the football away. Lorenzo would violate agreements and then turn on his legendary "smooth talk" to charm pilots with new promises. Then, like Lucy, he would jerk the football away, depositing his pilots once again on their rumps.

The TXI pilots eventually figured Lorenzo out, but at the time desperate action became necessary in the New York Air case, they simply lacked the stomach for it. Instead of striking, the TXI pilots waged a lengthy slowdown, called in sick well past the limit permissible under their contract, and challenged New York Air in court for violating the "scope" clause of their contract.

"We decided to stay put, sitting in our cockpits while fighting our fights with Lorenzo," says Dennis Higgins, MEC chairman at the time.

Lorenzo sued over the "sick in," won every round in court, and thrashed ALPA solidly. New York Air would survive every challenge until Lorenzo folded it into Continental after the strike—thus proving that the airline was, as ALPA had always maintained, merely antiunion corporate thimble-rigging.

When the crisis on Continental emerged in August 1983, the stresses of merging still affected the pilot group. Continental's pilots were determined to preserve their contract from Lorenzo's bullying, and their new TXI colleagues had every reason to support them.

Because Lorenzo had targeted his pilots, he became a close student of what made them tick. He had to know that the ancient factors that made pilots, when united, formidable would soon emerge to limit his freedom of action on Continental.

In fact, the process of melding and fence-mending among Continental's pilots (after an admittedly rocky start) made good progress. Neither the "old" Continental pilots nor the TXI newcomers were fools—they knew that unity was a prerequisite for dealing with Lorenzo. They were also professionals who understood that mergers were an unavoidable consequence of the modern airline industry, which no amount of bellyaching would change. Like other professional airline pilots on other airlines in other times, the pilots of "old" Continental and TXI would, given enough time to work things out, put aside their differences and get on with the business of flying the line.

Frank Lorenzo's challenge was to keep his pilots off balance while he maneuvered to destroy their contract. Continental's MEC Chairman Larry Baxter, as even his detractors admitted, was tough, intelligent, and far from naive about Lorenzo. He moved rapidly to devise a strategy to counter Lorenzo and, in fact, fought an excellent delaying campaign that stymied Lorenzo for many months. Had it not been for the pressure and timing of events ("fate," if you will), Baxter might have succeeded. How he failed must now concern us.

The story begins with the ill-fated "Prosperity Plan," Lorenzo's highly touted opening gambit. Continental's pilots knew that the airline was in precarious financial condition even before the advent of Frank Lorenzo and the merger with TXI. This financial weakness was at least partially responsible for the failed Employee Stock Ownership Plan (ESOP).

Desperate to block Lorenzo's takeover of their ailing carrier, Continental's unionized employees, under the leadership of Paul Eckel, a Continental management pilot who was widely respected by the airline's ALPA pilots, launched the first serious effort at an employee buyout in the airline industry's history. Despite the full support of Al Feldman, Bob Six, and Continental's top management, Eckel could not persuade lenders that an enterprise the size of the Continental could (or should) be run by its employees.

"Under Paul Eckel as chief pilot, life was pleasant," recalls former ALPA EVP Phil Nash. "He was a very fair, bright, vibrant guy."

Eckel's qualifications were so strong and the support he generated among Continental's unionized employees was so widespread that many Continental pilots attribute the ESOP's failure to a sinister antilabor conspiracy among bankers. Lorenzo, seriously worried about the possibility that the ESOP might succeed, fought it bitterly, undoubtedly using his influence to discourage potential ESOP lenders. His argument against the ESOP stands clearly revealed in an April 21, 1981, letter that Al Feldman (Bob Six's chosen successor as CEO of Continental), wrote to Lorenzo.

"Your continued assertion that the ESOP is no more than an effort to maintain entrenched, inefficient management is ludicrous," Feldman said. "From the outset, you have been urging me to operate the combined carrier. If we had really wanted to entrench ourselves, all we had to do was permit you the easy takeover of Continental you seek. Your assertion that the ESOP is being foisted by management on our employees is an insult to them. The ESOP is the result of their own dedication and enthusiasm to control their own destiny. Bob [Six] and I have concluded it is a great idea, a model for the industry, not simply an attack on your efforts to take control."

With the collapse of Eckel's ESOP effort on Continental in April 1981, Frank Lorenzo's takeover became inevitable. When he finally seized the prize, on Aug. 9, 1981, a distraught Al Feldman put a pistol to his own head.

During Lorenzo's hostile leveraged buyout of Continental, his duplicity fooled no one, although he tried to reassure people. In a letter to AL Feldman dated March 13, 1981, Lorenzo wrote: "We would expect that the [merger] agreement would protect the most valuable resources of our two companies—our employees."

Aside from his gushing praise of Bob Six ("we have long admired Bob Six's creative leadership"), Lorenzo's merger letters are chiefly interesting because he habitually referred to himself as "we." Mark Twain once said that one should beware of any man who uses the "royal we" when referring to himself—unless of course, he has a tapeworm.

In any case, Lorenzo didn't fool old Bob Six, ailing with heart trouble though he was. On April 24, 1981, in his capacity as chairman of Continental's Board, Six showed great prescience when he denounced Lorenzo's "junk bond" method of acquiring Continental.

"Frank, I find your [merger] proposal would create a company so overburdened with debt that it would, in my judgment, be unfair to the employees," Six wrote. "The bottom line is you are asking our employees to help pay for your purchase of Continental. That is clearly unfair."

But old Bob Six came from another generation and another era, a time when some degree of fair play seemed to matter in corporate boardrooms. To Frank Lorenzo, a representative of the new corporate ethic of the "greed decade" of the 1980s, Six's values were anachronistic.

So Frank Lorenzo outmaneuvered everybody and acquired control of one of the proudest names in airline history. He wasted no time in proving Bob Six a prophet—Lorenzo would make his employees pay for their own airline.

Lorenzo's initial target would be the International Association of Machinists (IAM). But before he took them on, Lorenzo needed to temporarily neutralize ALPA—hence the "Prosperity Plan." Easily slipping into his "Frankie Smooth Talk" persona, Lorenzo wooed Continental's pilots with promises of a golden future *if they would only make sacrifices*. By August 1982, he succeeded in wringing additional concessions out of a pilot group that had already made substantial givebacks during the pre-Lorenzo period.

Then, the "Lucy Syndrome" kicked in. In January 1983, with the Prosperity Plan only recently in place, Lorenzo demanded additional concessions. Continental's pilots, like Charlie Brown with Lucy, believed they had a deal with Frank Lorenzo. But their $100 million giveback over a two-year period wasn't enough, Lorenzo said, even though it gave him work rules concessions that resulted in some 400 furloughs and reductions in funding of the pilots' pension plan.

MEC Chairman Larry Baxter, who had played a crucial role in selling the Prosperity Plan to a reluctant rank and file, felt betrayed. During 1982–83, two Negotiating Committees, composed of a rotating cast made up of Scott Henderson, John Huber, Dennis Duffy, Kirby Schnell, Guy Casey, and Lou Colombo, wrestled with Lorenzo's demands as they tried to find a way to save their airline without sacrificing their contract.

After agreeing to the Prosperity Plan, Continental's pilots had swallowed hard, rolled up their sleeves, and prepared to live with it. Then they discovered, just as the TXI pilots had warned them, that signed contracts meant nothing to Lorenzo. The effect on Larry Baxter was particularly devastating.

"Larry was a highly intelligent individual who could be quite persuasive," says Guy Casey, who would later become strike coordinator. "But he misjudged Lorenzo, in that he felt Lorenzo did have some moral character."

Phil Nash, who was an ALPA EVP at the time and never a fan of Baxter's, called the Prosperity Plan "an accommodation with the devil," a view shared by most rank-and-file pilots. "We were going to have to live with it, and we would have. Then Frank came back to us for the second money in January, and then the third money in June. I smelled a rat."

The rat Phil Nash smelled (although nobody knew it at the time) was Lorenzo's underlying purpose in negotiating the Prosperity Plan. Put simply, Lorenzo wanted to keep his pilots off balance while he destroyed the IAM, *exactly* the pattern he had used earlier at TXI. He offered the mechanics a raise if they would permit "outsourcing," a fancy name for subcontracting their work out to nonunion shops. Naturally the IAM resisted, for Lorenzo's plan would eventually lead to the layoff of about half their members. While he dragged out the IAM negotiations, Lorenzo feverishly trained scab mechanics.

Matters came to a head in a confusing welter of events in August and September 1983. In the midst of his carefully laid plans to break the IAM while flying through a strike with his pilots' support, Lorenzo abruptly changed course. This change originated in Lorenzo's desperate need to service the enormous debt he had undertaken in the purchase of Continental—the debt Bob Six had warned about. Although Lorenzo claimed Continental was broke, its parent corporation, TAC, boasted $288 million in cash, securities, and accounts receivable (with virtually no debt), *according to his own filing with the bankruptcy court*! It was a preview of the "upstreaming" technique Lorenzo would later use to strip Eastern's assets before the strike of 1989. Lorenzo's corporate shell game permitted him to shield assets in TAC, while arguing that high labor costs were breaking the very companies that generated the cash he "upstreamed" to his holding company. But Lorenzo told the *New York Times* that debt wasn't his problem. "Our sole problem is high labor costs," Lorenzo said.

The IAM struck Lorenzo on Aug. 13, 1983. Continental's pilots honored their contract and continued flying, largely because Lorenzo threatened to take the airline into bankruptcy otherwise. Immediately upon seeing that the pilots and flight attendants would cross the IAM's picket lines, Lorenzo pushed his psychological advantage by demanding further concessions.

While not refusing Lorenzo's demands outright, Continental's pilots wanted him to at least prove his financial need. For months they had asked him to "open the books" and to agree to joint meetings with the airline's lenders. Lorenzo finally did open his books after a fashion, but he steadfastly refused to permit joint meetings between the holders of his debt and his unions.

Lorenzo's resort to bankruptcy followed a precedent set by Universal Airlines (Zantop) to break its ALPA contract in 1971. As tensions with the IAM mounted, Lorenzo hired the New York law firm Weil, Gotshal, and Manges, which specialized in bankruptcies, to take Continental into Chapter 11. This action would permit Lorenzo not only to suspend payments on his debts (one of the first of a wave of junk bond failures that would help bring down the U.S. savings and loan industry at the end of the 1980s) but break his unions as well.

So to recap, during the prolonged maneuvering of 1983, Continental's pilots found out that the TXI pilots weren't exaggerating about Lorenzo. He reneged on "Prosperity Plan I" almost before the ink was dry and demanded "Prosperity Plan II," which involved further concessions. MEC Chairman Larry Baxter stalled off Lorenzo's demands from January to August 1983. Meanwhile, Lorenzo attacked the flight attendants and mechanics, finally provoking the IAM's August strike. A critical decision now faced the Continental pilot group—should they cross the IAM's pickets, or should they be good labor unionists?

"When the IAM went out on Continental, I did roadshows urging them to honor the lines," recalls Hank Duffy, who was still relatively new to the job of ALPA president. "They rejected what I said."

One reason the Continental pilots decided to honor their contract and cross the IAM's picket lines had to do with that union's sorry history of internal unity in strike situations. Historically, the IAM has not been able to control its own membership. Many Continental pilots felt that the strike on their airline would see large numbers of crossovers among the mechanics, and that the IAM was a very weak reed to lean on in a critical situation, a point with which Hank Duffy could only agree.

"When I made the roadshows, I knew that the IAM had not delivered when they went out," Duffy says in explanation of the Continental pilots snubbing his advice. "On Alaska, their own units crossed them; the main mechanic unit stayed out, but the crew scheduling unit went across. They couldn't even hold their own people."

Duffy, mindful of this IAM trait (one that would figure prominently in the Eastern strike of 1989), certainly was not as forceful in his roadshow advice as he could have been. The Continental pilot group had a history of crossing other unions' picket lines, but this time it was a very close decision, made with grave misgivings and at the price of much internal distress.

"I came on the MEC in late June, just as it got called into session to handle the issue of the IAM strike," recalls Phil Nash, who served as ALPA EVP from 1980 to 1982. "My pilots didn't have a stern resolve to stop Lorenzo then. It was the 'Frank's a bad dude, we'd-better-do-anything-he-wants' syndrome. So we crossed the picket line, and so did everybody else, including a large percentage of the IAM guys. It smelled real bad, and I felt bad—I couldn't even look those guys in the face. Some of my pilots didn't want to come to work; they called in sick. Some of the pilots who had been mechanics said we were lily-livered, and others called me an idiot for voting to go on strike. I took guff from both ends."

From the beginning of the IAM strike on August 13, Continental's MEC was in almost continuous session, dealing with a series of emergency demands from management.

Then on Sept. 11, 1983, under the signature of Stephen Wolf, Lorenzo's titular president of Continental, an apocalyptic telegram went out to all Continental pilots _over the head of the MEC_, with hand deliveries to ALPA's national officers. Wolf demanded an additional $60 million in pilot givebacks, "all or nothing," over the previously negotiated $100 million.

"We have to get our costs down," Wolf said. "Today's marketplace prices are being set by Southwest Airlines, which is trying to drive us out of market after market."

"That was funny," recalls Dennis Duffy. "He told us Southwest was beating us to death. So we took a Southwest contract, ripped the cover off, and put a Continental cover on it. We said we'd sign it just like it is. They sent it back to us, wouldn't touch it."

At this point, Continental's pilot leaders, fearing for the future of their airline, were in same the kind of whip-sawed state that Lorenzo had previously induced among TXI's pilots. Rank-and-file pilots divided all over the lot, with some urging surrender while others wanted war. Larry Baxter wanted nothing further to do with Lorenzo. He became moody and uncommunicative, leaving the Negotiating Committee adrift.

"Baxter's attitude was we gave Frank enough," recalls Phil Nash. "He embarrassed Frank by telling him, 'In less than ten months, you've gone through a hundred million? You said you could run an airline with that, now go run an airline!'"

Meanwhile Lorenzo kept pressing. He set a deadline of 4 p.m. on Saturday, Sept. 24, 1983, for the pilots to capitulate. Either they would abandon their contact, or he would file for bankruptcy.

The astounding thing about the 1983 Continental strike is that the pilots _did_ _capitulate_! During frantic negotiations that began with the IAM strike, and intensified meetings in September (brought on by Lorenzo's threat to file for bankruptcy), the Negotiating Committee publicly committed Continental's pilots to "do whatever it takes" to save their airline. Lou Columbo, who chaired the Committee, made that explicitly clear as early as September 19, when he told company negotiators formally: "We are not limited. We are committed to _do whatever it takes_ (emphasis added) to return this airline to profitability."

The white flag was up, but Lorenzo, already secretly committed to his bankruptcy strategy, would take no prisoners. Instead, he used the trumped-up excuse of MEC Chairman Larry Baxter's lack of formal communication with him to reject Columbo's offer. Although Baxter, moody and withdrawn, argued that the pilots had a valid contact and needn't negotiate further, Continental's Negotiating Committee thought otherwise. Baxter, sulking in his tent, was not involved in the late September round of negotiations. During a meeting at the Greenspoint Marriott Hotel in Houston on September 23, Continental's negotiating team accused the pilots of a "refusal to participate," citing Baxter's absence.

"Unless you give us a firm proposal," said John Adams, Continental's negotiator, "we must conclude that you won't give us anything. We have an _immediate and permanent_ requirement to lower costs."

For Lou Columbo and his fellow negotiators, the only real question was _how_ to implement the concessions Lorenzo wanted and _what_ technical steps had to be taken to insert them into their existing contract. The historical record is clear and unequivocal on these points: Lorenzo had no intention of agreeing to anything; he had already decided to take his airline into bankruptcy; he wanted a "blank check"' from his pilots instead of a contract; and he expected them to "fly to the FARs."

In short, evidence shows that Larry Baxter was absolutely right—no amount of good-faith bargaining would have deterred Lorenzo. During one frantic session preceding the strike, Stephen M. Wolf, the Lorenzo lieutenant who would later become United's boss, did something remarkable.

"We were in the room negotiating when Wolf walked in and asked us—Lou Columbo, Kirby Schnell, and myself—to take a 10-minute recess," recalls Dennis Duffy. "'Gentlemen,' he says, 'I have just resigned from Continental. I won't be part of this,' and he walked away. The girls [flight attendants] told Wolf they were with us on the 'do whatever it takes' thing. Wolf thought that was enough, but Lorenzo wouldn't accept it."

"Lorenzo pulled Wolf from his team at a very strategic point," agrees Seth Rosen, the ALPA staff lawyer assigned to Continental, who believes it was a case of Wolf jumping ship before Lorenzo pushed him. "It was a real blow because we had confidence in Wolf. Once Wolf was out of the picture, Lorenzo wasn't doing anything except trying to figure out a way to break the contract."

The Continental pilot negotiators, flabbergasted at this turn of events, nevertheless continued good-faith bargaining. It all came to a head in one final bizarre episode. Lorenzo demanded that Larry Baxter _personally_ respond to his specific demands by phone, no later than 4 p.m. on Friday, September 23. Under severe stress, and at the urging of his Negotiating Committee, Baxter finally did make the call, only to be told that it was too late—he had missed Lorenzo's deadline by a few minutes!

"You mean to say that even with a big chunk from the pilots and from the girls [the Union of Flight Attendants], he would shut it down?" asked an incredulous Lou Columbo of Tom Matthews, Lorenzo's representative.

"He will do it," said Matthews.

"We're working with two crazies," Columbo screamed. "For one phone call, you sacrifice 12,000 jobs!"

Seth Rosen, the ALPA staff attorney, who met frequently with Lorenzo during 1981–83, believes the pilots never had any chance of averting bankruptcy.

"Lorenzo kept upping the ante that summer," Rosen says. "Every time we saw him, Lorenzo became less precise, more general. We ended up with double talk. Where he wanted relief, it was much greater than the dollars attributed to it. He was really setting us up for bankruptcy. When he got to court, he would have this track record of having made all these requests, that he was acting in a good-faith manner, when he was really engaging in a lot of superficial nonsense."

At 6:30 p.m. on Sept. 24, 1983, in the dry, technical language of law, Continental filed for "reorganization" under Chapter 11 of the U.S. Bankruptcy Code in Houston, Texas. Throughout the United States and overseas, Continental's video terminals went blank, and flights were canceled, stranding stunned passengers and crews alike. Coming hard on the heels of Braniff's 1982 bankruptcy, Continental's action seemed to foreshadow the doom of an industry.

Continental's pilots, now massing in unaccustomed numbers on the ground, were shocked, full of disbelief and anger. Everybody wanted answers; nobody had any. Confusion reigned.

Lorenzo, simultaneously with his bankruptcy petition, promulgated Continental's new "Emergency Work Rules," which would replace ALPA's contract. The new rules called for drastic 50 percent pay cuts, increases in duty time, and out-of-seniority flying. Through the weekend, Continental's pilots held mass meetings, anxiously awaiting "the word" from their MEC and ALPA's national officers. On Monday, September 26, following consultations with ALPA's attorneys, Continental's leaders declared that their existing contract remained in effect. What should line pilots do then, with respect to the company's limited, out-of-seniority callback?

In what everybody later agreed was a mistake, Continental's MEC, operating in conditions approximating the "fog of war," told pilots to return to their cockpits "under duress." During the 72-hour shutdown, Lorenzo had restructured his airline to cover only about 40 per cent of the pre-bankruptcy operation. He offered *outrageously* low $49 fares (to all destinations) to entice customers back to Continental and recalled pilots to suit his needs, not the contract's. The few pilots who were recalled following this 72-hour shutdown were "in the castle," so to speak, psychologically scabs already, with ALPA's consent. Many would not come out.

On September 29, an emergency meeting of ALPA's Executive Board convened in Houston at the Sheraton Crown Hotel. United's Chuck Pierce, ALPA's secretary, announced that the meeting was closed to the news media. Hank

Duffy took the rostrum to preside over one of the tensest meetings in ALPA's history. Significantly, his first action was to recognize the presence of Capt. Bob Malone of American, who was formally representing the Allied Pilots Association. The industry's crisis, building since deregulation, had brought the APA home, if only temporarily.

"The crisis in our industry, as evidenced in Denver [a reference to Frontier's threat to create "Frontier Horizon," an alter-ego airline similar to New York Air], as evidenced in Miami [a reference to Eastern's on-going crisis], and especially as evidenced here in Houston," Duffy warned solemnly, "is starting to engulf all of us. For five years, we have been complaining about deregulation. In April, we told Congress that this industry is unraveling. In the month of September, our testimony has become prophesy. My assessment is that we have been too understanding, too trusting, and most of all, too patient. The airline pilots of this country are going to have to stand up and act like a labor union if we are going to save this industry."

Hank Duffy's charge to the Executive Board struck a responsive chord. Following presentations from the MEC chairmen of each of the three most threatened airlines, Larry Baxter of Continental, Wes Davis of Frontier, and George Smith of Eastern, the assembled Executive Board delegates unanimously and virtually without discussion approved drastic measures. For Continental's pilots, ALPA would modify its strike benefit policy to pay each pilot striker an amount comparable to the salary Lorenzo was paying under his "Emergency Work Rules." Lorenzo proposed to halve the compensation called for in the Continental contract, paying captains $3,585 per month and the new "pilot officers" (he dispensed with distinctions between first officers and second officers), $2,335 per month. Subsequent to approval by a mail ballot of the membership (with immediate "loans" that would be wiped out once the vote was official), striking Continental captains would receive $3,800 per month, while first and second officers would receive $2,500—to be paid for by special strike assessments the membership would vote to impose upon itself.

With extraordinary strike benefits approved, the balance of the Executive Board's work was devoted to a discussion of a possible suspension of service (SOS), "ALPA's nuke." Under the direction of TWA's Harry Hoglander, the Executive Board approved an SOS, but only with a membership ballot and only "after suitable education" of the membership. Nobody wanted to call another SOS and then have it fizzle.

The delegates agreed with Hank Duffy when he said: "I am occasionally soft-spoken, but that doesn't reflect the anger I feel at the management of Continental and Frontier _and at a government that has not been responsive to us. I will not hesitate use the full force of everything you have given me, including the SOS._" But, Duffy continued, "those of you who have been through an SOS before know that it is a long way from here to getting the line pilot to do it. If we could have had the collective membership here to listen to Moffitt Tinsley today, I have no doubt that we would march 34,000 strong in the same direction."

Duffy's reference to Moffitt Tinsley deserves explanation. Tinsley, a Continental pilot since 1968 and a first officer representative on the MEC, moved the

Executive Board delegates in a way they will always remember, not with bombast, but with sober, honest confession and a call for renewal that was almost religious in its intensity.

"I had no intention of speaking,"Tinsley remembers."I had attended several meetings, and I'd never stepped up to a microphone to make any utterance.J.J. O'Donnell once asked me, jokingly, if I was every going to have anything to say. Before the debate on strike benefits, Larry Baxter said, 'Moffitt, I want you to make a speech.' I had all of five minutes to think about what I was going to say."

With unforced eloquence and passion, Tinsley summed up what being an airline pilot meant to him. He said that he had never wanted to be anything else, that he prized being part of the brotherhood of the air above all else. Then, with great contrition, Tinsley noted that he had betrayed the brotherhood during the Braniff bankruptcy, that his first reaction was, "Gee, I wonder if Continental's going to pick up the South American routes and will this make me a captain?" Tinsley's frankness touched deep wellsprings of feeling, and his call to redeem the profession handed to them by the Old Guys who had sacrificed so much provided a unifying theme.

Airline pilots in general and the Continental pilots in particular would need stirring words like Tinsley's in the ordeal to come. On September 29, the same day the Executive Board met, Continental's MEC voted to "withdraw from service" as of Oct. 1, 1983.

The strike was on.

CHAPTER 14

THE CONTINENTAL STRIKE
ALPA's Dark Night of the Soul

In June 1992, the U.S. Senate failed to end a Republican filibuster to block passage of a law that would have protected workers against being "permanently replaced" during a strike. George Bush had vowed to veto it in any case, but 36 GOP senators saved him the trouble by talking the law to death, even though it would have exempted employers who agreed to arbitration. Because professional airline pilots had recently suffered "permanent replacement" during the "Lorenzo Wars" on Continental and Eastern, ALPA lobbied strongly for a political solution to the problem. As old Dave Behncke knew, politics matters—particularly in a fight.

ALPA had gotten into a *real* fight with Frank Lorenzo in 1983. For the 1,000 Continental pilots who stuck it out to the bitter end (Continental counted 2,000 pilots—1,600 active and 400 furloughed, at the time of the strike), a friend in the White House might have made a difference. National Airlines pilots had Harry Truman in 1948, the Southern pilots had John F. Kennedy in 1963. But the Continental pilots would have no such luck with Ronald Reagan.

Being "permanently replaced" has always been the single greatest fear of any union member during a strike. The Railway Labor Act of 1926 and the so-called "pilots' amendment" to it in 1936 provided legal machinery that lessened, but did not entirely eliminate, the possibility of "permanent replacement." Political times unfriendly to labor (as the Reagan–Bush years most emphatically were) greatly increased the likelihood of this most devastating of strike outcomes. That's why Democrats friendly to organized labor in 1992 sought to pass a law to protect future workers against what Frank Lorenzo had done to his pilots.

The Continental strike began in a welter of confusion and disarray. On the union side, nobody was ready for it, no plans had been made, no communications were established, and nobody knew what to do. Continental's pilots had to immediately shift gears from thinking about how to make their airline work to thinking the unthinkable—how to *stop* it from working. It was a wrenching transition.

The most appropriate historical analogy to the Continental Strike of 1983–85 would be the outbreak of the Korean War in 1950. The United States then had no combat units on the Korean peninsula, and the only forces available were poorly trained garrison troops in Japan, unaccustomed to field operations. General MacArthur threw in typewriter clerks and motor pool mechanics piecemeal, to be ground up while they tried to remember how to field-strip an M-1 rifle—a weapon most of them hadn't touched since boot camp. With the United Nations forces crushed back to the Pusan Perimeter at the southeastern tip of the Korean peninsula, the enemy juggernaut stood poised for victory. Then MacArthur rallied, staged the brilliant end-run amphibious landing at Inchon, and won the war—temporarily. Had MacArthur not crossed the 38th parallel and pressed on to the Yalu River, the summer of 1950 would be remembered today as a victory without parallel for American arms.

Perhaps the unhappy outcome of MacArthur's post-Inchon march to the Manchurian border explains why George Bush ended Desert Storm so abruptly in 1991. He apparently didn't want to risk his partial victory and be mistaken for another Douglas MacArthur. He won't be. At the end of Desert Storm, Saddam Hussein still ruled Iraq, and George Bush contented himself with other victories, among them (as professional airline pilots will always remember), a veto of congressional legislation that would have created a Presidential Emergency Board (PEB) to investigate ALPA's final "Lorenzo War," the Eastern strike of 1989. In all probability, this PEB would have settled the Eastern strike in ALPA's favor. PEB intervention had saved ALPA's bacon in similar strikes before. In some faraway old-pilots' Valhalla, Dave Behncke must surely have been repeating what he said so often in life—"politics matters."

The Continental strike of 1983–1985 would have no Inchon Landing to redeem it. Continental's pilots took terrific losses in the early going while they got their internal problems sorted out, then rallied in their own version of the Pusan Perimeter for a while, only to suffer crushing reverses in the courts. Following the Bildisco Decision of February 1984 (which we will discuss shortly), only the hard core of Continental pilots held out against Lorenzo. If the result wasn't total defeat, it clearly wasn't victory either. The hard core hunkered down, doggedly kept faith with each other, and ALPA finally secured their reinstatement—the much maligned "Order and Award" of Oct. 31, 1985 (grimly nicknamed the "Surrender Agreement"), which satisfied nobody. Getting 1,000 loyal ALPA members back into their cockpits, however bloodied, constituted a victory of sorts, even though they returned to work without the ALPA contract that had caused the strike in the first place.

Lorenzo's bankruptcy court tactics and the judge's tilting of the playing field in Lorenzo's favor would permit him to fly through the strike, but we must remember that historically, any airline boss determined to scab out his pilots has always succeeded in doing so. ALPA has _never_ won any strike in its history on pure economic muscle alone, or because a determined opponent like Frank Lorenzo couldn't find pilots willing to cross picket lines. Even in 1932, at the profession's beginning, when the sense of brotherhood among airmen was very strong, E.L. Cord was able to staff his Century Airlines against the determined opposition of Dave Behncke _and_ a Congress friendly to organized labor. In 1983, Hank Duffy faced a vastly different situation, one that cried out for a pro-labor President in the White House.

The Reagan Administration created a hostile political climate nationally, which, had it existed during any other ALPA strike historically, would almost certainly have resulted in a crushing defeat. In addition, deregulation spawned a witches' brew of collateral problems that ALPA had never faced in a strike situation. A festering problem on Frontier, whose management was threatening to create Frontier Horizon, an alter-ego airline similar to New York Air, preoccupied ALPA's national officers. At the time of Lorenzo's bankruptcy filing, the September 1983 issue of *Air Line Pilot* was devoted almost exclusively to Frontier Horizon, which would remain a threat until Frontier itself died. Meanwhile, Frank Lorenzo got a free ride at Continental.

So Hank Duffy would receive a rough baptism in this first great crisis of his presidency, as he fought Lorenzo through a thicket of bankruptcy court decrees no other ALPA strike effort had ever encountered. In the long run, ALPA could claim a qualified victory in that Congress changed the bankruptcy law to prevent any future Lorenzo-style use of it for union-busting. But in the short run and as viewed from the trenches by striking Continental pilots, long-term victories were hard to appreciate.

Events that occurred in the first three weeks of the Continental strike almost foreordained its unhappy outcome. As we have seen, Continental's dazed MEC told pilots to report to work "under duress" (whatever that meant), following the initial 72-hour bankruptcy shutdown. Lorenzo would not have been able to fly the schedule he planned if the Continental MEC had ordered a walkout *from the start.* When the Continental MEC belatedly initiated the strike three days later, on October 1, some pilots, accustomed by now to Lorenzo's Emergency Work Rules, stayed in their cockpits. This group (about 75 pilots) would be joined by approximately 200 more crossovers in October. These "October scabs" would split almost evenly between former TXI and "old" Continental pilots. One of those "urban legends" that plagued the strike effort had a higher number of TXI pilots scabbing than "old" Continental pilots.

"It was quite common for the Continental pilots to believe the Texas guys were scabbing in greater numbers," recalls Guy Casey, the steady ex-USAF pilot who served as strike coordinator. "I had access to all the records, I checked on it, and it just wasn't true. I had to go around to all the bases where Continental pilots lived to tell them the percentages were basically the same."

So, with these pilots (about 20 percent of the prestrike workforce, counting the relatively large contingent of management pilots pressed into service), Lorenzo would be able to fly, if only just barely, about 20 percent of his prestrike schedule, despite ALPA's "job action." If weather delays had burned up crew time, Lorenzo would have faced an early shutdown. But placid high pressure dominated October's weather—a bad omen.

Lorenzo's success in getting that first group of pilots to cross during the early days of the strike owed much to the skill that earned him the nickname "Frankie Smooth Talk." Using a technique familiar to old TXI pilots, Lorenzo began to phone pilots *personally.* Armed with specific details about each pilot's family situation, such as whether he had a wife or child who might be ill, Lorenzo could be a formidable salesman. Rather than threats, Lorenzo's most effective tactic was to project a sense of concern, an earnestness that he really *needed* each pilot. Lorenzo had an undeniable gift for this kind of cajolery, as do all good salesmen. Lorenzo telephoned so many pilots, at all hours, that many wondered when he slept! It was devastatingly effective—Lorenzo's verbal magic even persuaded one member of Continental's MEC to cross!

"Look, Frank's a savvy guy, and he can really be slick," says Dennis Higgins, former TXI MEC chairman and veteran of many one-on-one confrontations with Lorenzo. "A guy would go home at night from the picket line a strong strike supporter, showing not a flaw in his defenses. The phone rings, and it's Frank Lorenzo! The pilot sits there with his mouth wide open, and Frank says, 'I want you to understand that I understand why you are doing what you're doing. All I want is a chance to explain why we are doing what we are doing, and also to let you know that I need you badly and that I want you to come back so we can put this thing back together just exactly the way you have envisioned.' Now if the guy hasn't hung up by this point, he's hooked! The next day, it's like he's kidnapped; we can't find him, and somebody reports he's crossed. Frank was good, you bet! The only defense was to say 'Merry Christmas, Frank,' and hang up before he started talking."

Certain aspects of the modern airline pilot's lifestyle also gave Lorenzo an advantage. Although no statistics exist to specifically prove it, a consensus of opinion holds that airline pilots tend to live up to the limit of their credit—and sometimes a little beyond. A lifestyle full of expensive toys, boats, and second homes left many Continental pilots "financially challenged." Lorenzo had sources that allowed him to target these pilots with his phone calls—particularly the divorced.

"As soon as a guy's captain bid comes out, he and his wife start looking for a captain's house," Dennis Higgins observes wryly. "Lots of guys were financed to the hilt, particularly those with second wives and new families. The wife would, in the privacy of the home, ask, 'Are we going to have to move out of the house, take the kids out of the private school, deliver a car back to the bank?' A pilot's got to carry the uncertainty of the strike home to her and be able to justify it when the phone rings and she says, 'It's Frank Lorenzo!'"

The "might-have-beens" of history, although fascinating, are usually fruitless. But there can be no doubt about the importance of those first few strikers Lorenzo personally persuaded to cross the line. There is a vast difference between the "October scabs" and those who succumbed to sheer hopelessness many months later, particularly after the Bildisco Decision, when it was apparent that Lorenzo would be able to sustain his operation with full approval of the federal courts.

If the Continental strikers had been able to hold those first critical 300 pilots on their side of the picket line in October, Lorenzo _almost certainly would have capitulated_. For three nervous weeks, Lorenzo trembled on the edge of defeat. He didn't have enough management pilots to fly his projected schedule for more than a few days, and the sheer logistics of requalification meant that he couldn't get enough of the 400 Continental furloughees or "off-the-street" new-hires into his cockpits in time to save the situation. In any case, Lorenzo didn't advertise for "permanent replacement" new-hires until November.

But as October progressed, he was getting enough picket-line crossers to hope that he might not have to hire any pilots "off the street."

"In the first two weeks, vast numbers were crossing the picket line," says Dennis Higgins. "There was a lot of concern as to whether we could get that hemorrhaging under control."

As things steadied, and when it looked like ALPA's lines were going to hold at the first batch of crossovers, Lorenzo would find pilots elsewhere. But he would have lost without those October "in-house" scabs, particularly a group of 110 who crossed during the third weekend of the strike when the MEC seemed to be in turmoil owing to the recall of Larry Baxter (which we will discuss shortly). As Lorenzo's skeleton pilot force nearly ran up against the maximum FAA-imposed flight time limits and a shutdown loomed during the closing days of the month, he grew desperate. Proof of Lorenzo's desperation lay in his quite uncharacteristic willingness to resume *serious* negotiations in late October.

"In the early stages, Lorenzo wasn't sure he was going to pull it off in terms of adequate numbers of pilots," believes Kirby Schnell, whose 553 combat missions as a Marine pilot in Vietnam engendered a toughness that would sustain him as the Continental pilots' Negotiating Committee chairman throughout the strike. "Once we stabilized our lines, the negotiations were probably as close to real as anything we ever had. But when large numbers of our own pilots started back to work [during the third week], from then on, Lorenzo's negotiating was nothing more than maintaining a posture for public consumption."

Once Lorenzo had survived that first month and he realized that he would have a breathing space in which to hire "permanent replacements," to tap into the reservoir of unemployed pilots who would unhesitatingly cross ALPA's pickets, negotiations became a sham. By November, the second month of the strike, only hard, remorseless struggle remained.

Although the conventional wisdom holds that after the first month the decks were stacked against the Continental pilots, they were not without weapons, and they made a good fight of it. The courts provided a promising avenue of attack. Because of Lorenzo's use of the bankruptcy laws, ALPA had standing as a litigant. Continental's pilots were creditors under the bankruptcy rules because Lorenzo owed them money for unpaid salaries and unfunded pensions. Furthermore, there was always the possibility that he would lose—that a judge would disallow cancellation of union contracts under the bankruptcy code. Eventually, as we shall see, these court actions would not turn out well for ALPA, but they did provide the fulcrum from which ALPA would exert leverage to force Lorenzo into court-ordered negotiations that would bring about the "Order and Award" settlement of 1985. But for many months to come, nobody could be sure of the outcome of these legal actions, so the war had to continue as if they didn't exist.

In another Korean War analogy, despite the fact that peace talks began at Panmunjom in July 1951, U.N. forces had to continue fighting for two more years, because nobody could be sure that the maddeningly slow negotiations would ever produce anything. The role of embittered, unemployed ex-Braniff pilots in this drama was as critical as the intervention of Chinese "volunteers" on the side of the defeated North Koreans.

"The big difference at Continental was that 4,000 surplus pilots were out there," Hank Duffy said sadly in his 1990 interview. "The Braniff pilots were pushing each other out of the way to get in."

Here again, a statesmanlike gesture on the part of Hank Duffy quite unintentionally aggravated the situation. When Braniff emerged from bankruptcy in March 1984, it did so under a new ALPA contract with pay and working conditions many striking Continental pilots thought equivalent to Lorenzo's. News of this new Braniff contract came almost simultaneously with the Bildisco Decision, angering many weary Continental pilots, who were wavering as their strike settled into its sixth month.

"My first involvement with Braniff was signing that contract," Hank Duffy explained later. "I debated it and decided I would bring that inferior contract in with an ALPA imprimatur. We held out for all the boilerplate, seniority, and grievance, but anything that cost money we just weren't going to get."

Duffy's contractual lenience toward Braniff's new owner, Jay Pritzker of Hyatt Hotel fame, struck many Continental strikers as oddly out of sync with ALPA's policy toward Lorenzo. Of course the great difference between the new Braniff contract and the conditions Lorenzo offered was that the Pritzkers *negotiated* with ALPA, whereas Lorenzo imposed his terms *unilaterally*. Duffy hoped that once Braniff was on its feet financially, the "B-scale" contract he signed could be upgraded. As it turned out, he was right, although in 1989, immediately after agreeing to the "industry standard" contract that the first agreement was calculated to procure, "Braniff II" would succumb to "Bankruptcy II."

So it all came to nothing, but that lay in the future. For the moment, the Continental pilot's view from the trenches lacked this foresight, and the substandard Braniff contract produced considerable grumbling on the picket line and an increased willingness to cross.

The peculiar nature of the strike's inception added another handicap. Repeatedly, Lorenzo would ask pilots he telephoned how they had voted on the strike. Lorenzo knew full well that there had been no formal strike ballot, merely a show of hands in crowded mass meetings at the various domiciles, under the kind of confused, "fog of war" conditions any combat veteran would remember.

"There never was a formal mail ballot," Guy Casey agrees, "but there were voice and hand votes at all the local council meetings, and they were all decidedly in favor of striking."

These expressions of mass sentiment in favor of fighting Lorenzo were so vociferous that many observers believe they distorted actual strike sentiment and silenced less committed pilots.

"The strike vote in Houston was like a college pep rally, rather than a union business meeting," complains one disaffected former ALPA member who still flies for Continental and prefers to remain anonymous.

His complaint has a certain validity, one that thoughtful observers believe magnified prostrike sentiment—a sure guarantee of later trouble. No strike can succeed without wholehearted support from the rank-and-file, and union leaders who invent such support take a grave risk. In Continental's case, there was ample reason to doubt the commitment of rank-and-file line pilots long before the strike began.

"The Continental pilots had a real history of not being good trade-union guys," says former Executive Vice-President Skip Eglet of Northwest, who like most pilots from that strife-wracked airline, became a close student of the subject. "They'd crossed both the flight attendants and the mechanics, so their rank-and-file pilot just wasn't prepared to respect a picket line."

Ironically, ALPA's offer to sustain the strikers financially, although an unaffected expression of good will and *technically* made independently of the Continental pilots' decision to walk out, similarly served to amplify a commitment that was far less certain than it appeared. ALPA's prestrike benefits policy at the time called for flat payments to each striker, regardless of rank.

"Our paying strikers the same as Lorenzo was a significant gamble," recalls Continental's Dennis Duffy, who was serving as an executive vice-president at the time. "But if we could have kept Lorenzo down for a week, he would have quit."

To ALPA's national officers, paying the Continental pilots not to work seemed the surest way to guarantee that they would stand solidly together. But there were long-range hazards in this short-range approach, as Guy Casey explains: "Striking captains would get captain pay, striking first officers would get first officer pay. But if a copilot crossed, he would get promoted and draw captain's pay."

So ALPA's policy of paying generous strike benefits was less effective than hoped and turned out to be a financial sieve as well. As the strike dragged on, the monthly strike assessments became an onerous burden and a divisive issue within ALPA. Generally, pilots from airlines that were doing relatively well, such as United, Delta, and Northwest, paid their assessments. Pilots from troubled airlines, like TWA and Eastern, did not. Making up the shortfall strained ALPA's financial resources tremendously and would lead to the creation of the Major Contingency Fund (MCF). ALPA's leaders hoped the MCF, a kind of permanent strike assessment, would eventually eliminate the need for specific strike assessments and the internal strife they generated.

"Strike benefits at Continental were enormous, and we learned that we needed a special contingency fund, a war chest," said Hank Duffy in his 1990 interview. "Before Continental, the cost of strikes had always been just strike benefits. But because of the bankruptcy aspects of Continental, we drew down the equity on the building [ALPA's Washington Office] and our financial reserves. Obviously, we couldn't do that anymore."

ALPA's BOD, in an unusual June 1985 special meeting, would recommend creation of the MCF, to be financed by dues increases of 1 percent of each member's income. The membership, finally convinced that deregulation and the turmoil it created in the industry warranted it, subsequently approved the MCF levy in August 1985 by mail ballot.

While a historian may see possible glimmers of success in several aspects of the Continental strike, for the pilots actually in the trenches, the view was a good deal murkier. The fall of MEC Chairman Larry Baxter provides a classic illustration. In mid-October 1983, as the Continental pilot group struggled to whip their strike effort into shape under crisis conditions, Baxter seemed to reach the limit of his endurance.The pressures on him were enormous.He had pursued a hard-line course of action with Lorenzo, and he had been wrong—Lorenzo wasn't bluffing. JFK once said, "Victory has a thousand fathers, but defeat is an orphan."The tragic result was that Baxter, father to this orphan, collapsed from exhaustion during a special Executive Committee meeting in Washington, D.C., where he had gone to present a strike budget for the national officers' approval.

Continental's MEC had no choice but to recall Baxter for what it believed were valid medical reasons. On October 13, in an emergency meeting at the Sheraton Hotel in Houston, the MEC replaced him with Dennis Higgins.The vote was unanimous.

"I was doing a little PR work, but I didn't have a title," Higgins remembers of the strike's first days [no former TXI pilot had been elected to the new combined MEC, but Higgins was their unofficial "minister without portfolio"]. "I got a call at two o'clock in the morning; I was home in bed; they wanted me down at the Sheraton, said they'd wait till I got there. I walked in, and they said, 'Larry's been removed for very private reasons, and we want to elect you.'"

Baxter would recover shortly and challenge his removal. But his support on the MEC had been eroding even before the events that caused his colleagues to think his removal medically justified. Higgins's sole demand as a condition for assuming the chairmanship was that Floyd Carpenter, the veteran TXI ALPA activist, have a seat on the Negotiating Committee.

Higgins' first task was to put into concrete terms Lou Columbo's "whatever it takes" pledge of September, which Baxter had resisted.Within 24 hours of taking over, Higgins had a proposal for $30 million in concessions approved by the MEC. But the turmoil on the MEC had unnerved a big batch of 110 shaky pilots, who crossed the line.This freshet of crossovers during the third week of the strike emboldened Lorenzo, who toughened his negotiating stance. So nothing came of the so-called "October Concessions."

"Upon taking over the MEC, the bleeding from our own ranks slowed down, and I could focus on finding a process that would put us across the table from Frank and get us back to work," Higgins declares. "I asked the leaders of other unions to jointly discuss a new negotiating initiative. I suggested we offer to return under the EWRs [emergency work rules] and at the 50 percent reduction in pay. We had to make a major jump like that. The other unions were unwilling, so I went ahead anyway."

But Lorenzo, encouraged by the poor solidarity ALPA was displaying through the first half of October, stalled for time. Until the Continental strikers proved they weren't going to totally collapse, Lorenzo would hang tough.ALPA would have to find another way to carry the war to him.

One promising avenue of attack proved to be a blind alley. Because Lorenzo's scaled-down strike operation included some new, high-profile international flights, ALPA tried cashing in on its overseas connections with various labor groups.The idea was that militant British, Australian, and Japanese unions, in the spirit of international solidarity, would refuse to service Continental aircraft, perhaps even capture a B-747, jack it up, pull the wheels off, and turn it into a permanent ground monument. The AFL-CIO supplied a consultant named Ernie Lee, who was supposed to coordinate this overseas campaign against Lorenzo.

"That was a big fizzle," Hank Duffy recalls sourly. "Lee made trips, accompanied by Continental pilots, to talk to all the unions. We were told that the Australians and British labor unions could do things for us. What you quickly find out is that you don't ask people to do things you can't do yourself. If we couldn't shut the damn airplanes down in this country, why should we ask them to do it in their country? Lorenzo's first airplane landed in Australia five minute early and departed three minutes early!"

For all its weaknesses and false starts, the Continental strike began to pinch Lorenzo once Dennis Higgins took command of the MEC. The surge of October crossovers ebbed and was not followed by any more "in-house" scabs in November. With the arrival of Captain Bob Kehs, the legendary "Dr. Strike" of Northwest's many skirmishes with management, detailed by ALPA to supply technical and organizational know-how to the Continental pilots, their lines stiffened. Although plagued from beginning to end by a shortage of picket-line manpower, under Kehs' expert tutelage (and, one must admit, a threat to cut off strike benefits), the Continental pilots bent to their unpleasant task, often joined by wives and children as they carried placards through airport terminals. They began mastering the arcane aspects of a strike, something other airline pilots in other days had done before them, not willingly, but with grim effectiveness.

Too grim, in some cases. Sporadic episodes of violence marked the strike: a bloody, decayed elk head tossed through a plate glass window of one crossover's house; two Continental strikers, carried away by their fury, caught with a bomb they intended to plant in a scab's garage (both later drew lengthy prison sentences); innumerable acts of petty harassment directed at nonstriking pilots. In short, the standard fare of labor strife, that ugly shadow that always emerges when livelihood and career come under threat—what old Dave Behncke once called "the heavy boot."

The purpose of this increasingly efficient strike operation was to generate pressure for serious negotiations. As we have seen, fear that Lorenzo would run out of pilots before the end of October motivated him to talk, but he was also under court order to do so. With canny old Floyd Carpenter, veteran of many run-ins with Lorenzo at TXI, massaging every conceivable pressure point, the Continental negotiators *did* come up with a settlement Lorenzo would buy— sort of. In point of fact, these negotiations were heavily concessionary on ALPA's part, little better than the EWRs Lorenzo had spelled out upon announcing his bankruptcy action.

During tense negotiations in late October, when Lorenzo still wasn't sure he could staff his airline and while ALPA worried that the Continental strikers might continue to cross the picket line in large numbers, a compromise seemed to emerge. As a steady veteran of the Lorenzo Wars at TXI, new MEC Chairman Dennis Higgins was anxious to see these negotiations succeed, but he recognized the disastrous effect dashed hopes would have.

"How do you hold a pilot group together when it runs from emotional peak to valley?" Higgins asks rhetorically. "They would look at some event, like a court date, and attach great significance to it. When it didn't work, they really hit bottom emotionally. I had to shallow these emotional swings out of the pilot group, to play down their expectations while looking for a negotiated solution. So, at the various crew bases, I started a series of meetings in which I told them, 'Frank's got us off the property and he's not going to let us back unless we keep a steady hand.'"

By November, the Continental pilots' negotiators seemed successful. But well aware of Lorenzo's supple mind and devious abilities, Higgins remained wary—for good reasons.

"The company said it needed an additional $50 million in work-rule concessions," Higgins recalls bitterly. "We gave them a proposal that met the $50 million, but the company said it didn't. We told them to rewrite our proposal to where it met their $50 million, and we would accept it. They refused to rewrite it."

The Continental pilots had thus all but surrendered, and they were under the impression that Lorenzo would settle once the technicalities in the "back to work" portion of the agreement were ironed out. From ALPA's point of view, some of these technicalities involved serious concessions, among them Lorenzo's insistence that about 100 "permanent replacement" strikebreakers hired "off the street" in November remain in place—seniority not withstanding. To this ALPA couldn't formally agree, but that shouldn't have scuttled the whole effort. Just as the National pilots would make life too unpleasant to bear for the post–1948–strike scabs they were forced to accept, so the Continental pilots would surely have been able to do the same. The National pilots had successfully handled a much larger group than the 100 scabs to whom Lorenzo had promised "permanent" jobs at that point. Perhaps Lorenzo knew this. So, in an episode similar to one he had played out against the TXI pilots in 1980, Lorenzo, backed off from a deal to which he had previously committed himself.

During this standoff over implementation of the back-to-work portion of the settlement, Lorenzo seems to have come to the conclusion that his accelerating hiring of ex-Braniff pilots would shortly allow him to win without further concessions. He appeared to enter a "take no prisoners" mode, just as Continental's pilot negotiators, unaware of this development, rather naively believed they could resolve back-to-work differences through an arbitrator. UCLA Professor of Law Benjamin Aaron, who undertook this role in early November, would find himself on a fool's errand.

Any arbitrator, as a prerequisite to bringing two bitterly divided positions into agreement, will insist that each side make concessions. By the time Aaron got the case, Continental's pilot negotiators were only quibbling over implementation of the back-to-work agreement—they had beaten a heavy retreat on all economic questions. Lorenzo insisted that "work rules" had economic implications, and he demanded that the pilots accept totally the Emergency Work Rules, which largely dispensed with bidding and seniority rights. ALPA wanted to quibble—it would give up any work rules that had serious economic implications, but wanted to at least bargain about them. Lorenzo adopted an "all or nothing" position. By Thanksgiving, Professor Aaron admitted defeat and quit with a blast at Lorenzo.

"I required the parties to come to the table willing to make substantial changes in their demands," Aaron declared. "The pilots' union has met those demands and exceeded them. The company has shown a continued unwillingness to move from its position."

So the strike moved into 1984, with both sides now awaiting the decision of the courts. Short of winning the economic contest outright, something ALPA had never been able to do during any previous strike, the judges and lawyers controlled the future. Eventually, Lorenzo would win on two fronts. A series of decisions by Judge R.F. Wheless between January and June 1984 found Lorenzo's bankruptcy filing legitimate and not merely a dodge to void union collective bargaining agreements—decisions that flew in the face of Lorenzo's public admission that he had a "labor problem," not a "bankruptcy problem." Saying that Lorenzo had made "reasonable efforts to negotiate a voluntary modification" of his labor contracts, Judge Wheless then allowed him to impose the Emergency Work Rules. ALPA immediately appealed Judge Wheless's preliminary ruling in January, but before a higher court could hear it, the Bildisco Decision dealt ALPA a fatal blow.

In February 1984, *by a single vote*, the U.S. Supreme Court upheld the essence of the Houston court's preliminary finding. For ALPA, the critical part of the Bildisco Case came in a closely divided 5–4 ruling that union contracts could be canceled *even before a bankruptcy court ruled on that business's request*! This was, of course, exactly what Lorenzo had done and what ALPA had been contesting so vociferously in its appeals. Ultimately, ALPA's campaign in Congress to overrule this aspect of the Bildiscoe Decision with new legislation would succeed, but too late for the Continental strikers. Even worse, the Bildisco Decision reversed a previous finding by the National Labor Relations Board (NLRB) that Bildisco had engaged in an "unfair labor practice" by canceling its union contracts unilaterally. ALPA had been counting on this NLRB finding to defeat Lorenzo.

The Bildisco Decision was an unmitigated disaster for ALPA, carried by five Republican justices appointed by Nixon and Reagan. The only two Democratic appointees remaining on the court, Justices Byron R. White and Thurgood Marshall, joined with moderate Republicans Harry Blackmun and William Brennan in dissent. Answering William Rehnquist's opinion, these dissenters wrote: "The majority has completely ignored important policies that underlie the NLRB."

Calling the Bildisco Decision a "puzzling misreading of congressional intent," Chairman Peter Rodino of the House Judiciary Committee announced that he would begin immediate hearings on a law to overrule the Bildisco Decision. But the new legislation would be many months in coming, and useless to Continental's striking pilots because it was not retroactive.

When Congress subsequently outlawed what the 5–4 Republican majority on the Supreme Court had done, ALPA won a victory of sorts, and Lorenzo's action at Continental would stand as an isolated footnote to labor history. But the damage was done. Politics matters, because politicians determine who sits on the Supreme Court.

With the Bildisco Decision, the Continental strike was effectively lost.

"In hindsight, it's easy to see that once Bildisco came down, the appeals process wasn't going to lead anywhere," admits Seth Rosen, director of ALPA's Representation Department. "It would have been better calling the strike off right there, because it was a total victory in busting the union. Continental had no desire to negotiate at that point."

A huge block of 300 Continental strikers crossed the picket line immediately after Bildisco. The Continental strikers had held their lines with virtually no crossovers for nearly five months, but Lorenzo had a large contingent of "out-house scabs" nearing the end of training, and something approaching panic set in as these post-Bildiscoe crossovers saw their jobs disappearing forever.

Among the 600 "in-house scabs" who crossed during the strike, there was a vast difference between these post-Bildisco scabs, who crossed after the fight was lost, and the "October scabs," whose early betrayal was so crucial.

"I supported the strike like a good union member for six months," says former ALPA LEC member Captain Jim Minor, still anguished at finally crossing the picket line. "Going back to work for Frank Lorenzo, the guy who ruined my career, was the single most traumatic event of my life, and that includes both my divorces. But we were told that he didn't have the legal right to void our contract. Well, the courts said differently. What was I supposed to do, after all those years of beating the ice off the wings of a DC-3, trying to make it to the next stop, trying to build an airline? Go to work for Southwest and pull gear for some guy half my age for $18,000 a year? Or take the forty-three grand Lorenzo was offering?"

Captain Don Henderson, the ex-Navy pilot who was later ALPA's "custodian" on Continental, says sadly of these late crossovers: "Many of the old Continental pilots will now admit privately that they made a mistake, that the company lied to them when they made the decision to get in bed with the company. But once they made it, they had to live with it."

By June 1984, an accumulation of adverse court decisions meant that ALPA would, realistically, have to pull down the Continental strike on unsatisfactory grounds at some point. Although the die-hard Continental strikers, by now engaged in a "holy war" against Lorenzo (much like their brethren at Eastern later), continued to do their utmost, the only effective means at their disposal was the deeply abhorrent one of making total war on the airline itself. By pressuring travel agents not to sell Continental tickets (a critical factor in Braniff's demise), Continental's striking pilots, _if they succeeded_, stood to destroy the very airline they had spent their lives building.

So ALPA would have to retreat, but until a way could be found, Continental's strikers would soldier on, pursuing a variety of stratagems. ALPA's "corporate campaign," designed to pressure Lorenzo both morally and financially through pleas to lenders and vendors, found little support among Lorenzo's fellow CEOs. The 1980s, with the "Reagan Revolution" at floodtide, proved unreceptive to concepts like "fairness" and "corporate responsibility."

ALPA's challenge to the safety of Continental's scab-ridden operation was another matter, however. With an inexperienced pilot force, incidents multiplied. By December 1983, ALPA had already documented almost daily infractions, ranging from busted altitude assignments to inadequate crew rest. On Nov. 9, 1983, a DC-9 with Lorenzo himself aboard landed *on a taxiway* at Denver. In February 1984, a hard landing resulted in aircraft damage that went unreported until non-Continental ground personnel finally noticed wrinkled skin. Meanwhile the aircraft continued in line operations *for three days*!

ALPA tried mightily to interest the news media and the FAA in these safety violations. In April 1984, CBS's *60 Minutes* ran a program on them, but the FAA regarded these charges as merely "union stuff" and resisted becoming involved. Expressing deep frustration with FAA Administrator Donald Engen, Hank Duffy told congressional investigators in June 1984, that federal officials were ignoring ALPA's reports of safety violations and actively favoring Lorenzo. In one midair near-miss incident, ALPA's Director of Accident Investigation Harold Marthinsen provided the FAA with ATC tapes that the FAA *later erased*! It was just an inadvertently hasty "recycling of tapes," Engen explained.

In June 1984, Hank Duffy presented congressional investigators with a detailed list of 152 similar safety violations committed by Continental during the strike and cited the FAA as a "classic example of an agency that either can't or won't do its job." Stung by congressional criticism following ALPA's complaints, the FAA launched an investigation of Continental, and ultimately cleared it. "Continental continues to provide safe service," Engen said publicly.[1]

One small episode in the strike deserves mention. Under the leadership of Paul Eckel, the Continental management pilot who had tried to prevent Lorenzo's takeover with an employee stock ownership plan (ESOP), a group of striking Continental pilots started their own airline, Pride Air, to compete on selected routes with Continental.

Pride Air was vaguely reminiscent of the Southern Airways pilots' 1961 attempt to fly their own "strike airline," which they called Superior Airlines. The difference between the two airlines—Superior and Pride—was that ALPA got financially involved in Superior, whereas Pride came mostly out of the Continental pilots' own pockets, primarily their pension funds. Superior was a financial quagmire that taught ALPA a lesson. The Continental pilots who invested in Pride should have paid attention to history—they lost everything.

How then, did the strike finally end? Lorenzo had won all the economic and legal battles to this point and had no incentive to negotiate. Only the bankruptcy court's order that he do so perpetuated desultory negotiations.

"In fact, the guy across the table told me, 'We're not here to do anything but play games,'" recalls Seth Rosen. "'But you can't say that as a matter of record, or I will deny it.'"

By August 1985, Continental had a full complement of 1,600 pilots, 1,000 "permanent replacements" hired after the strike began and 600 who had crossed picket lines—its full prestrike strength. About 1,000 ALPA loyalists remained on strike, with approximately 400 others either having found jobs elsewhere or retired. Their last connection with Continental was the prestrike ALPA contract, which still retained legal standing in the bankruptcy court.

Then Lorenzo outsmarted himself—finally.

On Aug. 26, 1985, Lorenzo moved to terminate the ALPA contract. Declaring that Continental's original acceptance of ALPA as the collective bargaining agent for its pilots was "voluntary" and had never been certified by a formal vote, Lorenzo announced that he was withdrawing the recognition. With 1,400 of his pilots having signed a petition requesting it, Lorenzo declared that a majority of all his pilots, even if the 1,000 strikers were included in the total, favored decertification of ALPA. He then _unilaterally_ broke off the court-ordered negotiations, which had been sputtering on ineffectually.

At this point, cocky and overconfident, riding the crest of dozens of puff pieces in the business press describing him as "the wonderboy who took on the unions and won" and "the man who proved deregulation would work," Lorenzo stubbed his toe. Notwithstanding that Bob Six had "voluntarily" accepted ALPA as the bargaining agent for Continental pilots back in 1942, Lorenzo could not unilaterally withdraw that recognition.

Established precedent in NLRB case law required a formal, supervised ballot—not the informal ballot Lorenzo announced. Having gotten away with canceling the wage and working conditions portion of the ALPA contract, Lorenzo figured the bankruptcy court would now permit total cancellation of the entire contract under the same rationale, and without going through the formal decertification process.

So without waiting for the bankruptcy court to rule on his high-handed action, Lorenzo announced an expansion of Continental's flight schedule. Ironically, Lorenzo had been so successful at breaking the strike that he now needed more pilots. On Sept. 9, 1985, thinking ALPA's legal challenge to his decertification would fail, Lorenzo announced a "vacancy bid" for nearly 500 captain and first officer positions, plus the hiring of an undetermined number of second officers "off the street." Lorenzo believed his "decertification" of ALPA meant that striking pilots would have no standing to bid for these positions.

One final crisis now loomed for the Continental MEC. While ALPA tried to persuade the bankruptcy court of the illegality of Lorenzo's decertification, the leaders of Continental's pilot group would get one last grab for a very tarnished brass ring. Reluctantly, under severe prodding by ALPA's outside legal counsel Bruce Simon, they agreed to submit bids for these new "vacant" pilot positions.

"It was two o'clock in the morning, and we were read the riot act by Bruce Simon, who told us it's going downhill from here," Vice-Chairman Pete Lappin recalls of the MEC meeting. "Most of us didn't want to call off the strike for anything less than total victory. But we were losing people to suicide! Simon persuaded me that we had to swallow this piece of shit, save some jobs _and_ some lives."

Lorenzo promptly filed a petition with the court stating that the strikers were "not entitled to any of the bid vacancies under any circumstances," because all of them had already been awarded to "permanent replacements." The federal bankruptcy court thought otherwise.

On Oct. 31, 1985, Judge Roberts entered an "Order and Award" (O&A) of the bankruptcy court imposing a settlement on Lorenzo. Often denounced as the "Surrender Agreement" by militant Continental strikers, the O&A was, in fact, far better. Describing his O&A as a "global settlement," Judge Roberts required that Lorenzo offer his pilots three options, ranging from reinstatement in order of seniority (according to a complicated formula) to severance pay of $4,000 for each year of service. Pilots who wished to retain their right to litigate further would also be reinstated, but only *after* all pilots who waived that right. Although not all former Continental captains moved immediately into the left seat, Lorenzo had to guarantee a substantial number of them captain's pay anyway.

Within a year of the O&A, *most* Continental strikers were back in their cockpits—but not all. Guy Casey, Dennis Higgins, Dennis Duffy, Larry Baxter, Pete Lappin, to name but a few, did not appear on Continental's seniority list. From the beginning, Lorenzo *privately* made it clear that he would never accept pilots who had played a leadership role in the strike.

Poststrike harassment is nothing new in ALPA's history, but the subtlety of Lorenzo's campaign set a new standard. His primary weapon was the polygraph machine, or "lie detector," a device premised upon the unscientific notion that lying triggers certain physiological changes in fibbers. Lorenzo used these contraptions on Continental's strike leaders in conjunction with legal depositions designed to ferret out knowledge of illegal acts committed during the strike. Although not admissible as evidence during a trial, the Texas bankruptcy court permitted Lorenzo to use them internally—a decision ALPA challenged unsuccessfully.

Armed with polygraph results, Lorenzo set out to make life difficult for Continental's strike leaders during requalification.

"There were about a dozen individuals who were very active, vocal, and visible during the strike that the company didn't want back under any circumstances," says Kirby Schnell, who now works for the FAA. "Ed Nash [one of the few strike leaders who currently flies for Continental] is probably still looking over his shoulder, and that is nothing derogatory about Ed."

"On days off, the company kept wanting Pete Lappin and me to submit to polygraph tests," says Guy Casey, who finally found the harassment too much and went to work for United. "Then they said I had a heart problem, and I had to take a bunch of tests at my own expense—they showed I didn't."

One by one, all the principal strike leaders, when questioned about poststrike harassment, ask to "go off the tape." They can't prove what they say, and they know how litigious Lorenzo can still be. So they choose words carefully. But in every instance, they insist that they were privately warned by old friends in management (of which, surprisingly, there were more than a few) not to come back, that they would never make it through training. Save yourself the trouble, they were told, take "Option III," the $4,000 per year severance pay, and run. Most did.

"Frank hates me, so I never considered going back," says Dennis Higgins, whose consistent geniality masked the gut-fighter he had proven himself to be. Short and muscular, with a ready smile and disarming manner, Higgins built a nonflying career in labor relations after the strike.

"Without a union contract, when they get down on a guy and decide he's not going to make it on his simulator rides, there is no recourse," Higgins says. "Don

Henderson [MEC secretary-treasurer during the strike and later ALPA "custodian" on Continental] is an exception, but he didn't have a real public role in the strike. I would have been a major target."

Finally, one sad footnote. A few Continental strikers retained their right to sue under the O&A. A flurry of lawsuits resulted. Lorenzo won *every single one*. In their despair, they turned on ALPA itself, filing a "Failure of Duty of Fair Representation" lawsuit, which alleged that ALPA's acceptance of the O&A was a betrayal. In early 1991, the U.S. Supreme Court threw out their lawsuit and exonerated ALPA.

The Continental strike was finally over.   ✦

NOTE

[1] This episode provided an eerie foreshadowing of the celebrated ValuJet crash in May 1996, which brought the FAA's safety failures into bold relief—finally.

ABOVE: Appearing before the press on April 28, 1981, to kick off ALPA's "corporate campaign" against Texas Air Corporation—parent company of Texas International (TXI) and New York Air—were ALPA President J.J. O'Donnell (standing at lectern); TXI Master Executive Chairman Dennis Higgins (right of lectern); and Ray Rogers (left of lectern, the man who led organized labor's successful protest against the J.P. Stevens Company between 1977 and 1980. O'Donnell announced that ALPA had recruited Rogers to help expose the "interlocking directorships, stockholders, credit sources, and political power bases" that Texas Air is using to promote the nonunionized New York Air at the expense of TXI employees. O'Donnell said the techniques Rogers used against J.P. Stevens can also be used to stop Frank Lorenzo, chairman of Texas Air, from breaking the unions on his property. Rogers, who was based in New York, would work with ALPA a minimum of 6 months.

ABOVE: Trans Texas (TTA), which became Texas International (TXI) as it grew from piston power to turboprop to pure jet, would be Frank Lorenzo's first victim.
RIGHT: ALPA pilots participate in a a joint ALPA/AFL-CIO protest against New York Air.

ABOVE: Continental (CAL) Capt. Paul Eckel (center) went to the steps of the U.S. Capitol in late April 1981 to campaign for an employee stock ownership plan (ESOP) at Continental as an alternative to merger with Texas International. A few days earlier, almost 9,000 out of 10,400 Continental employees voted to support the plan, which would give the employees controlling interest in their company. Eckel called on the Civil Aeronautics Board to delay any takeover tactics by Texas International until Continental's Board of Directors had time to consider the ESOP. Eckel said he and his fellow workers were willing to give up future pay raises to buy Continental stock.

LEFT: Continental pilots walk the picket line after airline owner Frank Lorenzo filed Chapter 11, closed the airline, abrogated labor contracts, and started up again at half wages. The debacle at CAL was the culmination of the unrestricted laissez-faire Administration policies in the early years of deregulation.

BELOW: Capt. Dennis Higgins, who became CAL MEC chairman on October 13, 1983.

ABOVE: AFL-CIO President, Lane Kirkland speaks at a Continental strike press conference. **RIGHT:** Pilots picketing at Dulles International Airport...note mustachioed pilot to spokesman's right, future ALPA President, Randolph Babbitt.

ABOVE: Capt. Duffy pickets at Washington National Airport in 1984.
LEFT: Striking Continental pilots picket at Dulles International Airport in Virginia.

ABOVE: Capt. Duffy urges news reporters attending a 1983 seminar on "The Future of the Airline Industry" to examine closely how deregulation has hurt commercial air transportation and has prompted companies like Continental to abuse bankruptcy laws.

ABOVE: In December 1983, ALPA called a press conference to announce a corporate campaign against Continental for its ploy of using bankruptcy to reject its collective bargaining agreements. ALPA offered a reward for information on "insider" stock trading of Continental officials prior to declaring bankruptcy.
RIGHT: Testifying with Capt. Duffy at congressional hearings on airline safety are, from left, Capt. Don McClure (Eastern), psychologist Dr. Phillip McGraw; Capt. Duffy; former Continental chief pilot, Capt. William Laughlin; and ALPA's chief of accident investigation, Harold Marthinsen. Duffy blasted FAA's handling of alleged safety violations of the "new" Continental since the airline declared bankruptcy in September 1983.

ABOVE: Capt. Duffy presides over ALPA's 42nd Executive Board in 1983 as Capt. Dennis Higgins, Continental MEC chairman, and Continental pilot spokesman Gary Baker answer questions from the floor about the striking pilots' need for support.

ABOVE: Capt. Duffy accompanied AFL-CIO President Lane Kirkland and a delegation of other labor leaders in October 1983 to meet with House Speaker Tip O'Neill to discuss how companies were abusing bankruptcy laws to bust unions.

ABOVE: Global pilot concern over the union-busting activities of Continental Airlines was the topic of the International Federation of Air Line Pilots Associations Individual Study Group, which convened in Washington, D.C., in November 1984. Capt. Dennis Higgins, MEC chairman for the striking Continental pilots, represented ALPA at the meeting.

CHAPTER 15

BLUE SKIES AND MEC WARS:
The Origins of the United Strike of 1985

A n old axiom holds that all politics is local, that great historical events have humble, grass-roots origins. For example, during the election of 1860, Abraham Lincoln became the Republicans' choice, not because the party faithful recognized his transcendent virtues, but rather because his opponents for the nomination had fallen afoul of bitter local disputes over everything from prohibition of alcohol to curbing foreign immigration—small issues all but forgotten today. Lincoln could win the votes of German immigrants (which would be crucial in certain states during the election), whereas one of his principal opponents for the nomination, Missourian Edward Bates, would surely lose their votes because he had belonged to the anti-immigrant American (or "Know-Nothing") Party until 1856. So Bates was out. The general hubbub over slavery dominates our memory of that era today, but to understand the election fully we must take these lesser squabbles into consideration as well.

The same principle holds true of ALPA. Much of its history lies hidden at the master executive council (MEC) level, where complex struggles and obscure local issues have often dictated the outcome of historically significant events. On some airlines, like TWA for example, the internal wars at the MEC level have been positively byzantine, almost impossible to trace. The evanescent quality of these "MEC wars" on most airlines has been such that even those who participated actively in them at the time often give different interpretations of what they meant.

For example, the relatively simple question: "What caused the United strike of 1985?" elicits complex answers keyed to the local situation on United Airlines. Without knowing the internal dynamics of the United pilot group and the history of its MEC (particularly during the early 1980s), no genuine understanding of the 1985 strike is possible. Certainly, one cannot find the answer by studying ALPA's history at the national level alone. Rather, local factors as compelling as those that brought Lincoln to the White House in 1861 are central to the story.

Among the cast of characters who figured prominently in the strike, we must first deal with John Ferg, the MEC chairman who led the United pilot group into the 1980s. Ferg's relationship with Dick Ferris, the rapid-fire talker who shot meteorically to the top of United's corporate hierarchy, also figures. How did John Ferg emerge, and why did his relationship with Ferris lead to the now infamous "Blue Skies" contract of 1981? Unless we understand their motives, we cannot understand the origins of Blue Skies. Without understanding Blue Skies, we cannot know what the strike was about.

Because John Ferg flew during the 1985 strike, he would earn the loathsome nickname "Super Scab" from the pilots he once led. Adding to his everlasting infamy among the 95 percent of United pilots who honored the picket line, Ferg's son also flew, an action former ALPA President J.J. O'Donnell blamed on the father.

"His son has to live with being a scab for the rest of his life, and that is so sad," O'Donnell said in his 1991 interview. "If it were me, even if I were going to work, I'd have told my son '_You_ don't ever cross a picket line!'"

John Ferg came to United in the Capital merger of 1961. Readers familiar with _Flying the Line_ know just how difficult that transition was for the old Capital pilot group.[1] As we have seen in our previous look at the career of Bill Arsenault, the Capital pilots, although suffering a kind of second-class citizenship following the merger, came to exercise an influence in ALPA affairs far beyond their numbers. The typical Capital pilot had many attributes normally associated with blue-collar unionism—traits less pronounced among most "real" United pilots.

With the possible exception of Pan American in its salad days, the United pilot group earned a reputation as the most "aristocratic" in ALPA, particularly after World War II. United personnel managers, when hiring pilots, might as well have been interviewing for executive positions. By the 1950s, the typical United pilot was a college graduate with a military background and a managerial mentality that came so naturally that many people speculated United looked _specifically_ for such characteristics in hiring. Significantly, United would have no pilot strikes between 1951 and 1985—a span of 34 years. That was quite a stretch, considering that United, Dave Behncke's old airline, was ALPA's cradle, the original home to an assortment of flamboyant and individualistic Old Guys. But United's management had pretty well weeded them out by the 1950s.

Don Nichols, who served as ALPA Region III vice-president from 1967 to 1971, had definite ideas about the evolving "class system" on United. As an original "Tracey Ace" who began flying for United before World War II, Nichols encountered some condescension because he had learned to fly in the Civilian Pilot Training Program, instead of in the military, and also because he had dropped out of the University of Michigan's redoubtable engineering program without a degree during his senior year. Although he became a Boeing 247 captain in only two years (thanks to the departure of military reservists ahead of him on the United seniority list after Pearl Harbor), Nichols doubts that he would have been hired under United's post-World War II system.

"In later years, they began using all these different psychological tests to determine whether you would be a pilot for United Airlines or not," says Nichols, who retired in 1978. "Management was looking for what I call the 'placidity factor,' people who were easy to mold, placid, not strong individualists like Dave Behncke and the bunch who started ALPA. Those tests were designed to eliminate people like that and maybe to avoid union problems by hiring only people who would be more inclined to think along company lines."

The unintended consequence of United's hiring policies was that in the 1960s, "blue-collar" Capital pilots like John Ferg and Bill Arsenault began gravitating into ALPA leadership positions. By the 1960s, "real" United pilots seemed less interested in ALPA affairs than earlier ones, particularly after old hands like Chuck Woods, Scotty Devine, and H.B. Anders, all younger contemporaries of Dave Behncke, began retiring. Their departure from MEC leadership positions, coupled with the post-World War II new-hire's typical disinterest in ALPA, created a vacuum that the old Capital pilot group filled. Occasionally, some "real" United pilots would rouse themselves and wrest control from the Capital pilots, as happened to Bill Arsenault in 1975 and to John Ferg in 1965 during his first brief, dimly remembered tenure as MEC chairman. But because of retirements, new hiring, and general disinterest, few United pilots by the late 1970s either knew or cared about John Ferg's history. When he reemerged as a force in United's internal ALPA politics in the late 1970s, the old schism generated by the Capital merger had largely faded from memory.

Another twist in United's hiring policies added to this problem. For a brief period in the mid-1960s, a genuine pilot shortage existed. Between the end of the Korean War and the outbreak of the Vietnam War, military pilot training programs shrank. Thus, when the mid-1960s jet revolution took hold and vast numbers of new passengers expanded the need for airline crews, the traditional source of pilots had all but dried up. As the military downsized in the Eisenhower years, it not only cut back pilot training programs, but also increased the length of obligated service for people who underwent training, which meant that many pilots would remain in the service for a full career.

United tried to remedy this shortage by hiring and training its own pilots, who were usually college-educated young men with just a private ticket and only a few hours of single-engine time. Possibly management saw these low-time new-hires as adding to the antiunion "placidity factor" among its pilots. If that was indeed the goal, it failed miserably. Two future MEC chairmen, Roger Hall and Frederick "Rick" Dubinsky, came from this category of new-hires and, as we shall see, proved far less than "placid." But in the short run, United's hiring of low-time new-hires might have contributed to the rank-and-file disinterest that allowed old Capital pilots like John Ferg to rise.

Following Ferg's recall from the MEC chairmanship, he disappeared from ALPA affairs for the remainder of the 1960s. Then, in the early 1970s, he earned considerable notoriety among rank-and-file United pilots through the "Rainey Case," a termination action that saw him *voluntarily* testify against a fellow pilot in a safety-related matter. United's MEC formally censured Ferg; he sued the MEC over it, citing "freedom of speech" issues and "lack of due process" (the MEC had not granted him a hearing before the censure) and won an out-of-court settlement that included modest cash damages.

"Ferg didn't witness the events that led to this pilot's termination," says United's Doug Wilsman, who served as ALPA's grievance observer during the episode. "ALPA has never objected to a pilot testifying to what he actually witnessed in a termination case. But Ferg had no direct knowledge of the case that got this guy fired; he simply said Rainey was a bad pilot, and for that we censured him."

All this, when coupled with his considerable talent as a rhetorician and speech maker (a skill touching the edges of demagoguery, many old United hands thought), meant that John Ferg was by no means finished. But from his recall in 1965 until his old Capital colleague Bill Arsenault fell from power in 1975, Ferg generally kept a low profile. Then, in 1977, he returned to the MEC as the Denver captain representative. Within two years, Ferg would capture *de facto* control of United's MEC, able to command more support than MEC Chairman Dick Cosgrave. When Cosgrave's term ended in 1980, Ferg became chairman.

"As Denver LEC Chairman Ferg had access to a broad spectrum of pilots passing through our training center," recalls Charles J. "Chuck" Pierce, who would serve as MEC secretary-treasurer during part of Ferg's term as chairman. "He gave me the impression of someone who was very calculating and never did anything without a reason. He was a hard-hitter relative to ALPA, expressing dissatisfaction with where the national organization was going, and for taking a harder line with the company. Obviously, history showed that wasn't the real John Ferg! But there was always something about him I didn't quite trust."

Although current ruminations about Ferg's career bear an obvious bias owing to his joining management before the strike, they have an ominous tone nevertheless. Jerry Pryde, who served as MEC chairman before Dick Cosgrave and who subsequently went on to become ALPA's first vice-president at the end of the O'Donnell years, recalls being very worried when Ferg won election.

"I didn't really consider him the type of person United had historically been represented by," Pryde says without hesitation. "We had been at odds on many things, particularly on the way United's management was running the airline. I was in Washington as first vice-president, but I continued to fly the line so I pretty much kept in touch. I was aware of many things that he was involved with that other people didn't know. John Ferg, in my mind, never was a union person."

Future strike leader Rick Dubinsky, who would later break with Ferg, swims against the general tide by remembering him positively.

"I was a believer in Ferg," Dubinsky admits. "He was militant, he said all the right things, and I'm not so sure at that point he wasn't honest in what he was trying to achieve. I wasn't privy to the mechanics of how his alliance with Ferris solidified, except for one little anecdote John told me about. John got the royal treatment from Ferris, really introduced to the high corporate life, keys to the washroom and limousines and that kind of symbolic stuff. I remember John saying of Ferris: 'He thinks he has me right in his pocket,' and he tapped his shirt pocket in pantomime. 'Yep, he's got me right where I want him!'"

Jerry Pryde and other senior ALPA leaders worried about Ferg's increasingly chummy relationship with Dick Ferris, whom we have met before. Ferris was young and articulate, and the pilot group liked him—a lot! So much in fact, that they gave him an "honorary" ALPA seniority number. Ferris had learned to fly after becoming United's CEO, and he tooled around to various domiciles in a Learjet Model 24, favorably impressing the pilot group with both his plans for the future and his airmanship.

How many United pilots of that era knew that E.L. Cord had actually done the same thing a generation earlier? In Cord's case, flying his own Stinson Trimotor convinced him that there was really nothing much to flying, which justified cutting his pilots' salaries. Cord never went flying unless the weather was perfect, and his own personal pilot always came along in case the weather turned sour. Ferris's flying was a lot like Cord's, which was a bad omen. But oblivious to these portents, John Ferg, once he became MEC chairman, made Ferris's ALPA number *real*, rather than honorary. Should he ever choose to do so, Dick Ferris would actually be able to fly the line!

Ferg's relationship with Dick Ferris bears analysis within the United context. Following Bill Arsenault's recall in 1975, the next two MEC chairmen, Jerry Pryde and Dick Cosgrave, resumed a moderate approach to dealing with the company, which had traditionally characterized the United pilot group. Because of the "placidity factor" referred to by Don Nichols, the rank-and-file United pilot generally remained passive, thus inhibiting new initiatives by the MEC under normal circumstances. But this procompany passivity among pilots was beginning to wear thin, largely because United had become a stagnant carrier. As the largest airline in the free world, United got scant consideration from government regulators awarding new routes. Instead, smaller airlines got the route awards and consequently most of the growth.

As the 1970s came to an end, the typical United pilot, for all his managerial mentality, could look elsewhere and see five-year captains sitting in the left seats of other carriers. Meanwhile, the sight of graying pilots still holding only second officer bids was common on United. Although they liked and respected Eddie Carlson, Dick Ferris's mentor and predecessor as United's CEO, his tenure had done little for the United pilots' stagnant promotion list. When Dick Ferris took over, full of "piss and vinegar," most United pilots found his pitchmanship irresistible, thus making Ferg's activism possible.

At some point after the onset of deregulation in 1978, Dick Ferris and John Ferg made a deal. If Ferg would move the United pilot group toward liberalized work rules through a major contract revision, Ferris would use this form of "giveback" to "grow the airline." More pilots would then advance to captaincies, and when United soared into a brave new future, Ferris would do right by the pilots whose generous concessions had made it all possible. Presumably ALPA's example would leave United's other unions no choice but to follow.

The only problem with this rather straightforward deal was that it flew in the face of nearly half a century of pilot work rules—particularly the idea of flat monthly salaries, which Ferris advocated. John Ferg wasn't the first MEC chairman gripped by managerial fever, nor to fall victim to management blandishments. Attempts to "chisel" (as old Dave Behncke used to say) on a hard-won contract to gain some purely local advantage had a long history. To understand the gravity of this issue, we must take a brief look at the "givebacks" that characterized the recessionary early 1980s, and the instrument through which these contract concessions were often made—the "side letter."

The basic technical trick that underlay ALPA's four golden decades of collective bargaining success was Dave Behncke's *original and absolute rejection of any form of flat monthly salary.* By basing pilot pay on a complex system of "piecework," under which compensation depended upon the type of flying and equipment, ALPA and the airline piloting profession prospered. The early private airmail operators inherited this piecework pay system from the old Post Office Air Mail Service, and they didn't like it. It was cumbersome, expensive, and required a lot of record-keeping. These early aviation entrepreneurs were also smart enough to see that eventually somebody would use the piecework pay system to "jack up the house," as Dave Behncke put it.

Naturally, the private airmail operators preferred to pay their pilots a flat monthly salary. It was simpler, and when faster more productive equipment came on the line, management (not pilots) would derive the benefits. The private operators' effort to substitute a flat monthly pay scale for the old Post Office system was the root cause of ALPA's formation. Eventually, Dave Behncke threatened a nationwide strike over flat monthly pay scales in 1933.[2] When serious collective bargaining finally got under way in 1939, the original operators' fear of the "house jacking" technique proved justified.

This "piecework" approach to collective bargaining, coupled with government regulation, meant that when one pilot group got a contractual advantage, it inevitably flowed to other groups. The technical name for what Behncke called "jacking up the house" was "pattern bargaining," which meant that a *single* pattern of pay became the standard for the whole industry. Under government regulation, the airlines could pass along costs to consumers, so management had little incentive to resist "pattern bargaining." The drawback to "pattern bargaining" was that in a time of concessionary contracts, it would also serve to ratchet pay and working conditions *down*. Industrywide bargaining (the polar opposite of pattern bargaining), which management sought and ALPA resisted after World War II (thus precipitating the TWA strike of 1946), would work to ALPA's advantage in a deregulated environment.

Unable to secure industrywide bargaining, and increasingly buffeted by ALPA's skill at using pattern bargaining to fine-tune contracts across the nation, management occasionally won concessions and givebacks through local "side letter" modifications to existing contracts. In one notable case during Charley Ruby's term, the pilots of Piedmont signed a "side letter" that completely gave away the third crewmember on the B-737—and then kept it secret! Fearful that individual pilot groups would succumb to various blandishments and give away hard-won contractual principles for some local plum, ALPA began to require the same kind of national approval of "side letter" modifications that were required of a contract. As late as 1984, Hank Duffy would complain publicly that ALPA's national officers were frequently unaware of "side letter" givebacks and that once granted they were "hard to undo."

Of course, the economic downturn of the early 1980s, coupled with the adverse effect of deregulation, caused the avalanche of "side letter" givebacks. Eventually, the 1984 BOD meeting in Bal Harbour, Fla., would adopt stringent measures to keep individual MECs from giving away the shop. Henceforth, "side letter" negotiations would require the "physical or monitoring presence" of an ALPA national representative, plus formal notification of any changes generated by such an agreement. The game John Ferg played with Dick Ferris in the early

1980s triggered this unprecedented attempt by ALPA's national officers to look over the shoulders of local negotiators.

In the beginning, John Ferg's proposal to grant Dick Ferris drastic contract concessions to get United growing won support from many junior pilots. Felicitously labeled "Blue Skies," these work rules concessions would add about two days per month to each United pilot's flying. In return, Blue Skies raised pilot pay, but in a way that would have given old Dave Behncke fits—a version of flat monthly salaries.

Before Ferg took over as MEC chairman, Dick Ferris began pushing contract concessions using a variety of techniques. Arguing that the flood of post-deregulation "new entrant" airlines required a drastic response, Ferris warned United's pilots that if they did nothing, the airline might actually fail. Ferris was an acknowledged master at the art of "road shows"; so good in fact, that on the eve of the strike in 1985, United's MEC urged pilots to boycott them.

"There wouldn't have been a strike if we hadn't kept the guys away from those sessions," says Doug Wilsman, the captains' representative from Los Angeles, whose respect for Ferris's persuasiveness led him to organize the boycott.

Once John Ferg became MEC chairman in 1980, Ferris had an ally instead of a watchdog. Using every tactic at their command, Ferris and Ferg jointly painted a picture that was alternately bleak without Blue Skies and rosy with it. Flying around to various pilot domiciles in his Learjet, Ferris wowed the assembled pilots with visions of rapid captaincies. For pilots who could not make the meetings (which skeptics referred to as "Dog and Pony Shows"), Ferris installed VCRs in crew lounges. The videotaped wisdom of Dick Ferris, with John Ferg cheerleading, was omnipresent.

Another factor in the selling of Blue Skies rested on Ferg's appeal to a growing dissatisfaction with J.J. O'Donnell's leadership. Ferg's reputation as a fiery rhetorician accelerated during Operation USA in 1980, and he became quite adept at exploiting rank-and-file anger over the "giveaway" of the third crewmember by the 1981 Presidential Emergency Board. Ferg could be particularly vitriolic on the crew complement issue, which as we have seen was plaguing ALPA and causing the United pilot group (which stood increasingly alone in supporting it) to feel aggrieved at other pilot groups.

Deregulation also played a role in the selling of Blue Skies. Although United's pilots had loyally toed the line in opposing deregulation along with the rest of ALPA, their boss, Dick Ferris, was one of its foremost supporters. During Dick Cosgrave's MEC chairmanship, Ferris's arguments gathered steam, and quiet support for deregulation grew among rank-and-file United pilots.

"Because United was so large, the CAB [Civil Aeronautics Board] was giving routes to everybody else, and we suffered dramatically," says Rick Dubinsky, who served as Cleveland first officer representative under Dick Cosgrave in the late 1970s. "United pilots found themselves with 15-year flight engineers, while the Piedmonts of the world were rapidly moving seats. Ferris said: 'Take the shackles off us, and we are going to kick ass, because United is the 500-pound gorilla who's going to take its resources and pent-up energy and go out in a nonregulated industry and *grow*!'"

The Ferg–Ferris alliance both reflected and helped to mold a new militancy taking root among the previously "placid" United pilot group. This transformation took place rapidly, a quite surprising about-face for a pilot group whose distinguishing characteristic had heretofore been cool detachment. In the aftermath of the 1985 strike, with United pilots wearing their militancy on their lapels, displaying a bewildering array of "battle stars" under ALPA tie-tacks and pins, they self-consciously saw themselves as the profession's "Prussians," the tough guys who had put it on the line and rescued *real* pilot unionism from its debilitating slide. But in the early part of Ferg's MEC chairmanship, United's pilots stood a chance of going in exactly the opposite direction, perhaps even leaving ALPA entirely! The celebrated three-day walkout by the United delegation at the 1980 BOD meeting in Los Angeles raised just such a possibility. It was the final factor in the coming of Blue Skies.

The United contingent's walkout at Los Angeles both outraged and worried other BOD members. The United pilot group was beginning to exhibit the same kind of long-term disaffection that had characterized the American Airlines pilots in the early 1960s. Was John Ferg bidding to become the next Gene Seal, the American master chairman whose poisonous relationship with Clancy Sayen lay at the root of that group's secession from ALPA? The historical parallels were ominous: in the early 1960s, the putative cause of the American group's disaffection was ALPA's crew complement policy; by the early 1980s, this issue's forlorn offspring still troubled United. If a dedicated leadership group on United was inclined to exaggerate ALPA's failures and thereby exploit this growing disaffection, things could get disastrously out-of-hand, much as they did on American in 1963, or so J.J. O'Donnell thought.

"The story of that 1980 walkout actually started earlier, when the United MEC passed a resolution to study the feasibility of pulling out of ALPA," O'Donnell declared in his 1991 interview. "They later expunged it from their records, but we had some good friends on the United MEC who kept us apprised. Henry Weiss thought it was a serious threat at the time. He said, 'John, you've got to visit the United MEC, let them take their pound of flesh. We can't afford to let United pull out of ALPA.' "

After much dickering, O'Donnell secured Ferg's permission to address a regular MEC meeting in Chicago in early 1980. Upon arrival, Ferg kept him waiting all day. "I flew up that morning; it was cold and snowy in Chicago. I was supposed to go on at two o'clock," O'Donnell remembered angrily. "Ferg went through the MEC meeting, had the committee meetings, everything else, and I didn't get to go on that day."

That night Ferg took O'Donnell to dinner. Reflecting the United pilots' growing dissatisfaction with ALPA, Ferg threatened to lead a "restructuring" of ALPA that would reduce the national organization to relative impotence. Such talk, often bordering on outright secession, had been a staple at United grousing sessions for years. But in 1980, O'Donnell feared words might give way to action.

"Because I was in enemy territory, I had one drink and watched Ferg get pretty well sauced," O'Donnell recalled later, although Ferg had no reputation for overimbibing. "At the end, he starts blurting out: 'We're going to set up a separate Airline Pilot Confederation. Eastern and TWA are going to come in, *and American*! We'll send you a percentage of our dues; you can handle legislative in Washington, but we'll handle everything else.'"

How genuine was United's 1980 threat to secede from ALPA? It has been the subject of debate ever since, but ALPA's national leadership took it seriously at the time, which Rick Dubinsky believes was warranted.

"I don't think the average United pilot had thought that far down the road, but Ferg was looking forward to separating us from ALPA as early as 1980," Dubinsky says flatly.

The mere possibility of such a breach brought O'Donnell scurrying to Chicago to head it off. When O'Donnell met with the full United MEC the next day, the anti-Ferg minority rebuked Ferg for not allowing O'Donnell to speak the previous day and moved that he be put on immediately at the beginning of the 9 a.m. session. This motion provoked a heated debate, during which O'Donnell had to patiently tolerate a long harangue from Ferg, basically on crew complement, but other things, too.

"The failure of ALPA financially, the failure to do things in Washington, the failure to establish negotiations, the failure to get a single national seniority list," O'Donnell recalled Ferg's laundry list with a snort. "National seniority list! Hell, we tried that in 1958; I was on the committee that studied it. We couldn't get anybody interested."

Because of what O'Donnell considered the dire threat of secession, he felt he had no choice but to quietly take these attacks and endure Ferg's humiliating treatment. Once O'Donnell got the speaker's rostrum, he emulated Andrew Jackson during the "Nullification Crisis" with South Carolina during the early 1830s. Although boiling mad and threatening privately to lead the U.S. Army south to hang nullification leader John C. Calhoun (who was, coincidentally, Jackson's own vice-president during his first term), "Old Hickory" adopted a public tone of calm reasonableness in his celebrated "Proclamation to the People of South Carolina." Like Andrew Jackson, O'Donnell controlled his anger while he argued for the ancient advantages of union, declaring that the strength of numbers outweighed any temporary gains that might come from independence.

"It was an awful beating, and I just stood there and took it for two and a half hours," O'Donnell later recalled of that 1980 MEC meeting. "But I was really prepared by Henry Weiss, Jack Bavis, and Jerry Pryde, who was at the meeting, probably the best MEC chairman United had ever had, along with Dick Cosgrave, those two are number ones! I got a standing ovation from the MEC, which knocked me off my feet. John Ferg stood up and shook my hand after the speech and says to the MEC, 'That's why he's president!'"

O'Donnell's bravura performance at the MEC meeting, along with the considerable help he received behind the scenes from an antisecession faction led by Hal Osteboe and Jim Engleman, temporarily scuttled Ferg's plans, whatever they were, for either outright secession or a new "confederation." But Vice-Chairman Pat Austin disputes that Ferg had ever set up any formal "secret study committee."

"Ferg made O'Donnell wait around longer than I thought was proper," recalls

Austin, a Ferg ally who was nevertheless embarrassed by his rudeness. "I definitely remember the episode, but J.J. was clearly overreacting. There was no big secret campaign to get out of ALPA."

"There were enough people like Doug Wilsman and Hal Osteboe on United to stop it," O'Donnell insisted in his 1991 interview. "When the committee report was finally finished, Ferg wouldn't let it come to the MEC because it said they could solve their problems from inside of ALPA."

But Ferg was gnawing on a big problem for ALPA, as even O'Donnell admitted. Deregulation, then in its first full year of operation, was causing small new-entrant airlines to spring up like dandelions after a rain. What *did* the United pilot group have in common with these new groups? Although many were becoming affiliated with ALPA, their airlines competed ruinously with the established carriers, and their wages and working conditions had a depressive effect.

"It could have been the little pebble that destroyed ALPA," O'Donnell admitted later. "The small carriers' pilot groups could not exist by themselves. John Ferg said there was a conspiracy in Washington to deprive the United pilots of their fair share, they weren't getting enough resources. They were paying about $4 million in dues then, and they were getting back probably a million and a quarter. A million goes to Washington, and the other two million is spread out amongst these smaller airlines."

O'Donnell countered Ferg's argument by citing the necessity of using ALPA's financial resources to sustain and organize the pilot groups of these new-entrant airlines. Transplanting ALPA to these new-entrants served everybody's long-term interests, O'Donnell contended, and the price in lost dues money was small indeed when compared to the damage they might do if they remained *outside* ALPA. O'Donnell struck a responsive chord, actually converting most United MEC members, and Ferg, too, remarkably.

Logically, if United was to benefit from deregulation (as the Ferg–Ferris alliance vowed it would), new-entrant carriers would be inevitable. Organizing these new-entrant pilot groups was the obvious way to safeguard existing contracts—by bringing everybody else up to the major carriers' level. Later, one subordinate cause of the 1980 Los Angeles walkout was the United pilots' belief that the BOD had not given O'Donnell sufficient support in organizing Pacific Southwest Airlines (PSA), the non-ALPA carrier that would later merge into USAir, now US Airways.

O'Donnell's promise to meet regularly with the United MEC to keep it apprised of how its money was being spent defused the secession issue. In all probability, United's MEC would not have supported it in early 1980, even if O'Donnell had not acted with such alacrity. Ferg, still in his first year as chairman, did not have firm control over the MEC on this issue. But this setback did not derail Ferg's drive toward secession for long. At the 1980 BOD meeting later that year, Ferg would be in a much stronger position.

As we have seen, the crew complement issue finally came to a resolution through Operation USA and the PEB that followed it. But in the months leading up to Operation USA, the United pilot group was arguably becoming the most militant in ALPA, with crew complement as the principal cause. Certainly, John Ferg deserves some credit for this transformation of the United pilot group. By repeatedly stressing that the third crewmember meant jobs, talking about "solidarity," and urging ALPA to "act like a real labor union," Ferg in some sense midwifed the rebirth of the United pilot group's militancy. The walkout that this militancy precipitated at the 1980 BOD meeting in Los Angeles profoundly startled everybody. But J.J. O'Donnell could see it coming as the various committees shaped up.

At BOD meetings, committees composed of delegates do the basic work and then make recommendations back to the general session. While that body theoretically has the last word, in fact the committees do the critical work. Each committee usually has an experienced core of pilots who have previous experience in ALPA affairs and who are able to lead their less knowledgeable colleagues. Typically, at that time, more than half the nearly 300 delegates at each BOD meeting were attending for the first time.

Each delegate gets assigned to at least one BOD committee, but an old policy allows voluntary switches, which ALPA's president cannot control. As O'Donnell saw the list of names switching to the critical crew complement committee at the 1980 BOD convention, he sensed trouble.

"To be honest with you, I would take a critical issue and shift it to a particular committee that we were sure had solid citizens," O'Donnell admitted in his 1991 interview. "At the time of this BOD meeting, United had 27 members on the MEC, so that meant at least one or two United guys were on each committee. Well, on the floor anybody can shift committees, and I could see, by the guys United was shifting to crew complement, that we had problems. They were radicals and crazies."

When the committee dealing with crew complement came in with a report that dissatisfied the United contingent, they walked out. Actually, the United group had walked out on a previous ALPA BOD, in 1974 at Kansas City, over the failure to be granted a recess. But that trivial episode lasted only a few hours. In Los Angeles, their walkout was longer and far more threatening, with the United delegates leaving *en masse*, checking out of the hotel, wives, baggage, and all. But the walkout was *not* about seceding from ALPA, according to Chuck Pierce.

"Our intent was never to leave the Association," Pierce says. "It was to demonstrate our anger with the BOD and particularly the actions of the Delta pilots. Pat Austin and I were the last to leave the hotel; we paid the bill and made sure our message got delivered to O'Donnell correctly and not by innuendo. Our last conversation was with Jack Bavis [O'Donnell's executive administrator]. I believe now that our walkout was abrupt, arrogant, and too extreme. It led to the average United pilot being viewed as someone who is willing to tell the rest of ALPA how things should be done but isn't willing to listen to somebody else's opinion."

For three days, nobody knew where the United pilots went or whether they would return. Henry Weiss and J.J. O'Donnell were visibly upset, preoccupied to the point of distraction over the walkout. For Henry Weiss, the episode seemed like an ugly replay of the American Airlines split 17 years earlier.

"I was greatly concerned," ALPA General Counsel Henry Weiss admits. "I felt that whatever the intention of the walkout, which was like a military operation, with the whole MEC getting up and leaving as one man, that the longer it continued, the more likely it was that what may have started as a maneuver might become translated into a reality. It was simply unacceptable for the United pilots to be separated from ALPA for any length of time. I told J.J., 'You and I better go looking for these people and work out some kind of understanding.'"

Rick Dubinsky confirms Weiss's fears.

"If it had gone one more day," Dubinsky believes, "we would have been gone."

For the next three days, Weiss and O'Donnell scoured Los Angeles, looking for the United delegates without success. Only Rick Dubinsky remained at the BOD hotel to act as United's representative. Why Dubinsky?

Although Rick Dubinsky bore a surname famous in labor history, he was not related to David Dubinsky, founder of the politically powerful International Ladies Garment Workers Union. Rick Dubinsky would eventually become well-known in ALPA because of his leadership during the 1985 strike, but in 1980 he was just a first officer representative from Cleveland of middling seniority, or so it seemed. But ALPA insiders understood very well that by the United pilots' choice of Dubinsky to represent them, they were sending an unsettling message. Carrying himself like a middleweight boxer, Dubinsky brought to mind a character in an old Bowery Boys movie, the grim kid who'd never shrink from a street fight. But did that mean secession was imminent?

"There really wasn't a consensus in favor of leaving ALPA," Dubinsky explains, "but a significant number of United pilots would have gone home and worked for decertification."

O'Donnell later speculated that Ferg had the support of slightly more than half his MEC, with the views of United's rank-and-file a mystery. But only MEC members were at Los Angeles, so they were O'Donnell's first concern.

Dubinsky knew where the United pilot group had gone and that they had not left Los Angeles. With the crisis growing steadily worse, Henry Weiss finally met with Dubinsky, after several fruitless cab rides to various hotels where Don Skiados, ALPA's Communications Director, thought the United pilots might be.

"I asked Rick Dubinsky, 'Are you here to further a separation of the United pilots from the Association?'" Weiss recalls of their discussion. "He said, 'Oh no, I'm an ALPA man.' So we arranged a meeting between myself, O'Donnell, Pat Austin, and John Ferg. I was a little surprised that Rick was not invited to participate."

In fact, Dubinsky's absence from the meeting evidenced a degree of internal opposition to Ferg, which would become significant later. Although known as one of the "Ferg Dogs" (a tongue-in-cheek internal nickname that arose from jokes about Ferg's ability to "sic his dogs" on opponents), Dubinsky was in the beginning stages of doubt about Ferg, particularly his advocacy of separating from ALPA. Dubinsky's reluctance to throw out the baby with the bathwater would spread among United's MEC until eventually the whole idea reached the stage of denial.

"We worked out a face-saving agreement," Weiss declares, reluctant to be more specific about the details that brought the United pilots back into the fold at Los Angeles. "Years later, John Ferg and Pat Austin invited me to dinner. They said, 'You know, when we walked out, that was only a maneuver.' 'Well,' I said, 'that wasn't the flavor I got.'"

The exact terms of the deal worked out between O'Donnell and Ferg remain something of a mystery, but its general outlines are clear. The United pilots would return *symbolically* to the BOD meeting by sending three delegates, a captain, a first officer, and a second officer representative, each bearing proxies for their group. But the rest would stay away to dramatize their unhappiness.

As for the coming concessionary contract, which would be known as "Blue Skies," Henry Weiss sums things up succinctly: "Ferg made it clear that he was not any longer going to allow ALPA policy to hinder him in making a deal with United."

In one way or another, J.J. O'Donnell would have to accept Blue Skies and agree to whatever deal Ferg worked out with Ferris. In so doing, O'Donnell paid a huge price politically, for to say that the average delegate attending the BOD meeting was outraged at the United pilot group considerably understates things.

"The fact that the United MEC walked out of the convention brought us to a complete halt for three days," remembers Northwest's Skip Eglet, who was elected executive vice-president at the meeting. "O'Donnell, during that time, appeared to do nothing except grovel at their feet to try to get them to come back. It really hurt him with the rest of the Association."

O'Donnell, worried about the consequences of United's disaffection, saw himself as doing what his job required. He also felt a genuine sympathy for United's pilots, which transcended the mere political fact that they had supported him before and would do so again during the 1982 presidential election.

"I had to take the heat and listen to their arguments," O'Donnell says. "They said, 'We're the big guys, we provide most of the money, and everybody dumps on us.' Which was kind of true. They felt they weren't being listened to by the Association, *that* was really their biggest bitch. I satisfied the United MEC by courteously listening. If I hadn't felt they had legitimate grievances, I wouldn't have busted my hump to keep them in."

So from the end of the October 1980 BOD meeting, Ferg had control of the situation. He would cut his deal with Ferris, confident that O'Donnell could do nothing to stop him. While the negotiations that would eventually result in Blue Skies progressed, the outcome of the third crewmember controversy went badly from the United pilots' perspective, thus strengthening Ferg's hand even further. The cycle of LEC elections brought several more Ferg supporters to the MEC in early 1981, thus placing him in a commanding position internally. Only a few ALPA activists were now bucking the "Ferg Dog" tide, one of whom was Harlow B. "Hal" Osteboe, a respected "nuts and bolts" type who would eventually win a first officer representative's position on Council 12 in Chicago.

"Following the Los Angeles BOD meeting, Ferg made a concerted effort to get his people elected locally, particularly in Los Angeles and Seattle," recalls Osteboe. "That meant he had solid support on the MEC for Blue Skies, and there was absolutely no question in my mind that because of the walkout, J.J. was going to have to sign the Blue Skies contract."

Roger Hall, chairman of United's Negotiating Committee, received his marching orders from the MEC shortly after the 1980 BOD meeting. By early 1981, reflecting Ferg's successful politicking at the LEC level, the Negotiating Committee was composed entirely of new members, something of a departure for United's pilots, who had a history of continuity on this important committee. But the new committee's inexperience was mitigated somewhat by the fact that Hal Stepinsky, an ALPA staff negotiator with 20 years of service, would assist them. The technical details of Blue Skies would be worked out quickly once Hall and Ferg, who were allies at the time, got their signals straight. Although Hall had been Ferg's personal choice to conduct the negotiations and had resigned from the MEC to take the committee chairmanship, he was nevertheless troubled by Dick Ferris's influence over Ferg and the process that surrounded the coming of Blue Skies.

"John Ferg became enamored with Dick Ferris; and before Blue Skies was done, they developed a very close relationship—too close, in fact," Hall believes. "Ferris was doing a lot of nice things for John, picking him up at the O'Hare terminal and spending the evening at lavish dinners. John loved it, and there was no doubt Ferris was trying to buy Ferg. Ferris was very charismatic, and he could charm anybody. He wanted flexibility so he could go out and fly aggressively in the marketplace. Ferris came to the Negotiating Committee and said, 'You guys can either give me relief in the work rules so I can buy airplanes and make United grow, or you can choose not to and we can continue as a stagnant airline, or even retrench a little.'"

For Roger Hall, a reserved engineering graduate of Bradley University in Peoria, Ill., Ferris's proposals had obvious personal appeal. At the time, he was still only a B-727 first officer, after 17 years with United. Hall knew that Ferris's proposal extended the scope of contract negotiations beyond the envelope ALPA had previously found acceptable, so he referred the matter to the MEC itself.

"What Ferris wanted was not the Negotiating Committee's decision to make," Hall believes. "It was a matter for the MEC and ultimately the entire pilot group to decide. Our attitude was that we really didn't know where this thing was going. So when Ferris came to the MEC to make his pitch, the Negotiating Committee also went and just listened."

Ferris proposed an ongoing type of contract that he said would address what United needed to expand. While the contract would have an amendable date, negotiations would continue on a regular basis, with constant meetings to solve problems that might arise. Ferris's proposal made a certain sense, for there were so many uncertainties in what he eventually might need to "grow the airline" that until the pilots actually started living with Blue Skies, predicting its effect was nearly impossible.

"If the pilots had a problem with Blue Skies, he would take care of it," Hall recalls Ferris promising. "He sold the MEC on the concept, and this is where his personality came into play. The man was extremely dynamic. So the direction we were given as a committee was to go off and negotiate the kind of agreement Ferris wanted. It seemed plausible and workable at the time."

In return for substantial work rules concessions, which added about two days of flying per month for each pilot, Blue Skies called for a series of 6 percent pay raises sprinkled at intervals throughout the life of the contract, payable henceforth as flat monthly salaries. The actual dollar amount of concessions in Blue Skies is difficult to assess, but best estimates measured them at about 15 percent.

Things moved rapidly. By March 1981, Roger Hall's Negotiating Committee had worked out the basic agreement. In August, the MEC gave its approval to Blues Skies following an 83 percent favorable ratification vote by the United membership at large. Negotiations on certain aspects of pension funding would drag on into 1982, but by September 1981, Blue Skies was an established fact. Everybody was pleased. Dick Ferris publicly declared "a new partnership between United and its pilots." Peace, harmony, and satisfaction reigned. The millennium seemed to have arrived. What could that curmudgeonly 17 percent of United pilots have been thinking about when they voted "no" on Blue Skies?

Everybody was about to find out.   ✈

NOTES

[1] See "Jets and Thin Ice," *Flying the Line*, Ch. 23, particularly pp. 251–53.
[2] See "The Perils of Washington," *Flying the Line*, Ch. 7, particularly pp. 62–67.

CHAPTER 16

OF B-SCALES AND ALPA's FUTURE
The United Strike of 1985

A n ancient Chinese curse says:"May you live in interesting times."
Professional airline pilots were discovering the true meaning of that curse by the mid-1980s. "Interesting times," filled with tragedy and turmoil, conflict and loss, make for dramatic history—but they're hard to live through. The fate of winners and losers dramatically counterpoised, "sad tales of the death of kings," have absorbed us since the dawn of human history. Indeed, losers often generate more interest than winners. How else can we account for the endless fascination with Adolph Hitler's last days in his Berlin bunker?

A strike always carries the possibility of loss. Before deregulation, ALPA's fights with management mainly ended in victory. Ask National Airlines' Ted Baker, Southern Airways' Frank Hulse, or the notorious E.L. Cord of Century Air Lines about that. But in the antilabor 1980s, with political conservatism rampant on a field of deregulation, Frank Lorenzo had reversed that historical tide. Could ALPA win a fight in this brave new world, where government tilted *against* labor instead of *toward* it? The pilots of United Airlines would confront that question directly.

Blue Skies became Frankenstein's monster in record time. What the United pilots thought would inaugurate a golden age turned into a time of troubles within a year. As a result, MEC Chairman John Ferg, the man most responsible for Blue Skies, saw his standing with United's pilots plummet. Dick Ferris had sold Blue Skies to him using all the trappings of friendship, ego enhancement, and one must admit, rational calculations of his pilots' self-interest. Better leaders than John Ferg might as easily have succumbed to Ferris's silky persuasion. So the question of Ferg's motivation confronts us. Rick Dubinsky, originally a Ferg supporter, began feeling uneasy about him after the "second videotape," a 1982 attempt to allay rising pilot suspicion of Blue Skies, paid for by the company but produced by the MEC.

"It was a real propaganda operation," Dubinsky asserts. "I confronted John about the tape. Where was the other side of the coin? It was just a giveaway. And he just grinned at me. He knew I had figured it out. At this point, I became convinced that the pilots were being taken to the cleaners *and that Ferg knew*!"

Unanswered questions linger. Was John Ferg ALPA's Benedict Arnold, or merely mousetrapped by Dick Ferris? Should we fault Ferg for not recognizing the Faustian nature of the bargain he struck with Ferris? And what of Dick Ferris himself? Was he genuine, or simply a con man? How did Blue Skies, undertaken with such high hopes and vows of mutual cooperation, become a grim joke so quickly? Most importantly, why *didn't* Ferris use Blue Skies to "grow the airline?"

Put simply, Blue Skies failed to accomplish what Ferris promised either because he never intended to use it that way, or because he miscalculated its effectiveness, or because he was incompetent—or some combination of all three. And, as we shall see, a mid-course correction inspired by Frank Lorenzo might have affected Ferris.

But in one sense, Ferris used Blue Skies beautifully. United's balance sheet showed record profits by 1984, and in cost per seat-mile, the airline ranked as the most efficient *unionized* carrier. By early 1985, the Air Transport Association listed only People Express, Southwest, and Continental (all nonunion or with independent unions) as having lower seat-mile costs than United.

But what had United's pilots gotten out of it? By the summer of 1982, barely a year into the new contract, they looked increasingly foolish as it became clear that Ferris's only real use of Blue Skies so far had been to increase United's profits by exploiting its more relaxed work rules.

Indicative of Ferris's flush coffers, on April 22, 1985, he signed an agreement with Pan Am's C. Edward Acker to buy the *entire* Pan Am Pacific route structure and *all* the aircraft required to fly it (11 long-range Boeing 747SPs) for $750 million. This incredible deal, which shifted fully one-fourth of Pan Am (with all the employees, pilots included) to United, was a blockbuster—the biggest single deal in the history of commercial aviation. But it was hardly the kind of expansion United's pilots expected, and it benefited them little in terms of promotion, always Blue Skies' most attractive promise. Because ALPA was involved in the purchase, it could ensure proper application of merger policy, and Pan Am's 430 transferring pilots would count themselves lucky because of it. Coming as it did during the spring of 1985, just as contract negotiations intensified, the Pan Am acquisition undercut Ferris's arguments that United had to have additional concessions from ALPA to survive. Important stockholders would also raise questions about the purchase, not only because they thought Ferris overpaid Pan Am, but because something didn't smell right about it. Leafleting pilots outside the Westin O'Hare Hotel, site of United's annual stockholders' meeting, made a point of sharing these misgivings.

One aspect of the Pan Am buyout merits comment for its labor implications. When compared to Eastern's 1982 purchase of Braniff's Latin American routes, the United pilot group comes off very well. The Pan Am pilots who now wear United uniforms owe a lot to the fact that United's pilots wanted no part of any "expansion plan" that would shove brother pilots out of their cockpits and off their routes. The fact that this came up in 1985, as the strike neared and as United's pilots were desperately building internal unity and a sense of professional brotherhood, probably had something to do with it, too. But in the long and sorry history of merger animosity, United's pilot group stands out for its sense of fair play and commitment to justice, particularly in this instance.

Thus, by 1985, as the Blue Skies contract came up for renewal, Ferris's talk about using it to turn United into the big monkey that would "kick butt" in the airline industry seemed hollow. Not only that, but in a classic example of the "law of unintended consequences," neither Ferris nor Ferg seemed to consider how the 500-pound gorilla in the next cage might react. United was, after all, not the only big primate in the airline zoo.

Almost immediately after news of Blue Skies hit the industry in 1981, Robert Crandall, the powerful CEO of American Airlines, began using it as a wedge to split open his own pilots' contract. Leaders of the Allied Pilots Association (APA), the ALPA clone that resulted from the 1963 split, were susceptible to Crandall's pressure tactics for many reasons, not least being that they saw Blue Skies as aimed at them. Crandall cleverly exempted American's *current* pilots from United-style across-the-board givebacks by proposing a two-tier scale that would pay new-hires substantially less. He would first impose a B-scale on American's mechanics in 1982 and then immediately target the APA for a similar contract. American's pilots were on Crandall's B-scale agenda in any case, but Blue Skies provided a convenient excuse and plenty of leverage.

In 1983, the APA's leaders agreed to a contract that would pay newly hired pilots approximately one-half the going rate. Deregulation had rekindled the traditional rivalry between United and American, historically the two biggest airlines in the industry. To leaders of the APA, Blue Skies seemed like naked aggression against their carrier, amply justifying a response. Crandall sweetened the deal by granting a small pay raise (in lieu of one that the APA had given back earlier), agreed not to lay off any pilots for the life of the contract, promised to recall 500 furloughed pilots by 1986, and established a profit-sharing plan. So in effect, this first major-airline B-scale bribed American's 3,400 pilots with some middling benefits, but it boiled down to selling their patrimony *on faith* for a mess of Crandall's pottage.

But initially, the American pilots' gamble paid off. Crandall, unlike Ferris, *did* use his givebacks constructively to "grow" the airline. Not that it benefited American's pilots all that much. By the early 1990s, despite American's phenomenal growth and the near doubling of its pilot force, lagging pay and increasingly harsh working conditions had made American's flight crews among the angriest in all of aviation, driven to the desperate expedient of a wildcat "sick out." This massive action forced Crandall to cancel 11 percent of his flights over the holidays in January 1991 and to run full-page ads headlined "AApology" (with American's familiar eagle logo cutely placed between the redundant double "AA"). In a startling lapse, American's publicity flacks mistakenly *identified their own pilots' union as ALPA*! So they had to spend more money correctly identifying the APA in additional ads!

Thus, the sins of the fathers were visited upon their children. The roots of their transgression lay in the unprecedented B-scale "giveback" the APA's leaders handed Crandall in 1983, which went far beyond Blue Skies. At least United's pilots shared the pain with those who would inherit their cockpits. The APA's leaders sacrificed nothing themselves, while passing the pain to their professional posterity, an act redolent of generational betrayal, replete with threats to safety, and with profound implications for the very future of pilot unionism. If the B-scale worked as planned, in the run of time a majority of pilots would be second-class citizens, resentful of their elders *and the union* that had sold them out. When the United's pilots' own B-scale crisis came in 1985, they argued strongly that the resentments of underpaid new-hires would inevitably affect not only unionism, but also crew coordination and hence safety.

Ironically, almost at the exact moment the APA was gambling with the future, Blue Skies started unraveling on United. By 1982, barely a year into Blue Skies, scattered results from LEC elections indicated a small wave of opposition. In Chicago, Cliff Sanderson displaced Dick Kuhn, a strong Ferg supporter, as chairman of Council 12. This LEC election dramatized both incipient disillusionment with Blue Skies and John Ferg's political slippage as well. Sanderson, a former B-29 pilot who spent half a career in the Air Force before signing on belatedly with United in 1964, changed his mind about Blue Skies after seeing it in action.

"To be honest, I thought Blue Skies was a very good thing at first," says Sanderson, a University of Maine graduate who majored in foreign languages. "Like most United pilots, I accepted John Ferg's assurances that Dick Ferris would not use Blue Skies to exploit us. But Ferris interpreted Blue Skies as a sign of our weakness, and it snowballed through the whole damn industry. Everybody blames the givebacks on American, but United under John Ferg caused it."

ALPA loyalist Hal Osteboe, who helped squelch Ferg's secession plan in 1980, also won election in 1983 as first officer representative from Chicago's Council 12. By then, the "Ferg Dogs" were in full retreat. Chicago's Council 12, the largest on United, provided an excellent barometer of rank-and-file pilot opinion.

"I would say that within 90 days of Blue Skies going into effect, Ferg's reputation began to sink," says Osteboe, a precise, studious man who could easily be mistaken for a professor. "The LEC election cycle began to reverse in 1982 and then became an anti-Ferg landslide in 1983 because Ferris didn't take any advantage, in a business sense, of the givebacks in Blue Skies."

In all probability, Dick Ferris didn't use Blue Skies to "grow" the airline because he simply didn't know how, at least in the beginning. As we have seen, aside from his *What Makes Sammy Run?* glibness, Ferris's qualifications for United's top job were thin. His career after leaving United seems to confirm that he was, as the saying goes, an "empty suit."

"As time went on, it became apparent to me that Ferris was a good huckster, but not a good businessman," says Roger Hall, who negotiated Blue Skies and knew firsthand how little use Ferris made of it. "I became disillusioned with him very quickly. If he had all this business acumen, I would have thought he'd have found another top management job after leaving United. But he's been basically just unemployed ever since."

Hall might be correct in his belief that Ferris's failure to put Blue Skies to productive use stemmed from simple incompetence—at least in the beginning. But we must remember that just as Blue Skies arrived, Ferris had another powerful role model to observe—Frank Lorenzo. Ferris might have entered on Blue Skies in good faith and then, noticing the success and news media attention Lorenzo was getting with his hard-line approach to labor, changed his mind to become a "copycat killer."

In the rarefied world of top airline executives, not all decisions need have economic justification. In fact, a plausible case can be made that intangible considerations of prestige and status played a powerful role in motivating top airline executives like Ferris, Lorenzo, and later, Carl Icahn, the corporate raider and financial manipulator who would seize TWA in 1986. Perhaps their drive to cut pilot salaries sprang from competitive urges run amok, a kind of antilabor feeding frenzy among boardroom sharks. To be able to walk into the exclusive forums where these top CEOs rubbed elbows, where they could revel in their colleagues' approval (or envy) of the way they had stood tall against labor, *particularly the haughty pilots*, might explain a lot. Certainly, rational economic analysis cannot entirely explain the economic damage that Lorenzo and Ferris did to ALPA, their airlines, *and ultimately themselves.* Answers might be available in the field of abnormal psychology, however.

"In hindsight, it's easy to see that people like Lorenzo and Ferris were not going to be satisfied with anything short of destruction of ALPA on their property, and you have to ask yourself *what do they gain?*" says Northwest's Skip Eglet, who pondered this question from an executive vice-president's vantage. "I mean, ALPA was willing to grant deep concessions, anything they wanted really, and they wanted *more*, is what it amounted to. There really isn't any logic to it, because they could have gotten what they wanted without doing what they did. It is something I will never understand."

Maybe these airline executives believed their own propaganda. Many of them seemed to believe that modern pilots were unworthy of their heritage, that they were unwilling to take risks that might jeopardize their affluent lifestyles. Perhaps the airline industry's Ferrises and Lorenzos believed that, unlike the Old Guys who had bled real blood and risked cherished careers to build ALPA, this new generation of pilots, with their Rolex watches and Porsches, had no *real* fight in them. Maybe they were patsies, easy marks who would meekly submit to any CEO steely enough to take them on frontally. Certainly, the national political climate, with the "Reagan Revolution" at full antilabor tide, encouraged such ventures. If ALPA's house had rotten walls, and its modern inhabitants lacked the iron will of the Old Guys who had built it, then the times almost demanded action—all a bold airline boss had to do was kick the door down, as Frank Lorenzo had already demonstrated.

If that's what Dick Ferris thought, the pilots of United were about to prove him mistaken. The rapid transformation of this pilot group, as they reacted to Ferris's misuse of Blue Skies, stunned everybody. Hank Duffy, who became ALPA's president just as the phenomenon became full-blown in January 1983, had a box seat.

"The whole personality of the United pilot group changed," Duffy said in his 1990 interview. "They were involved in everything, coming to meetings, much more into mutual assistance to each other. It would really be interesting for an industrial psychologist to study how that group changed so dramatically, from Blue Skies, where they couldn't give Dick Ferris enough, to the hard-line militants they became."

A sense of betrayal spurred this militancy. It began among United's best-informed pilots, particularly among a segment of the MEC led by Hal Osteboe, Jim Engleman, Doug Wilsman, and by 1983, Rick Dubinsky. As awareness of Blue Skies' inadequacy grew, it turned to anger and spread to the rank-and-file. Ironically, Negotiating Committee Chairman Roger Hall, long considered a Ferg acolyte, had also slipped into opposition as he came to doubt the agreement he had brokered.

"The pilots weren't unhappy with the pay, because some really good raises were scattered through Blue Skies," says Hall. "But the airline wasn't growing, and Ferris was beginning to complain very loudly about his payroll costs. The understanding in Blue Skies was that we would have continuous negotiations. Ferris didn't live up to his part of the bargain, and getting our problems addressed was like pulling teeth."

For John Ferg, who unquestionably had ambitions for national ALPA office, the clouding over of Blue Skies had devastating consequences. Without the support of his own MEC, he would not be able to challenge for ALPA's presidency in 1986. His MEC support began to erode in 1982 and expanded among rank-and-file United pilots in early 1983. When leavened by the informed arguments of his MEC critics, the inchoate dissatisfaction of ordinary line pilots rapidly swelled into an anti-Ferg majority. Nearing the end of his second term as MEC chairman, Ferg desperately needed another term to keep alive his chances of ousting Hank Duffy. But a long-standing United policy limited the chairman to two consecutive terms *unless* the MEC approved a third term by a two-thirds majority.

In June 1983, the MEC meeting at the Bond Court Hotel in Cleveland, Ohio, dashed Ferg's hopes for a third term. He could not secure even a simple majority, let alone the two-thirds MEC vote he needed. Ferg furiously denounced the MEC he had so recently controlled.

"It finally came down to a shouting match in a hotel corridor," says Hal Osteboe. "Ferg screamed that we had stabbed him in the back, that we couldn't see the noses on our own faces, that he knew where the industry was going and nobody else did, and that only he could save us."

Blocked from a third term by his own disaffected MEC, his prestige in tatters among rank-and-file line pilots, Ferg responded by becoming even more adamantly committed to Ferris's view of Blue Skies. He would shortly damage his standing with the pilot group beyond repair by *unilaterally* deferring one of the regular Blue Skies pay raises to which Ferris was objecting.

One of flying's oldest tongue-in-cheek aphorisms has it that a pilot doesn't become a "professional" until he starts asking, "Who pays me?" Ferg's deferral of the pay increase nipped at each United airline pilot's wallet-to-heart nerve, and everybody flying the line, no matter how remote from the center of action, had an opinion about that!

"As we approached the fourth pay raise, John Ferg took it upon himself to defer it, and that was a big bone of contention," says ex-naval aviator Bill Stewart, a Los Angeles-based B-747 captain who would later serve as communications director for his LEC during the strike. "The fact then came out from some of the older people that Ferg was MEC chairman once before and got recalled. Most of us didn't know that—I didn't. I guess we deserved what we got for not being better informed as to Ferg's previous history."

Actually, Ferg's recall in 1965 had less to do with his shortcomings than with a quirk of MEC politics at the time. At the first combined MEC meeting following the 1961 merger of Capital and United, voting for chairman was "one MEC member, one vote." Because Capital had more crew bases than United, that meant a majority of MEC members were, like John Ferg, former Capital pilots. Because each domicile, regardless of the numbers of pilots based there, elected representatives to the MEC, a "tribal vote" easily put Ferg into the chairmanship. The "old" United pilot group, vastly larger than the number of former Capital pilots, found this intolerable. So, without even considering Ferg's merits, at the very next MEC meeting, the MEC recalled him, which they could do because a recall vote, unlike the chairman's election, went by roll call based on the membership totals at each crew base.

"I was about to come on the MEC at the time," recalls John LeRoy of Ferg's recall. "Ferg got to go to only one MEC meeting as master chairman. He always bore a grudge about that."

When Ferris eventually created a management position for Ferg on the eve of the strike, perhaps this ancient slap made it easier for him to accept. But nobody who lived through that episode thinks Ferg's managerial status was genuine, and almost everybody harbors deep suspicions about Ferg's role in encouraging Ferris to challenge ALPA.

"I have no doubt that Ferg was telling Ferris we could be had," Rick Dubinsky asserts.

"I lay 80 percent of the blame for the strike right at the feet of John Ferg," Roger Hall agrees. "He became so bitter when the MEC would not agree to a third term that in short order he went into management and began telling Ferris that if he ever wanted to take on the pilots, do it now, that we were divided, we'd crumble."

By January 1984, with Roger Hall taking over a faction-ridden MEC from John Ferg, Dick Ferris had to be thinking of the similar situation on Continental, which Lorenzo had exploited. Ferris probably concluded that the time was right to emasculate ALPA on United, if not to break it entirely. Roger Hall was the junior captain on the airline when the MEC elected him chairman at Honolulu in October 1983, *by a single vote*, over the vastly experienced former chairman Jerry Pryde, one of United's most senior and respected captains. Hall could only barely hold a captain bid and hadn't even gone to school yet. Would the airline's senior pilots follow this relatively junior MEC chairman into a strike? An ancient prejudice against junior pilots holding high MEC office still existed on United, which had never elected a noncaptain MEC chairman.

"Had I not had the captain bid, I don't think I would have been elected," Hall says simply.

On the surface, it appeared that Roger Hall would continue Ferg's program, slightly modified, because he was closely identified with Blue Skies. But Hall had parted company with Ferg sometime in 1983, largely because he thought Ferg's relationship with Ferris had degenerated into an unequal and unhealthy dependency that was undermining the fundamental tenets of unionism.

"I did not feel we must always be confrontational with management," says Hall of his evolving position. "We have many areas of mutual interest, but to some degree labor relations *is* confrontational. John had been delivering all kinds of things to Ferris, really in bed with management. I believed the integrity of the process had been violated and required a more arms-length negotiating stance."

Simultaneously with Hall's taking office, a new Negotiating Committee chaired by Bill Brashear began working on a contract to replace Blue Skies. A high degree of continuity characterized this new committee. Under Hall's chairmanship, the committee members had been Brashear, Dick Brace, and Al Santmeyer. Brace would hold over on the new committee, Deke Clark would take Santmeyer's slot, and Warren Nelson would become the fourth member of Brashear's team. As MEC chairman, Hall effectively remained on the committee, actively participating in selected phases of the negotiations. The new committee had need of Hall's experience, for the talks went badly almost from the start.

"I had a number of meetings with Ferris one-on-one as the talks began," Hall says. "He just got more and more strident, hard-nosed, and demanding. As the summer went by, we were having a difficult time, and I began to feel Ferris was setting us up for a strike, looking to outdo Frank Lorenzo."

After all the years of dealing with John Ferg, Roger Hall's calm demeanor must have struck Ferris as too lacking in fire to provide the strong leadership United's pilots would need in a strike. The soft-spoken Roger Hall had no Ferg-style bombast, so how could he function effectively as a leader in time of crisis?

The answer lay not in Hall's forensic skills, but in his talent for organization, preparation, and most of all, picking subordinates. Hall established a Strike Preparedness Committee in September 1984, appointing Rick Dubinsky chairman. His first order to Dubinsky's committee was, "Go to school on Continental."

Dick Ferris had seen the future at Continental, and he wanted to be part of it. United's pilots had seen the same future and wanted no part of it.

"They were to look at what went wrong on Continental," Hall says of his charge to Dubinsky. "If we were going to find ourselves in a strike situation, which I really hoped we could avoid, we weren't going to make the same mistakes Continental did."

A cold panic gripped the United pilots' leaders, forcing them to focus their attention the way an engine-out emergency would. Like a classic barroom bully, Ferris taunted and probed United's pilots, who had not been on strike since 1951—a "job action" that lasted either 11 or 12 days, depending on how one counted certain events. During that long-ago strike, pickets marched, leaflets circulated, and meetings met. Nobody flew—nobody! The airline shut down completely. But 34 years is a long time between strikes, and the current generation of United pilots would have to learn everything afresh. Were they up to it? On the few occasions when they had honored other unions' picket lines during the intervening years, United's pilots had really done nothing significant, other than quietly not fly.

Given the history of then-recent strikes at Wien, Northwest, and the ongoing debacle at Continental, one can only imagine the United pilots' state of mind. But the gauntlet was down, and United's pilots had to either respond or crawl away.

The job of whipping United's line pilots into fighting trim fell on Dubinsky's committee, which included Ray P. Schlage, Keton Barnes, Felix Isherwood, Bruce Wilkinson, and Pat Palazzolo—all canny veterans. They received valuable indirect aid from volunteers like former MEC Chairmen Scotty Devine and Dick Cosgrave, both retired by 1985. These older pilots played an important role in mentally toughening younger pilots, with advice both practical and historical.

"Fighting between management and labor isn't all bad," Cosgrave said. "But you've got to fight fair, like you do with your wife, because you've got to crawl back in bed again."

Both Cosgrave and Devine worried that line pilots might have an overly romanticized view of United's history, particularly when it came to the semilegendary W.A. "Pat" Patterson, the former Wells Fargo banker who became president in 1931. For all his father-figure image, Patterson had fired Dave Behncke, and he would have done the same to others had not ALPA stopped him. The Old Guys knew how to close ranks when a brother pilot was being abused. The Pat Patterson of rosier later years would brag about his pilots' high salaries and United's cozy labor/management relations. But that was true only because Patterson had learned from bitter experience that he couldn't kick his pilots around.

"With all his positive attributes, Pat Patterson was still a hard-headed banker," says Scotty Devine, who began flying for United in 1940 and knew Patterson well. "I think we remember him fondly because he never backed himself into a corner like Ferris, and he showed a great deal of wisdom in strikes, so when it was all over there were no bitter feelings to be overcome. But times weren't all that easy back then."

In a sense, United's pilots confronted a fight as irrepressible as the U.S. Civil War. The record is abundantly clear that no concession United's pilots could have made at this point would have averted the storm rumbling toward them. Historical details about negotiations, therefore, matter little. Dick Ferris was going to have his test of strength. He had already cowed the mechanics and flight attendants into accepting a two-tier wage scale by 1985. Only the pilots were left standing in his way. They didn't want a strike, the ultimate test of any union, and they didn't seek it.

If a fight must come, Dick Ferris made an ideal opponent because by 1985 he had so little credibility with his pilots. Following Braniff's bankruptcy in 1982, United's pilots experienced the same unease as others in the airline industry, and they had slowly come to doubt not only Ferris's integrity, but his business sense as well. As we have already seen, the incompetence of airline executives had become a mounting concern not only of ALPA's national officers, but of rank-and-file line pilots as well. Clearly, Ferris's grandiose plans to make the airline but one cog in "Allegis," his "integrated transportation company that would remake the industry" (to quote him) struck most United pilots as dubious. They had a healthy suspicion of diluting the company's basic business, which was flying airplanes, with risky expansions into areas in which United had limited experience, such as hotels and car rentals. Put simply, they feared that Ferris's incompetence would do to United what Harding Lawrence's unchecked grandiosity had done to Braniff.

Eventually, United's pilots, acting on plans Roger Hall had concocted under a cloak of secrecy approximating the Manhattan Project, would try to wrest control of the airline from Ferris and Allegis. Through an instrument unique to "progressive capitalism," an employee stock ownership plan (ESOP), Hall led United's pilots into a full-blown attempt to buy their own airline. Although this audacious poststrike effort failed to achieve its primary goal of an employee-owned airline during the period of time covered by this history, it did succeed in ousting Ferris. In 1987, largely because of stresses that the ESOP battle generated, United's board replaced Ferris with Continental's former president, Stephen Wolf, who had at least _some_ credibility with pilots because he broke with Lorenzo just before the Continental strike.

As we shall see later, the ESOP effort had a far-reaching effect because it returned United to its airline roots, thus warning every airline executive in the industry that pilots would take extreme financial countermeasures to preserve their profession, and that reckless corporate maneuvers would invite retaliation. The fall of Dick Ferris was a warning to every executive in the industry that their actions could have profound personal consequences.

But all that was in the future. For the present, 1985, negotiations deadlocked over Ferris's insistence on givebacks that almost made Blue Skies look good by comparison, among them a B-scale like Crandall's. In April 1985, John LeRoy pointed out at the annual stockholders meeting that United's pilot pay scales were already lower than American's. But Ferris, answering LeRoy from the podium, insisted on comparisons with Continental's pilot pay!

"Does it make sense to damage the corporation over this?" LeRoy asked the assembled stockholders, while outside uniformed pilots conducted an "informational picket."

United's pilots were in no mood to make Continental-style concessions, for under Blue Skies the company had returned to profitability. Roger Hall, a methodical man who took on one problem at a time, would not let Ferris stampede him. While the unproductive talks dragged on, United's pilots were far from idle. To pressure Ferris into signing a decent contract, the pilots had, in 1984, tried various forms of in-cockpit job actions, most notably a program they called "Withdrawal of Enthusiasm," or WOE, essentially the ancient tactic of "working to the book," doing just what the job required and no more.

But nothing worked. The ultimate test loomed, with the question hanging in the air like MacBeth's ghostly dagger—would United's pilots actually strike? Each pilot had to make that decision alone—there would be no place to hide. Against that moment of truth, Roger Hall and Rick Dubinsky, assisted by many others (the Strike Committee had expanded to 20 members by then) laid their plans and made their preparations, insisting that nothing be left to chance, so that no distractions would divert United's pilots from the main matter.

One bright spot emerged. Should it come to a strike, money would not be a problem. For years, United had paid more into ALPA's national treasury than any other pilot group. Now they wanted it back. Hank Duffy, still embroiled in the long contest at Continental, knew the stakes as he met with Rick Dubinsky in late 1984 to talk about money.

"Dubinsky and his leadership group came to Washington, D.C., several months before the strike and laid out their program for me," Duffy recalled in his 1990 interview. "They talked about some unusual preparations, for example 'family awareness groups,' that needed extra funding. It made a lot of sense, and I approved it. At the time, I thought we were talking about half a million dollars. They wound up spending nearly $2 million in preparation, but well worth it in the results we got. Typical of the United pilot group, they did very careful planning."

The United pilot investigators, early in their study of what went wrong at Continental, isolated the role of spouses, which, as we have seen, proved critical. The key to keeping family members on board would be prestrike education about ALPA's history and role, plus innovative communications during the strike, entailing many novel approaches, such as regular videotape updates, traditional telephone chains, and nontraditional satellite communications links among mass meetings at United's various domiciles. All this would not only cost a lot of money, but also require months of advance preparation. Rick Dubinsky's study group, now officially designated the Strike Committee, began receiving full funding from ALPA in October 1984.

Eventually the 29-day strike would cost ALPA $10 million, and that *did not* include any strike benefits to United's pilots. Everybody knew that if, on the heels of the Continental debacle, United's pilots lost this battle to Dick Ferris, ALPA's future looked dim. In a very real sense, United's pilots would be fighting for ALPA's survival. The stakes were so high nearly everybody was "in denial," as psychological jargon puts it, hoping against hope that a strike wouldn't happen.

"It was about March 1985 when I finally felt that Ferris had made the decision to maneuver us into a strike," says Roger Hall. "He was convinced he could win a strike. I talked with Hank Duffy about the difficulties we were having with negotiations, but his feeling was that it wouldn't come to an all-out confrontation."

Duffy agrees with Hall's recollection, noting that United's corporate history indicated a preference for accommodation with labor, rather than confrontation. Then Duffy had a personal encounter with Dick Ferris—in full bluster—which indicated otherwise.

"About three weeks before the strike. Ferris came into my office, took off his coat (he's a very muscular guy), and sat on the arm of a chair so as to purposely look down at me," Duffy said in his 1990 interview, laughing at this sophomoric intimidation tactic. "They must have taught him this trick at the Cornell hotel school. Ferris then proceeded to tell me that if there was a strike he already had a group of working pilots, that he'd have 10 percent operations by the first week, 20 percent by the end of the first month, 30 percent by the second month, and at that point our people would crack. He said he had a $1 billion line of credit that he was perfectly willing to use, that we were broke, and that there was no way we could stand that. This was a huge ego we were dealing with. Somewhere along the way, he'd decided he could hammer us."

As summer approached and negotiations remained deadlocked, Ferris rather surprisingly made an attack on Rick Dubinsky the centerpiece of his appeals to the United pilot group, going over the heads of their elected representatives. By this time, the Strike Committee was in full battle harness, and Dubinsky was visibly and combatively out front, bringing the same energy and drive to the task that he had invested five years earlier in Operation USA, which first gained him a measure of national attention. Perhaps Ferris listened to Ferg, who told him Dubinksy was too radical, or he had heard that some pilots had alliteratively nicknamed him "Mad Dog." Back in 1975, as a very young MEC secretary-treasurer, Dubinsky had angrily resigned over Bill Arsenault's recall, an episode some United pilots still remembered with distaste.

As part of Ferris's ill-fated "road show" between April 29 and May 5, which the pilots generally boycotted, he floated the canard that Dubinsky was willing to lead the strike only because he was _independently wealthy_ and didn't need his job! This classic bit of disinformation actually had many United pilots believing it.

"That was a story the company was spreading going into the strike," says Dubinsky. "Corporate leaders are capable of the basest actions imaginable. They were trying to discredit my leadership, because if I had nothing to risk, what did I care if we went on strike?"

In fact, Dubinsky insists he was as dependent on his salary as any other pilot, despite a settlement he had received from a hospital because of negligence in the death of his wife some years earlier. The son of a union meatcutter from St. Louis, Dubinsky had grown up in a working class family. While studying mechanical engineering, he worked part-time as a research assistant for Monsanto, the St. Louis chemical giant. He paid for his own flying lessons, and United hired him during the 1965 pilot shortage. Dubinsky had 275 _total_ hours at the time. In the early 1970s, Dubinsky achieved some fleeting notoriety as one of the "hair grievers." United insisted on military haircuts for line pilots, regardless of the modishly long styles then in fashion. Because corporate regulations on hair length were imprecise and clashed with the ideals of several young pilots, they filed grievances. This episode illustrated not only a bit of nutty historical trivia, but also Dubinsky's willingness to resist authority when he thought it wrong, a trait he picked up while working for Monsanto.

"I absolutely cannot abide the arbitrary exercise of power over people when there's no good reason for it," says Dubinsky. "At Monsanto, I worked with some extremely talented engineers who put their heart and soul into projects, lived for months and years making products, not so much for the compensation as for love of the process. Yet, some bean counter could cut them off at the knees with two weeks' notice. It was devastating, and they had nothing to say about it. From my first exposure to ALPA, I saw that unionism was the reason airline pilots didn't have to put up with that, or get on their knees to anybody."

Roger Hall entrusted leadership of the strike to Dubinsky for a variety of reasons.

"Rick was a strong unionist, and I had high respect for his organizational ability, the way he could lead a group," Hall explains. "He had sort of separated himself from Ferg during the Blue Skies period, he was not at all in agreement with it, so he seemed to me an ideal person to organize and lead the strike."

In April 1985, United's pilots got final proof that no concession short of abject surrender would avert a strike. United's pilot negotiators agreed to some form of B-scale—*in principle*. It was a major concession, one that the pilots believed would be the basis for further negotiations leading to a settlement. But to make sure that Ferris didn't interpret this concession as a sign of weakness, United's MEC also recommended a strike authorization vote. United's 5,000 pilots supported their leaders by approving a walkout, set for May 17, 1985. Armed with this authorization, intensive negotiations under National Mediation Board auspices entered the final phase. Hank Duffy, following these developments closely, still believed a settlement likely.

"I thought Ferris was like Bob Crandall, in that he would take on the unions but that he was not suicidal," Duffy said in 1990 of his meeting with Ferris. "Our people were trying to be reasonable, and I thought right up to the eve of the strike that Ferris would see that and make a settlement. For all his bluster, he *said* he was open to further discussions. So I set up another meeting between him and Roger Hall, but that didn't go anywhere."

Finally, with the traditional high-traffic months of summer nearing, the two sides reached an impasse, and the NMB "released" the parties, freeing them to engage in self-help. In the last negotiations, attention focused not on Ferris's demand for a B-scale (which United's pilots had already conceded), but on its nature. Ferris wanted a B-scale that would end for new-hires only after they made captain, which meant, in effect, that it would penalize the next generation of United pilots well into paunchy, balding middle age. If history was any guide (which in this case it wasn't), no United new-hire could expect to make captain for at least 20 years. The pilots held out for a B-scale that would merge after six years. American's B-scale at that time would *never* merge.

As the May 17 strike deadline neared, Ferris played his trump card. Through carefully orchestrated news releases, Ferris announced that he would hire "permanent replacements" in the event of a strike. To put teeth in his threat, Ferris had, since December 1984, trained, *but not hired,* 570 new second officers, telling them that they would be used for "expansion." Clearly, Ferris expected to lure first officers across the picket line with promises of instant captaincies and to use "the 570" (as they came to be known) to fill out scab crews. The 570 were thus in an anomalous position, clearly contingent scabs, having neither union protection nor standing as employees.

Only happenstance let United's pilots know about the 570 or the nasty surprise Ferris intended them to be. Ferris had trained them quietly in small groups at United's Denver training center, a very large facility where anonymity is the rule, and the 570 went virtually undetected. But Jamie Lindsey, a second-generation airline pilot whose father had flown for both United and American, became concerned about them while he was undergoing first officer upgrade training in January 1985.

"Several people had wondered who these people at Denver with strange nametags were," says Lindsey. "But I was the only one dumb enough to walk up and ask one of them directly."

The young trainees with the odd nametags told Lindsey they were "pre-hires" who would be coming on the line as soon as ALPA signed a new contract. Lindsey, who had been an active "committee puke" at the MEC level, promptly phoned Roger Hall in Chicago to find out what he knew about them—which was nothing. Delegated by Hall to investigate these strange creatures further, Lindsey discovered that they were receiving only 19 days of training instead of the usual four to six weeks, that they were being paid a flat per diem rate of $26, with no allowance for either food or lodging, and that they were as bewildered about their status as ALPA was about them.

"Contacting them was real easy," Lindsey laughs. "All I had to do was put up a sign that said, 'Pre-hires Welcome Meeting, ALPA—FREE FOOD.'"

In short order, it became clear to everybody that the 570 were a strikebreaker force in training and that ALPA had better reach them quickly. With the assistance of Steve Forte, Bruce Lasch, and Raoul Bouher, Lindsey set up a systematic "contact program" aimed at the 570 as they came through the Denver training center each month. A key element in Lindsey's "outreach" program involved offering the "pre-hires" tutoring and a "study hall" each evening staffed by ALPA volunteers. Since the 570 were getting nonstandard training but still had to go through the regular exams, they were very grateful. This assistance proved to the 570 in concrete terms that ALPA was more interested in their welfare than was management.

But ALPA had other things than the 570 to worry about. On May 1, 1985, United began advertising for "fleet qualified" pilots who could step immediately into United cockpits. Ferris offered potential scabs "personal services" contracts, which paid captains a flat salary of $75,000 per year and noncaptains $50,000.

Ferris's actions infuriated United's line pilots, who knew that United was _already canceling revenue flights because it lacked crews._ The 570 were needed immediately, but Ferris kept them off the line as part of his prestrike maneuvering.

To thwart him, ALPA representatives made sure the 570 were fully aware that by resisting a nonmerging B-scale, ALPA was fighting _their_ battle. Still, no one could be sure what the 570 would do, and ALPA had no way of influencing (or even contacting) the "fleet qualified" applicants.

So current United pilots themselves would win or lose the strike. If Ferris could get a "critical mass" of pilots to cross early enough in the strike, he would win. United's pilots were fully aware that Lorenzo had won at Continental because just such a critical mass deserted the strike early on. It was an unstated fact that, if such a critical mass crossed, United's pilot leaders would have to call down the strike and admit defeat. But how many pilots would that be?

"I knew going into the strike that if the line started to crumble, we were going to have to settle," Roger Hall admits. "If we lost more than 15 percent, that was my mental number, we would have to take whatever terms were there."

And so the strike came.

On May 17, United's 5,000 pilots "hit the bricks" like any traditional labor union, picket signs in hand. It was the moment of truth, for down deep, each striker knew that the best job in the world was at stake. One popular lapel button said it all:"Cross and the Great Job Dies!" Each striker's story was different, yet somehow the same. It became a shared moment like none other save combat, the kind of experience that would later be taken out and unwrapped, like a precious heirloom, to be examined at leisure in a thousand pilot lounge conversations.

Whatever United's pilots were before the strike, they would never be the same afterward. For those who stood the test and now wear their "battle star" lapel pins (designed to instantly identify scabs, to whom no ALPA loyalist will speak socially outside the line of duty), who so rattled scabs by "clicking" children's' Halloween noisemakers as each one walked into their pilot lounges that Ferris finally had to get a humiliating court order against it, the strike lives in memory. It was a transforming moment akin to the experience U.S. Civil War soldiers would recall through the haze of years: Chickamauga, Antietam, Shiloh. This litany of humble U.S. placenames forever etched in memory would have counterparts in United's strike lore.

How could you tell a scab? He was the guy in the toilet stall with his baggage stuffed in, too, lest it get sent to Hong Kong. Veterans of the strike tell these stories and smile. What those who broke faith and crossed the picket line do as they look each morning into their mirrors, no one can say.

One thing any airline executive should always think about before provoking a strike—it gives pilots a chance to get to know each other. Most pilots lead professional lives of relative isolation, never really getting acquainted with very many of their colleagues. During normal operations, a big percentage are always flying. But in a strike, with everybody grounded and engaged in a cooperative effort, real solidarity and attendant friendships can emerge.

"We developed great closeness during the strike, many friendships that are still very strong with United people living half a mile from us that we didn't even know," says Bill Stewart, whose view from the trenches in Los Angeles will have to serve as surrogate for the stories of 5,000 other pilots. "Six months before the strike, if asked about it, I'd have probably said, 'Well, I'll try it for a while, but I can't risk my whole career just because the union tells me to.' But as we got into the strike, we discovered, Hey, we're not some kind of white collar professional association, we're a labor union, and if we don't stand together, they'll kill us individually. We had 95 percent honoring the picket line that first day, and that didn't change an awful lot. You're talking about people who never went to ALPA meetings, who all of a sudden realized what the situation was. So, ever since then, we've had this comradeship, or this togetherness, or this unity, whatever you want to call it, because it became painfully obvious that this was a noneconomic strike aimed at destroying us as a profession."

Round one went to ALPA, when all but 6 of the 570 not-quite-hired second officers refused to work. This development was critical, because *if* the 570 had crossed, it might have undermined many weak or greedy first officers who would have jumped at the chance to achieve "instant captaincies." Stung by the refusal of all but 6 of the 570 to cross the picket line, Ferris accelerated his hiring of permanent replacement "fleet qualified" scabs, but he couldn't find enough of them to break the strike. It all came down to the same old rub—United's pilots could control their own fate *if they could hold their own lines*.

On May 1, Ferris had predicted to the *Chicago Tribune* that 40 percent of his pilots would cross the picket line. Keeping in mind his private prediction to Hank Duffy that he expected victory when 30 percent crossed, how close did he come?

"Rick Dubinsky predicted that we would lose no more than 4 percent the first 48 hours, and that prognosis was essentially correct," says Roger Hall of the critical early hours. "Ferris was convinced that he would have 20 percent across the line within five days, and Ferg was telling him the strike would crumble within 48 hours or less. After 29 days, we ended up right at 6 percent who went to work, and that held."

Confronted by a unified pilot group, with the strike costing United literally millions each day, Ferris reluctantly, under shareholder and lender pressure, agreed to a five-year B-scale with negotiations and binding arbitration to follow. He could have had such an agreement earlier with far less trouble and expense. By the simple act of sustaining their picket lines, United's pilots had succeeded in calling his bluff. The B-scale game was no longer worth the candle, so five days after the strike's inception, Ferris settled.

The strike would continue for another 24 days because of difficulties over the back-to-work agreement, often the most wrenching aspect of any strike. At issue was the fate of the 570 and the flight attendants who had honored ALPA's lines. Ferris had also sent termination notices to a number of strike leaders, including Rick Dubinsky, which created another stumbling block.

"It was vindictive and just strengthened the resolve of the pilots," says Hall, who did not get one of the dozen termination letters. "There was no way the pilots would go back under those circumstances, and sane people in management knew it."

When the strike finally ended on June 14, critical post-mortems began coming in from outside. Pilots from other airlines, perhaps reflecting a touch of envy, spoke of the United pilot group "leaving their wounded on the battlefield." Stories circulated that United's pilots called down their strike only because massive numbers were on the verge of crossing. Such speculative disaster scenarios, like all "what ifs" in history, can be neither proven nor disproven. But Roger Hall offers a patient, logical explanation for which corroboration exists.

"At 26 days into the strike, the line was holding very well," Hall insists. "We legally had no choice but to settle the status of the 570 through court action, and the only remaining issue was the flight attendants getting a back-to-work agreement. At that point, Patty Friend [president of United's Association of Flight Attendants unit] came to me and said, 'We want you to go back to work. We cannot negotiate a back-to-work agreement; we intend to go to court, but our people need to get back to work, and the only way they can do that is if the airplanes are flying.' We gave financial support to the flight attendants until they got back to work, and eventually they were successful in court."

"We were accused of paying blood money for leaving our wounded, the flight attendants, on the battlefield," says Hank Duffy, confirming Hall's account. "But that's not it at all. They asked us to go back—at the national level they asked me, and at the local level they asked Roger. The flight attendants could not stay out any longer. They said, 'If you have an agreement, go back, because financially our organization is broken, and we have got to go back to work.' They asked for financial assistance *later*. They gave us absolution to go back because it was in *their* interests. Our people did all the honorable things in that strike."

As to the speculative charges, which are incapable of proof or disproof, that massive numbers of United pilots were preparing to cross the line if the strike had gone on only a few more days, all one can say is *if that were true*, it constitutes a tribute to the leadership and perspicacity of Roger Hall and Rick Dubinsky. The *essential* attribute of strike leadership is to recognize the precise moment, neither too late nor too early, when the time to settle arrives. Too late, and a strike becomes a holy war, which means that even in victory, the union loses because it destroys its company or its own jobs, as the Eastern strike of 1989 proved.

"If the tide was changing, then Roger Hall was very good at sensing it, and he caught it just as it changed, before we had to deal from an adverse position," says Hank Duffy. "But they *were* winning."

At the very worst, United's pilots won a clear-cut draw. Given the way things had been going recently for ALPA, that counted as a victory. Criticizing the outcome of the strike is a little like complaining about George Washington running away from the British early in the American Revolution. During the Battles of Long Island and Brooklyn Heights, Washington realized that, by pressing the issue, he risked getting cut off from the mainland. So he disengaged, strategically retreated his army across the Hudson River into New Jersey, and kept intact his striking power, the fabled Continental Blues, made up primarily of long-term enlistees. So long as Washington's army remained whole, the Revolution and the nation lived. But if Washington pressed a battle past the point of prudence, he risked not only losing just a battle, *but everything*. Only the last battle in a war counts.

ALPA was in the midst of what would inevitably be a long war. Deregulation had wrought changes that profoundly altered the relationship between labor and management. United's pilots fought ALPA's Battle of Long Island in 1985. If they had lost, their epitaph would also have been ALPA's as a viable union. Their victory, however qualified, proved to be a watershed, for aside from Frank Lorenzo's suicidal attempt on Eastern, it discouraged any further assaults on ALPA during the 1980s.

In one sense, United's pilots came away with a clear-cut victory, for they had dared to strike and, once engaged, had held their ranks against a determined opponent. They were still fit to fight at the end, but to have pressed the strike to a finish over the 570 or the flight attendants would have been foolish. Although for while the 570 lost, on average, something like 600 numbers of seniority to scabs (and some nonscabs hired after the strike), ALPA's legal actions eventually won for them the right to fly the line without betraying their profes-sional heritage—at a stiff price, but in the opinion of many, well worth it. In 1993, ALPA won a complete victory for the 570, when the courts ruled that United had illegally denied them their rightful seniority. They were immedi-ately jumped over the 600 scabs who had been hired during the strike.

Every professional airline pilot still covered by an ALPA contract owes the 570 a debt of gratitude. By courageously acting in concert with United's strik-ing pilots, the 570 allowed the pilots to settle the issue directly, without fear of their flank crumbling.

United's pilots had stanched the debilitating slide that had afflicted ALPA since the onset of deregulation. They had bought the profession time. It was now up to the "politicians" in ALPA's national offices to make the most of it. ✈

CHAPTER 17

NATIONAL POLITICS AND MERGERS
The Election of 1986 and Beyond

Picture MacBeth's "weird sisters" and their bubbling cauldron laced with "eye of newt and toe of frog." Slimy stuff, but if Shakespeare had really wanted nasty in the pot, he would have dropped in a merger. For making a political "hell-broth boil and bubble," merging an airline pilot group's seniority has it all over "adder's fork and blind-worm's sting!"

Politics, according to an old definition of the term, is how we decide who gets what. As an arena for the resolution of conflict, politics stands just shy of the theater of war. In the famous Clauswitzian dictum, war is the "extension of politics by other means." That politics often adopts the language and symbolism of war, with rivals waging "campaigns" and planning strategy with military intensity, should come as no surprise.

In reality, *successful* politics rests upon consensus and compromise—a willingness to take half a loaf. Because the solution will inevitably have losers, the structure of politics must accommodate them. Where peoples and nations are concerned, failure of political consensus leads to war, civil or foreign. In organizations like ALPA, political failure brings factionalism and disunion—the 1963 defection of the American Airlines pilots, for example.

But another dimension to politics bears more directly upon ALPA's history. Sir Lewis Namier, the eminent historian of 18th century British politics, noted that for all the disputations between Whig and Tory, very little in the way of substantive issues actually divided them. The aristocratic English gentlemen who fought out political campaigns with such venom were linked by kinship, class, and a basic value system. This underlying consensus allowed them to *safely* dispute political issues. By the 18th century, the so-called "Age of Reason," neither Whig nor Tory feared that victory by the other would bring prison or property confiscation. Their heated political campaigns simply illustrated yet another ancient political axiom—the closer the relationship, the warmer the contention. Or put plainly, there's no feud like a family feud, even when it's only about what 18th century British politicians called *place* (office and status), not matters of life and death.

The trick to *successful* politics lies in keeping passions from getting out of hand over nonessentials—not an easy task. Historians can see these old political wars in dispassionate retrospection, but those who actually lived through them had a harder time of it. Once immersed in the tangled underthickets of politics, where personal ambition, private vanity, and naked ego could fester unchecked, warring factions can easily lose sight of the consensus they all know, *down deep*, they share.

"Some of us still don't realize that the enemy is *out there*, not *in here*," said Hank Duffy in his opening remarks to the November 1986 BOD meeting at Bal Harbour, Fla. In what was sure to be a hotly contested election for ALPA's leadership, Duffy was making a point that was as true for 18th century Whigs and Tories as it is for modern airline pilots—that far more unites than divides them. Amidst all the disagreements over specific problems that confronted the profession, from the vexations of crafting new seniority lists for the 12,000 dues-paying ALPA members facing mergers to Frank Lorenzo's ominous takeover of Eastern, Duffy emphasized the fundamental truth that airline pilots share basic interests.

"Every one of our enemies is out there; not one of them is in this room," Duffy repeated for dramatic effect, earning a round of applause from BOD delegates.

It was a nice try at defusing the palpable tension in Bal Harbour. During Hank Duffy's first term, he had labored under an internal political burden that complicated nearly every aspect of ALPA's mission. His narrow victory over J.J. O'Donnell in 1982 left ALPA with a divided Executive Committee. Tom Ashwood, the TWA pilot and O'Donnell protege who emerged as ALPA's first vice-president, anchored an anti-Duffy faction that always regarded his victory as a fluke. Either Ashwood or Jack Bavis, ALPA's executive administrator, could easily have won ALPA's presidency in 1982, Duffy's critics believed, had not O'Donnell sabotaged their candidacies by seeking a fourth term. As the 1986 election approached, they saw Duffy as vulnerable.

But Hank Duffy thought otherwise. Thanks to United's pilots, the delegates had some breathing space for calm reflection. Likewise, the phasing down of the financial burden caused by the Continental strike (which would eventually cost ALPA $70 million) bought Duffy some slack. If the BOD delegates would only step back from the intense struggles of the recent past and consider his leadership on its merits, Duffy believed, he would win another term.

"You will note that these remarks don't contain the doom and gloom flavor of some of my previous reports," Duffy told the November 1985 Washington, D.C., meeting of the Executive Board, which effectively began the 1986 ALPA presidential campaign. Relieved that for the first time he was addressing the delegates "without some major crisis brewing," Duffy could point with pride to ALPA's successes. He justifiably cited the new $100 million Major Contingency Fund, or war chest, "the accolades given ALPA over the United Strike," and ALPA's increasing expertise in "protecting pilots threatened with corporate takeovers" as reasons for re-electing him. Duffy's opening remarks also contained a strong endorsement of close ties with the AFL-CIO and promised continued support for unemployed pilots, particularly those from Continental.

"First and foremost, we must take care of our casualties, those people who have given everything for ALPA," Duffy said. "I'm calling on each of you to use all the leverage you have with your managements to place these fellow pilots in jobs on your airlines."

Tom Ashwood, who followed Duffy to the rostrum for his address as ALPA's first vice-president, adopted a less sanguine tone, particularly on the Continental strike.

"Let's not fool ourselves," Ashwood countered. "We lost this one."

Perhaps asking pilots who had been through the recent fires to consider their leadership choices calmly was asking too much. Historians might easily recognize an almost Whig-vs.-Tory quality to the upcoming Ashwood–Duffy contest, but more casual observers, enmeshed in all the heated rhetoric, would not.

A peculiar feature of the 1986 election was that for the first time in ALPA's history, all national officers would be elected to simultaneous four-year terms. Historically, ALPA had favored staggered terms to preserve continuity, but internal changes in governance had lessened the need for that safeguard. Consequently, the opportunity to make a sweeping "mid-course correction," as Hank Duffy put it during the May 1986 meeting of the Executive Board, was never better. But Duffy expected no such outcome. Despite niggling criticism by rank-and-file pilots (part of the historical baggage all sitting presidents carried), Duffy was confident that the BOD delegates, who generally had a more sophisticated understanding of the difficulties confronting ALPA, would reelect him. Then the unexpected happened—complications arose in the Northwest/Republic airline merger.

"Going into the election, I felt I had a pretty comfortable margin," Duffy recalls. "But I was basing that largely on having the Republic pilots' votes. Because of merger-related issues, we lost Republic, and that made the election a lot tighter."

Short of bankruptcy and unemployment, nothing has bedeviled ALPA's internal politics the way mergers have. Acrimony, bitterness, paranoid suspicions—all these and more have resulted from mergers. Making matters worse, ALPA has *always* been the scapegoat for pilots dissatisfied with mergers. Since Hank Duffy's election in 1982, aside from the continuing trouble with Frank Lorenzo, ALPA's single most contentious internal political issue had been the spate of deregulation-generated mergers.

Honoring a campaign promise to be more "responsive" to rank-and-file members, Duffy spent a lot of time personally answering letters of complaint during his first term. The angriest letters in ALPA's bulging "President's File" during these years concerned mergers, some of them long past.

"I will no longer be a member of an association that turns its back when unfair treatment occurs within its ranks," wrote Jack Fehling, a former Northeast Airlines pilot who came to Delta in the 1972 merger. In a 1987 letter to Duffy, Fehling, his old resentments stirred anew by the 1986 Delta/Western merger, resigned from ALPA over what he saw as the injustice of ALPA's merger policy. "Why is a pre-1972 Delta pilot with my length of service 800 numbers senior to me?"

"I was very disappointed to receive your letter of resignation," Duffy patiently responded to Fehling. "In both the Delta/Northeast and Delta/Western mergers, both sides sent merger representatives in to achieve not only the best for their own pilots, but also a fair and equitable settlement. I'm convinced that the system we use under ALPA Merger Policy, whereby an attempt is made to achieve a result through direct negotiations before finally relying on binding arbitration, is a good one. It is fair and provides due process with an ultimate decision by a neutral, and I think that's the best any union can do. Jack, to blame your union and to resign from it over a single issue is extremely shortsighted. There are simply too many forces at work attempting to tear down the piloting profession for us to fight as individual pilots."

Duffy was obviously forgetting yet another ancient political truth—"All politics is local!" Fehling was simply expressing a resentment that was understandable among those who had to settle for half a loaf—the inescapable requirement of successful politics. On some airlines, merger fights so blinded pilots to the principles of conciliation and compromise that they actually sought to decertify ALPA. On TWA, for example, trouble involving the 1986 Ozark merger forced MEC Chairman Harry Hoglander to doggedly beat back a decertification effort by a splinter group calling itself the "Airline Pilots Union." Proving that there was really nothing new under the historical sun, this episode was eerily reminiscent of a similar attempt, led by Waldon "Swede" Golien, a disaffected ALPA pioneer, to form a splinter union called "The TWA Pilots Association" *in 1933!*[1]

Airline mergers have produced some wacky feuds over the years. For example, the 1953 merger of Delta and Chicago & Southern Air Lines caused an improbable falling out between Charles H. Dolson and Stewart W. Hopkins, two authentic ALPA pioneers. Before moving on to airline careers, Dolson and Hopkins had served together as U.S. Navy carrier pilots in the late 1920s. Each man had organized his airline for ALPA in 1935—quite remarkable feats considering the hostility toward unions that characterized the South. Dolson (who was older than Hopkins and senior to him in the Navy, went to work for American in 1931, a year before Hopkins signed on with Pacific Seaboard Airlines. But then Dolson got furloughed because of the air mail cancellations of 1934. He caught on with Delta in 1935, but Hopkins meanwhile had "continuous service" as Chicago & Southern acquired Pacific Seaboard in 1934. When Dolson's "broken service" with American was disallowed, that made Hopkins *one number senior* on the new Delta list.

Dolson was furious. Now keep in mind, neither man had ever flown copilot for anybody and their piddling seniority difference had no practical effect whatsoever on their professional careers. Dolson, who died in 1992 at the age of 86, would rise from Delta's chief pilot to chairman of the Delta Air Lines Board of Directors—far and away the most successful executive career any airline pilot has ever had. Hopkins, who at 83 was still alive at the time of this writing, was no slouch either. Not only did he become an admiral in the Naval Reserves, but he also served as ALPA's first vice-president and was an authentic "king maker" in ALPA politics who almost single-handedly saved Charley Ruby from being recalled in 1966. But that *one number* rankled Dolson to his dying day, maybe because Hopkins puckishly kidded him about it, giving Dolson a nickname ("Cheerful Charlie") he could neither live down nor appreciate.

At least the Old Guys like Hopkins and Dolson didn't sue each other over seniority problems. By the 1980s, pilots unhappy with a merged list were, like so many other litigious Americans, quick to file lawsuits—against ALPA! The 1986 Delta/Western merger (which stirred up Jack Fehling's old resentments) generated a long, complicated, and expensive lawsuit that did nothing except enrich lawyers.

Ironically, the disaffected Western pilots, consisting mostly of a contingent based in Salt Lake City, would almost certainly have been without jobs had not Delta acquired their airline. Western almost surely would have followed Braniff into oblivion otherwise. But no matter, ALPA *(and by inference, the merger committee negotiators from Western itself)* would wind up on the receiving end of yet another lawsuit that would require justification of its merger policy before a federal court.

"I've got to tell you I think our merger with Delta was fair," says Chuck Tully, a Western pilot since 1966, dismissing the complainers from his own airline. "I was a B-737 captain before the merger, and I was still a B-737 captain after. If a guy the day after a merger is doing the same thing he was the day before the merger, it's fair. No Western pilot lost like that, and we were given access to widebody equipment that we would not have had otherwise.

'I don't want to sound insensitive to the guys at the bottom of the seniority list [where most of the unhappiness existed, primarily because of age discrepancies], but I think there were a lot of unrealistic expectations out there that no merger committee could have met," Tully says. "Our committee wasn't really looking at 'fair' so much as they were looking at a comparison to arbitration, the bird in the hand compared to how much more they could gain as to how much they could lose."

In February 1990, a federal judge would confirm Tully's views by dismissing the lawsuit filed by "Rick Herring *et al.*" (popularly known as "Pilots for a Fair Seniority List"). With some exasperation, the judge ruled that there was an element of the irrational about lawsuits challenging ALPA's merger policy. Perhaps the judge was only saying, in legalese, what everybody who had ever examined merger disputes already knew—that some animosities would persist until the last pilot involved retired!

Nothing illustrated the inherent contentiousness of mergers better than the Northwest/Republic merger of 1986. Like Western, Republic (originally an amalgam of Southern, North Central, and Hughes Air West) was flirting with bankruptcy when Northwest acquired it. The merger of the two airlines, which operated disparate equipment because their differing route structures and histories, generated a bitter political fight that spilled over into ALPA's 1986 election.

For all the controversy that ALPA's Merger Policy has generated over the years, nothing particularly complicated or sinister underlies its *principles*. It called for negotiations between the two affected pilot groups who ideally would agree on a new integrated seniority list. But what if they couldn't agree? Then ALPA policy specified binding arbitration by a neutral third party chosen by the principals. ALPA *recommended* (but did not require) that the negotiators and arbitrators *consider* certain guidelines in making a settlement. Always high on the list of these factors were the twin totems of airline pilot seniority—date-of-hire and length-of-service.

As is inevitably true of such seemingly simple, straightforward, and principled "guidelines," the devil was in the details. What, for example, should be done about a conflict between date-of-hire and length-of-service? Which should take priority? During the 1980 merger of PanAmerican and National, some furloughed Pan Am pilots had dates-of-hire earlier than National pilots who had longer length-of-service. Should date-of-hire for a pilot who had been cleaning swimming pools for the past 10 years take precedence over length-of-service for one who had hustled up another flying job? What was fair?

Further merger complications involved "class and craft" considerations, to use traditional labor terminology. What should be done about a Pan Am pilot with 20 years of unbroken service who, because of that airline's stagnant promotion list, held the rank of only first officer, while a National pilot with 10 years of unbroken service held a captaincy? Should the first officer and captain lists be integrated separately? And what about gross disparities in equipment flown by two merging airlines? Should Northwest be required to upgrade (at tremendous expense) a grizzled old Republic DC-9 captain to the B-747, even though he was nearing retirement?

Clearly, rigid adherence to merger "guidelines" in all cases was impractical. After all, the purpose of mergers was economic—to ensure the survival of an airline so as to preserve pilots' jobs. But putting together a merged seniority list was a fiendishly complex, intrinsically contentious process that would have taxed the wisdom of Solomon. What should be done about timetables for complying with upgrade training on new equipment, verification of employment data for accuracy, and dozens of other technical details? And finally, what should ALPA do about an arbitrator who does something really stupid—like cutting the baby in half?

The bitter 1986 merger between Air Wisconsin and Mississippi Valley, two small airlines with fewer than 100 pilots each, stands as a case in point. Because the pilots could not agree on a merged seniority list, the final decision fell to an arbitrator who imposed a settlement that left 15-year Air Wisconsin first officers flying copilot for Mississippi Valley captains with 7 years of service!

Air Wisconsin's outraged pilots blamed ALPA (not their own negotiators' hard-nosed insistence upon a "stapler" merger—simply adding the Mississippi Valley pilot seniority list to the bottom of the Air Wisconsin list). Eventually, ALPA had to impose a "trusteeship" over the merged airline after the Air Wisconsin pilots (who outnumbered the Mississippi Valley group by five pilots) voted to pull out of ALPA to overturn the arbitrator's decision. With ALPA's good faith on the line, Hank Duffy had no choice but to resist their move and appointed United's redoubtable Cliff Sanderson as trustee.

All this happened because the breakdown of *direct* negotiations between the two pilot groups threw the final decision into the hands of an arbitrator who blew it. Such are the hazards of letting outsiders decide things.

"Since 1985, all of ALPA's internal political crises have been about mergers," Sanderson declares simply.

Through the years, ALPA has struggled mightily to devise some way to resolve the Merger Policy dilemma. At the very least, ALPA's policy ought to shift the onus of resentment to the place where it properly belongs—the recalcitrance, unreasonableness, or stupidity, whatever might be the case, of the pilot group negotiators themselves. Many bright and knowledgeable people have fruitlessly sought a "magic bullet" that would provide a painless solution to mergers. By the late 1980s, "final offer arbitration" took its place as the latest in a long line of utopian solutions to merger disputes. Under this scenario, the arbitrator would be obligated to accept either one or the other pilot group's "final offer." This would put a premium on reasonableness (assuming that the arbitrator was knowledgeable enough to recognize it), and perhaps bring the two groups into actual agreement. But in any case, ALPA itself would be spared. All this did Hank Duffy no good, however, in the Northwest/Republic merger, which took an inordinate amount of time to resolve. Inevitably (if unfairly), Duffy became the lightning rod for the Republic pilots' anger.

Part of the problem was that the arbitrator, Thomas Roberts, took so long to make his decision. During the three years (from 1986 to 1989) while Roberts sorted out his options, the merged airline had to operate with cumbersome "fences," which kept the two pilot groups artificially separate, much to management's irritation. Then, when Roberts finally made his decision, he departed from tradition by arranging the list by date of hire but using a "career-expectation rubric" with fences that muted its effect.

Under terms of the "Roberts Rights," senior Republic pilots, no matter what their premerger seniority, would be "fenced off" from bidding up to heavy Northwest equipment (under certain circumstances), until the "career expectations" of *some* Northwest pilots had been met. Put simply, this meant that until the group of Northwest pilots who had hired on with the "career expectation" of becoming widebody captains had been met, they would have first bidding rights. Since most Republic pilots had hired on with "career expectations" no higher than the left seat of a DC-9, they would have to wait for their turn at heavy equipment—in some cases until 2006!

This extended "fence" was only one of several bitter disputes between the "Red Tail" (original Northwest) and "Green Book" (former Republic) pilots. A variety of arcane details, such as "dispute resolution" over the B-757/767 type rating, resulted in yet another welter of lawsuits filed by everybody on all sides with multiple targets—ALPA, the opposition pilot group, the former managements, and arbitrator Roberts himself! Each group had grievances over specific aspects of Roberts' award. An old adage holds that when *everybody* is unhappy with a merger, it must be fair!

One other aspect of the Northwest/Republic merger deserves comment. In their leadership choices, each pilot group selected men better known for pugnacity than persuasiveness. The Northwest pilot group chose ALPA's original "Dog of War," Bob Kehs, whose nickname of "Dr. Strike" was a recognition of his skill at confrontation. Perhaps to counter Kehs, the Republic pilot group selected his mirror image, Earl J. ("E.J.") Lawlus for a prominent role. Neither would win any shrinking violet contests.

The carrier's economic burden of retraining crews, one traditional reason for an arbitrator imposing "fences," played little role in Roberts' original arbitration.

In mitigation, Republic pilots who were most affected by these "fences" actually got paid the same as if they were flying the heavy aircraft from which they were "fenced off," thanks to their ALPA contract. It was actually a fairly generous reward for sparing the company (in some cases) the expense of upgrade training for pilots nearing retirement.

But many Republic pilots, feeling psychologically aggrieved, blamed ALPA for "betraying the guidelines" contained in the Merger Policy. Actually the Northwest/Republic merger did no such thing. The Republic pilots could see only that the "fence agreement" violated the date-of-hire priority. But ALPA's Merger Policy had always subordinated straight date-of hire/length-of-service to the overriding necessity of "preserving jobs" and other considerations as well. By 1988, to break this fixation on date-of-hire, ALPA's revised Merger Policy would explicitly state that "the application [of these criteria] *should not preclude* the consideration or use of any integration method which could balance the equities [emphasis added]."

The Northwest/Republic merger undoubtedly made the former Republic pilots feel like "second-class citizens," but it did not violate ALPA's policy, and in the way of such things, the actual injury done them wound up being magnified in the retelling. Smarting over arbitrator Thomas Roberts's handling of the merger, Republic's pilots abandoned Hank Duffy, for whom they had cast all 1,684 of their votes by "unit rule" in 1982. Four years later, they would cast 1,726 unit-rule votes for Tom Ashwood.

With the TWA/Ozark merger generating similar stresses, Hank Duffy suddenly found himself facing a growing and quite unexpected coalition of pilot groups who blamed him for the perceived shortcomings of ALPA's Merger Policy.

"I think maybe the pilots unfairly expect ALPA to fix things that are really not fixable," admits Lawlus. "I've flown with former Eastern and Braniff pilots, and while they're all thankful to have a job, that underlying resentment directed at ALPA doesn't seem to go away, and that's also true of mergers. There are former Northeast pilots who are still pissed off at Delta's pilots after all these years."

But Lawlus, a former Marine pilot who began flying with Bonanza in 1956 (and consequently takes a back seat to no one in "merger experience"), despite his philosophical commitment and long service to ALPA, feels bitter about the way his "Green Book" Republic pilots were treated in the merger with Northwest's "Red Tails." He blames Northwest's management for a pattern of discrimination, which the original Northwest pilots encouraged, against former Republic pilots. Lawlus also believes Duffy ignored it to gain the political support of the Northwest pilot group in 1986.

"I would have preferred to see things in a different way, and I hate to be so critical of Duffy and ALPA," Lawlus says, "but they made us feel like we had a damned tattoo on our foreheads."

"Going into the 1986 election, I thought Hank would win in a landslide," says Northwest's Skip Eglet, who was an ALPA executive vice-president at the time. "Then, a tremendous coalition of airlines who had the same merger philosophy, who publicly and vigorously defended date-of-hire as the *only way* to merge seniority lists, carried the policy debate over into the convention and voted as a block against him, and that was some big airlines—United, TWA, USAir."

When combined with Tom Ashwood's undeniable brilliance as a campaigner, the festering animosities brought on by the avalanche of mergers suddenly made the election of 1986 a toss-up. Ashwood had made identification with the larger trade union movement a centerpiece of his campaign, even before pilot opinion began to shift on the issue in the 1980s. Constantly urging pilots to solve their problems in the "good old union way," Ashwood was a master at anecdotally praising unionism _in principle_, calling on pilots to not only play a role in the AFL-CIO, but to lead it as well.

"Now we hear talk about 'Let's join the labor movement,'" Ashwood chided Duffy at the November 1985 Executive Board. "We should be leading it!"

While Duffy's aristocratic bearing and former role as a Republican Party county chairman made him an unlikely labor leader, no one could doubt his commitment by 1986. Spurred not only by Ashwood's criticisms, but also by the antilabor bias of the Reagan Administration, Duffy began to emerge as a conspicuous spokesman for the AFL-CIO—something ALPA's leaders had been wary of, historically.

"The strong antiunion stand of this [Republican] Administration is unchanged, and we cannot expect any help," Duffy told the May 1986 Executive Board. "If we want to survive, we have to toughen up as a union. We tend to look too much to other people. During Continental, we looked to the Australians to shut down the South Pacific [a slam at Ashwood, who believed Aussie trade unions would refuse to fuel Lorenzo's planes]. The catalyst for our transition from an elitist association to a labor union has been communications. In 1982, I told everybody who would listen that we needed communications across company lines. If that program had been in place during Continental, I think the results would have been far different."

Citing regional meetings with spouses, "family awareness," increased use of VCRs, computer nets, and the introduction of "Viewpoint Cards" in every issue of _Air Line Pilot_, Duffy took credit for the success of the United strike and the new militancy and self-confidence that were rippling through ALPA. He noted that, under his leadership, ALPA had placed pilot representatives on several AFL-CIO councils, had become affiliated with the Maritime Trades Department of the AFL-CIO and the International Transport Federation, had joined the "union label" movement, and was advertising the "Don't Buy" list among rank-and-file pilots.

""These things have nothing to do with the airline industry," Duffy proclaimed, "but a lot to do with the trade union movement. We have come a long way from the days when at every BOD meeting we had a resolution on the floor that said, 'Get out of the AFL-CIO.'"

Ashwood, who constantly cited the British trade union tradition in his anecdotal speeches to ALPA groups, believes he forced Duffy into a more militant, prounion rhetorical mode as the 1986 campaign evolved.

"I believe I was the first national officer to ever use the word 'union' on the record," Ashwood says. "O'Donnell, who actually switched us from a professional association to a union, used to suck on his teeth when I would do that, because union wasn't a popular word until the Continental strike."

With nothing to differentiate Duffy and Ashwood on most substantive issues, the election of 1986 would ultimately turn on matters of personality and the struggle for "place," as 18th century Whigs and Tories understood it. But Ashwood did urge one rather remarkable change internally—a change that might have backfired on him. Insiders knew that Ashwood was unhappy with Henry Weiss, and Ashwood let it be known that if he won election, ALPA's historical connection with the law firm of Cohen, Weiss, and Simon, would end.

"Cohen, Weiss, and Surrender, I like to call it," snorts Ashwood.

Ashwood had become disillusioned with Weiss while serving as first vice-president. He would later come to believe that ALPA was "outlawyered" during the Icahn takeover of TWA, but his core complaint against Weiss was that he had become too involved in ALPA's *internal* politics. Ashwood was deeply suspicious of Weiss's role as parliamentarian, particularly some technical decisions in 1982, which Ashwood maintains kept the pilots of recently bankrupt Braniff, who would have supported O'Donnell, from voting. In 1986, as Ashwood sees it, Weiss was instrumental in letting the Frontier pilots vote, even though they were in essentially the same condition as the Braniff pilots had been in 1982.

"Frontier had gone belly up, and there was not a chance that they were ever going to come back," Ashwood maintains. "But Weiss ruled they were still alive as far as ALPA was concerned, while the Continental pilots, who were getting back to work, 1,600 votes that were for me, Weiss ruled could not vote, even though they were represented at the BOD. Pure politics—I would have won, and Weiss would have been out of a job."

To many ALPA insiders, Ashwood's criticisms of Henry Weiss were jarring. Weiss's service to ALPA dated back to the Behncke era, and his reputation for remembering ALPA's history is renowned. As ALPA's "chief legal counsel," Henry Weiss has been at the heart of ALPA's courtroom battles for nearly half a century.

"There was never any *legal* establishment as 'general counsel,'" says Henry Weiss. "It's just a name that sticks to us."

Legally established or not, Weiss was the rock upon which ALPA's legal edifice was built. Largely owing to Clarence "Clancy" Sayen, ALPA's second president, Henry Weiss and his law firm became inextricably linked to ALPA, serving both as "outside" counsel and, through a curious set of historical circumstances, as godfather of ALPA's current Legal Department.

In the mid-1950s, Clancy Sayen, dissatisfied with the way ALPA's in-house Legal Department was handling *routine* casework (grievances and the like), gave Weiss an angry ultimatum. It was a surprising development, because Sayen and Weiss were close friends. The raging firestorm of the 1953 Behncke ouster, which they had fought as allies, had built a bond between them that was like the bonds men retain from experiencing war together. They even shared each others' homes, rather than stay in hotels when they found themselves in Chicago or New York. Suddenly, here was Clancy Sayen storming into Henry Weiss's office with blood in his eyes.

"Sayen came to New York and said to me in plain terms, 'If you don't handle our grievance cases, you're not going to do *any* of ALPA's work!'" Weiss recalls. "Previously, with few exceptions, I had handled only those grievance cases that had special note of some kind. The Legal Department had messed up a lot of things, and he wanted to disassemble it completely. He said, 'You'll become vice-president of Legal.' I remember it was wintertime, and I was sick with a cold. I said, 'Clancy, let me alone! I don't work as an employee for institutions. Take your anger out some other way.'"

After Sayen cooled off, Weiss agreed to supervise the building of a new legal staff for ALPA. With Sayen's backing, Weiss cleaned house, interviewed and hired new lawyers, and reorganized ALPA's administrative procedures in so far as they applied to routine legal matters.

"The long and the short of it," Weiss remembers, "is that I got a mandate to reestablish a reoriented Legal Department."

Sayen gave Weiss a year to complete the job. Building upon Harold Bennett and Maurice Schy ("Both very good men," says Weiss), the newly restructured ALPA Legal Department emerged from the chaos of the early 1950s with a new sense of direction.

"I tried to give these lawyers a sense of their client," Weiss says with intensity. "Lawyers were being sent all around the country with no sense of connection with United Airlines or the United pilots, or National Airlines and their pilots."

To develop this sense of identification with pilots flying the line, Weiss insisted that ALPA's lawyers be assigned to serve specific airlines and *physically* dispersed around the country.

"I saw that if we would out-base the lawyers at the various domiciles, where they might handle two or three airlines, because business was not so intense as to require one lawyer for one airline at that time, they would have a sense of the guys they represent *and to whom they are responsible.*"

Henry Weiss emphasizes this last point with a flinty glance, one that has been honed over nearly six decades of intense courtroom battles.

Although Weiss admits to being Clancy Sayen's soul mate in every way (words like "brilliant" recur in his conversational remembrances of Sayen), ALPA founder Dave Behncke, not Sayen, first brought Weiss on board. The United States is a litigious land, so any confrontational organization (like a union), must necessarily find itself enmeshed in legal snares. Just such a snare brought Dave Behncke to Henry Weiss's door in 1946.

Weiss is convinced that the airline operators intended to destroy ALPA after World War II. The post-war surplus of pilots qualified to fly military transports was the operators' ace in the hole. Using these pilots as leverage, the airline operators expected to get rid of ALPA once and for all. The effort began on Ted Baker's National Airlines, and it would eventually culminate in the celebrated strike of 1948. But all Henry Weiss knew when he met Dave Behncke for the first time was that ALPA wasn't going to be an easy outfit to work for.[2]

"Dave was a very demanding person, and you had to do precisely as he wanted, or else you were fired; and he fired ruthlessly, in a very arbitrary fashion," Weiss recalls.

Indeed, Henry Weiss and his law partner, Sam Cohen, became ALPA's lawyers only because the eminent labor lawyer, Henry Kaiser, had quit ALPA because he found Behncke impossible.

"I soon encountered that problem myself," Weiss recalls.

Behncke expected a lawyer simply to be a mouthpiece who would parrot long, rambling statements that Behncke himself had previously written. At his first legal proceeding representing ALPA, Behncke handed Weiss such a statement. Finding it both inappropriate and demeaning, Weiss began editing Behncke's prose severely.

"Stick to the script!" Behncke hissed.

Weiss flatly refused. Having just lost one prominent labor lawyer with these tactics, Behncke retreated and allowed Weiss to do his job.

"I don't know how we made our peace," Weiss recalls of his refusal to knuckle under to Behncke. "But somehow we came to an understanding."

Behncke and ALPA desperately needed a topflight labor lawyer to pursue legal action against National's Ted Baker, who was making a shambles of ALPA's dearly bought collective bargaining contract, refusing to honor parts of it and threatening to fire any pilot who acted as a union officer. Desperate, Behncke turned to his old friend Fiorello La Guardia, the mayor of New York City, who recommended Henry Weiss. Weiss had never heard of ALPA when Behncke lumbered into his New York City offices in 1946.

By folklore and custom, the best way to deal with litigation is to have a legal pit bull to turn loose on opponents. Henry Weiss already fit that description, and it was a good thing. Ted Baker's lawyer in the first round of legal sparring that followed Weiss's hiring was none other than Roy Cohn, who would later achieve notoriety as Senator Joe McCarthy's hatchet man.

"That was before his Red-baiting days," Weiss recalls with more than a hint of disdain.

By taking the measure of Roy Cohn and Ted Baker, Henry Weiss made an impression on Behncke, thus beginning a relationship between his law firm and ALPA that has endured through the 1990s. What began as a temporary legal assignment, a one-time job for a union Weiss never expected to hear from again, would lead him into a parallel life—half spent with the law, the other half with ALPA.

Like the *grillot* tale-tellers of West Africa, who bear within their own memories the rich oral traditions of their people, Weiss has accumulated a vast store of knowledge about ALPA's history—much of which does not appear anywhere in the written record. There was practically nothing about ALPA he didn't know, hadn't seen, and most remarkably for a man of 80 (at the time of an oral history interview in 1990) couldn't remember.

Henry Weiss was born on March 31, 1910, the second son of a successful, hard-driving Baltimore clothing manufacturer who cannot be credited for making him a labor lawyer—quite the contrary. His father hated unions and warred with them continuously. In 1925, when Henry was only 15, he entered Cornell University in Ithaca, N.Y. Graduating from college at the tender age of 19, Weiss went on to Columbia Law School, emerging with his degree in 1932—at the bottom of the Great Depression. Ironically, he did not initially practice labor law, the field in which he became so prominent.

Although Weiss retired from the active management of his law firm in 1985, he continued as ALPA's parliamentarian, much to Tom Ashwood's dismay. Weiss reflected upon these distant events during an interview in August 1990. He was still keeping an office on the 25th floor of the unpretentious building at 330 West 42nd street (next door to the New York Port Authority bus terminal), an area gone seedy with panhandlers and trashy businesses.

It wasn't always this way. Once, in another time, through these very doors walked Behncke, Sayen, Ruby, and all the other great names in ALPA's past. Now that "Behncke's Tomb," the old headquarters building at 55th and Cicero in Chicago, has fallen to the wrecking ball and Midway's expansion, perhaps these offices are the closest we can get to a "historic" ALPA site.

The surroundings are a perfect reflection of Henry Weiss—straightforward and no-nonsense. The office accoutrements of a practice devoted to labor law are usually somewhat spartan, and Henry's digs are, to put it mildly, no exception—clients of Cohen, Weiss, and Simon needn't worry about being charged for the overhead of this utilitarian layout. No deep pile carpets, no fancy art work, no hushed atmosphere, no elegantly coiffured secretaries—just plain, working-class New York simple. Henry's office, which commands a sweeping view of the Hudson River and Manhattan's Lower West Side, is hard-edged and spare. Instead of drapes to hush the din rising from the adjacent theater district along Broadway, the windows have plastic venetian blinds. The only thing in the office that bespeaks luxury is a single Japanese wood block print by Hiroshige—a souvenir of Weiss's World War II service as a U.S. Navy officer. The normal buzz of the great city below occasionally rises with the wail of a siren, making it necessary to turn off the tape recorder until the emergency vehicle has passed.

Henry Weiss sat for two days, patiently answering questions, choosing his words carefully, weighing their impact. He scrupulously avoided any mention at all of Tom Ashwood personally, but he denied charges of interfering in ALPA's politics.

"I have from time to time been called into discussions that were certainly about policy," Weiss said carefully. "I would not under any circumstances attempt to influence or shape a judgment or policy without feeling that this really resonates with what the members want done. Of course, I will enter discussions as to the merits of some particular issue. But it's up to them to decide, to make their choice."

Weiss would say no more about the unpleasantness of the 1986 election. His conversation ranged from the merely anecdotal (fascinating stories about ALPA's dominant personalities and their foibles) to the kind of sere, linear analysis of events one would expect of a law school professor (which Henry Weiss has been). He was far more interested in the future of the airline piloting profession than in settling old scores.

Weiss worried most about two things—the effects of the internationalization of the airline industry and deregulation. Henry Weiss is not a man to mince words. "Capital doesn't have any patriotic strain in it," Weiss declared. "Capital flows where the capital gets paid most for its use. Because transportation has become so fluid and efficient, we know that it is seeking globalization, really a searching out from one market to another for the cheapest labor."

Weiss doubted that the U.S. government will be of much help to airline pilots seeking to protect their jobs from cheap foreign competition.

"The State Department has been willing to give away these intrusions [by foreign airlines] into American domestic markets without getting anything in return," said Weiss. "This represents a major threat to the pilots of this country. Unless airline pilots have some kind of national agenda, for example one that includes internationalization high on the list, they're going to find themselves very hard-pressed as a profession. Unless they speak with a single voice on major issues, unless they damn well act as a unified group, they're going to wake up someday and find their jobs are disappearing."

After nearly half a century of valuing Henry Weiss's advice on an enormous range of subjects, Ashwood probably made a mistake in attacking him. Nor was Weiss's decision to keep Braniff's pilots from voting in 1982—Ashwood's core complaint against him—clearly improper.

Duffy's victory over O'Donnell was so narrow that every vote was crucial, but we must remember that the Braniff situation was unique in ALPA's history at that point. Braniff's pilots represented an airline, which, _at the time_, had ceased flying and seemed dead. In 1986, Frontier was not yet technically in bankruptcy. Weiss's decision to allow the Frontier pilots to cast their 407 votes was admittedly arguable, but Duffy would eventually win by a margin of 570 votes. Similarly, Continental's ALPA loyalists were clearly in the minority on their airline and had already lost a decertification vote. In any case, even if Weiss had ruled that they were eligible to vote, the Continental pilots might have gone for Duffy, anyway—they had voted for him over O'Donnell in 1982.

So the situation was murky, the political equivalent of the "fog of war." Still, Ashwood had definitely touched a nerve by bringing the role of Cohen, Weiss, and Simon into political play. Whether it was the cultural inclination to criticize lawyers or substantive legal issues of the past, the law firm had been around so long and had engaged in so many critical actions that it had built up a backlog of pilots who could find reason to be disappointed with it in some way or other.

"I think the role of Cohen, Weiss and Simon was a fair question," says United's Chuck Pierce, ALPA's secretary and Ashwood's ally. "I think they were in over their heads in some areas, but maybe that's inherent with having a general firm in whose basket you put all your eggs."

But in fact, the role of Henry Weiss in the election of 1986 was always peripheral. The merger issue was dominant insofar as policy considerations played a part. After that, the choice of leaders came down primarily to a struggle for "place" among men who shared a consensus—far more than they would admit in the heat of the campaign. The BOD delegates would ultimately have to make their choice based upon personality, style, and hunch—not policy.

Randy Babbitt, ALPA's executive administrator since replacing Western's John Erickson in January 1985, came aboard after the Duffy-Ashwood split was already full-blown and had a ringside seat at the 1986 election. Babbitt, whose talents as a conciliator would later play a pivotal role in winning ALPA's presidency in 1990, brings considerable insight to the questions of personality and style in ALPA's politics.

"I thought I could mend some fences, so I devoted a lot of energy to that,"

Babbitt says of the Duffy–Ashwood rift. "But after a year of trying, I conceded it was unredeemable, there was just too much scar tissue. I never knew whether there was already so much damage done there was no repairing it. I will probably go to my grave wondering."

As the campaign of 1986 moved into high gear, Babbitt realized that the Northwest/Republic merger might throw the election to Ashwood, but even here the candidates' personalities and styles figured prominently. Babbitt saw Duffy as an effective campaigner in small groups, but less convincing with large groups. Ashwood was just the opposite.

"Hank could sit down with three or four board members, and they'd walk out absolutely convinced," Babbitt mused. "As for the larger groups, his style, which was very cerebral, hampered getting his message out. Ashwood, conversely, was very polished, but I found the clarity of his vision doubtful, and I didn't think Tom had the savvy to do the decision-making that was going to be in front of us. While Tom was convincing audiences, I was always more comfortable with Hank making the tough decisions, particularly in 1986. That was just an unbelievable nightmare with Northwest and Republic fighting, all those mergers—USAir, Piedmont, PSA—testing pilot groups' wills, and what gets squeezed is ALPA as an institution."

As the election campaign heated up, Duffy got a break when Roger Hall, United's MEC chairman, unexpectedly entered the race, thus diluting the anti-Duffy vote. Hall's sudden entry angered Ashwood's friend, Chuck Pierce.

"I can't remember seeing Hank Duffy so elated," says Pierce. "The fact that Roger Hall was running made Duffy's job significantly easier, because the Delta people came down to Miami saying, 'Look, the opposition can't even make up their mind who they want, the train is about to leave the station, Hank is the next president, and you'd best be on board.'"

Hall had told Pierce in March 1986 that he had no interest in running for ALPA's presidency. Then a combination of things intrinsic to United's politics changed his mind. Hall, who had been elected MEC chairman by a single vote, led an unstable coalition whose heart really belonged to Rick Dubinsky, whom many considered United's leader of the future. Still, Hall's many strong admirers at United thought that he had done a superb job during the strike and that this prestige would carry over into a large vote by uncommitted BOD members. In addition, more than a few United activists, for all their dislike of Hank Duffy, were lukewarm about Ashwood. As these pressures mounted, Hall belatedly entered the campaign.

"A lot of people were pushing me to run against Duffy," says Hall, admitting that it was a question of disillusionment with the choices that motivated them. "United had become a very cohesive pilot group, and I happened to be the leader."

"Roger's decision to run divided the opposition," says Pierce. "The two campaigns, Ashwood's and Hall's, went on until just before the election process, when Hall conceded to step down and run for first vice-president. But by that time, the damage had been done. If the United pilots had gotten behind Ashwood right from the beginning, in my opinion he would have beaten Duffy."

Perhaps, but in the opinion of many others, Duffy's incumbency and the good relationship he enjoyed with the Group Five airlines, when coupled with the undeniable tactical skills of the fabled "Delta Machine," doomed Ashwood's candidacy. By 1986, Group Five had more than 5,000 votes—taken together, these "ants" made up a big airline. These smaller airlines depended upon ALPA and its administrative and financial support far more than the larger airlines. Because of this working environment, the personal relationships they had developed with their contacts in ALPA had a definite political impact. Randy Babbitt, who had helped negotiate so many contracts for these "ant" airlines, would eventually owe his election in 1990 to the simple fact that pilots working for the Group Five airlines *liked* him.

The same was true of Duffy in 1986. When the balloting was all done, Duffy's strongest support clearly came from Group Five. Among the large airlines, Duffy took only Delta, Northwest, Pan Am, Piedmont, and less than half of Eastern. Ashwood took TWA, United, the lion's share of typically splintered Eastern, nearly all of USAir, and Republic by "unit rule." The "ants" (the Alaskas, Suburbans, Simmonses) generally favored Duffy.

In a curious reversal to the pattern that saw most pilots affected by mergers vote for Ashwood, the pilots of Frontier voted for Duffy out of anger at Roger Hall (despite his withdrawal) and United. Because Hall and Ashwood effectively made up a "ticket," the beleaguered Frontier pilots, reacting to the failure of their proposed merger with United, punished Ashwood—thus earning Henry Weiss the Ashwood faction's ire, as we have seen.

Politics often comes down to the old notion that "My enemy's friend is my enemy." Dick Ferris, angry at the 1985 strike's outcome, had sought to sabotage it by offering a merger to Frontier *conditioned upon* that airline's pilots' willingness to accept a B-scale, which of course they would, because the alternative was bankruptcy and unemployment. United's pilots had just taken a strike over this issue, so they could not allow Ferris to subvert their victory through the backdoor via this merger.

If Frontier's pilot were to don United's uniforms, they would do so under the same contract that United's pilots had bled for in 1985.

So the United/Frontier merger fell through, not that it was ever much more than a maneuver on Ferris's part. Abundant evidence shows he never had any intention of merging with Frontier, that he merely wanted to pick off some of Frontier's assets while embarrassing United's ALPA loyalists.

Duffy's total vote came to 14,714, as compared to Ashwood's 13,604. In a somewhat surprising development, indicative of the ambivalence of many BOD delegates about "politics," Roger Hall (the other half of the Ashwood "ticket") won handily over Northwest's Skip Eglet, 18,086 to 10,331 for first vice-president.

Eglet fell victim to an internal political dynamic worked out in the corridors and hospitality suites, during those long hours the night before ALPA's elections when "the elephants dance," as the saying goes. The big airlines, groping toward unity and a show of harmony, moved toward Hall as an outsider who would carry none of the acrimony that had characterized the Duffy–Ashwood years. In addition, thanks to Hall's leadership during the strike, he had taken on the aura of a folk hero, and many delegates saw a vote for him as a symbolic gesture of solidarity with the United pilots and their stand against Ferris.

The remainder of the national officer races settled out for a variety of reasons. Probably indicative of a desire to keep political power "balanced," the delegates reversed course again after electing Ashwood's putative ally Roger Hall, by electing Eastern's Larry Schulte secretary, to replace the incumbent, United's Chuck Pierce, a staunch Ashwood supporter—although by a much closer margin of 15,116 to 13,304. Finally, genial Jack Magee of Ozark/TWA, by 1986 virtually a permanent fixture as ALPA's treasurer, turned back yet another in a long series of challenges, outpolling USAir's Bob Spates 15,502 to 12,918.

When the election was all over, Duffy observed the rituals of politics, declaring: "To those who voted against me, let me pledge that we are going to draw a curtain on all the division at the end of this election. It is emotionally draining, and it pits us against each other. I am going to come out and visit with each of you and discuss our differences; and when we come out of that meeting, we will all be marching in the same direction."

True to his very British roots, Tom Ashwood accepted defeat with grace and equanimity. He returned to flying the line as a TWA B-727 captain and eventually reentered the maelstrom of TWA's internal politics. He locked horns with Carl Icahn, got drafted as MEC chairman, and then recalled—a common fate on that airline. Hank Duffy would eventually name Fred Arenas, a loyal "committee puke" and self-described "foot soldier," to take over temporarily as TWA's MEC chairman during one of that airline's constant emergencies. Arenas lasted one day!

"We were surprised at United and TWA combining because they had been in virtual open warfare over the TWA pilots crossing the flight attendants' picket line, United being in support of almost anybody on strike," said Hank Duffy in retrospect in 1989. "They had open hostility on the picket lines, so I thought there was no possibility of them throwing their forces together. Fortunately my campaign manager [Bill Brown of Delta] was more pessimistic about that, and he turned out to be right. I was doubly surprised that Roger Hall agreed to take second position on that slate, because I thought, if anything, it would be the other way around. They had a real chance to carve me up. They missed, but it was closer than we thought it was going to be."

"A lot of it was painful, but I don't regret it," Ashwood says. "People have asked me after 1986 how I would have changed my campaign. I wouldn't, that's why I can live with the loss, because I did everything I possibly could do within my own set of standards. And I lost. That's O.K., that happens in politics."

Sir Lewis Namier couldn't have said it better of any Whig or Tory. Now was the time to lick wounds and come together for Duffy's second term. Frank Lorenzo, poised at Eastern like Hitler on the Polish border of the Soviet Union in July 1941, was about to launch his own version of Operation Barbarossa. ✦

NOTES
[1] See "The Rise and Fall of the TWA Pilots Association," _Flying the Line_, Ch. 9.
[2] See "The National Airlines Strike of 1948," _Flying the Line_, Ch. 13.

CHAPTER 18

LORENZO'S LAST GAMBLE
The Origins of the Eastern Strike

By 1987 the little copper box had lain beneath the steps of ALPA's old Chicago headquarters at 55th and Cicero adjacent to Midway Airport for 36 years. When Dave Behncke placed it there during the building's dedication in 1951, the artifacts in the "time capsule" already belonged to an era that was fading fast, as was Behncke himself.

"This is the very soul of ALPA," Behncke had intoned as he consigned the copper box to wet cement (which would partially crush it and damage some of the items—a collection of photos, membership lists, and documents.) The "Old Man," as everybody called Behncke, had been increasingly concerned with ALPA's history of late, and he frequently complained that younger pilots didn't appreciate the struggles he and the "Old Guys" had endured. Behncke, wan and ill, looked all of his 54 years. He would be dead by 1953, and ALPA, the entity he had brought to life, would teeter on the verge of collapse, partly because of the building in which he was burying his "time capsule."

If we may indulge in a little dime-store psychology, Behncke was clearly having intimations of mortality. He didn't much like modern aviation, already so alien to the world of wooden wings he had known, so he retreated into the past. He saw the squat, utilitarian building (complete with bunkrooms and shower facilities no airline pilot would ever use) as a monument to his leadership. Consequently, Behncke lavished time and money on his dream building, insisting that it be built to "aircraft specifications." He spent endless hours sidewalk supervising its construction when he should have been taking care of ALPA's business. It was not a happy time—either for ALPA or Behncke—as the sad fate of the building and the copper box buried under in steps would show.

Behncke would never conduct ALPA's business from his dream building. In 1969, ALPA moved to Washington, D.C., where most of its real business had always taken place (the only reason for ALPA's home office having been in Chicago was that it was Behncke's home), and his cherished building was abandoned to an indifferent fate on the Chicago real estate market.

Midway Airport itself went into a long eclipse following the opening of O'Hare, and the ALPA building finally wound up in the possession of a trucking company. Everybody forgot about the little copper box beneath its steps, unmarked now even by the brass plaque emblazoned with ALPA's motto, Schedule with Safety, which somebody had scavenged.

Ironically, Behncke's time capsule saw the light of day again on Dec. 10, 1987, largely because of deregulation. The pilots of Midway Airlines, at the time a promising "new entrant" carrier and inspired by the stiff fight United's pilots waged in 1985, had recently organized and won an ALPA contract. Under the leadership of former TWA pilot Jerry Mugerditchian, Midway's pilots now needed office space for their new MEC. Mugerditchian asked his vice-chairman, Frank Anthony, to investigate renting office space in the old building across the street from Midway—which neither of them knew had once been ALPA's national office.

"The first thing I discovered," Anthony recalls, "was that the building was coming down as part of Midway's renovation, so we couldn't rent office space in it."

But while checking out the building, Anthony noticed a brass mail drop with the letters "ALPA" on it. From this lucky break, everything else flowed. Tom Dalton, director of ALPA's Office Administration Department, vaguely recalled the time capsule, thus setting in motion a recovery effort that would involve the pilots of many airlines. United MEC Communications Director Jim Damron, a second-generation airline pilot with a keen interest in ALPA's history, and his assistant, Hank Krakowski, helped with the salvage effort.

"We were excited to learn of ALPA's historical connection with the building," recalls Mugerditchian, who would become ALPA's secretary in 1990. "At first, we just wanted to save the brass mail drop and present it to Hank Duffy and ALPA for all the help we had received in organizing Midway. The existence of the time capsule came as a big surprise to us."

The time capsule returned to a world in which airline pilots were confronting their history in the most painful way possible—by reliving it. Frank Lorenzo's imitation of E.L. Cord had plunged ALPA into times Behncke and the Old Guys would have recognized instantly—a world of turmoil, bankruptcies, and ruined careers.

Despite these trials, ALPA's future was far from hopeless as Hank Duffy began his second term. The rash of deregulation-inspired new-entrant airlines seemed, to some observers, to preface a tremendous new diversity of carriers in the industry, much like conditions at the time of ALPA's founding. For every Braniff that failed, an optimist could see a Midway rising to take its place. If the future of the industry was to be one of diversity, ALPA could survive by conducting "outreach" efforts to educate the pilots of these new airlines. With proper preparation, these nonunion pilots would, when the time was right, be brought to see ALPA's advantages.

Which did not mean that pessimists had surrendered the field. They predicted that the unfettered free market would eventually result in a semi-monopolistic "Big Three" airlines dominating a swarm of small, nonunion carriers whose pilots worked for peanuts. In their dark vision of the future, it would be either feast or famine professionally for airline pilots, depending upon where they worked, and the ancient ALPA principle of unity across company lines could hardly survive in a world of princes and paupers. The cofferdam United's pilots had erected against the antipilot tide in 1985 was merely temporary, pessimists feared. While the failure of Dick Ferris to break ALPA seemed to discourage other airline executives from trying it themselves, Frank Lorenzo still lurked out there, undefeated; and he had just acquired control of Eastern Airlines, one of aviation's most prestigious namesakes. Critics warned of Lorenzo's spreading empire, which would eventually include upstart People Express and revived Frontier. They cautioned that deregulation would lead to more airline failures. But, at that time, few pessimists foresaw the fates of Eastern and Pan American.

History needs a little distance, both in time and emotional involvement, before making firm judgments. Otherwise history might be wrong, and it would become indistinguishable from journalism—history's "first rough draft." Not that journalism is unimportant. No historian will ever be able to write about the Eastern strike of 1989 without it. Most of the important contemporary books dealing with Eastern and its fate were written by "beat" journalists covering it almost daily as it unfolded. No historian will ever be able to write about this subject without consulting Aaron Bernstein's *Grounded: Frank Lorenzo and the Destruction of Eastern Airlines* (1990). Bernstein, a reporter for *Business Week*, covered Eastern from 1985, which was before Lorenzo took over, until Bankruptcy Court Judge Burton Lifland finally removed him from control in April 1990. But when Bernstein finished his book in 1990, Eastern was still alive, albeit barely.[1]

But history must cover "the rest of the story," so what conclusions might we venture about ALPA's history during the late Duffy era?

The most obvious generalization might be that the nature of Duffy's power was comparably weaker than that of any previous ALPA president. We can get an inkling of this by comparing him to J.J. O'Donnell, who until 1978 worked in a regulated environment. Before 1978, O'Donnell unhesitatingly took the leaders of errant MECs to task, often pressing them brutally. As we have seen, in the mid-1970s, O'Donnell repeatedly lambasted the Continental pilots—quite a major group at the time. But *after* deregulation, pressing a major pilot group like that was unthinkable—witness O'Donnell's reticence in the case of United's "Blue Skies" contract in 1981.

From the moment Duffy took office in January 1983, his presidency had essentially been reactive, with strategic long-range planning necessarily taking a back seat to the kind of tactical, short-range thinking the burgeoning crises demanded. At the beginning of his second term, with the storm seeming to abate somewhat and the internal division symbolized by Tom Ashwood's challenge resolved, Duffy hoped he could devote his full attention to ensuring ALPA's effectiveness in the deregulated airline industry of the future. If ALPA was to survive as the profession's voice into the 1990s and beyond, Duffy knew, he would have to move it beyond the fingernail-scratching fight for survival that had so far characterized the 1980s.

But nothing came easily for Hank Duffy. He would have no let-up from the agony of deregulation-induced mergers, with all the internal discord that implied. Nor was Frank Lorenzo finished. After acquiring control of Eastern in early 1986, Lorenzo made promises of peace and cooperation with ALPA and remained quiescent throughout the remainder of Duffy's first term. But that was only the lull before the storm. Duffy's trials would continue to the bitter end of his eight-year tenure, culminating in an ALPA presidential election of unparalleled historical divisiveness.

"The major test of my administration has been holding ALPA together," Duffy declared flatly, during an interview in the summer of 1990, shortly after announcing that he would not seek a third term. "What with the pilot groups who have threatened to get out of ALPA because they didn't want me to enforce merger policy or because they didn't think I *had* enforced it, didn't do this or didn't do that, it's been tough. Keeping this outfit together has taken a real diplomatic effort and a lot of compromises that weren't always too pleasant."

Although Duffy's mind was clearly on his place in ALPA's history, his concern for the future was obvious. By the beginning of his second term, deregulation had brought about a set of circumstances within the airline industry that no other ALPA president had faced. If the critics of deregulation were right and the industry degenerated into a semi-monopoly, what was ALPA's future? The evolution of the industry into a few mammoth airlines with their associated "elephant" pilot groups could take ALPA into unexplored regions. Could an ALPA president withstand a determined assault by one of these new postderegulation "megacarriers?" More to the point, could ALPA survive a concerted effort by the pilots of one of these new super-airlines to secede outright, as the pilots of American Airlines had done in 1963?

"Keeping ALPA together is the real challenge, and it's going to be tough," Duffy warned darkly in his 1990 interview. "With four major carriers, any one of which could afford to leave and operate on its own, that's going to be the test of leadership. If you get the wrong people in charge, who for selfish motivation would lead their pilot group away from ALPA, this profession's going to be in trouble."

With the airline industry increasingly dominated by giant carriers, each supreme in its own sphere of "hubs and spokes," many thoughtful observers believed it would only be a matter of time before Duffy's fears materialized and the pilots of one of them threw out the baby with the bath water. As we shall see, at the end of Duffy's administration, following the bitter and controversial election of Randy Babbitt, that hour seemed to have struck. The pilots of United, against all odds, seemed perched upon the precipice of disunion, so bitter was their reaction to the defeat of Roger Hall.

"The real challenge for whoever comes after me is to make sure ALPA doesn't break up into a loose federation of independent unions," Duffy fretted in 1990. "It's been suggested that we might lure American back into ALPA with promises of autonomy. But I'll tell you, that wouldn't be worth the price. The biggest advantage ALPA has is its ability to speak with one voice. The chairman of the House Aviation Subcommittee doesn't get the United pilot position whispered in one ear and the USAir position whispered in the other. He hears one position from *airline pilots*! ALPA is effective in Washington [D.C.] because of that, and the American pilots are simply nonplayers. If we ever split our voice, our enemies will have us for lunch. Actually, what I'd really like to know is what ALPA's going to be like when they open that time capsule a century from now."

Duffy was determined that ALPA would survive, speaking with one voice, into the 21st century. At times he could be very tough, but like O'Donnell after deregulation, his power was stronger when dealing with "ant" airlines than with "elephants." Duffy would impose a trusteeship during the Air Wisconsin–Mississippi Valley merger dispute, much as O'Donnell had done to the Frontier pilots in 1978. But if the pilots of a megacarrier insisted upon doing things their own way, even in contravention of ALPA policy, Duffy had, like O'Donnell after 1978, recourse only to the weapons of conciliation and persuasion, rather than arbitrary force.

"We have had to meet trouble by heading it off before it happens," Duffy admitted at the end of his presidency. "You have to stay on top of things, know what they're doing, so you can come to a consensus before you ever get into trouble."

As we have seen, after a rocky start that saw Piedmont's pilots (among others), sign away major contract provisions through "side letters," Duffy engineered a new collective bargaining system that subjected negotiations on each airline to the direct supervision of ALPA's national officers. The savage impact of mergers, notably Northwest–Republic, caused Duffy serious trouble. Northwest had no B-scale before the merger, while Republic did. The pilots of Northwest were determined to grant their management a B-scale, and if Duffy had resisted they might well have seceded from ALPA. The newly merged Northwest (by now one of the "Big Four") was certainly capable of standing alone.

"Some things are so egregious that you'd have to risk a pilot group's leaving ALPA," Duffy believes. "But in the Northwest thing, I lobbied them, trying to get them to hold ground against signing any kind of a B-scale, but it wasn't the kind of thing we could draw the line on, because it was better than anybody else's B-scale. If it was something predatory that was going to give a pilot group some intrusion into another pilot group's work, I'd have to say 'no' and suffer the results. But I can't think of an example where this couldn't be headed off."

Duffy makes a plausible argument. Even presidents of the United States, with all the raw power of military might at their command, are prone to note in their memoirs that the power to persuade, the fact that opponents *have* to listen (the "Bully Pulpit," if you will), gives them their *real* power. Duffy believes that the kind of conciliatory, consensus-building approach he had no choice but to embrace might have worked as well for ALPA in the past as it *must* work in the future.

"In today's environment, with proper coordination among the pilot groups, we might even have held off the whole B-scale" Duffy said in 1990. "I think the American pilots would be very reluctant today about undercutting another pilot group."

But the biggest problem Duffy faced was Frank Lorenzo. Regardless of the bodycheck United's pilots had dealt copycats like Dick Ferris, or the fact that other airline executives seemed less eager to follow his example, nothing ALPA or Hank Duffy could have done would likely have dissuaded Lorenzo from the course of action upon which he had embarked. His *modus operandi*, as we have seen, was established in the mid-1970s at Texas International (TXI), and it never really changed. Lorenzo was a "one-trick pony" pursuing the main chance, carrying a load of junk bond debt that typified everything that was wrong with deregulation, Reaganomics, and amoral "Yuppie" greed.

The biggest historical question, which will always haunt the Eastern strike, is why any government would allow a man with Lorenzo's reputation to acquire such a respected and venerable airline in the first place. After all, Lorenzo was operating Continental under protection of the bankruptcy laws, thus in a *de facto* sense, competing unfairly with other airlines that were paying their bills. In the old deregulated system, the Civil Aeronautics Board, which underwent "sunset" in 1984, would surely never have allowed a man of Lorenzo's cancerous reputation to metastasize to another airline. Even under deregulation, Lorenzo's acquisition of Eastern was so fraught with antitrust and conflict-of-interest problems that any Department of Justice except Reagan's thoroughly ideological outfit almost certainly would have disallowed it. But ideological conservatism not withstanding, Lorenzo's careful cultivation of the Reagan Administration insulated him from such scrutiny.

These larger issues aside, the specific question that will always haunt Eastern's pilots is, *Why did Lorenzo do what he did?* The answer lies in his history, and perhaps in the ancient adage that a leopard never changes spots.

At TXI and Continental, Lorenzo first attacked the mechanics, provoked strikes, and then tried to manipulate his pilots into breaking them for him. His plan hadn't worked, but because he had won the subsequent strikes anyway, he was sure to try it again at Eastern. Before the strikes on each airline, the pilots, in saving their jobs, would have done almost anything to accommodate Lorenzo. In a classic example of the "Lucy Syndrome," in 1978, during Lorenzo's attempt to acquire National Airlines from Lewis B. "Bud" Maytag, *Newsweek* quoted "a veteran pilot" as saying: "Almost anybody would be better than Maytag." Incredibly, the International Association of Machinists' local newsletter encouraged Lorenzo with the following headline: "TAKE US, WE'RE YOURS!" That willingness to give Lorenzo the benefit of the doubt never really changed—even Eastern's unions were cooperative at first.

Lorenzo acquired Eastern through a fluke. It happened in February 1986, when a gamble by Frank Borman to coerce Eastern's unions into concessions (including a B-scale for new-hire pilots) went badly awry. In late 1985, Borman had tried to bluff the pilots by threatening to sell the airline to Lorenzo if they didn't grant concessions. Eastern's pilot group responded by taking a strike vote, which passed by a 96 percent margin. But more troubling than that, Borman's bluff stirred up the "outside" members of Eastern's Board of Directors. These directors, whose fiduciary responsibility required them to consider any reasonable offer for the troubled airline, insisted that Lorenzo be allowed to bid. Lorenzo himself, surprised that he was being taken seriously (he was running a bankrupt airline under Chapter 11 rules at the time), seized the main chance and put together a financial package consisting mostly of junk bonds. Then he waited for the mouse to fall into his trap.

With ALPA's strike deadline exerting pressure, Borman, who had no intention of selling Eastern, responded by pushing his bluff to a higher level. Probably at his urging, Eastern's creditors announced a February 28 deadline for the unions to make concessions or they would foreclose on $2.5 billion in loans, thus forcing the airline into bankruptcy, with potentially catastrophic consequences for existing union contracts *and* the possibility of Lorenzo grabbing control anyway. Lorenzo had led a charmed life under the bankruptcy laws, and he had excellent financial connections to Michael Milken, the Drexel, Burnham, Lambert junk bond king and future felon. (Although not part of this story, deregulation of the savings and loan industry paved the way for looters like Milken to channel S&L money to fast buck operators like Lorenzo, with taxpayers taking all the risks. The savings of ordinary people, invested by corrupt or incompetent S&L managers in Milken's junk bonds, provided the capital that allowed the likes of Lorenzo to flourish.)

Exasperated with Borman, to whom they had made hefty concessions in 1983, only to watch him turn around and give the IAM a *raise*, Eastern's pilots were worried and suspicious. Under August H. "Augie" Gorse, the MEC chairman who had been instrumental in swinging a large bloc of votes away from J.J. O'Donnell to Hank Duffy in 1982, Eastern's pilots had granted Borman $100 million in deferred pay raises, increased flying time, and reduced vacations. By 1986, the MEC was bitterly divided between two strong polar opposites, Chairman Larry Schulte, a moderate who wanted to help Borman despite his previous missteps, and Charles "Skip" Copeland, a veteran New York-based ALPA activist, who was militantly opposed. Arguing that concessions were the only way to ensure that Lorenzo would not take over their airline, Schulte got the MEC to agree (by the barest of margins) to a new contract. Randy Babbitt, in his capacity as ALPA's executive administrator, had a ringside seat as the fiasco played itself out.

"It was the wildest MEC meeting I ever witnessed," Babbitt recalls of the complex negotiations between unions, management, and Eastern's creditors preceding the bankers' February 28 deadline. "It went around the clock Saturday. The only group to reach a deal was the pilots, but ultimately the airline was sold Sunday evening. There was terrible miscommunication between the unions, and a lot of mistrust directed at ALPA national, too."

The selling of Eastern during the early morning hours of Feb. 24, 1986, was a cathartic moment. Betrayed by IAM leader Charlie Bryan, undercut by some of Borman's own subordinates (who apparently fancied their chances in a reorganized airline), and outmaneuvered by Lorenzo, Borman was an emotional wreck. He was 57, had invested nearly 12 years in Eastern, and had little likelihood of future employment in the industry. Borman had fought desperately to cap his career by saving Eastern, thereby linking his name with such legendary giants as Rickenbacker.

Eastern's pilots had also invested a lot, both in emotions and givebacks, in Borman, and his failure was also theirs. Larry Schulte at one point had to be restrained from a fistfight with an Eastern executive gloating over Borman's fall. The next day, Hank Duffy talked Borman into formally signing the new contract that Schulte had hammered out, which granted a B-scale plus $150 million in concessions. Schulte and Borman ratified the agreement before the MEC, then embraced, crying. The MEC gave them a standing ovation.

"That was a tough time," Randy Babbitt observes. "I remember talking to Borman about 30 minutes after the airline was sold, and he had tears running down his face. He was a devastated man."

The famed astronaut proved he was still a pilot at heart. He would give Eastern's pilots what protection he could against Lorenzo by signing the new contract. A mere contract, however, was a slender reed upon which to lean when dealing with Lorenzo.

Lorenzo, delighted that this prize had fallen into his lap for such a pittance, promptly announced that he would accept the pilots' contract Borman had signed. He denied any unionbusting intentions and agreed to a 7 a.m. breakfast meeting with Hank Duffy at the Miami Marriott the next morning. The meeting went well. Lorenzo vowed to let bygones be bygones. Duffy promised that ALPA stood ready, as always, to help anybody—even Frank Lorenzo—make an airline work.

In the interim, the employees, while they allowed Lorenzo a chance, saw no reason not to try to find an employer who was more suitable—a "white knight." To this end, over the next two years, Eastern's unions, operating through the Eastern Employees Acquisition Corporation, approached a wide variety of "movers and shakers" about supplanting Lorenzo. They talked to former Baseball Commissioner Peter Ueberroth, Dallas billionaire Ross Perot, Denver mogul Marvin Davis, and corporate raider T. Boone Pickens, among others. Also, because Eastern's unions had substantial stock holdings from the 1984 "Cooperation Plan," they were simultaneously exploring an Employee Stock Ownership Plan (ESOP), by which they could become their own bosses.

All these efforts failed for one of two reasons. The first was that Lorenzo could not be *forced* to sell Eastern. He had picked up the airline for a song, and its net asset value, should it be liquidated, was nearly $3 billion. Lorenzo was thus in a position to ask an enormous price. Second, to meet this enormous price would require not only hundreds of millions in givebacks from the unions, but an enormous amount from their pension funds as well. ALPA and the flight attendants were willing to invest substantial amounts from their pension funds, but the machinists were not. So all efforts to displace Lorenzo through a white knight or an ESOP came to nothing.

As we have seen, Lorenzo was really not interested in aviation. He was essentially a corporate raider and financial manipulator, more like his friend Michael Milken or his rival Carl Icahn, than like Bob Six or Eddie Rickenbacker. The daily details of actually running an airline held no charm for Lorenzo. Rather, the heady rush of *the deal*—the maneuvers, the ploys, the sharp advantage to be gained over an opponent by shrewd "one up-manship"—was what attracted him.

To fully understand Lorenzo's obsessive character and his visceral attack on unions (particularly ALPA) requires a detour into abnormal psychology, which is beyond the scope of this history. As Aaron Bernstein wrote in *Grounded*: "Eastern had problems, but labor was not foremost among them. The pilots and flight attendants had just cut Eastern's labor costs to reasonable levels. For equity's sake, the machinists should have kicked in, too, but their cuts were not sufficient to make or break the company. Lorenzo was so obsessed with beating labor that he never faced Eastern's real dilemmas. His employees had shown a willingness to do almost anything to keep their jobs and the company going. Lorenzo never saw that. Instead, he stripped Eastern and made off with millions in assets."

Lorenzo's looting of Eastern began slowly. Throughout the remainder of 1986, things remained relatively quiet as ALPA gave Lorenzo every chance to save the airline. But ALPA's good faith was in vain, for Lorenzo was merely biding his time, following his familiar strategy of dividing labor by targeting the IAM first. The truce would end when the machinists' contract came up for renewal in February 1987.

The IAM refused Lorenzo's demands for wage cuts and instead asked for a raise. Lorenzo launched a publicity war, denouncing "$45,000-per-year baggage handlers."

This time ALPA wouldn't be taken in. A memo to all ALPA members contained the following statement: "How do you think an employee will feel if you're 51 years old, you're a baggage handler, you've worked your way up to $30,000 a year, and they come in and say, 'I'm going to cut your salary to $18,000. If you don't like it, you're fired!'"

Amazingly, the preceding statement wasn't from some IAM official. Rather, it was a direct quote from Robert Crandall, CEO of American Airlines, in a June 1987 *Airline Executive* interview.

For the next two years, the acrimony between Lorenzo and the IAM continued, as the contract talks underwent mediation. Although the pilots' contract was not open, Lorenzo nevertheless sought $114 million in additional concessions simultaneously with his demands for givebacks from the IAM. When the pilots refused, Lorenzo followed yet another of his familiar strategies, suing to invalidate the contract Borman had signed during the takeover—the very contract Lorenzo had sworn to accept!

February 1987 marked the beginning of sustained conflict between Eastern's pilots and Lorenzo. Unlike the Texas and Continental pilots, Eastern's pilots vowed to be ready for Lorenzo this time. While they had extended their wholehearted cooperation during the 1986 truce, the pilots had also simultaneously prepared for a fight, should it come to that.

Building upon the experience ALPA had gained in the United strike, Eastern's pilots instituted a "family awareness" program to build internal solidarity. Under the leadership of former Executive Administrator Jack Bavis (who became MEC chairman after Larry Schulte won election as ALPA's secretary in November 1986), Eastern's pilots prepared to launch preemptive strikes at Lorenzo to keep him off balance.

Chief among these stratagems was one aimed at organizing their Texas Air Corporation (TAC) siblings to bring them all together under ALPA's umbrella. Reasoning that a formal program sponsored by ALPA national would meet resistance, Eastern's MEC pilot group began a "pilot-to-pilot" program they called

"TAC Unity," which encouraged Eastern pilots to *individually* seek out pilots they knew personally at Continental.This bridge-building program didn't work, less because of the lingering animosity of the 1983–85 strike than because of internal divisions on Continental itself.

"On Continental, it was like the old Kingston Trio song, everybody hated everybody," recalls Randy Babbitt, who had specialized in difficult organizational efforts since becoming Hank Duffy's executive administrator."The Frontier pilots were angry at the People Express pilots, who were angry at the New York Air pilots, who were angry at the original TXI guys, who were still angry at the Continental guys. Plus you had different degrees of scabs, ranging from the 'walk-backs' to the 'crawl-backs.' Organizing them was impossible."

And, of course, nearly all Continental's pilots were angry at ALPA for something, even many of the striking loyalists, who still resented the "Surrender Agreement." Confidential internal assessments supplied by ALPA field organizers detailed the problems.

"The best reading I can get from talking to line pilots, scabs, strikers, and new-hires alike," wrote Jim Abney to Seth Rosen, "is that a reasonably viable union could probably organize the Continental property. ALPA, however, continues to suffer from a largely unfair understanding of earlier situations, such as the Braniff and Frontier bankruptcies."

Nevertheless, TAC Unity worried Lorenzo. Operating with a grant of $2.5 million from the Major Contingency Fund (MCF), Eastern's pilots seemed to be making inroads among Lorenzo's disgruntled pilots, who chafed under substandard wages and poor working conditions. Lorenzo wasn't at all sure his Continental pilots wouldn't sign enough "Authorization to Act" cards to force a representational election under National Mediation Board (NMB) auspices, so he countered by announcing a retirement plan (the bankruptcy court had invalidated the original one) and wage increases (which he had to do because Continental was losing pilots to other airlines). Lorenzo also struck back with a panicky letter to all Continental pilots in September 1987.

"If ALPA wins, they plan to merge the Continental and Eastern seniority lists," Lorenzo warned. "Many of you would go *right to the bottom* [italics Lorenzo's], and many more would lose their positions—just as ALPA has always wanted. So when ALPA approaches you, remember that they were willing to sacrifice you and your family."

Proof that Lorenzo was seriously worried came in a series of personal meetings with his pilots at Continental domiciles—something he hadn't done since the strike. He promised that they would be only the first of regular quarterly meetings to build the "Continental family." Lorenzo invariably began these meetings with pilots by telling a favorite horror story about ALPA.

"You might recall the story of the eight-year Western Airlines veteran after ALPA merged their pilots with Delta's," Lorenzo declaimed. "He was placed on the seniority list below a Delta pilot *who wasn't even out of training*" (emphasis Lorenzo's).

Lorenzo's horror story deserves explanation. As we have seen in earlier discussions of ALPA merger policy, if date-of-hire was to be the *only* method of integrating pilot seniority lists, it could lead to grave injustices. In the Western–Delta merger of 1986, negotiators accepted a "stove-pipe standalone" seniority list integration. Under this system, pilots were integrated according to the equipment they flew at a ten-to-one ratio (the size of the two pilot groups), structured so that *no pilot on either airline would lose his domicile or be forced to change his seat.* The main deviation from date-of-hire arose because of a category of aircraft, the B-767, which only Delta flew, so there was some distortion in favor of Delta pilots.

Lorenzo's attack on ALPA merger policy for deviating from date-of-hire contains a supreme irony, for if Continental and Eastern ever were to be integrated as a "single carrier," the method used in the Western–Delta merger would *protect* the junior pilot group—namely Lorenzo's own scabs. So the celebrated horror story with which Lorenzo warmed up his apprehensive Continental pilot audiences was a distortion Joseph Goebbles would have admired.

"Boy, would I like to have had equal time for a reply on that one," says former Executive Vice-President Frank Mayne of Delta, an ex-Western pilot. "The case Lorenzo always cited involved a guy who had been on medical leave for five years before the merger. The company wanted relief on training costs, so anybody already in training was guaranteed a number. So one Western guy on medical leave gave Lorenzo the basis for his horror story."

In fact, Jack Bavis did formally request "equal time" to refute Lorenzo's misrepresentation of ALPA merger policy. In September 1987, he received the following reply from John Adams, Continental's human resources vice-president: "If you have so much time available, I suggest you visit the two ALPA pilots still serving 13-year prison sentences for carrying explosive devices."

ALPA upped the ante by filing with the NMB a "single carrier" petition that would have declared Eastern and Continental to be one airline. This petition, if the NMB supported it, would result in a representational election for the combined airlines. Continental's pilot leaders (known derisively as the "Student Council" to ALPA loyalists) hued to Lorenzo's line by trying to derail the single-carrier petition by launching a campaign to revive "racketeering" charges against ALPA. Lorenzo had once filed a $510 million lawsuit alleging a racketeering conspiracy by ALPA, but had dropped it as part of the strike settlement in 1985.

"ALPA has never changed," screamed "Student Council" memos to all Continental pilots. "It is the same group led by unprincipled, power-mad individuals."

By late 1988, Eastern's pilots faced a more serious challenge—Lorenzo's "cherry-picking" of Eastern assets. This technique, also called "upstreaming," saw Lorenzo loot Eastern by selling off such valuable properties as the shuttle service to Donald Trump, the New York real estate speculator.

Lorenzo had warmed up by selling Eastern's SODA computerized reservations system to TAC (effectively himself) for a fraction of its actual value in 1987. The total of these transactions amounted to nearly $1 billion and would later be ruled illegal by David Shapiro, the examiner assigned to the case by bankruptcy judge Burton Lifland. Shapiro ruled that in 12 of 15 asset transfers, TAC (Lorenzo) paid "unfairly low prices" to Eastern.

In the case of the SODA sale, Lorenzo had paid Eastern only $100 million, and then *charged* Eastern $130 million to use it! Even worse, he later sold *half* the SODA system for $250 million. Subsequent to Examiner Shapiro's finding, Lorenzo belatedly paid Eastern $280 million extra for SODA, although typically only $133 million was in cash—the rest was junk bonds.

By the fall of 1987, it was clear that Lorenzo had no intention of working cooperatively with ALPA. Working conditions deteriorated, with ALPA pilots insisting that supervisors were pressuring them to violate federal aviation regulations and fly unsafe aircraft. ALPA responded with the "Max Safety Campaign" to call attention to Lorenzo's shortcuts. By holding Lorenzo accountable, Eastern's pilots were intervening on the behalf of an unsuspecting public, thus fulfilling the most ancient and primary responsibility of the airline piloting profession. Unfortunately the FAA, exhibiting a Reagan-Bush–inspired lethargy, dismissed ALPA's safety complaints as "just a labor dispute."

Later, after Lorenzo had effectively destroyed the airline, the FAA would reverse itself and fine Eastern and several individual supervisors for falsifying maintenance records—just as the pilots had charged. In July 1990, Eastern and nine high-level managers were formally indicted for "conspiring to falsify safety and maintenance records to avoid costly flight delays and cancellations." These *criminal* indictments, unprecedented in the history of commercial aviation, charged that mechanics had been ordered to falsify log books.

Working at Eastern, an airline with no future, became so stressful and unsatisfactory that junior pilots began leaving for other jobs, which they could do at the time because the industry was prospering and pilot hiring was high. Lorenzo worsened "pilot flight" by announcing stringent new requirements for sick leave, and he instituted a new system, in apparent contravention of FAA regulations, for countermanding a captain's ancient authority to determine airworthiness. More than 600 senior pilots retired early in the two years after Lorenzo took over, leaving Eastern so short of flight deck crews that Lorenzo had to begin emergency hiring. He also accelerated his plan to shift Eastern's routes to non-union Continental, along with the aircraft to fly them, including several of the fuel-efficient Airbus Industrie A300s for which Frank Borman had mortgaged Eastern's future.

To many pilots, this transfer of routes and equipment was the last straw. A kind of fatalism set in, as Eastern's pilots concluded they must either get rid of Lorenzo or lose their careers. Increasingly, the pilots came to favor drastic, even radical, action. The powder keg was open. All it needed now was a spark. That came in March 1989, when the long-stalled IAM contract talks, which had been in "super mediation," finally broke down and the NMB "released" the parties to "engage in an economic contest," or strike.

Frank Lorenzo's plan was right on schedule, unfolding at Eastern precisely as it had at TXI in 1975 and at Continental in 1983. The only issue now at stake was the pilots. Would they cross the IAM's picket lines? There was so much bad blood between ALPA and Charley Bryan, leader of the Eastern machinists' union, that Lorenzo could reasonably hope they would. If Eastern's boss had been anybody but Frank Lorenzo, they probably would have. But Lorenzo had made Eastern's pilots desperate. Their goodwill had been met with cynical maneuvers, best illustrated in the following anecdote from Aaron Bernstein's *Grounded*. Shortly after Borman formally resigned, Joe Leonard, an executive sent over from TAC, called in Bob Shipner, a veteran Eastern pilot (and 1978 ALPA presidential candidate) who was at that time the airline's vice-president for flight. Leonard summarily fired Shipner and sent him back to the line. When Shipner asked why, Leonard said: "You don't have the stomach to do what we're going to do to the pilots."

Little did Lorenzo know, this time ALPA would be ready for him.　　　✈

NOTE

[1] *Hard Landing: The Epic Contest for Power and Profits that Plunged the Airlines into Chaos* (1995) by Thomas Petzinger, Jr., and *Rapid Descent: Deregulation and Shakeout in the Airlines* (1994), by Barbara Peterson and James Glab, are also essential "journalistic" books.

CHAPTER 19

THE EASTERN STRIKE AND THE FALL OF LORENZO
"How do you spell 'Pyrrhic Victory,' Frank?"

Former B-727 Captain Wayne Dolan, a 25-year Eastern Airlines veteran, makes his living today as an independent painting and roofing contractor in Baltimore. He has seen his own American dream evaporate. But like nearly all the last-ditch fighters against Frank Lorenzo, Dolan radiates a kind of quiet satisfaction, despite the terrible price he paid personally.

"I don't have a job, but Frank doesn't have an airline, either," Dolan said during a 1991 interview.

After getting out of the army in 1964, Dolan learned to fly in a Colorado civilian flight school, then caught the great hiring wave of the mid-1960s with Eastern. He was a loyal ALPA member throughout his career and during the strike willingly did any task assigned to him. In the summer of 1989, with the battle against Frank Lorenzo at its height, Dolan was philosophical.

"I'll always be grateful to Eastern for giving me a chance to be an airline pilot," Dolan said at the time. "There's nothing I wouldn't do to save Eastern, the old Eastern the way it was before Lorenzo. But the job isn't worth having now. It was either die fighting Lorenzo or watch him kill the airline one cut at a time."

From being one of ALPA's staunchest loyalists during the strike, Dolan became one of 2,504 former Eastern pilots suing ALPA under a "failure of duty of fair representation" lawsuit.

"Hell, I don't want ALPA's money," said Dolan in 1991. "I just want a job flying the same airplane that somebody else is flying right now with another paint job. I think ALPA owes me that. I was up on a two-story house near BWI [Baltimore–Washington International Airport] last week, putting on a roof, right under the ILS path. Talk about eating your heart out."

As a "50-something" pilot several years out of currency, Dolan's anguish was palpable. He knew his chances of ever getting another airline job were slim. He could only laugh grimly at a letter of rejection from Delta saying he did not meet "minimum qualifications," despite his years of airline experience. He knew ALPA was not really responsible for what happened to him; nevertheless he felt betrayed. Like many ex-Eastern pilots, Dolan believed ALPA's "fragmentation policy" should have guaranteed him a cockpit seat somewhere in the industry. Implicit in Dolan's complaint is the idea that if ALPA only had the *will*, it could have forced its fragmentation policy on a recalcitrant airline industry.

"There is always a tendency to blame ALPA when a strike goes badly," Hank

ALPA Secretary Charles Pierce, United MEC Chairman Roger Hall, MEC Secretary-Treasurer Tom Sashko, and MEC Vice-Chairman Jim Engleman speak with a reporter during the UAL strike of 1985.

ABOVE: AFL-CIO President Lane Kirkland (center sign bearer) and ALPA Secretary Jack Magee (sign bearer to Kirkland's right), march in support of the United pilots.
LEFT: United Capt. Rick Dubinsky coordinated pilots' efforts as chairman of the United Pilots Strike Preparedness Committee, and later the Strike Committee. Dubinsky, later as MEC chairman, was a driving force behind the United pilots' early attempts to create an ESOP.

ABOVE: From right, Capt. Bill "Bubber" Rushing, national coordinator for the United Pilot Strike Coimmittee Family Awareness Program, F/O Dave Koch, executive producer of the video teleconferences, and husband-wife team Leslie and Michael Avery, communications experts and founders of Chicago-based Human Resources Development, were key people in developing and implementing the multifaceted communications plan that was critical to the success of the strike.

ABOVE: Capt. Felix Isherwood types at bulletin transmitter system developed by Isherwood and ALPA staffer Charlie Murphy.
RIGHT: John LeRoy (public relations) and Joe Keown (family awareness) getting information to send out on phone tree.

LEFT: Using satellite and computer technology, sophisticated communication programs that include one-on-one contact with pilots and with news media reporters are an effective tool in influencing the collective bargaining process. Here John LeRoy is interviewed at the pilots' Strike Center.

BELOW LEFT: United Capt. Clifford Sanderson's election as chairman of Council 12 in 1982 was the beginning of opposition to United's Blue Skies agreement and to John Ferg's political strength. Capt. Duffy later appointed Sanderson as trustee for Air Wisconsin during a merger dispute with Mississippi Valley pilots.

ABOVE: In October 1985 Capt. Henry Duffy and Gary Green, director of ALPA's Legal Department, urge members of the House Aviation Subcommittee to enact LPP legislation to protect employees who might be adversely affected by sale or merger. During his testimony, Duffy criticized the Transportation Department for abandoning the employee protection doctrine established 20 years before by the Civil Aeronautics Board.

LEFT: Two gunmen take combat positions as TWA Capt. John Testrake's B-727 prepares to take on fuel in Beirut, Lebanon, 8 days after it was hijacked in June 1985.

ABOVE: Capt. Duffy presents his opening report to the Spring 1985 Executive Board.
BELOW FROM LEFT: ALPA First Vice-President Tom Ashwood, Treasurer Jack Magee, and Secretary Charles J. "Chuck" Pierce, report to the Executive Board. Pierce was crucially important in healing the internal wounds caused by dissidents at United during the Ferg era.

ABOVE: ALPA's secretary, Capt. Chuck Pierce, explains membership balloting procedures to a committee drafting a recommendation for continued support for the Continental strikers during a special Executive Board session in July 1985. The committee also drafted language for United strike support and a dues increase to 2.35 percent to create the Major Contingency Fund.

LEFT: Capt. Harlan B. "Hal" Osteboe (United), was instrumental in defusing the defection of the UAL pilot group during the John Ferg era.

BELOW: The National Officers elected at the 1986 BOD were Capts. Hank Duffy (Delta), president; Roger Hall (United), first vice-president; Jack Magee (TWA), treasurer; and Larry Schulte (Eastern), secretary.

ABOVE: Eastern's Master Executive Council chairman, Capt. Jack Bavis, addresses ALPA 57th regular Executive Board meeting in Washington, D.C.
RIGHT: Henry Duffy opens the special Executive Board meeting held in Washington, D.C., Dec. 11–12, 1989, on the Eastern crisis.
BELOW: Eastern pilots walk the picket line with Machinist Union President William Winpisinger.

ABOVE: "Hey yo! Lorenzo has gotta go!" ALPA's "family awareness" approach involved spouses and kids—a lesson learned the hard way during the Continental strike.
LEFT: Eastern strikers walk the line at Washington, D.C.'s National (now Reagan) Airport.
BELOW: Eastern pilots had been portrayed as meaner than a junkyard dog—now we know why. Bankruptcy by Lorenzo brought a real junkyard to Atlanta and other sites, where aircraft were being cannibalized for parts to keep other aircraft in the air.

Capt. Roger Hall (United), below, whose leadership brought about the ESOP, making United the largest employee-owned corporation in the United States. Hall narrowly lost to Capt. Randy Babbitt (Eastern), right, in the controversial 1990 presidential election.

Duffy said with resignation during the summer of 1989, as the strike was starting to unravel. "The Eastern pilots did everything right. If you took a snapshot when they went out on March 4, it was the absolute right thing to do. They had the resources, they had the ultimate enemy, and they were together. For it not to be going well brings out all the residual hostility toward ALPA, because they think their union should be able to stop that from happening."

In February 1989, Lorenzo rejected binding arbitration with the International Association of Machinists (IAM) after two years of sabotaging meaningful negotiations. Walter Wallace, head of the National Mediation Board, blasted Lorenzo's refusal to negotiate fairly and asked U.S. President George Bush for a Presidential Emergency Board (PEB) to resolve the impasse. Lorenzo denounces Wallace (a Republican appointed by Dwight Eisenhower), who had more often supported management than labor, as a "shill for organized labor."

The NMB, acting under its mandate to prevent strikes in the airline industry, had stalled the strike Lorenzo wanted as long as it could. Now the machinists, Lorenzo's perennial first target in his unionbusting pattern, were finally in range.

Since 1928, the NMB had asked for a PEB 211 times, with no refusals from the occupant of the White House. George Bush broke the pattern. It really shouldn't have surprised anybody.

"We knew the Bush Administration was not prolabor," Hank Duffy said. "But we had no comprehension of the depths to which they would stoop to carry Frank Lorenzo's water."

At the beginning of the Bush presidency, Duffy believed a change for the better might be in the offing. Bush had made a point, publicly and most unusually, of his intention to clean up the shoddy ethical practices of the Reagan years, often referred to as the "sleaze factor." Duffy hoped in vain. The Department of Transportation (DOT) proved unwilling to curb Lorenzo. ALPA asked the DOT for a "fitness review" of Eastern on Dec. 7, 1989. DOT head James Burnley denied the fitness review a mere seven days later, an unusually short period of time for such an administrative action. He also used injudicious, biased language, calling ALPA "irresponsible" and declaring that it had "unclean hands." Burnley did this _at the same time he was negotiating for a job with the law firm that represented Eastern_—a clear conflict of interest.

The internal politics of the Republican Party also damaged ALPA's chances of getting a sympathetic hearing from the Bush Administration. During his first year in office, Bush had been looking for some way to emulate his predecessor, Ronald Reagan, who during _his_ first year had broken the PATCO strike to almost universal applause, including most airline pilots. Bush, always on shaky ground with right-wing conservatives in his own party, saw backing Lorenzo as a risk-free way to enhance his popularity. If Lorenzo won, Bush could bask in the approval of his party's traditional antiunionism. If Lorenzo lost, Bush could make pious noises about the sanctity of collective bargaining and walk away.

Given the revolving door between Republican administrations and Lorenzo's business associates since 1981, Bush could hardly have done otherwise. ALPA would later document 30 top officials who had rotated between service to Bush and employment by Lorenzo. During the 1988 presidential election campaign, Lorenzo had contributed $100,000 to the Republicans. That kind of money buys a sympathetic ear.

Still, George Bush's precedent-breaking failure to create a PEB was a bitter disappointment to Eastern's pilots. Who could blame them for hoping that old naval aviator Bush might do a favor for his fellow airmen? But Frank Lorenzo's cozy relationship with the Republicans doomed these hopes. George Bush would give Lorenzo the strike he wanted.

At first Eastern's pilots appeared to hold all the cards. Lorenzo had made arrangements with outside mechanical contractors to service his airplanes, and he knew from past experience that he could circumvent the IAM. Eastern's pilots were the key. If ALPA honored the IAM picket line, the airline would shut down. But if ALPA crossed, Lorenzo would find the IAM action merely an annoyance.

Armed with this certainty, Eastern's pilots made demands on Lorenzo. MEC Chairman Jack Bavis (who had been J.J. O'Donnell's executive administrator for 12 years) made clear that pilots wanted four distinct things, backed by ironclad guarantees, or they would walk.

First, they wanted "objective, measurable actions" (a "business plan") from Lorenzo, one that would make Eastern a viable airline again.

Second, they wanted a "fence" between Eastern's operations and Continental's to prevent any future asset looting.

Third, they wanted a contract with Lorenzo's holding company, Texas Air Corporation—*not with Eastern*—because they knew that a bankruptcy court could invalidate any promise that Lorenzo made to them in Eastern's name.

Fourth, they wanted Eastern's operations merged into Continental's, because they knew Lorenzo was playing a corporate shell game that isolated them as union orphans in his nonunion house. They also figured that once the two airlines were unified, they had a puncher's chance to bring the combined operation back into ALPA.

On March 1, three days before the strike "release," Lorenzo responded to ALPA's four-point demand by dusting off his "Frankie Smooth Talk" routine. He mailed to all 3,400 Eastern pilots a 15-minute video of an informal interview with him sitting relaxed on a sofa. On the surface, the talk sounded good— Lorenzo seemed to agree to their demands. But on closer analysis, Lorenzo's promises proved a sham, for he had, in *every case,* left himself a loophole. Past experience suggested that if a loophole existed, Lorenzo would use it.

With ALPA's support, Eastern's pilots had become quite expert at financial analysis. They had hired a Touché Ross analyst named Farrell Kupersmith to advise them. Kupersmith, whose no-nonsense style appealed to Eastern's pilots, had conducted an extensive analysis of Lorenzo's jerrybuilt empire, and he was convinced that if Lorenzo didn't agree to the four-point plan, ALPA could find the financial pressure points to nail him.

But Lorenzo was nothing if not wily. He decided to gamble that the pilots' long-standing animosity to Charlie Bryan, leader of the IAM, would prevent meaningful cooperation between the two unions—a 1986 "cooperation agreement" notwithstanding.

On March 2, Lorenzo rejected ALPA's four-point plan ultimatum. He publicly stated his belief that 800 of Eastern's 3,400 pilots would cross the IAM's picket line if ALPA's leaders were foolish enough to authorize a sympathy strike. Counting 200 management pilots plus assorted instructors from the Miami training base, Lorenzo figured he could operate a large part of his schedule for almost 10 days—just long enough to shift some of his excess Continental capacity to Eastern's routes. Seeing Lorenzo operate their former routes with Continental crews and equipment, he believed, would so unnerve Eastern's remaining pilots that the strike would collapse within two weeks.

With his former "wonder boy" reputation slipping, particularly on Wall Street, Lorenzo was also counting on a sharp, quick strike victory to once again make him the darling of the antilabor movement. It would also simultaneously catapult him to the very top of the industry, placing him in command of the largest airline in the free world, without a single union to brook his will.

At midnight on March 4, Eastern's pilots put their careers on the line. They walked out in sympathy with the IAM, and the great test began. It was, in the history of the airline industry, the equivalent of Napoleon's crossing of the Niemen River to invade Russia in 1812, or Hitler's launching of Operation Barbarossa from nearly the same spot in 1941. Lorenzo should have heeded the fate of his historical soul mates. But he seemed oblivious to the fact that most Eastern pilots hated him so much that they would call artillery in on their own position before surrendering.

Lorenzo's boast that 800 pilots would immediately cross the IAM's picket lines proved hollow—only a piddling 120 of Eastern's 3,400 pilots crossed during the first week.

ALPA responded furiously. The MEC chairmen, meeting as the Executive Board on March 13, voted strike benefits of $2,400 per month plus a package of loans. Hank Duffy announced that the entire $37 million in ALPA's Major Contingency Fund would be made available to defeat Lorenzo. To nail down this fight with Lorenzo once and for all, the Executive Board also adopted strong resolutions on fragmentation and "first right of hire" should Eastern go into liquidation. Ominously for pilots like Wayne Dolan, the Executive Board had to qualify these guarantees by noting that they would be "subject to negotiation with the pilots and management of an acquiring carrier."

With good solidarity, good financial support, an excellent strike organization, and popular backing that ranged across the political spectrum from Ralph Nader on the left to William Safire on the right, Eastern's pilots should have been able to win this fight with Lorenzo. The pilots of American Airlines, through their ALPA clone, the Allied Pilots Association, contributed $100,000 to the Eastern pilots' "welfare fund." Lorenzo was widely unpopular, a fact he seemed unaware of and considerably rattled by when asked on a national TV newscast: "How does it feel to be the most hated man in America?"

On March 9, confronted with a labor solidarity he had never experienced before, Lorenzo filed for bankruptcy. The key player in the strike would now be Judge Burton R. Lifland, whose reputation for favoring management over labor was well-established. Owing to his pro-Lorenzo rulings, in hindsight it is easy to see that it would have been wiser had ALPA ended the strike immediately upon the bankruptcy filing. Lorenzo had pulled one of his typically dubious legal maneuvers by filing for bankruptcy in New York, instead of Miami, where Eastern was based. Bankruptcy judges in New York had a history of cooperating with the "debtor in possession," while Florida judges tended to side with creditors. Pension obligations and unpaid salaries would have given Eastern's unions standing as major "unsecured" creditors. More sinisterly, Lorenzo's principal bankruptcy lawyer, Harvey Miller, had a "long-standing relationship" with Judge Lifland, according to Aaron Bernstein, the reporter who covered the story for *Business Week*.

Rank-and-file Eastern pilots were probably more militant about the strike than their leadership. Almost unanimously, they figured that Lorenzo had left them no choice but to strike. Lorenzo's mismanagement of Eastern and internal harassment of employees had become legendary. The employees pinned their hopes for victory on several factors, first among them a "white knight" to buy out Lorenzo.

"They could have gone back to work unconditionally, but they were not psychologically ready," Hank Duffy said in his 1990 interview of Eastern's pilot group at the time of the bankruptcy filing. "We had this son-of-a-gun on the run. There were buyers, and we wrongly believed we could force a sale on him. But the bankruptcy court so tilted the deal against us that unless Lorenzo wanted out, the airline was not for sale."

Why wasn't Eastern sold? Within days of the March 9 bankruptcy filing, a suitable candidate had emerged. He was Peter Ueberroth, former commissioner of baseball. He had solid financial backing, a seasoned airline manager to run Eastern (Martin Shugrue, a former Texas Air Corporation official who, like so many others, Lorenzo had fired), and union support.

Only Lorenzo stood in the way of a sale. Lorenzo *said* he was amenable to a sale, Judge Lifland *said* he favored it and even appointed an "examiner," Washington lawyer David Shapiro, to facilitate the search for a buyer. The basic reason Lorenzo was able to sabotage a sale was because Lifland *let him*.

Lorenzo undermined the sale to Ueberroth by his usual trick—shifty bargaining. Every time Ueberroth's negotiators thought they had a deal, Lorenzo backed off and suggested changes. Pilots had long complained about Lorenzo's negotiating tactics. Now his fellow businessmen were getting a taste.

"I can understand now why the unions are so angry with him," one frustrated Ueberroth lieutenant said.

Aaron Bernstein wrote in *Grounded*: "Lorenzo's bargaining style—his demands to change terms in a deal even after he had agreed to it—destroyed any faith Ueberroth might have had in anything Lorenzo said."

But Lorenzo's style of negotiating a sale was possible only because Judge Lifland put up with it. Delay worked to Lorenzo's advantage. Because Lifland continued to let him strip assets from Eastern, the airline was worth less to a potential buyer every day.

Eastern's pilots were powerless to prevent this slow dwindling away of their airline's assets. The worst example of which was Lifland's approval, in May 1989, of the sale of the shuttle to Donald Trump for $350 million. With the profitable shuttle service stripped from the airline, its economic viability was doubtful.

Still a sale seemed *so close*. In early April, a month before Lifland allowed the shuttle sale, major newspapers ran stories indicating the sale to Ueberroth was a "done deal." Eastern's pilots were so certain they were rid of Lorenzo that they had a memorable party in Miami that lasted until 3 a.m.

The sale would never happen, but it took a couple of months before the pilots realized that fact. During this time, Eastern's pilots clung to the hope that either Judge Lifland would replace Lorenzo with a "trustee" or *force* him to sell out. By mid-April, it should have been apparent that Lifland would do neither.

Farrell Kupersmith began warning Eastern's pilots shortly after the Ueberroth sale collapsed that Judge Lifland was allowing Lorenzo a free hand and that perhaps they ought to reconsider their strike decision. By leaving Lorenzo as "debtor in possession," Judge Lifland permitted him to sell enough assets to satisfy creditors. In bankruptcy, the interests of creditors are paramount. So long as lenders thought Lorenzo could service their debt by cannibalizing the airline, they were willing to go along—regardless of the effect upon the airline's long-term employees.

Perhaps Kupersmith's warnings were too subtle for rank-and-file pilots to understand. By early summer, Eastern's leadership group, particularly MEC Chairman Jack Bavis, began to realize the trouble they were in. He began to urge pulling down the strike when it became clear that Lorenzo could not be forced into a sale. But for rank-and-file pilots, their blood inflamed, the struggle against Lorenzo had become a holy war.

"The line pilots wouldn't accept any deal like that," Randy Babbitt observes. "The flaw was that the strike had made us feel strong. We had shut Eastern down with a handful of pilots and pocket change. Just the thought of having the oppressive harness of Lorenzo lifted gave line pilots all these great visions of a wonderful airline surging forward. That became the new goal, not getting a new contract. If there was a point in time that we lost our focus as a pilot group, it was about six weeks into the strike. We became obsessed with finding a white knight. We wanted Lorenzo gone."

On April 17, Lorenzo announced publicly that Eastern was not for sale. The pilots refused to believe that Judge Lifland would permit him to wriggle out. Indeed, the Judge ordered Examiner Shapiro to continue the search for a buyer. So many potential buyers seemed to be lining up to take Ueberroth's place, that Jack Bavis created a committee to vet them. Raymond "Buzz" Wright and Jack Suchocki handled this task. Eventually Eastern's pilots settled on a 42 year-old Chicago commodities trader named Joe Ritchie. They offered Ritchie the same concession package they had previously offered Ueberroth. But Ritchie stumbled—he couldn't nail down his financing.

"Lorenzo was of a mindset to prevail," says Randy Babbitt. "If it meant tearing Eastern apart bolt by bolt, he was hell bent to do it."

Unfortunately, nearly everybody was slow to recognize that Judge Lifland was going to let him do it. In desperation, ALPA engineered a joint effort by organized labor to buy Lorenzo out. Several major unions promised $5 million each out of their pension funds. But Examiner Shapiro rejected the idea of an employees' buyout, and Judge Lifland supported him.

These maneuvers took until late May, and in the meantime, Lorenzo had embarked upon a Continental-style effort to break the strike. Enraged Eastern pilots, their fury growing, could only watch as Lorenzo announced a reorganization that would reduce the airline's size to barely half its prestrike level. Lorenzo had quietly hired 700 scabs, so there weren't enough jobs for every striker, if they did pull down the strike "unconditionally."

"All of us or none of us," rank-and-file pilots vowed, as they voted to continue the strike against the advice of their own leadership.

Increasingly, the Eastern strikers pinned their hopes for victory on "ALPA's Nuke," an industrywide suspension of service—an SOS. Hank Duffy's refusal to endorse an SOS generated enormous anger among them.

"When the strike started to go bad, they wanted a national action, but I told the Eastern MEC going into the strike, and anybody can research the record, that they could not expect us to shut down the country to win a strike," Duffy asserted in his 1990 interview. "There are some issues—cabotage and hijacking—that involve everybody where an SOS may be possible. But no single strike, even against Frank Lorenzo, will penetrate all the local interests on an individual property. So nobody who does not bargain nationally so that all the local units are involved, commits a national action like an SOS."

At a July LEC meeting of several hundred furious Eastern pilots in an Alexandria, Va., hotel, Farrell Kupersmith, Randy Babbitt, and Jack Bavis faced a hostile reception. Bavis argued that Lorenzo was winning through bankruptcy again, and the issue now was simply between saving some jobs or losing them all to scabs. When the 700 scabs had completed their initial operating experience (IOE), Bavis warned, there would be no way to get rid of them. Another large group was in ground school.

"We see the landscape out there as bleak," Bavis admitted.

If they voted to call down the strike and go back to work unconditionally, Bavis said, between 1,300 and 1,700 of them would have jobs (although Lorenzo was saying at the time only 950 strikers would be rehired). For a pilot group that numbered 4,500 dues-paying ALPA members at the time of Lorenzo's accession in February 1986, and 3,400 at the beginning of the strike in March 1989, this was totally unacceptable.

Angry questions assailed Kupersmith, once so popular as a teleconference participant that he was nicknamed "Captain Video." He tried patiently to explain that the bankruptcy process had "co-opted all the points of financial leverage" that existed at the beginning of the strike.

Kupersmith also announced that he would take no further payment or fees from ALPA but would continue to serve. The general tone of the questions directed at Bavis, Babbitt, and Kupersmith indicated that the rank-and-file was in no mood to surrender. They would fight Lorenzo to the death—regardless of their leadership's advice. It was an ugly scene, rife with charges of bad faith, incompetence, and worse.

"Don't go shooting at ALPA," Bavis pleaded with angry pilots demanding that

Hank Duffy shut down the entire airline industry. "Hank Duffy told us from the very beginning that there would be no SOS."

"If we go back, we'll be nothing but a bunch of damned scabs working for Continental," Skip Copeland argued, his craggy face a mask of determination.

Bavis, fighting for his life, committed himself to staying on strike for as long as the pilot group wanted, but he insisted that duty required him to render his best advice, which was to call it off. Hank Duffy agreed with Bavis.

"Kupersmith became something more than a consultant to the Eastern pilots," says Hank Duffy. "He became a hero because he had a great way of communicating and great credibility. When Bavis decided it was time for them to go back, Kupersmith agreed. He went out on road shows and told them it didn't make sense to stay out any longer. That was not the message the Eastern pilots wanted to hear, so they rebelled. A lot of them said Kupersmith changed his story. He may have put a little different spin on things, but the facts had changed and our situation had changed."

By July, Duffy had become convinced, after assessing all factors, that ALPA's best interests nationally would be served by ending the strike. Strike assessments that individual members had agreed to impose upon themselves were becoming onerous and controversial. Inevitably, as the prospects for an outright victory over Lorenzo faded, pilots resented paying. Their resignations from ALPA would generate internal problems for years to come. The only thing keeping Eastern's pilots from seeing the light, Duffy believed, was their forlorn hope that he would call a national SOS. Duffy had to disabuse them.

On August 20, the Executive Board did so by formally rejecting an SOS. To Eastern's hard-core strikers, this was _prima facie_ evidence that Jack Bavis had failed them. Early in September, reflecting rank-and-file anger, they recalled Bavis and elected his long-time antagonist, Skip Copeland. This turmoil had the predictable effect of unnerving many wavering strikers. About 500 of them crossed the picket line late that summer. Most of this leakage came a full five months into the strike. Until then, the Eastern pilot group had displayed remarkable solidarity, holding their lines tenaciously. But for the last-ditch holdouts, the strike had become a war with no quarter asked and none given.

In October, with the strike obviously weakening, the Executive Board recommended a reballot on the strike assessment—a critical test of ALPA's willingness to continue the battle. For a strike that seemed to be losing steam, it would be remarkable indeed if ALPA's rank-and-file voted to continue financially supporting Eastern's pilot group. Individual ALPA members would have to literally put their money where their mouths were. Strike assessments have been unfailingly controversial in ALPA history, and the outcome of this referendum was in doubt. In an "all member" mailing, Duffy urged every pilot to keep the faith by voting to continue the assessment. ALPA's 34,000 members heeded his advice, but only narrowly.

Like the Continental loyalists before them, Eastern's pilots waged a good fight against overwhelming odds. Had the national political climate been more favorable, they would have won. They engaged in a variety of effective and innovative tactics, including a 3,000-mile picket line that stretched, symbolically and actually, across the continent. When the nationwide picket line was completed on September 6, a bevy of major politicians, including Sen. Edward Kennedy and Congressman James Oberstar, chairman of the House Aviation Subcommittee, joined Hank Duffy and AFL-CIO President Lane Kirkland on the steps of the Capitol building, calling for George Bush to support a Presidential Emergency Board (PEB) to resolve the strike with justice for all parties. Kennedy, whose Senate Committee had midwifed deregulation in 1978, had turned against it by then.[1]

All the while, Eastern's striking pilots kept up their picketing and publicity activities. The damage inflicted on Lorenzo by these actions was substantial, as the steady downward trend of his passenger loads showed. The strikers made sure the public knew about the marginal quality of the scab pilots Lorenzo was hiring. Confidential documents leaked by an ALPA sympathizer at the Hartley Training Center in Miami showed that an astounding 40 percent of Lorenzo's scab new-hires failed to complete training! Even nationwide TV ads featuring a scab pilot lauding the quality of the "New Eastern" couldn't burnish the airline's tarnished image. A skittish public, worried about safety, stayed away in droves.

Toward the end, with every avenue of attack stymied by Judge Lifland, Eastern's pilots placed all their bets on a tactic old Dave Behncke would have approved. By the fall of 1989, six months into the strike, their only hope was a direct political solution. To this end, Eastern's pilots, supported by the entire apparatus of organized labor, lobbied Congress furiously to *impose* a "back door PEB," a bipartisan commission which would *force* George Bush into action. They hoped that, confronted by such an expression of congressional support for Eastern's strikers, Bush would come to his senses. Experts warned that there was virtually no chance of Congress overriding a Bush veto, so everything depended upon his being willing, at long last, to break ranks with Frank Lorenzo. Given the antilabor bent of the Republican Party, it was a forlorn hope.

On November 21, Bush vetoed Congress's version of a PEB, saying it would "hinder saving Eastern." The Republican minority in Congress sustained his veto. Lorenzo wrote Bush a chummy note thanking him for his "courage and clear vision."

That was it—the strike had to be stopped. Lorenzo had won the battle, if not the war. On Nov. 23, 1989, the Eastern MEC, on a motion by "Buzz" Wright, a veteran widely respected for his financial acumen, called off the sympathy strike. MEC Chairman Skip Copeland opposed Wright, but he knew it was over. If Buzz Wright thought the game was up, the MEC would agree. In symbolic protest, Copeland refused to participate in the vote.

As early as the summer of 1989, Hank Duffy believed that Eastern would not survive, regardless of whether the pilots called down their sympathy strike. Lorenzo's mismanagement had gutted the airline, Duffy believed, and nothing ALPA could do would save it. The effect on Eastern's pilots would be extreme, Duffy knew. Their only hope lay in ALPA's *somehow* persuading various airline managements to take the Eastern loyalists aboard voluntarily—preferably in seniority, but, a job being a job, at the bottom of the list if need be. To this end, Duffy began contacting MEC chairmen, urging them to approach management about taking a quota of Eastern strikers. He also editorialized in the July 1989 *Air Line Pilot* on the moral obligations of all pilots to persuade their airlines to hire Eastern strikers.

"A willingness to share seniority is not only the moral way to operate—even though it may impinge upon one's own advancement—it is also an important check of our Association's character," Duffy wrote. "Conversely, a move that results from Eastern equipment sales to 'our' company is a move up off the backs of striking pilots. To profit thusly is a serious breach of faith."

Duffy tried to practice what he preached. He arranged a personal conference with Ron Allen, CEO of Delta, his own airline. It came to nothing.

"Ron Allen looked me in the face and said, 'Why should I hire trouble?'" Duffy recalled in his 1990 interview. "He said he could hire all the 28-year-old ex-military pilots he needed. He believed that these new-hires wouldn't come out of an 'alien corporate culture' like the Eastern pilots did. I couldn't move him."

One of those supreme ironies is that some Eastern equipment did wind up at Delta, by way of Pan Am. When Eastern spun this equipment off to Pan Am, no pilots were included. By the time Pan Am went under, Duffy's moral suasion had taken sufficient root that Delta finally agreed to take Pan Am pilots, "alien corporate culture" notwithstanding. The newly radicalized Delta pilot group, which was beginning to experience the same tensions as other ALPA pilot groups, also exerted pressure to take Pan Am pilots. But no Eastern pilot benefited, despite the fact that the airplanes had originally been *theirs*. Braniff pilots at last had their revenge.

Midway's pilots, under the leadership of Jerry Mugerditchian, also tried to honor the spirit of sacrifice Duffy encouraged. When some Eastern equipment and routes went to Midway, Mugerditchian opened negotiations with management, trying to get 400 Eastern strikers hired, *in seniority*. Management refused. Finally, the only way Midway's pilots could have forced their airline into compliance with ALPA fragmentation policy was by going on strike themselves!

The only bright spot came at United, whose battled-hardened pilots *demanded* that Eastern's strikers be given first-right-of-hire, or something approaching it. Eventually, 600 Eastern refugees would wind up in United cockpits, including former MEC Chairman Larry Schulte.

Because Rick Dubinsky marched into the office of Bill Traub, vice-president for flight, and threatened to go to the mat over jobs for former Eastern pilots, United's Training Center at Denver became a haven for nearly 300 of them. This served a double purpose for United's pilots—it acquitted their moral obligation to the profession and it also cleaned house at Denver, which had become a cesspool of scabs trying to hide from the wrath of their former line pilot colleagues. The pressure of United's ESOP effort gave Dubinsky part of the leverage he needed to "de-scab" United's training center, and a successful grievance action provided the rest.

But isolated successes like those at United only lessened the sting. Eastern's pilots believed ALPA's efforts to implement "fragmentation policy," which had been formally promised to them, were inadequate. While other airlines skimmed the cream of Eastern's routes, equipment, *and pilots*, rank-and-file strikers could only watch helplessly. Formal promises to implement fragmentation policy for them were so hedged about with qualifications that they proved unworkable. For the 1,600 pilots who remained unemployed after ALPA called off its sympathy strike, the only solace was the bitter pleasure they took in the fall and final disgrace of Frank Lorenzo.

Unfortunately for Lorenzo, the nationwide recession (which ended the "seven fat years" of the Reagan boom) had begun by 1989. Lorenzo had once again beaten his unions, but at a terrible price. Now he needed a thriving economy like the one that had saved him after the 1983 Continental strike. This time his luck had run out, but it wasn't immediately apparent.

By June 1989, Lorenzo was clearly winning his battle with the unions. Judge Lifland rejected ALPA's petition to have a trustee installed to run Eastern in Lorenzo's place. The creditors had bought Lorenzo's promise that he could, by a combination of asset sales and downsizing the airline, pay them back at 100 cents on the dollar. Judge Lifland, ever mindful of the creditors' views, publicly stated that he wanted to see the airline flying again. If Shapiro and the unions couldn't effectuate a sale, then Judge Lifland would get Eastern back into the air by helping Lorenzo break the strike.

On July 21, Lorenzo filed his reorganization plan and announced that he would immediately bring Eastern up to speed by using "leased" nonunion Continental crews and aircraft. Judge Lifland approved this arrangement with no objections. Aside from proving, as ALPA had always contended, that Continental and Eastern really were a "single carrier," this move forced Jack Bavis to conclude that he had no choice but to negotiate the best deal he could with Lorenzo. Owing to changes in the bankruptcy law following the Continental strike, Lorenzo also had to negotiate. Bavis, too, had to negotiate; otherwise Lorenzo could petition Lifland to abrogate the contract. But rank-and-file militants saw Bavis's *required* negotiations as a sellout. Bavis was finished politically when the MEC rejected, in late August, the back-to-work agreement he negotiated, because it would leave some 2,000 strikers on the street.

With crossovers, scabs, and the Continental lease, Lorenzo had his shrunken version of Eastern flying again by December 1989. But the economy now intervened. Nothing he tried generated enough passengers to turn a profit, and the creditors were getting restless. Finally, Judge Lifland also began to lose confidence in Lorenzo—at last. In January 1990, Lorenzo reneged on his promise to pay back creditors fully and offered instead only 50 cents on the dollar. Most of the money to pay them would come from the proposed sale of Eastern's Latin American routes to American Airlines. Perhaps these routes carried a curse. These were the same jobs that Eastern's pilots had taken from Braniff's pilots in 1982, in clear violation of the spirit of ALPA's fragmentation policy.

In March 1990, Examiner Shapiro found that Lorenzo had indeed "cherry picked" Eastern's assets and had not paid a fair price for them. In 12 of the 15 asset transfers Shapiro examined, he found that Lorenzo had cheated Eastern and, by inference, its creditors. Lorenzo settled out of court, in effect pleading guilty to looting. ALPA had won a moral victory and again petitioned Lifland to appoint a trustee to run Eastern. To do otherwise, ALPA's lawyers argued, would be tantamount to allowing a parent found guilty of child abuse to retain custody. The judge still refused to remove Lorenzo, but he was clearly beginning to have doubts. Because Lorenzo's asset-stripping had damaged the unsecured creditors, ALPA, as one of them, had standing to sue. But Lifland stayed the suit.

"We filed a lawsuit charging Lorenzo with fraudulent conveyance, a crime," says Randy Babbitt. "I have been around labor a while, I had the warm-up rounds for Continental. I wrote that off as Texas politics. But I had no idea how unbalanced bankruptcy could be. I can't think of a worse place to be as a labor union. Every grievance is stayed, every piece of litigation is stayed. You prevail in an arbitration, it's stayed."

Judge Lifland's forbearance toward Lorenzo had as its object to save Eastern—as a nonunion carrier, of course—but nevertheless to save it. So long as he thought Lorenzo could do that, he went along, ALPA's objections notwithstanding. Lifland had accepted Lorenzo's original plan, which envisioned full repayment of the creditors, and Lifland grumbled only briefly at Lorenzo's second plan, which contemplated paying off only 50 percent of the unsecured debt.

Meanwhile, the Judge was learning what many veteran Lorenzo-watchers already knew, that Lorenzo had no idea how to run an airline, other than beating up on labor. With Phil Bakes as Lorenzo's nominal president of Eastern, losses mounted. For the entire period (March 1989 to April 1990), Lorenzo *lost* $1.2 billion.

Matters finally came to a head on April 2, 1990, when Lorenzo proposed paying creditors only 25 cents on the dollar, of which a mere 5 cents was cash. The remainder would be in junk bonds. The creditors had finally had enough. Lorenzo had to go, they told Judge Lifland, echoing the position ALPA had taken since the beginning of the strike. Lifland finally agreed and, on April 18, named Martin Shugrue, the former TAC official Lorenzo had fired, who had been Ueberroth's choice to actually run Eastern, as trustee. Lorenzo, humiliated and publicly revealed as the incompetent ALPA had always known him to be, was out.

It needn't have ended that way. The historical record is abundantly clear that Eastern's pilots had done their utmost to meet Lorenzo halfway, and more. But most Eastern pilots saw what Lorenzo was doing to them as so provocative, so redolent with violations of basic safety doctrines, and so absolutely destructive of their professional futures that they saw no alternative to fighting him.

Eastern would linger on under Shugrue's trusteeship until Jan. 18, 1991, before finally succumbing. During the eight months of life remaining to the airline between Lorenzo's fall and the liquidation, the usual ebb and flow of hope mingled with despair, for both ALPA's loyalists and the scabs.

With Lorenzo gone, his scabs stood naked, clearly expendable. Phil Bakes resigned as Eastern's president two days after Shugrue took over as trustee. Shugrue owed the scabs nothing, and they knew it. In a panic, they tried, pathetically, to protect themselves by forming their own union. On May 30, they announced something called the Eastern Pilots Association, claiming to represent 93 percent of the 1,775 pilots then employed by the airline. They petitioned the NMB for an election, claiming to "better represent the real interests of the men and women who are flying Eastern's planes every day." It was exactly what George T."Ted" Baker's scabs had done following the 1948 strike on National Airlines. The results were about the same.

In every single labor dispute in the modern history of aviation, with the single exception of the Continental strike of 1983–85, management has always thrown scabs out like dead rats when they became inconvenient. Every pilot considering crossing a picket line should be acquainted with the sad historical fate of scabs, and be reminded forcefully that airline managements change, and when they change, the new boss owes scabs nothing. The new management does, however, have to make a profit, which requires the cooperation of ALPA. As the scabs at United found out after the 1985 strike, management has *always* left them to their fate in the end. As every modern airline pilot capable of rational analysis knows, pilots are just numbers to management. Scab pilots, however, are *embarrassing* numbers.

Frank Lorenzo's failure at Eastern was so complete that he was, for all intents and purposes, finished in the airline industry. In 1986, he had taken control of America's *third largest* airline, which was making respectable profits at the time and had a new *concessionary* ALPA contract that was quite reasonable by industry standards. By the time Judge Lifland summarily canned him, Lorenzo had reduced Eastern to a shadow of its former self, primarily by selling off $1.5 billion in assets, while *still* piling up huge losses. A failure more complete than Lorenzo's is hard to find in the annals of commercial aviation.

Nor was Eastern Lorenzo's only failure. Continental was a disorganized, debt-ridden mess, with the worst customer service "image" in the industry. Lorenzo's normally pliant board of directors had become restless, largely owing to the fear that they might be held liable for approving some of his more outrageous financial manipulations. Wall Street analysts, once so high on Lorenzo because he had taken on the unions, now saw him as a liability. His money man, Michael Milken, who had bankrolled Lorenzo's ventures with junk bonds, was under indictment and would eventually be found guilty and sentenced to 10 years in prison. Pressure mounted on Lorenzo to resign from the active management of Continental.

In August 1990, Lorenzo sold his interest in Continental Airlines Holding (TAC's new name since 1989) to Scandinavian Air Service (SAS), for $30 million. He signed a "noncompete" agreement that barred him from any role in the airline industry for seven years.

"Hell, we'd have paid him $30 million to just go away," said Pat Broderick, an Eastern pilot whose "My Turn" article in *Newsweek* laid bare the damage Lorenzo had done. In fact, when all the tabulations were complete, ALPA spent about $200 million fighting the Lorenzo Wars—$70 million of it on Eastern *alone*!

As for striking ALPA loyalist Wayne Dolan, fate had one more disappointment. Trustee Shugrue reached a back-to-work agreement with the Eastern MEC that would affect about one-third of hard-core strikers. Dolan, because of his seniority, received a bid to begin training on Jan. 18, 1991—the day Shugrue shut the airline down.

"I was getting packed to go down to Miami," Dolan recalls. "I got a phone call from somebody, who said, 'Don't come.'"

For nearly 20 years, Frank Lorenzo had waged an absolutely unnecessary war on labor that finally resulted in the destruction of one of the proudest airlines in aviation history. During his career, he ruined thousands of lives. To win his war with ALPA, he had to destroy himself—a pyrrhic victory in the classic sense. The former wonder boy had become a pariah and a bad joke. Lorenzo must have worried that his associates were winking and snickering at his pretensions behind his back. The loser who dared to sit in the chairs once occupied by Bob Six and Eddie Rickenbacker was completely humiliated. So great was his humiliation that _Air Line Pilot_ felt it unnecessary to do more than mention his drunken driving arrest several months later. With Lorenzo universally despised for the failure he was, ALPA concluded that refusing to dwell on "King Lorenzo the Drunken" was a far more elegant way to emphasize his downfall.

Dennis Higgins, who began the fight with Lorenzo back in 1974 at little Texas International, adds one final story to illustrate the state to which Lorenzo had fallen.

"A guy who was a day-one picket line crosser, an adamant scab who sang Lorenzo's praises, called me up when Hollis Harris took over Continental," Higgins recounts. "He said, 'Well, now that that asshole is gone, are we ready to organize this property?'"

"I said, 'Jesus!'"   ✦

NOTE
[1] In a memorable public confrontation, Kennedy cursed his erstwhile committee staffer, Phil Bakes, who had become Lorenzo's CEO at Eastern: "This goddamned deregulation. Phil, you doublecrossed me; you lied to me."

CHAPTER 20

AFTERMATH
The Disputed Election of 1990 and ALPA's Future

Sir Walter Raleigh, writing his *History of the World* while imprisoned in the Tower of London, put it this way: "Whosoever, in writing history, shall follow too near upon its heels, it may haply strike out his teeth."

Contemporary history is never easy, as Raleigh would find out on the headsman's block. Those who walk on history's edge, who actually make it happen, are often so busy keeping their balance that they have little time for reflection on "what it all means." That's fine for participants, but a trap for historians, who ideally should wait until the dust settles.

Oliver Cromwell, rebuking the bloodlust of his "Witchfinder General," issued a stern warning equally applicable to religious zealots *and* historians: "I beseech you, in the bowels of Christ, think you, *you might be wrong!*"

Sometimes, historians must wait decades to make certain they're not wrong. The sinking of the British ocean liner *Lusitania* in 1915 provides a classic example. At the time, the *Lusitania* affair seemed to confirm British propaganda that Kaiser Wilhelm was the reincarnation of Attila the Hun, the vicious Asiatic marauder whose 5th century A.D. invasion of Europe still haunts our collective memory. But with the passage of time another story emerged. Not only was the *Lusitania* a "semiwarship" (it carried some light munitions, mostly rifles), but many decades later declassified British cables revealed a hint of conspiracy as well. The *Lusitania*'s captain had orders *not* to "zigzag," thus making the ship an easier target for German U-boats. They made short work of the *Lusitania*, with predictable results—a profound shift in American public opinion in favor of the Allies. Getting the United States into the war meant national salvation for the British—well worth the lives of a few innocents.

How long does passion take to cool and "the truth" to emerge? Talk to any former Eastern pilot, and you know their fires are still burning. Former Braniff pilots still seethe with anger over the failure of their airline. What did Hank Duffy or J.J. O'Donnell either do or not do during their tenure that their critics still denounce? Talk to anybody who was ever disappointed by some decision they made, and you know the heat of contention persists. What *really* happened during the fiercely contested presidential election of 1990 between Roger Hall of United and J. Randolph "Randy" Babbitt of Eastern? How long will the anger of Hall's supporters persist?

And what about ALPA a century from now? Will it persist?

If ALPA does survive to see the opening of another time capsule a century from now, it will almost certainly be because of the holding action Hank Duffy fought for eight years. Not that progress was lacking during his era, but planning for the future necessarily had to take place in the lull between battles, any one of which could have spelled ALPA's doom.

Hank Duffy's successes were like his personality—careful, precise, controlled, and not much given to flamboyance. He favored long-range planning, and he was always distrustful of impatient short-range projects. Transient enthusiasms couldn't move him to impolitic or hasty action. Hank Duffy preferred the long view, one that proceeded from thorough planning to achieve well-defined goals.

Nothing illustrates this better than the successful organization of 30 "new entrant" airlines during Hank Duffy's administration. In February 1983, at the very beginning of his first term, the pilots of TWA began pressuring Duffy for an organizational campaign directed at these new-entrant airlines. While noting that new-entrants commanded only 7 percent of the market, TWA's pilots worried that this share would grow, and they also feared that even if new-entrant carriers remained relatively small, the depressive effect of their low wages would inevitably have an adverse effect on the pilots of major airlines. The TWA MEC passed a resolution directing Duffy to "engage in a widespread and dynamic public relations campaign" to win the allegiance of new-entrant pilots, and it called for "support of a program that will organize these new-entrant carriers."

Duffy seemed genuinely interested in the futures of new-entrant airlines and their pilots. But the debilitating effects of deregulation meant that the pilots of these "code sharing" airlines, who flew for the likes of American Eagle or United Express, often wearing remarkably similar uniforms and flying aircraft bearing the same corporate logos as their major airline partners, would find their relative share of ALPA's pie diminishing in the late 1980s. A steady and inexorable concentration characterized the airline industry, a pattern of consolidation that caused the pilot groups of major airlines to grow in relative numbers and influence. In short, deregulation caused the "elephants" to get bigger and the "ants" to get smaller. Which didn't mean that the pilots of smaller airlines played an insignificant role in ALPA's history—far from it.

Randy Babbitt, whom Duffy had appointed as his executive administrator in January 1985, would probably not have won the election of 1990 had it not been for *one particular pilot* from one of these small airlines. Babbitt, almost from the moment he became Duffy's executive administrator, acted as a roving troubleshooter and goodwill ambassador for the organizational effort directed at small airlines. Whenever ALPA had to "show the flag" of official concern, Randy Babbitt was Hank Duffy's point man. As Duffy's chief assistant, Babbitt's involvement indicated to the pilots of small airlines that ALPA's commitment to them originated at the top. Thus for many of these pilots, Babbitt became an almost totemic figure, the national officer who was there for them at times of crisis in their struggle to achieve decent working conditions and fair wages.

"Where Hank used me most was on the collective bargaining side," Babbitt recalls of his five years as executive administrator. "He liked my background on ALPA's Collective Bargaining Committee. The regional airline industry didn't really get under way until 1982, and we didn't get serious about organizing them until 1985. Then, when we got them organized, what do we do with them? It took some educating of these pilot groups. They'd say, 'We're part of ALPA, now where's that Delta pay scale?' We had to convince them that first you get a basic contract, then the company has to get used to the whole idea. The industry was filled with colorful entrepreneurs, such as Joe Murray of Simmons Airlines, who'd fuss and carry on and swear at their pilots before finally saying, 'What do I have to pay to shut them up?' When negotiations ran aground, I would get involved."

The pilots of small airlines were actually living and working under conditions that ALPA's founders, the Old Guys, would have recognized—long hours, dangerous operations, unsympathetic and often autocratic managements. In some strange, indefinable way, Babbitt seemed like an Old Guy himself. He first attracted national attention in 1976 through his service on a national ALPA committee studying a national seniority list, something the Old Guys had dreamed of almost from the moment of ALPA's creation.

"John LeRoy and I worked very hard on that, but couldn't get anywhere," Babbitt recalls. "We advocated driving a stake in the ground and doing a national seniority list for the future. If we had been able to do it in 1977, 75 percent of ALPA would be under that list today. We couldn't do it because of the practicalities of how it would work. Are you going to furlough somebody to make room on the list? Today, I would consider it a major victory if we could ensure that when people lost their jobs they could get priority to go to the next open job."

Because Eastern's Washington, D.C., domicile was small, Babbitt became increasingly active, graduating from LEC service to work on various national committees. He came to Duffy's attention through his work as chairman of the national Collective Bargaining Committee, which J.J. O'Donnell established in 1982 to limit the spread of United's "Blue Skies" contract to other airlines and also to combat the B-scale epidemic that was then spreading outward from its epicenter on American Airlines. Fred Kozak of Piedmont and Bill Daugherty of Delta rounded out the three-man committee. Daugherty, who was very close to Duffy, liked Babbitt's work and told Duffy about this bright young DC-9 captain who bore a famous ALPA name. But the fact that Randy was the son of W.T. "Slim" Babbitt of Eastern, an authentic Old Guy whose service dated back to the Behncke era, benefited Randy Babbitt only indirectly. Slim Babbitt, who retired in 1970 and died in 1986 at the age of 76, always warned his son, perhaps tongue-in-cheek, to stay out of ALPA work. Young Randy Babbitt knew his father never meant him to take this advice seriously.

"Having grown up with it, I didn't realize how active in ALPA my dad was," Babbitt remembers. "I just assumed everybody's father was always involved in union meetings and committee work. I knew a lot about ALPA just by things that went on at home. I would typically go with my dad to the ALPA office and see things that went on. The first matchbook cover I remember reading said, 'Don't Fly National,' which is how I learned what a strike was. So I just kind of grew up with ALPA."

Slim Babbitt's prominence in ALPA had nothing to do with his son's rise, however.

"Although my father held elective ALPA office without interruption from 1937 to 1967, I really was fairly anonymous," Babbitt laughs. "You'd be amazed at how fast people forget."

Born in 1946, Babbitt grew up in south Florida, learned to fly as an adolescent, then began instructing and flying charters. He attended both the Universities of Georgia and Miami, leaving in 1966 without a degree to catch the great hiring surge at Eastern. At the tender age of 20, he was wearing Eastern's uniform, flying as a copilot on Lockheed Electras. By 1968 Babbitt had moved up to the B-727, becoming a "seat swapper," qualified as both a flight engineer and a copilot. Then, when dual qualification was eliminated in 1970, he settled in for a short stint on the panel.

"That wasn't a lot of fun, so I took the first copilot's seat I could get, which turned out to be on the DC-9," Babbitt remembers.

For 10 years, Babbitt slowly worked his way back to the right seat of the B-727 and then upgraded to the A300 Airbus. In 1983, 17 years into his Eastern career, but still only 37 years old, Babbitt achieved his captaincy on the DC-9. He would fly that position until Duffy tapped him as executive administrator to replace John Erickson of Western Airlines in January 1985.

Erikson's position was frankly political, in that he had been a key player in Duffy's 1982 victory over J.J. O'Donnell, and Duffy owed him. Historically, ALPA presidents have chosen executive administrators either for political balance or because of a long-term working relationship. Jack Bavis fit the latter mold—he had worked with O'Donnell for years on Eastern. Erikson illustrates the former case, and although neither he nor Duffy will speak ill of the other, Babbitt's appointment clearly resulted from a simple failure of "chemistry" between Erikson and Duffy, with perhaps the improved career advancement opportunities available to Erikson as a line pilot (because of the Delta–Western merger) also a factor.

The original Collective Bargaining Committee was composed of Executive Board members. That didn't work, largely because they were too busy. The restructured committee, with Babbitt as chairman, set in motion a series of steps that would eventually lead to the formation of the Association of Independent Airmen (AIA) at the height of the Eastern strike. The AIA was simply a better version of the Union of Professional Airmen (UPA), an O'Donnell-era effort. Created in July 1989, the AIA, with its low-cost benefits and positive identification with ALPA, was designed to give every pilot working under a non-ALPA contract good reason not to be a potential scab. The AIA was a good example of the kind of long-term project Duffy favored.

By 1989, Randy Babbitt's organizational skills had won contracts for several small airlines, including little NPA, a United code-sharer, based in Pasco, Wash. The initials had, long ago, stood for "National Parks Airways," a small airline serving the mountainous Northwest with single-engine Fokker "Super" Universals and Stearmans. During its 10-year existence, from 1927 to 1937, NPA became celebrated for the skill of its pioneer mountain fliers. Western Air Express, which eventually merged into TWA, bought NPA, and the famous initials by which the little airline was known lapsed into history. Years later, following deregulation, a group of entrepreneurs resurrected the initials, originally as Northern Pacific Airlines, a name they later dropped entirely for the historically significant initials, which the airline's 200 pilots joked stood for "No Particular Airline."

NPA would have little interest for this history except that in 1990 it sent, as its first officer representative, an ex-naval aviator named Dean Brouillette to the BOD meeting. As we shall see, Dean Brouillette's tiny airline would determine the victor in the Hall–Babbitt contest.

Hank Duffy announced in the summer of 1989, more than a year before the election, that he would not be a candidate again. Aside from the technical problem that Duffy would be past the airline pilots' mandatory retirement age of 60 by the end of another term, he also had a political calculation behind his decision. Although Duffy was certain he could win another term of office, he knew it would come only after another close and divisive election like that of 1986—exactly what ALPA didn't need at this juncture. Allowing ALPA to start the 1990s fresh with new leadership was a selfless act on Duffy's part, which is not to say that neither Hall nor Babbitt were untainted by association with him. As national officers, both carried some of the same baggage as Duffy.

The election of 1990 shaped up as a two-man contest almost from the beginning. Joe Kernan of USAir would wage a campaign, but more for the purpose of symbolically unifying his own airline than as a serious challenge for the presidency. Both Hall and Babbitt had extensive track records and instant name recognition. Hall had the advantage of having won ALPA's most significant victory of the postderegulation period, the United strike of 1985, and he also seemed on the verge of achieving an ESOP that would make United the largest employee-owned corporation in the world. He had also won plaudits for having made globalization a central issue for the future.

Almost from the moment Hall won election as ALPA's first vice-president in 1986, he had warned pilots of the dangers of globalization. If foreign airlines were allowed to penetrate the domestic U.S. market to carry passengers between two U.S. cities (cabotage), then the fate of U.S. airlines might be the same as that of the U.S. merchant marine—driven from the skies by putative "Air Slobbovias," the kind of cheap foreign competition old Dave Behncke worried about in the 1940s.

"Pilots want to hang onto the past very much," Hall declared in a postelection interview. "We don't like the idea of change because it has worked very much to our detriment. Globalization of the airlines is the second wave of deregulation; and if we don't act as a cohesive group, the same trauma we experienced in deregulation is going to revisit us."

Hall openly warned of the political battles ALPA would have to fight to stop cabotage, and he made no secret of his belief that ALPA should work for a change from Republican to Democratic administrations in Washington as a first step. The ideological bias of the Republican Party in favor of free trade, even when confronted with clear evidence of protectionism by our trading partners, was such that Republicans simply could not be trusted to handle the transition to a global airline system, Hall believed.

"The fight against cabotage must be waged collectively; it can't be done by just one pilot group," Hall says. "Pilots everywhere have to understand the threat that the Reagan and Bush administrations' policies pose to labor, and specifically labor in the airline industry."

By the summer of 1990, as electioneering reached its peak, Roger Hall seemed the clear front runner. A remarkable political transformation had affected airline pilots. Although no hard proof confirms it, anecdotal evidence suggests that airline pilots had voted overwhelmingly Republican since 1980. By the beginning of the 1990s, however, the ideological antiunionism of the Reagan-Bush years had become so manifest that even die-hard Republicans among airline pilots could scarcely stomach it.

Sickened by George Bush's support for Frank Lorenzo, rank-and-file ALPA members were primed and ready to abandon their traditional Republicanism. Roger Hall was out front, riding this political crest.

Hall's only serious opposition, Randy Babbitt, bore major handicaps. First and most significantly, Babbitt stood likely to become an orphan—a pilot without an airline. Although Eastern was still alive in the summer of 1990, its vital signs were weak, and its pilots were almost all scabs. Even worse, true to its fractious heritage, what remained of the Eastern pilot group, now led by Skip Copeland, was cool to Babbitt's candidacy. Many Eastern strikers denounced him as "just a guy who owns an Eastern uniform—not a real pilot," a reference to the fact that Babbitt had flown very little since becoming executive administrator.

"When Jack Bavis was executive administrator, he didn't fly anything for twelve years," Babbitt recalls. "I really wanted to keep my hand in with the flying, not so much for the mechanical skills but for keeping in touch with what's going on out on the line. The way our system worked, especially on the DC-9, you go in and out of Atlanta every other leg, hang out in the crew lounge and see everybody, all the different political factions, believe me, you know what's going on. Every airline has a soapbox, a political wailing wall, a great exchange place. But after about a year, it became obvious that I couldn't work in the office all week and fly on weekends. Hank would remind me of it every time I would go fly. To be able to leave Washington, go out and fly a trip for a couple of days, lay over in Mobile, was a nice break, a day off.

"But as time went on" Babbitt says,, "it became more difficult. Keeping my qualifications up became a pain. I went down and took a check ride right after the United strike ended. I hadn't been in the airplane in 75 days! I passed the check ride, and I'm still happy to say that I've never busted a check in my life. But taking check rides when you're flying only 20 hours a quarter is tough. I realized that if I kept this up, I would wind up embarrassing myself and ALPA."

Roger Hall, on the other hand, continued to fly regularly as first vice-president. Admittedly, his duties were less bound to office routine than Babbitt's, and most of Hall's predecessors had also continued to fly their trips. But in politics, symbolic factors play a large role; and for line pilots, the fact that Hall stayed out there, braving weather and icy runways, added to his appeal.

Only two negative factors figured in Hall's candidacy. The first, that he was from United, ALPA's 800-pound gorilla, the legatee of more than a decade of extremely testy relationships with other ALPA pilot groups, Hall couldn't do anything about. The second, that he had negotiated the infamous "Blue Skies" contract of 1981, could have been a problem—except that Randy Babbitt gave him a bye on it.

"I had an agreement with Roger early on to run as clean a campaign as we could," Babbitt says. "I did not bring up Blue Skies, although I was well aware it could have hurt him politically."

Had it not been for ALPA's prederegulation system of allocating executive vice-presidencies, the election crisis of 1990 might never have happened. As we have seen previously, in 1974 the BOD eliminated regional vice-presidencies in favor of executive vice-presidencies to be elected by "groups" of airlines selected by size. While this system worked reasonably well before deregulation, afterward it invited trouble because it _guaranteed_ a contest between the two largest airlines. Given the history of tribalism that had characterized ALPA's politics, this system was a ticking time bomb. Airlines in each group tended to develop political animosities over "place," if nothing else. Under the strains of deregulation, these animosities increased to the point that they threatened ALPA's very existence. By 1990, the Delta and United pilot groups could almost be counted upon to oppose each other politically, no matter what the issue.

At the summer 1990 Delta MEC meeting in Chicago, both Roger Hall and Randy Babbitt made full-fledged campaign speeches. Hall got a polite reception, but Randy Babbitt would clearly be the Delta MEC members' choice, partly because they saw him as Hank Duffy's favorite. Duffy remained popular with his fellow Delta pilots, most of whom resented the United pilot group's sniping at him. Although Duffy maintained a strict _outward_ neutrality, it was no secret that he preferred Babbitt.

"I was in the fortunate position of being able to live with either Roger or Randy, because both of them were committed generally to the direction I believed ALPA had to go," Duffy said later. "Now if the BOD had elected somebody like Joe Kernan, who attacked me personally, that would have been different."

Although Duffy meant to absent himself from any _public_ role in the election of 1990, he privately encouraged the fabled "Delta Machine" to support Babbitt. As a pilot from a beleaguered, strike-torn airline, Babbitt would have had no chance at all had Duffy not engineered support for him early. Without Delta's support, Babbitt would not have had the manpower to carry on the lobbying, personal contacts, and politicking in the corridors and hospitality suites at the Sheraton Hotel in Bal Harbour, Fla., when the BOD convened that October.

In Hank Duffy's "farewell address" opening the meeting, he urged the delegates to control expenditures. He was particularly severe in his attacks upon putative "outside experts," describing them as "anybody who's guessed right twice." But Duffy reserved his harshest words for merger attorneys, whom he accused of exploiting pilots' fears to increase their own fees. "God must have placed merger attorneys on Earth to challenge the skunk as nature's most offensive animal," Duffy said. He begged the delegates to strive for internal unity, to "think we, not me." He was clearly warning the delegates to remain cool during the election to come.

"As I have gone through a series of end-of-term interviews with the news media, most often they have asked, 'What was the high point and the low point of your time in office?'" Duffy told the BOD. "The high point was easy. Lorenzo discredited—driven from the industry. The low point I've been reluctant to discuss because it's internal to ourselves. My greatest source of discomfort was not Ferris or Icahn or Lorenzo. My most troublesome problems arose because of internal dissension between pilot groups, usually merger-related, that put them at each others' throats and put ALPA in the middle—with one or both pilot groups threatening that if they were not declared the winner they might pull away and fend for themselves. I knew that such a rupture could result in the destruction of the entire organization. More time than I care to admit was spent in figuring out how to keep those groups with us. Every pilot group faced with that choice during my tenure opted to work within the system. I'd like to thank their leaders for working through the emotion of the moment and allowing logic to prevail. I believe unequivocally that anything less than a strong centralized national union in today's environment is suicide for the profession and eventually for every pilot group."

And so, with Duffy's warning ringing in their ears, the delegates moved to elect their new leader. Hall jumped off to an immediate lead. With two of the "Big Four," United and Northwest in his column, Hall seemed unbeatable. Delta went for Babbitt, of course, while USAir committed itself by unit rule to its favorite son, Joe Kernan. Although Kernan had no chance of winning, he brought the delegates to their feet with a rousing speech, given in full uniform. But USAir's unit rule vote holds a hidden agenda, which requires some explanation.

USAir was the Oakland of airlines. Gertrude Stein once said of Oakland: "There is no 'there' there." USAir had grown so fast and was such an amalgam of previous airlines that it had no discernible identity of its own. USAir pilots habitually thought of themselves as old Piedmont, or old Pacific Southwest (PSA), or old Allegheny. Its leaders—Roger Hall (not *the* Roger Hall, but a USAir pilot of the same name), Joe Kernan, John Kretsinger, Chip Mull, and Bob Hammarley—had agreed that to establish a sense of internal identity, they ought not to be seen as puppets. In the days preceding the election, they had agreed that as an airline made up entirely of refugees and former local service carriers, their best interests would be served by voting for Kernan through two full ballots. On the third ballot, USAir would add its votes to the total for either Hall or Babbitt and determine the victor. The BOD members assumed that USAir would *not* vote by unit rule on the third ballot and would spread its votes. In any case, USAir would become a player of the first rank.

But, as we have said, a secret agenda existed. Bob Hammarley, like so many other USAir pilots, was a deregulation refugee. As a former Frontier pilot, Hammarley could be reasonably expected to oppose Roger Hall. As we have seen, Frontier's demise coincided with the end of the 1985 United strike. Dick Ferris had made what was almost certainly a spurious offer to absorb Frontier *if* he could do so with a B-scale. Having just taken a strike on this very issue,

United's Roger Hall could not possibly accede to Ferris's machinations, which amounted to a backdoor plot to snatch victory from the jaws of defeat. So Frontier went bankrupt, and Bob Hammarley, like hundreds of pilots from other airlines, notably Braniff, found new homes at the bottom of the seniority list of rapidly expanding USAir. But USAir's sizable former Frontier contingent always believed, perhaps unfairly, that United's pilots should have saved them.

Hammarley's position as USAir's MEC chairman left him in an ideal position to influence his amorphous airline. He honestly believed Babbitt was the better choice, but he agreed that, at first, USAir pilots should park their votes with Joe Kernan. But if Babbitt could just stay alive through two ballots, Hammarley had a surprise up his sleeve. He had persuaded the USAir MEC to go for Babbitt by unit rule, which would certainly clinch his victory, _on the third ballot._

But the USAir pilot group would never have been able to spring this surprise if it had not been for little NPA and First Officer Representative Dean Brouillette. With his measly 43 votes, Brouillette was an unlikely king maker, and nobody had paid him much attention during the intensive lobbying for the votes of Group 5 airlines—except for Patrick M. Broderick of Eastern. A 23-year Eastern veteran, Broderick acted as Babbitt's campaign manager. In fact, Broderick was instrumental in persuading Babbitt to run in the first place.

"I believe I was the first person to approach Randy about running," Broderick said in a postelection interview. "This was during the strike, and the airline was deteriorating badly. He said he had no constituency, but I thought Randy had the skills to be a fine ALPA president. I also thought he could mobilize ALPA to either get us back to work, or get us on with another airline so we could continue our careers."

The fact that a "mover and shaker" like Pat Broderick would solicit his vote impressed Brouillette. Broderick had noticed the tiny "tailhook" tie tack Brouillette wore during a social hour at one of the hospitality suites. A former naval aviator himself, Broderick engaged Brouillette in conversation, lobbied hard for Randy Babbitt, and believed Brouillette had committed to his candidate. As a former admiral's aide who had forsaken a fast-track military career for the airlines, Broderick could be quite persuasive. He had a winning personality and the dark good looks of somebody in show business. Imagine Broderick's consternation when, toward the end of the first ballot, little NPA went for Roger Hall _by unit rule_!

At this point, history gives way to personal observation, and perhaps it ought to stop. As Hank Duffy's guest, invited to observe the election of 1990, I had by the purest chance, met both Broderick and Brouillette socially in a hospitality suite earlier that week. Perhaps my miniature navy pilots' wings, worn on my lapel, had linked the three of us together. When the first ballot ended, I watched Broderick dash toward Broillette, who sat at the very last delegate table, separated from the visitors' section by only an aisle.

"I was for Babbitt all along," Brouillette said in an interview just minutes after the election. "I knew him personally—he had flown out at a moment's notice and helped us solve a merger crisis on NPA and WestAir. My captain and I got together with the WestAir pilots, with whom we are merging, and took a straw vote. It was split 50–50 at first, but then my captain, who had originally been for Babbitt, went over to Hall. We then agreed to go unit rule on the first ballot. I didn't feel right about it, because I had been for Babbitt for a long, long time. But that was nothing against Roger Hall. He has been one heck of an individual, good for the Association across the board. I just felt Babbitt would get his hands dirty down with the small carriers. Babbitt had just been a tireless worker. Well, I was arguing with myself when one of Babbitt's representatives [Broderick] asked me would I be willing to change my vote. I asked, 'Can I do it?' and he said, 'Yes, just go to the microphone and make the announcement.'"

At the time Broderick spoke to Brouillette, the first ballot was being counted and a lengthy delay was in progress. At that point, Hall had a bare majority of 50.1 percent. Randy Babbitt, listening to the results on an open mike in his room, actually began making his way to the convention floor to make his concession speech. But by the ancient parliamentary practice to which ALPA had long adhered, until a vote was officially announced from the rostrum, any member could change his vote. Brouillette's piddling 43 votes pulled Roger Hall infinitesimally below 50 percent, so a second ballot would be necessary. Babbitt had reached the door of the convention hall before being turned around and sent back to his room.

On the second ballot, Hall lost a few votes while the USAir pilots stayed firmly with Joe Kernan. Then, on the third ballot, Bob Hammarley sprang his surprise, and it was all over—Babbitt would be ALPA's new President. Maybe.

Roger Hall's furious supporters challenged Babbitt's victory, alleging that the voting had had "substantial irregularities." They carried a formal appeal all the way to a special hearing before arbitrator Lewis M. Gill, alleging that Broderick's contact with Brouillette, among other things, was illegal and asking that he set aside Babbitt's victory and declare Hall the winner. Gill rendered his verdict on Jan. 29, 1992. His reconstruction of events coincides exactly with what this historian witnessed personally.

Gill, noting that his investigation was a "novel proceeding more akin to fact-finding than arbitration," expressed surprise that a union with ALPA's "squeaky clean" reputation had come to this. While Gill's investigation also looked into such things as the Babbitt campaign's finances, and whether there had been a conspiracy to delay the vote count so that Babbitt's partisans would have time to switch some votes, the key finding had to do with the propriety of Broderick's contact with Brouillette.

"Under the agreed ALPA rules," Gill wrote, "the official results are not announced until two separate official tallies are checked against each other; and until that announcement is made, any of the delegates are entitled to change their votes and lobbying *among the delegates on the floor is permitted*" [emphasis added].

Hall's partisans noted correctly that Broderick was not a delegate and hence should not have had access to the floor. But Gill noted that with NPA's delegate table situated adjacent to the aisle dividing it from the visitors' section, Broderick stood in the aisle and was never technically on the floor. In any case, Gill found that even if Broderick had come onto the floor, it would not have been a "substantial irregularity" because the rule barring nondelegates from the floor had fallen into general disuse and was widely ignored.

As to a conspiracy to delay the vote count, Gill noted that with an "avowed Hall supporter" (Rick Miller of Northwest) chairing the voting process, that seemed unlikely. The clincher from Gill's perspective was that the United pilot group did not challenge the delay at the time, so it did not constitute a "substantial irregularity" either.

When the 32nd ALPA BOD meeting adjourned, a pessimist could have been forgiven for thinking that ALPA's future looked dim. The United pilot group had been completely frozen out of all national offices, and they had boycotted the remainder of the meeting—including Duffy's retirement dinner and the closing banquet. Steady Chuck Pierce of United, widely respected for his long and sober service to ALPA, had lost his executive vice-president (EVP) race to Delta's ebullient Jack Saux. Previously, after such a tough loss, the delegates had always tended to mend fences by electing an EVP from the airline that had lost the presidency. Northwest's Skip Eglet, a man whose long and important service to ALPA had made his candidacy for first vice-president strictly "no contest" in 1986, had lost to Roger Hall for precisely this reason. But in 1990, the BOD, tired of the United pilot group's truculence, was in no mood to balance the scales. The delegates openly speculated that a United walkout seemed likely.

But was it? While the mood was ugly in their hospitality suite, a solid cadre of United pilots indicated that despite their anger they had no intention of deserting ALPA. Of course, there were wild charges and air-clearing ventilations of anger among many United pilots attending the BOD meeting, but after calm returned, most of them seemed willing to hang on. As for rank-and-file United pilots, anecdotal evidence suggests that even if their leaders had tried leaving ALPA, they would in all likelihood have found nobody following. To their credit, there was never a hint of secessionist talk from United's *top* leadership. Neither Rick Dubinsky nor Roger Hall, despite their disappointment, ever breathed a word about forming an American-style splinter union. The mere fact that they fought to overturn the election *through channels* proved their loyalty and showed they had no intention of abandoning ALPA.

Time would have to do its healing work—time and Randy Babbitt's leadership.

Flash forward to the 1992 BOD meeting in Bal Harbour, Fla. The shoe is now on the other foot. United's pilots would shortly win a string of victories, in a scab harassment lawsuit and in restoring the rightful seniority of "the 570." Delta is now under pressure, its pilots threatened by a layoff of their most junior and vulnerable members as part of a management pressure campaign. Surely United's powerful pilot group should now be gloating.

What's wrong with this picture? Watch Delta's Jack Saux and United's Jamie Lindsay cooperating on a plan to prevent these layoffs. Two years earlier, they had nearly come to blows. See Delta's MEC Chairman Bob Shelton and Roger Hall (once again United's MEC Chairman) combining in cooperative actions, with Hall reading a resolution passed *unanimously* by the United pilots on the convention floor, *demanding* that their own company hire immediately all furloughed Delta pilots. What caused this turnaround?

The same thing that has turned ALPA around repeatedly during the first 60 years of its history. Somebody, some pilot group, some resolute individual, took it upon himself to mobilize his fellow pilots to *do something*! Somebody has always "sucked it up," refused to admit defeat, resolutely held the center when the flanks were giving way—damn the consequences. How many times has ALPA been given up for dead?

Who would have given the proverbial plugged nickel for ALPA's chances when, in December 1933, the affable, well-liked TWA pilot and former Dave Behncke intimate, Waldon "Swede" Golien lent his name and prestige to the "TWA Pilots Association" and thus betrayed Behncke. This company-sponsored attempt to destroy ALPA through a toothless, captive union was the direct result of Dave Behncke's greatest gamble, the threatened 1933 nationwide strike to keep ALPA out of the new National Recovery Administration's "wage guidelines" for the airline industry. When "Swede" Golien turned coat, unflappable Jimmy Roe put his career on the line to get TWA's pilots back into ALPA's ranks. Every pilot flying the line today owes Jimmy Roe a profound debt. Had it not been for Roe and dozens of pilots from other airlines like him who supported Behncke's bluff, the United States would never have had a "Decision 83," and ALPA in all probability would not exist today. Jimmy Roe and the other Old Guys had just as much to lose as any pilot flying the line today. Yet they held the center, just as in the crisis of 1990, *somebody* held it, too.[1]

Crises have dotted ALPA's history. The pessimists have always been a little too quick to count ALPA out. In 1933 they were wrong, just as they would be wrong again after the disputed election of 1990. Lots of people sucked it up, built bridges of trust, worked for reconciliation and mutual understanding, and patiently went about the business of explaining, once again, that ALPA is *us*— not *them*. Despite all the trauma that has beset ALPA since deregulation, these ancient arguments carried the day once again, just as they had in 1933 when the Old Guys pulled down the brims of their hats and hung tough.

Randy Babbitt seemed ideal for the task. He had absorbed the values of the Old Guys in the most direct and effective way imaginable—literally on the knee of his own father. Furthermore, with his own airline dead after 1991, one of ALPA's oldest problems—the necessity of separating its top leadership from the parochial concerns of their own airlines—had become moot. Randy Babbitt was ALPA's—he had no airline to go home to or parent pilot group his critics could accuse him of favoring.

Duane Woerth of Northwest, elected first vice-president along with Babbitt in 1990, was a perfect counterpoint. As a refugee from Braniff, Woerth came to his office with a gut level understanding that ALPA is *us*—not *them*. Literally thousands of pilots, moving from dashed hopes and failed carriers along the path Woerth had followed, were changing the face of ALPA. Maybe that's why ALPA surprised its enemies again. So many pilots had come to understand that nothing in life is certain, that no victory ever stays won. These pilots increasingly began to adopt the values and attitudes of the Old Guys, in ways that the intervening generations of pilots since the Old Guys had left the scene had abandoned. Duane Woerth understood.

On a frigid 15-degree Minneapolis day in 1989, Woerth (then a Northwest MEC officer) commuted in from Dallas, the city he would have been flying out of if Braniff were still alive. Away from home and family, disgusted with all the paperwork facing him, angry at the Bush Administration's support for Frank Lorenzo, Woerth was depressed and fed up. The phone rang. It was Ken Watts, vice-chairman of Council 1, ALPA's original LEC, the airline that Dave Behncke would have held seniority No. *1* on, had he not been fired for bucking management over safety in 1927.[2] Watts informed Woerth that retired Northwest Captain R. Lee Smith had died.

R. Lee Smith. The last surviving member of the original group of Old Guys who had conspired with Dave Behncke in 1929 to found ALPA. Watts suggested to Woerth that flowers be sent and maybe a letter of condolence to his family.

Woerth, by now really depressed, picked up a copy of *Flying the Line* and read a few pages. He had never met old R. Lee Smith while he was alive. But suddenly, in a moment of accidental epiphany, there was the Old Guy himself staring up from the page at Woerth.

"What's wrong, Duane?" Woerth imagined the Old Guy asking, his voice dripping with contempt. "Is it getting too tough out there for your generation of pilots? Do you think you're the first ever to suffer adversity, to feel the effects of government policy working in conjunction with hostile managements to bust your union? Suck it up, mister! You've got a legacy to live up to."

Old R. Lee seemed to be telling Woerth that leveraged buyouts, the threat of globalization, and Frank Lorenzo as the second coming of E.L. Cord were simply more of the same—the latest version of the battle pilots have been fighting ever since they first dared to lift up their heads and stare back at management defiantly—back in the days when pilots still sat in the slipstream to get the proper "feel" of their aircraft. And the Old Guy was telling Duane Woerth something else, too. He was saying that, without unity across company lines, they had no chance at all of preserving their profession.

"Every time I enter our Washington, D.C., office," Woerth wrote in a moving tribute to R. Lee Smith published in *Air Line Pilot*, "I can't help noticing the bronzed plaque that lists ALPA's founders, pilots from all airlines banding together to protect all pilots. They had learned the hard way that going it alone just got them killed one at a time."

Will professional airline pilots still be "sucking it up" in the 21st century? What will history have to say when the next generation of airline pilots inherits the cockpits of the current generation?

History is waiting for its answer—it always will be. ✈

NOTES
[1] See "The Rise and Fall of the TWA Pilots Association," in *Flying the Line*, Ch. 9.
[2] See "Dave Behncke—An American Success Story," *Flying the Line*, Ch. 10, pp. 97-98.

INDEX

PHOTO CREDITS

All illustrations *Air Line Pilot* photos